ZAGATSURVEY®

2005/06

NEW YORK CITY
NIGHTLIFE

Editor: Curt Gathje

Published and distributed by
ZAGAT SURVEY, LLC
4 Columbus Circle
New York, New York 10019
Tel: 212 977 6000
E-mail: nynightlife@zagat.com
Web site: www.zagat.com

Acknowledgments

We thank each of the following people who worked on this guide: our associate editor, Griff Foxley, and our editorial assistant, Jason Briker, as well as Betsy Andrews, Augustine Chan, Reni Chin, Larry Cohn, Victoria Elmacioglu, Schuyler Frazier, Jeff Freier, Shelley Gallagher, Natalie Lebert, Mike Liao, Dave Makulec, Bernard Onken, Emily Parsons, Robert Poole, Thomas Sheehan, Steven Shukow, Joshua Siegel, Carla Spartos and Sharon Yates.

Contents

About This Survey

This is our seventh annual foray into the wilds of New York City Nightlife, covering 1,304 bars, clubs and lounges in the five boroughs. By surveying a large number of local nightlife denizens, we think we have achieved a uniquely current and reliable guide. We hope you agree.

For this book, over 5,600 people participated; since they go out an average of 2.1 times per week, this *Survey* is based on roughly 620,000 nights out per year. We want to thank each of our participants, a widely diverse group in all aspects but one – they all love to party. Being based on their ratings and comments, this book is really "theirs."

In contrast to our *New York City Restaurant Survey,* where our respondents' mean age is 43, the participants in this *Survey* are relatively young. The breakdown is as follows: 43% are in their 20s, 37% in their 30s and a mere 20% in their 40s or above. As best we can tell, people in their 20s drink more than they eat, while the opposite is true of their elders.

To help guide our readers to best slake their thirsts by taste, mood and budget, we have prepared over 94 handy indexes and lists: see Top Ratings (pages 13–21) and Best Buys (page 22). We have also tried to be concise: our editors have synopsized our surveyors' opinions, with exact comments shown in quotation marks.

As companions to this guide, we also publish New York City restaurant, entertaining and shopping guides and maps, as well as guides to the surrounding suburban areas. These guides are also available on PDAs, cell phones and by subscription at zagat.com, where you can vote and shop as well. Not incidentally, our newly redesigned Web site now features nightlife content for the first time.

To vote in any of our upcoming *Surveys,* just register at zagat.com. Each participant will receive a free copy of the resulting guide (or a comparable reward). Your comments and even criticisms of this guide are also solicited. There is always room for improvement with your help. Just contact us at nynightlife@zagat.com.

New York, NY
June 13, 2005

Nina and Tim Zagat

What's New

NYC Nightlife continued to sizzle over the last year, in contrast to prior years when the banning of smoking and the politics of dancing garnered headlines. Downtown remained *the* destination of choice, though there were interesting arrivals turning up all over town. Here's what's happening:

Just Hatched: There's no stopping the Meatpacking District/West Chelsea nightlife juggernaut, a stilettos-and-martinis scene where high-end, banquettes-and-bottle-service clubs continue to open with no end in sight. Among this year's crop are Cain (arguably Gotham's hottest spot), as well as Aer, BED New York, Brass Monkey, Cabanas, Earth, 5 Ninth, Glo, Highline, Level V, Ono, Plunge, Quo, Ruby Falls and Salon. Equally hopping was the quickly gentrifying Lower East Side, which welcomed Dark Room, the Delancey, East Side Company Bar, Freemans, Girls Room, Libation and Stanton Social, among others. Elsewhere around town, notable arrivals included Brandy Library, Dizzy's Club Coca-Cola, Employees Only, Movida, NA, Pink Elephant, Snitch, Sugarcane, Supreme Trading and Table 50. Jazz fans celebrated the return of Smalls, the much-loved Village boîte that's reopened in its original location, while Uptown types were thrilled by the rebirth of Frederick's, a '90s scene on Madison Avenue now housed in a subterranean space on West 58th Street.

Micro Scoop: "Microneighborhood" is the latest real estate buzzword for small stretches of rapidly developing turf, and nightlifewise, these areas included: the Lower East Side's Allen Street corridor, showing some life with the arrival of Epstein's Bar, Lucky Jack's and Rockwood Music Hall; an expanse of Sixth Avenue in Chelsea where a number of new, singles-friendly high-rises have brought forth new, singles-friendly bars like Orchid, Rogue and xes lounge; and a swath of East Houston Street that's given birth to Martignetti Liquors, Stay, Vasmay Lounge and White Rabbit. On the other hand, rising microneighborhoods can threaten old-time establishments. This year's most talked-about example is the Bowery's punk landmark, CBGB's, which faces an uncertain future due to an imminent rent hike.

Rooftop Revival: At the turn of the last century, rooftop settings were all the rage (more than likely due to the lack of air conditioning), and in this new millennium that trend has been revived by some spectacular new aeries. Joining such tip-top spots as the Metropolitan Museum Roof Garden and the Pen-Top Bar were high-in-the-sky scenes at BED New York, Cabanas, the Delancey and Plunge.

Ciao Manhattan: A number of memorable places packed it in over the last year. Open closed, as did Centro-Fly, Chez Es Saada, Fez Under Time Cafe, Float, the Gaiety Theater, Hell, Lansky Lounge, Meow Mix, Pangaea, Plaid, Plant,

Suite 16, the Village Idiot and Yabby's (see page 252 for a full list). Also shut down was Bay Ridge's fabled Spectrum, where *Saturday Night Fever* was shot, though its illustrious illuminated dance floor has survived, auctioned off for $160,000. Traditionalists mourned the closing of the Plaza's classic Oak Bar, shuttered temporarily as the hotel undergoes condoization; it's promised back in late 2006.

Coming Attractions: In the pipeline are such scenes-in-the-making as Branch, the latest salute to fine mixology from the Milk and Honey folks; Pizza Bar, a pizzeria–cum–swanky lounge from the minds behind a comparable hybrid, Pop Burger; Subconscious, an underground lair in Midtown's Dream Hotel; an as-yet-unnamed redo of the hard-core dance palace Sound Factory; and the similarly unnamed Lotus spin-off, a more intimate, across-the-street adjunct of the Meatpacking District's very first hot spot.

Here's Looking at You: Designwise, tricky oversize lampshades continued to blanket the landscape as did the hundred-bottles-of-beer-on-the-wall concept first popularized by Schiller's. Taxidermy got hip at Barramundi, Duff's, Floyd and Freemans, while private yachts supplied the inspiration for the interiors of Lure Fishbar and Movida. Vying for the title of most dramatic design were eye-popping contenders like Duvet, Koi, Ono and Salon.

Random Notes: Beds in nightclubs are nothing new, but the Miami-born trend reached full bloom this year with the opening of two fully mattressed joints, BED New York and Duvet, serving food as well as drink . . . Theme bars showed new life with the appearance of arcade game–laden Barcade, salute-to-the-'90s Nerveana and pinup girl–friendly Tainted Lady; crime paid at two corruption-themers, Capone's and Crime Scene . . . The swanky hotel bar, a staple of the go-go '90s, showed renewed vigor with the arrival of Cabanas in the Maritime Hotel, Dream Lounge (Dream Hotel), Koi (Bryant Park Hotel), Ono and Plunge (Gansevoort Hotel), Silverleaf Tavern (70 Park Avenue Hotel) and the eponymous watering holes in the QT Hotel and The Hotel on Rivington . . . The name pool seemed to be shrinking with a rash of similarly monikered new venues: there was Snitch and Stitch, the Blue Room, the Green Room and the Dark Room. Hanger joined the already existing Hangar, B1 joined B61 and B3, and Eleven, Twelve and 17 added to the numbers game begun by One, 13 and 66.

New to This Edition: We've added 172 new listings to this guide, as well as new index categories for Beds, Photo Booths and Waterside spots. To all of our participants who shared their experiences with us and hung in there until last call, we raise our glass, with special thanks to the surveyor who coined our favorite new word of the year: "fratmosphere." Cheers!

New York, NY   Curt Gathje
June 13, 2005

NYC Neighborhoods

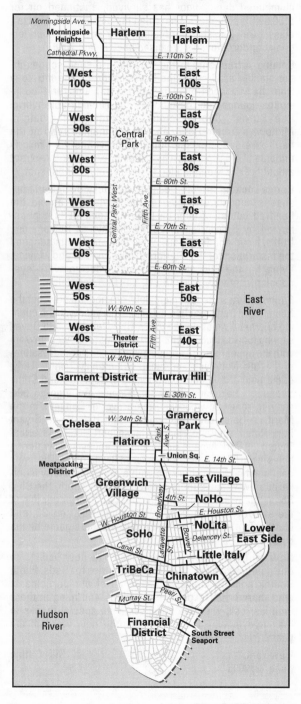

Ratings & Symbols

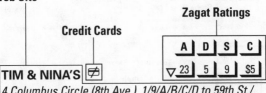

Name, Address, Subway Stop, Phone Number & Web Site

Credit Cards

Zagat Ratings

A	D	S	C
▽ 23	5	9	$5

TIM & NINA'S ⊘

4 Columbus Circle (8th Ave.), 1/9/A/B/C/D to 59th St./ Columbus Circle, 212-977-6000; www.zagat.com

Open 24/7, this "deep dive" bar with a bathroom and phone booth across the street resembles a "none-too-clean garage"; however, "dirt cheap" prices, a free-flowing tap and unlimited pretzels gratis draw "spaced-out crowds" of "multi-pierced patrons"; P.S. don't trip on any of the customers on the way out.

Review, with surveyors' comments in quotes

Nightspots with the highest overall ratings and greatest popularity and importance are printed in CAPITAL LETTERS.

Credit Cards: ⊘ no credit cards accepted

Ratings are on a scale of **0** to **30. Cost (C)** reflects surveyors' estimated price of a typical single drink.

A	Appeal	D	Decor	S	Service	C	Cost
23		5		9		$5	

0–9 poor to fair	**20–25** very good to excellent
10–15 fair to good	**26–30** extraordinary to perfection
16–19 good to very good	▽ low response/less reliable

For places listed without ratings, such as a newcomer or survey write-in, the price range is indicated as follows:

I	below $5	**E**	$9 to $11
M	$5 to $8	**VE**	more than $11

What's Hot

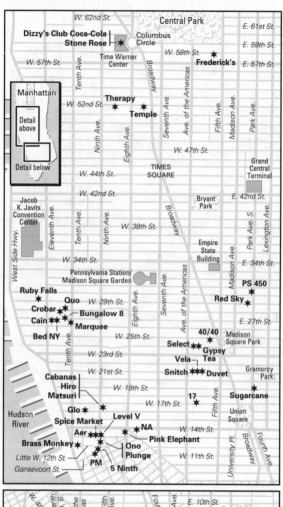

- Dizzy's Club Coca-Cola
- Stone Rose
- Central Park
- Columbus Circle
- E. 61st St.
- E. 59th St.
- W. 62nd St.
- W. 58th St.
- Frederick's
- E. 57th St.
- W. 57th St.
- Time Warner Center
- Broadway
- Tenth Ave.
- Therapy
- W. 52nd St.
- Temple
- Manhattan
- Detail above
- Detail below
- Ninth Ave.
- Eighth Ave.
- Seventh Ave.
- Ave. of the Americas
- Fifth Ave.
- Madison Ave.
- Park Ave.
- W. 47th St.
- W. 44th St.
- TIMES SQUARE
- Grand Central Terminal
- W. 42nd St.
- E. 42nd St.
- Jacob K. Javits Convention Center
- Eleventh Ave.
- Tenth Ave.
- Ninth Ave.
- W. 38th St.
- Bryant Park
- Park Ave. S.
- Lexington Ave.
- Broadway
- W. 34th St.
- Empire State Building
- Madison Ave.
- E. 34th St.
- West Side Hwy.
- Pennsylvania Station/ Madison Square Garden
- Seventh Ave.
- Ave. of the Americas
- PS 450
- Ruby Falls
- Quo
- W. 29th St.
- Red Sky
- Crobar
- Bungalow 8
- Cain
- Marquee
- Eighth Ave.
- E. 27th St.
- Bed NY
- W. 25th St.
- 40/40
- Madison Square Park
- Select
- Gypsy Tea
- W. 23rd St.
- Vela
- Tenth Ave.
- Cabanas
- Snitch
- Duvet
- Gramercy Park
- Hiro
- W. 21st St.
- Matsuri
- W. 19th St.
- 17
- Sugarcane
- Glo
- W. 17th St.
- Fifth Ave.
- Union Square
- Hudson River
- Spice Market
- Level V
- NA
- Aer
- Pink Elephant
- W. 14th St.
- Brass Monkey
- University Pl.
- Fourth Ave.
- Broadway
- Ono
- Little W. 12th St.
- PM
- Plunge
- W. 11th St.
- Gansevoort St.
- 5 Ninth

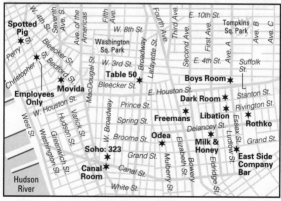

- Spotted Pig
- W. 4th St.
- Seventh Ave.
- Ave. of the Americas
- Fifth Ave.
- Fourth Ave.
- Third Ave.
- E. 10th St.
- Tompkins Sq. Park
- Ave. B
- Ave. C
- W. 8th St.
- Washington Sq. Park
- Broadway
- Lafayette St.
- Second Ave.
- First Ave.
- Ave. A
- Perry St.
- Bleecker St.
- Bedford St.
- W. 3rd St.
- E. 4th St.
- Suffolk St.
- Christopher St.
- Table 50
- MacDougal St.
- Bleecker St.
- E. Houston St.
- Boys Room
- Movida
- Dark Room
- Stanton St.
- Employees Only
- W. Houston St.
- Varick St.
- Prince St.
- Freemans
- Libation
- Rivington St.
- Rothko
- Hudson St.
- W. Broadway
- Spring St.
- Delancey St.
- Essex St.
- Ludlow St.
- Grand St.
- West St.
- Greenwich St.
- Washington St.
- Odea
- Broome St.
- Elizabeth St.
- Milk & Honey
- Soho: 323
- Grand St.
- Mulberry St.
- Bowery St.
- Eldridge St.
- East Side Company Bar
- Canal Room
- Canal St.
- White St.
- Hudson River

What's Hot

Aer	Milk and Honey
BED New York	Movida
Boys Room	NA
Brass Monkey	Odea
Bungalow 8	Ono
Cabanas	Pink Elephant
Cain	Plunge
Canal Room	PM
Crobar	PS 450
Dark Room	Quo
Dizzy's Club Coca-Cola	Red Sky
Duvet	Rothko
East Side Company Bar	Ruby Falls
Employees Only	Select
5 Ninth	17
40/40	Snitch
Frederick's	Soho: 323
Freemans	Spice Market
Glo	Spotted Pig
Gypsy Tea	Stone Rose
Hiro	Sugarcane
Level V	Table 50
Libation	Temple
Marquee	Therapy
Matsuri	Vela

It's hard to put your finger on what makes a place hot. Furthermore, what's hot one week can turn cold the next, only to warm up again the week after. The above list represents our take on what nightspots are generating the most heat as we go to press. If nothing else, it's a snapshot of NYC's ever-evolving, ever-happening scene.

Most Popular

1. Pastis	26. SushiSamba
2. Spice Market	27. Luna Park
3. Blue Water Grill	28. Bubble Lounge
4. Lotus	29. g*
5. Balthazar	30. PM
6. Park, The	31. Cielo
7. Brother Jimmy's	32. Campbell Apt.
8. Tao	33. Markt
9. APT	34. One
10. Heartland Brewery	35. Four Seasons Bar
11. Asia de Cuba	36. Sutton Place
12. Bungalow 8*	37. Cibar
13. Divine Bar	38. Suede
14. Gramercy Tavern	39. Serafina
15. Hudson Hotel Bar	40. Boat Basin
16. Coffee Shop	41. Level V*
17. Marquee	42. Dos Caminos
18. Son Cubano	43. Fifty Seven 57*
19. Chumley's	44. Schiller's*
20. Crobar	45. d.b.a.
21. Dt.Ut	46. P.J. Clarke's
22. Angel's Share	47. Bemelmans
23. McSorley's	48. Bar Veloce
24. XL	49. One if by Land*
25. Ginger Man	50. Pete's Tavern

It's obvious that many of the places on the above list are among the most expensive, but New Yorkers also love a bargain. Were popularity calibrated to price, we suspect that a number of other places would join the above ranks. Thus, we have listed 50 Best Buys on page 22.

---

* Indicates a tie with place above

Top Ratings

Excludes places with low voting, except where indicated by a ▽.

Top Overall Appeal

28 Rainbow Grill
27 Met. Museum Roof
 King Cole Bar
 Bemelmans
 Penthouse Exec. Club
 Cafe Carlyle
 Brooklyn Inn
 Milk and Honey*
 Room, The*
 Sakagura
26 MO Bar
 Gramercy Tavern
 Rue B
 Daniel
 Four Seasons Bar
 Boat House
 Regency Library Bar
 Floyd
 Bohemian Hall
 Eleven Madison Park

 Superfine
 Shalel
25 Otheroom
 Campbell Apt.
 SEA
 Whiskey Ward
 Megu
 Single Rm. Occup.
 Bond Street
 One if by Land
 Blue Ribbon Bklyn.
 Jean Georges*
 Grey Dog's
 Comedy Cellar
 Dylan Prime*
 House of Brews*
 Rise*
 Veritas*
 Top of the Tower
 Birdland

By Category

After Work
26 Four Seasons Bar
25 Campbell Apt.
24 Rink Bar
 Boat Basin
 Del Frisco's
 Tao

Art Bars
23 Passerby
 CB's 313
 Nuyorican Poets
22 Bowery Poetry
21 Galapagos
 Rififi

Beer Specialists
26 Bohemian Hall
25 House of Brews
23 Killmeyer's
22 Brooklyn Brewery
 Croxley Ales
21 Burp Castle

Bowling Alleys
22 Bowlmor Lanes
18 Chelsea Piers
15 Leisure Time Bowling▽

Cabarets
27 Cafe Carlyle
24 Oak Room
23 Rasputin
 Don't Tell Mama
 Feinstein's/Regency
 Joe's Pub

Cheap Drinks
26 Floyd
 Bohemian Hall
23 Corner Bistro
 Gowanus Yacht
22 Brooklyn Brewery
 McSorley's

Top Appeal

Cocktail Experts
27 Bemelmans
Milk and Honey
25 Angel's Share
24 Fifty Seven 57
23 5 Ninth
Flatiron Lounge

Coffeehouses
25 Grey Dog's
24 Caffe Rafaella
23 Dt.Ut
Cafe Lalo
22 Tea Lounge
21 Caffe Reggio

Comedy Clubs
25 Comedy Cellar
23 Gotham Comedy
22 Carolines
21 Stand-Up NY
20 Comic Strip
19 Dangerfield's

Dance Clubs
23 Copacabana
22 Cielo
21 Deep
Quo
20 Crobar
Gonzalez y Gonzalez

Dives
25 Whiskey Ward
24 Pyramid
21 Sidewalk
20 Bellevue
Library*
19 Cock, The

Fine Dining Too
26 Gramercy Tavern
Daniel
Four Seasons Bar
Eleven Madison Park
25 Megu
Blue Ribbon Bklyn.
Jean Georges*

Frat House
21 Bounce
20 Tortilla Flats
19 Doc Watson's
Ryan's Daughter
Jeremy's Ale
Fiddlesticks

Gay
24 Therapy
23 Boys Room
22 XL
21 Eagle, The
Posh
Starlight

Grown-Ups
28 Rainbow Grill
27 King Cole Bar
Bemelmans
Cafe Carlyle
26 Daniel
Four Seasons Bar

Hotel Bars
27 King Cole Bar
Bemelmans Bar
Cafe Carlyle
26 MO Bar
Regency Library Bar
25 Jean Georges

Irish
23 O'Lunney's
Molly's
22 McSorley's
Kinsale
Paddy Reilly's
21 Thady Con's

Jazz Clubs
25 Birdland
24 Jazz Standard
23 Village Vanguard
Blue Note
22 Smoke
Zinc Bar

Latin
25 ñ
24 Calle Ocho
23 Ideya
Copacabana
Son Cubano
Nuyorican Poets

Lesbian
22 Ginger's∇
21 Metropolitan∇
Starlight
18 Cubby Hole
17 Rubyfruit
16 Nowhere∇

Meat Markets

25 Hudson Hotel Bar
24 Cain
Therapy
Tao
23 Level V
Church Lounge

Music Clubs

24 Southpaw
Bowery Ballroom
23 CB's 313 Gallery
Living Room
Joe's Pub
Delancey

Newcomers/Rated

26 Floyd
25 House of Brews
Brooklyn Social
24 Cabanas
Cain
Freemans

Newcomers/Unrated

Aer
Duvet
East Side Co. Bar
Movida
Salon
Supreme Trading

Piano Bars

25 Brandy's Piano
23 Don't Tell Mama
22 Rose's Turn
21 Marie's Crisis
Helen's
19 Duplex

Pool Halls

23 Play▽
20 Slate
Q Lounge
18 Pressure
Amsterdam Billiards
17 Corner Billiards▽

Punk Bars

24 Ding Dong Lounge▽
22 CBGB's
20 Bellevue
Manitoba's*
19 Korova
18 Siberia

Quiet Conversation

28 Rainbow Grill
27 Milk and Honey
26 Four Seasons Bar
25 Otheroom
Angel's Share
24 Temple Bar

Roadhouse

20 Rodeo
Bellevue
Delta Grill*
Duke's (Gramercy)
18 Trailer Park
Hog Pit

Russian

23 Rasputin
Pravda
21 Russian Vodka Room
20 Russian Samovar
19 KGB
Anyway Cafe▽

Sports Bars

22 Croxley Ales
21 40/40
Bounce
20 Yankee Tavern
Tonic/Met Lounge
19 Riviera

Strip Clubs

27 Penthouse Exec. Club
23 Scores
18 VIP Club▽
Hustler Club▽
Flashdancers
16 Pussycat Lounge

Theme Bars

23 Zombie Hut
21 Burp Castle
20 Rodeo
Gstaad
Black Bear
Cowgirl*

Wine Bars

24 Bar Jamón
'inoteca
Bar Veloce
23 Enoteca I Trulli
Le Bateau Ivre
Ara Wine Bar

Top Appeal

By Location

Chelsea
24 Matsuri
Cabanas
Cain
Bar Veloce
Biltmore Room
23 Scores

East Village
26 Rue B
25 Angel's Share
24 Jules
Bar Veloce
Porch, The
Decibel

East 40s
27 Sakagura
25 Campbell Apt.
Top of the Tower
23 Morton's
22 Patroon
21 Thady Con's

East 50s
27 King Cole Bar
26 Four Seasons Bar
25 Harry Cipriani
24 Fifty Seven 57
Tao
23 Le Bateau Ivre

East 60s
26 Daniel
Regency Library Bar
24 Club Macanudo
Café Pierre
Geisha
23 Scores

East 70s
27 Bemelmans
Cafe Carlyle
26 Boat House
24 Mark's Bar
23 Sake Hana
Stir

East 80s
27 Met. Museum Roof
25 Brandy's Piano
23 Dt.Ut
Auction House
22 Manhattan Lounge
Bar @ Etats-Unis

East 90s & Up
22 Kinsale
19 Blondies
16 Brother Jimmy's
Big City
14 Bar East
13 Ruby's Tap House

Financial District
25 Rise
22 Bridge Cafe
21 Ulysses
19 Jeremy's Ale
Vine
Full Shilling

Flatiron District
26 Gramercy Tavern
25 Veritas
23 Flatiron Lounge
Gotham Comedy
SushiSamba
Pipa

Garment District/West 30s
23 Copacabana
Keens Steak
21 Uncle Jack's
20 Bellevue
19 Hammerstein Ballroom
18 Tír na Nóg

Gramercy Park
26 Eleven Madison Park
24 Bar Jamón
Jazz Standard
Tabla
Cibar
23 Enoteca I Trulli

Greenwich Village
25 Otheroom
One if by Land
Grey Dog's
Comedy Cellar
Otto
24 Chumley's

Little Italy
25 Odea▽
22 Double Happiness
21 M Bar
Onieal's Grand St.

Lower East Side

- **27** Milk and Honey
- **25** Whiskey Ward
- **24** Bowery Ballroom
  - 'inoteca
  - Freemans
  - Café Charbon

Meatpacking District

- **25** Spice Market
- **23** 5 Ninth
  - Level V
  - Pastis
  - Ono
  - Plunge

Murray Hill/East 30s

- **25** Asia de Cuba
- **24** Rare View
- **22** Wet Bar
- **21** Cherry
  - Dip
  - Ginger Man

NoHo

- **25** Bond Street
- **24** Temple Bar
  - Five Points
- **23** Table 50
  - Sala
- **21** Tom & Jerry's

NoLita

- **25** Public
- **23** Cafe Gitane
  - Pravda
- **22** Peasant
- **20** Vig Bar
- **19** Mexican Radio

SoHo

- **27** Room, The
- **25** ñ
  - Raoul's
- **24** Fiamma Osteria
  - Balthazar
  - Cipriani Downtown

TriBeCa

- **25** Megu
  - Dylan Prime
- **24** Harrison, The
  - Anotheroom
- **23** Church Lounge
  - Grace

Union Square

- **24** Union Sq. Cafe
  - Blue Water Grill
- **23** Luna Park
- **22** W Union Sq. Living Rm.
- **19** Coffee Shop
- **16** Heartland Brewery

West 40s

- **28** Rainbow Grill
- **27** Penthouse Exec. Club
- **25** House of Brews
  - Birdland
- **24** Royalton Lounge/Round Bar
  - Del Frisco's

West 50s

- **25** Single Rm. Occup.
  - Hudson Hotel Bar
- **24** Rink Bar
  - Pen-Top Bar
  - Hudson Hotel Library
  - Town*

West 60s

- **26** MO Bar
- **25** Jean Georges
- **24** Café des Artistes
- **23** Stone Rose
  - Tavern on Green
- **22** Rosa Mexicano

West 70s

- **26** Shalel
- **24** 'Cesca
  - Boat Basin
- **22** Beacon
  - Cafe Luxembourg
- **21** Citrus B&G

West 80s

- **24** Ouest
  - Calle Ocho
- **23** Cafe Lalo
- **21** Prohibition
  - George Keeley's
- **20** Rain

West 90s & Up

- **22** Smoke
  - Abbey Pub
- **21** Heights B&G
- **18** Cleopatra's Needle
- **16** Dive Bar
- **15** Eden

Top Appeal

Outer Boroughs

Bronx

22 An Béal Bocht ∇
20 Yankee Tavern
19 Stan's

**Brooklyn: Carroll Gardens/
Boerum Hill/Cobble Hill**

27 Brooklyn Inn
25 Brooklyn Social
23 Zombie Hut
Gowanus Yacht
22 BarTabac
21 Joya

Brooklyn: Fort Greene

27 Stonehome∇
21 Butta' Cup
20 Moe's
14 Five Spot∇
13 Frank's Cocktail∇

Brooklyn: Heights/Dumbo

26 Floyd
Superfine
20 Magnetic Field
Waterfront Ale House
13 Eamonn's
Water St. Bar∇

Brooklyn: Park Slope

25 Blue Ribbon Bklyn.
24 Southpaw
Gate, The
22 Patio Lounge
Miracle Grill
Tea Lounge

**Brooklyn: Williamsburg/
Greenpoint**

25 SEA
24 Pete's Candy Store
23 Teddy's
Brooklyn Ale
22 Brooklyn Brewery
21 Galapagos

Queens: Astoria

26 Bohemian Hall
25 Cávo
24 Cafe Bar
Central
19 Athens Café
16 Byzantio

Queens: Other

21 Uncle Jack's
19 Donovan's
Bartini's
17 Sidetracks
16 First Edition
Byzantio

Staten Island

25 Muddy Cup∇
23 Killmeyer's
21 Cargo
17 Jade Island∇
15 Big Nose Kate's

Most Visited

By Gender

Female
1. Pastis
2. Heartland Brewery
3. Coffee Shop
4. Blue Water Grill
5. Brother Jimmy's
6. Park, The
7. Spice Market
8. APT
9. Divine Bar
10. Asia de Cuba

Male
1. Heartland Brewery
2. Brother Jimmy's
3. Blue Water Grill
4. Coffee Shop
5. Balthazar
6. Hogs & Heifers
7. Asia de Cuba
8. Park, The
9. Pastis
10. XL

By Age

Twenties
1. Heartland Brewery
2. Brother Jimmy's
3. Park, The
4. Coffee Shop
5. APT
6. Lotus
7. Crobar
8. Joshua Tree
9. Pastis
10. Sutton Place

Forties
1. Blue Water Grill
2. Heartland Brewery
3. Balthazar
4. Pastis
5. Ruby Foo's
6. Asia de Cuba
7. Gotham B&G
8. Hogs & Heifers
9. Spice Market
10. B. B. King Blues

Thirties
1. Pastis
2. Heartland Brewery
3. Coffee Shop
4. Spice Market
5. Brother Jimmy's
6. Balthazar
7. Blue Water Grill
8. Asia de Cuba
9. Lotus
10. Tao

Fifties
1. Blue Water Grill
2. Gramercy Tavern
3. Heartland Brewery
4. Tavern on Green
5. Balthazar
6. P.J. Clarke's
7. Docks Oyster Bar
8. Ruby Foo's
9. Rosa Mexicano
10. Blarney Stone

Top Decor

28	Megu	Therapy
27	King Cole Bar	Asia de Cuba
	Daniel	Public
	Rainbow Grill	Cávo
	Spice Market	One if by Land
	Eleven Madison Park	Suba
	Campbell Apt.	**25** Taj
	Matsuri	Jean Georges
	SEA	MO Bar
	Met. Museum Roof	Stone Rose
	Bemelmans	Gramercy Tavern
26	Tao	Hudson Hotel Bar
	Villard	Guastavino's
	Sakagura	Café Pierre
	Hudson Hotel Library	Fiamma Osteria
	Biltmore Room	Brooklyn Inn
	Town	Geisha*
	Four Seasons Bar	Kemia*
	Shalel	Mark's Bar*
	Royalton Lounge/Round Bar	Brasserie 8½

Old New York

Bill's Gay 90's	McSorley's
Caffe Reggio	Old Town Bar
Campbell Apt.	Oyster Bar
Chumley's	Pete's Tavern
Ear Inn	P.J. Clarke's
Keens Steak	21 Club
Lenox Lounge	White Horse Tavern

Outdoors

Boat House	Moda Outdoors
Cabanas	One91
Cávo	Ono
Delancey, The	Park, The
5 Ninth	Rink Bar

Romance

Angel's Share	Le Colonial
Auction House	Milk and Honey
BED New York	Salon
Dove, The	Shalel
Duvet	Spice Market
La Lanterna	Villard

Views

Ava Lounge	Plunge
BED New York	Rare View
Boat Basin	Rise
Chelsea Brewing	Spirit Cruises
Met. Museum Roof	Stone Rose
Pen-Top Bar	Top of the Tower

Top Service

28	Daniel	Rainbow Grill
27	Gramercy Tavern	Superfine*
	Sakagura	Penthouse Exec. Club
26	Jean Georges	Union Sq. Cafe
	Bemelmans	Gotham B&G
	Café Pierre	Fifty Seven 57
	Four Seasons Bar	Tabla
	Veritas	V Steakhouse
25	Milk and Honey	Brooklyn Social
	One if by Land	Villard*
	Eleven Madison Park	Harrison, The
	Whiskey Ward	Harry Cipriani
	Blue Ribbon Bklyn.	Single Rm. Occup.*
	Cafe Carlyle	Del Frisco's
	Five Points	Club Macanudo
	House of Brews	Killmeyer's*
24	King Cole Bar	Blue Ribbon
	Morton's	Keens Steak
	Mark's Bar	Posh*
	Ouest	Café des Artistes
	Patrick Kavanagh's	Temple Bar
	O'Lunney's*	Abbey
	Chibi's/Chibitini	Brooklyn Ale*
	Otheroom	Cité Grill*
	Fiamma Osteria	Feinsteins/Regency*
23	21 Club	Regency Library Bar*
	Angel's Share	Tavern on Jane*

Best Buys

1. Gowanus Yacht
2. Brooklyn Inn
3. Whiskey Ward
4. Floyd
5. O'Connor's
6. alt.coffee
7. Brooklyn Social
8. Pete's Candy Store
9. Union Pool
10. House of Brews
11. Welcome/Johnsons
12. Brooklyn Ale
13. Gate, The
14. Motor City Bar
15. George Keeley's
16. Tea Lounge
17. Brooklyn Brewery
18. Patio Lounge
19. Enid's
20. Bellevue
21. McSorley's
22. Abbey
23. Zombie Hut
24. Magnetic Field
25. Teddy's
26. Great Lakes
27. Black Bear
28. Mug's Ale
29. Bowery Poetry
30. Boat
31. Dead Poet
32. Swift
33. Loki Lounge
34. McGee's
35. Bohemian Hall
36. Rudy's
37. Bar Reis
38. Corner Bistro
39. Trinity Public Hse.
40. Last Exit
41. Grey Dog's
42. Kinsale
43. Grassroots
44. Pine Tree Lodge
45. Rififi
46. Otheroom
47. Manitoba's
48. SEA
49. Stoned Crow
50. Hook and Ladder

Nightlife Directory

A&M Roadhouse
▽ | 19 | 18 | 20 | $7

57 Murray St. (bet. Church St. & W. B'way), 1/2/3 to Chambers St., 212-385-9005; www.amroadhouse.com

"Nothing's fancy" at this Financial District roadhouse, starting with the "down-to-earth" barkeeps who "keep the suds flowing" while "talking up a storm"; just-the-facts-ma'am decor, "tasty BBQ" ("don't wear white") and "rocking live music on weekends" contribute to the "simple, easy" vibe.

Abbey, The ⊅
21 | 13 | 23 | $6

536 Driggs Ave. (bet. N. 7th & 8th Sts.), Brooklyn, L to Bedford Ave., 718-599-4400

Sure, the decor's "boring" but the crowd's "hip" at this "laid-back" Williamsburg "staple" patronized for its "amazing jukebox" and "affordable" pops; amusements include "talking to old guys who have been there for years" or watching the "trucker-hat boys play pool."

Abbey Pub
22 | 15 | 19 | $7

237 W. 105th St. (bet. Amsterdam Ave. & B'way), 1 to 103rd St., 212-222-8713

Maybe "Columbiaville's best dive", this "multigenerational" West Side taproom draws an "odd mix of poets, drunks" and "grad students" to the "potentially indecent corners" of its "dark-wood" and "stained-glass" setting; it's just the ticket for a "shot-and-a-beer afternoon", abetted by "cheap" pours and a "lovely" staff.

Absolutely 4th
19 | 18 | 18 | $9

228 W. Fourth St. (bet. 7th Ave. S. & W. 10th St.), 1 to Christopher St., 212-989-9444; www.absolutely4th.net

Thanks to a "great location" and a nightly "two-for-one martini" deal, this Village lounge can get "a little too mobbed" – and a little too happy since the drinks go down like "liquid candy"; snobs say it attracts the "Murray Hill crowd", but songbirds trill it's a must on Wednesdays for some "serious karaoke."

Ace Bar
19 | 15 | 16 | $7

531 E. Fifth St. (bet. Aves. A & B), L to 1st Ave., 212-979-8476

"Totally group friendly", this "huge", "no-frills" East Villager boasts a "couple of pool tables", darts and "board games" galore, plus a "fabulous collection of vintage lunchboxes" that serve to "spur conversation"; since you won't be "dropping too much cash", there's "no need to get dressed up."

Ace of Clubs ⊅
– | – | – | M

(fka Acme Underground)

9 Great Jones St. (Lafayette St.), 6 to Bleecker St., 212-677-6963; www.aceofclubsnyc.com

"Listen to your favorite local band" at this "dark" basement venue, formerly Acme Underground and now newly renamed and lightly renovated; there's the same "gritty live music" as before, and the space is "not without its charm", particularly after a couple of "buckets of Rolling Rock."

AER
– | – | – | VE

409 W. 13th St. (bet. 9th Ave. & Washington St.), A/C/E/L to 14th St./8th Ave., 212-989-0100; www.aerlounge.com

There's plenty of breathing room at this latest Meatpacking District super-club contender, a sprawling 10,000-square-footer featuring dining, dancing and lounging in its vast, ground-floor space, with a slick, Lucite-and-white lounge downstairs reserved for VIPs and bottle buyers; while not exactly a red-hot scene, so far it's drawing a mixed crowd of hip and not-so-hip types.

Agozar!
18 | 17 | 19 | $9

324 Bowery (Bleecker St.), 6 to Bleecker St., 212-677-6773;
www.agozarnyc.com
"Pretty crowds" toy with "Latin drinks" at this "cool" Cuban bar/
restaurant on the Bowery where "mojitos and sangria rule" the roost;
the "tiny", "L-shaped" space is "perfect for small parties" or intimate
encounters, and in addition to a notable "happy hour", there's some
"darn good tapas" served.

Alamo, The
– | – | – | M

304 E. 48th St. (2nd Ave.), 6 to 51st St./Lexington Ave., 212-759-0590;
www.thealamorestaurant.com
Back after a three-year siesta, this resuscitated Mexican bar/eatery
near the UN still boasts the same deep tequila selection (and lethal
margaritas) that fueled many after-work fiestas in the '80s and '90s; it's
more of a local favorite than a destination watering hole, particularly
given the dearth of alternatives in Turtle Bay.

Algonquin Blue Bar
– | – | – | E

Algonquin Hotel, 59 W. 44th St. (bet. 5th & 6th Aves.), 7/B/D/F/V to 42nd St./
6th Ave., 212-840-6800; www.algonquinhotel.com

Algonquin Lobby Lounge
Algonquin Hotel, 59 W. 44th St. (bet. 5th & 6th Aves.), 7/B/D/F/V to 42nd St./
6th Ave., 212-840-6800; www.algonquinhotel.com
These dual watering holes in the Theater District's Algonquin Hotel
bring back "literary memories" of the Round Table wits who once held
court here; nowadays the Blue Bar is a cozy, conversation friendly
enclave decorated with Hirschfeld drawings, while the Lobby Lounge
offers prime seating for stellar, only-in-NY people-watching.

Alibi
20 | 19 | 18 | $8

116 MacDougal St. (bet. Bleecker & W. 3rd Sts.), A/B/C/D/E/F/V to W. 4th St.,
212-254-9996; www.alibiny.com
"One of the more swank locales along MacDougal Street", this "fun"
bar/lounge dispenses "gourmet" cocktails with "style"; although pretty
much "empty" during the week due to a "hidden", subterranean
location, it perks up on weekends thanks to a "loud DJ."

Alligator Lounge ⊅
15 | 12 | 22 | $6

600 Metropolitan Ave. (Lorimer St.), Brooklyn, L to Lorimer St.,
718-599-4440
"Strange but true": you get "free pizza with any drink" at this "only-in-
Brooklyn" East Williamsburg bar; cynics say the gratis slice "gimmick
won't last long" ("how can they afford it?"), but for distraction there's
always the "kitschy" back room decorated like a "small community
theater production of *South Pacific*."

All State Cafe ⊅
15 | 10 | 17 | $8

250 W. 72nd St. (bet. B'way & West End Ave.), 1/2/3 to 72nd St.,
212-874-1883
It "feels like home" at this Upper West Side "burger-and-beer" vendor,
even if it's "not entirely attractive" (and verging on "down 'n' dirty");
still, prices are "cheap", the mood's "low-key" and "if it's a stool you're
looking for, there are always plenty" available.

Alphabet Lounge
18 | 13 | 16 | $7

104 Ave. C (7th St.), L to 1st Ave., 212-780-0202
"Cheesy '80s music" fills the air at this "unpretentious", "no-frills"
East Village barroom; although "lacking in decor" (read: "grungy"),
it's still a "wonderful place to get lost" and is "packed on weekend
nights" with "easygoing" folks "out to party" hearty.

alt.coffee ⊘   21 | 17 | 20 | $5

139 Ave. A (bet. 8th & 9th Sts.), L to 1st Ave., 212-529-2233;
www.altdotcoffee.com
This "punk rock coffeehouse" opposite Tompkins Square Park offers "Internet access", "sunken-in couches" and a "hip staff" in one "funky", "cozy" package – and is "open late" to boot; sure, the house brew may be "kinda bitter", but so is its "grungy young" following.

American Spirits Saloon   10 | 9 | 14 | $6

1744 Second Ave. (bet. 90th & 91st Sts.), 4/5/6 to 86th St., 212-289-7510;
www.americanspiritsbar.com
"Rowdy" collegians and those who love them frequent this "typical" Upper East Side "dive" best known for its "cheap" drinks and American flag–festooned interior; foes fret it can be too much of a "sausage-fest", but at least the "loud music" will "drown out the drunken frat boy talking to you about nothing."

American Trash   12 | 9 | 14 | $7

1471 First Ave. (bet. 76th & 77th Sts.), 6 to 77th St., 212-988-9008;
www.americantrashnyc.com
"Just like it sounds", this "hard-core" East Side "bottom of the barrel" attracts "rocker/biker" types with "flowing shots", one of the "best [metal] jukeboxes in the city" and an overall "booty-call" vibe; for best results, "leave your ego at the door", be "already drunk by the time you get there" and "don't wear your Sunday best."

Amsterdam Billiards & Bar   18 | 15 | 16 | $8

344 Amsterdam Ave., 2nd fl. (bet. 76th & 77th Sts.), 1 to 79th St., 212-496-8180;
www.amsterdambilliardclub.com
"Billiards without sleaziness" summarizes this "upscale" Upper Westsider that's "classier than your average pool hall", with prices to match; "loads of tables", a "lovely fireplace" and plenty of "good-lookers" who "know how to handle a stick" are reasons for its popularity; P.S. scratch the East Side satellite, recently closed.

Amuse   20 | 20 | 18 | $11

108 W. 18th St. (bet. 6th & 7th Aves.), 1 to 18th St., 212-929-9755;
www.amusenyc.com
"Cool, calm and collected", this "sophisticated" Chelsea bar/eatery lures "mature" types with "plenty of room" and a "modest noise level"; some folks find the design "schizophrenic" what with the "gorgeous", circa-1889 bar surrounded by "minimalist" furnishings, but overall this "suave boîte" has "unexpected appeal" – and "the food's great" too.

Anatomy Bar   – | – | – | M

511 E. Sixth St. (bet. Aves. A & B), L to 1st Ave., 212-995-8889;
www.anatomybarandlounge.com
X-rays on the wall are a nod to the vague anatomical theme of this double-decker East Villager, with a zig-zag bar upstairs and a "funky", pool table–equipped space below; the sometimes "spotty attention" from the staff is reflected in the oftentimes spotty attendance.

An Béal Bocht   ∇ 22 | 18 | 22 | $9

445 W. 238th St. (bet. Greystone & Waldo Aves.), Bronx, 1 to 238th St.,
718-884-7121
Find "bohemia" near Manhattan College at this "tiny" Riverdale Irish pub that serves as an "updated Beat Generation hangout" for its "locals-and-students" crowd; "live music" on weekends and "friendly barmaids" who know how to pour a Guinness keep it "hopping right up until 4 AM."

Angelo & Maxie's
19 | 19 | 19 | $11

233 Park Ave. S. (19th St.), 6 to 23rd St., 212-220-9200;
www.angelo-maxies.com
"Men, men and more men" populate this "hopping" Flatiron bar/
steakhouse that's plainly a "good hunting ground" for single gals
(even if some find the scene too "loud, obnoxious" and "suburban");
now that cigar smoking is "nonexistent" here, it's perhaps best known
as the "home of the white chocolate martini."

ANGEL'S SHARE
25 | 22 | 23 | $10

8 Stuyvesant St., 2nd fl. (9th St. at 3rd Ave.), 6 to Astor Pl., 212-777-5415
"Precisely measured, accurately crafted cocktails" are the calling
cards of this "inconspicuous" East Village "drinker's paradise" that's
reminiscent of a "spy-novel rendezvous" given its "hidden", second-
floor location and "mostly silent" staff; this one's "guaranteed to
impress" if you obey the house rules ("no standing, no loud talking",
"no parties larger than four"), and thus the perfect spot in which to
"snuggle with your sweetie."

Angry Wade's
13 | 14 | 16 | $6

222 Smith St. (Butler St.), Brooklyn, F/G to Bergen St., 718-488-7253
"Not the usual Smith Street scene", this "serviceable" sports pub
may be a good "default bar" thanks to the "common bond of alcohol",
but analysts say its "eclectic mix of hipsters and boys from the 'hood
doesn't jell"; regulars relish its fireplace and pool table, not the "loud
TVs and even louder crowd."

Annie Moores
16 | 15 | 18 | $7

*50 E. 43rd St. (bet. Madison & Vanderbilt Aves.), 4/5/6/7/S to 42nd St./
Grand Central, 212-986-7826*
"Close proximity to Grand Central" makes this "big" Irish pub a
"commuter crowd favorite", especially since Metro-North schedules
are conveniently posted on video monitors; decorwise, there's "wood,
wood everywhere" and crowdwise, "suburban-bound family men"
killing time with "reasonably priced drinks and bar food."

Anotheroom
24 | 19 | 21 | $8

*249 W. Broadway (bet. Beach & N. Moore Sts.), A/C/E to Canal St.,
212-226-1418*
"Small, dark and quiet", this TriBeCa "boîte noir" attracts "stylish
thirtysomethings" with "interesting wine selections" and a "nice
assortment of beers on tap" (no hard liquor is served); insiders
"go early or late", since there's "no room to stand if you don't get a
barstool or banquette."

Antarctica
16 | 9 | 17 | $6

287 Hudson St. (Spring St.), C/E to Spring St., 212-352-1666;
www.antarcticabar.com
Located in the "middle of nowhere", this West SoHo "dive" keeps
cool with "affordable" pricing, an "attitude-free vibe" and bartenders
more than "generous with buy-backs"; if your name "matches the name
of the day" (posted on their Web site), "you drink for free."

Anytime
∇ 18 | 15 | 14 | $6

*93 N. Sixth St. (bet. Berry St. & Wythe Ave.), Brooklyn, L to Bedford Ave.,
718-218-7272; www.anytimeny.com*
What was originally a nondescript Williamsburg take-out/delivery
joint has been spiffed up and expanded to include table service as
well as a bar/lounge area; although no longer a 24/7 operation, a
choice location in the middle of happening North Sixth Street keeps
the trade brisk.

Anyway Cafe
▽ 19 | 14 | 18 | $8

34 E. Second St. (bet. Bowery & 2nd Ave.), F/V to Lower East Side/2nd Ave., 212-533-3412
1602 Gravesend Neck Rd. (16th St.), Brooklyn, Q to Neck Rd., 718-934-5988
111 Oriental Blvd. (West End Ave.), Brooklyn, B/Q to Brighton Beach, 718-648-3906
www.anywaycafe.com

"Hidden in plain sight", this "bohemian" East Village cafe (and its two Brooklyn siblings) is known for its "Russian-style" approach to nightlife, starting with those "homemade infused vodkas"; "passable live music" and "open-mike nights" lend a "hippie European vibe."

Apartment 138
– | – | – | M

138 Smith St. (bet. Bergen & Dean Sts.), Brooklyn, F/G to Bergen St., 718-858-0556

A former Boerum Hill apartment/office space reinvented as a bar/lounge, this new Smith Street arrival offers all the comforts of home along with strong specialty martinis and simple American grub; downstairs, there's a game room equipped with pool and foosball tables as well as access to garden seating.

Apocalypse Lounge
▽ 18 | 17 | 16 | $5

189 E. Third St. (bet. Aves. A & B), F/V to Lower East Side/2nd Ave., 212-228-4811; www.clubapocalypse.com

"You definitely know you're in the East Village" at this "arty" bar that's decidedly "not a pickup spot", but rather a "grungy, gritty, gamey" magnet for creative folk; "cheap beer", monthly changing art, two performance spaces and an ultra-funky basement seal the deal.

APT
22 | 23 | 16 | $12

419 W. 13th St. (bet. 9th Ave. & Washington St.), A/C/E/L to 14th St./8th Ave., 212-414-4245; www.aptwebsite.com

For a "real loft party experience without the mortgage", check into this smooth Meatpacking District lounge with an "at-home feel second to none"; upstairs looks like a "well-decorated" "bachelor pad" (complete with bed), while the lower level sports parallel bars and "great DJ talent"; maybe the "crowd's not as exclusive as before", but the door's still "hard" and policed by "annoying list checkers."

Ara Wine Bar
23 | 21 | 19 | $10

24 Ninth Ave. (bet. 13th & 14th Sts.), A/C/E/L to 14th St./8th Ave., 212-242-8642

A "welcome" change from all the neighboring "velvet rope nonsense", this "sophisticated little wine bar" stands apart from the rest of the "overly done" Meatpacking District; credit its "knowledgeable, friendly" staff, "wonderful" selection of vinos and a "cozy", "loungey nook" in the back that works well for "intimate social experiences."

Arlene Grocery
20 | 13 | 17 | $6

95 Stanton St. (bet. Ludlow & Orchard Sts.), F/V to Lower East Side/2nd Ave., 212-358-1633; www.arlene-grocery.com

"Emo boys and girls" dig this "bare-bones" Lower Eastsider, a "reliable default" bar showcasing "semi-decent up-and-coming" musicians; it's a "worthy enough scene even if the bands suck", and Monday's "punk rock/heavy metal karaoke" (replete with a "live band and tossed drinks") "brings out the big hair and acid denim in all of us."

Art Bar
17 | 16 | 16 | $8

52 Eighth Ave. (bet. Horatio & Jane Sts.), A/C/E/L to 14th St./8th Ave., 212-727-0244; www.merchantsny.com

An "old standby for a reason", this "low-key" Village bar is renowned for its "warm and fuzzy" back room replete with a "roaring fireplace" and "miscellaneous art splashed on the walls" (the ho-hum front room is "just a tease"); it's "always reliable for late-night drinks", "especially if seduction is on your mind."

Arthur's Tavern ⊭   22 | 15 | 19 | $8

57 Grove St. (bet. Bleecker St. & 7th Ave. S.), 1 to Christopher St., 212-675-6879; www.arthurstavernnyc.com

There's a "never a cover" at this "longtime neighborhood" music venue that "reminds you of what the Village used to be", starting with the "cheap" drinks; expect "characters galore" in the "lively, happy" crowd, all bopping to "really sweet" "classic Dixieland" and "New Orleans–style jazz."

ASIA DE CUBA   25 | 26 | 20 | $13

Morgans Hotel, 237 Madison Ave. (bet. 37th & 38th Sts.), 6 to 33rd St., 212-726-7755; www.chinagrillmanagement.com

Still "hanging in there", this "timeless" nightspot/restaurant continues to "ooze sex appeal" thanks to a potent mix of "amazing martinis", "Miami-hot" decor and a "beautiful", "hot-cha-cha" following; sure, it's "always crowded", "service at the tiny bar is slow" and you can expect to blow "major bucks", but "if you must go out in Murray Hill", this is the place to be.

Athens Cafe   19 | 17 | 16 | $9

32-07 30th Ave. (bet. 32nd & 33rd Sts.), Queens, N/W to 30th Ave., 718-626-2164

"Always packed", this "recently renovated" "über-Greek" cafe is like a "little piece of Europe" plunked down in Astoria; by day a "great chill-out" spot offering "people-watching for hours", it gets more "rowdy" after dark, when the "service can be trying."

Aubette   19 | 20 | 19 | $10

119 E. 27th St. (bet. Lexington Ave. & Park Ave. S.), 6 to 28th St., 212-686-5500; www.aubette.com

"Seductive" and "sexy", this "low-key", "high-ceilinged" Gramercy lounge has just the "right amount of edginess" to satisfy its "stylish" but "nonpretentious" following; regulars "head to the back", a "dark" nook with its own bar and fireplace that's got "make-out scene" written all over it.

Auction House   23 | 23 | 20 | $8

300 E. 89th St. (bet. 1st & 2nd Aves.), 4/5/6 to 86th St., 212-427-4458

Upper Eastsiders who "don't play beer pong" tout this "dark", "velvety" lounge as an "excellent alternative to the frat scene plaguing Second Avenue"; done up with "vintage bric-a-brac", "nude paintings" and plenty of cuddly couches, it's got "second date" appeal (i.e. "lots of necking going on") and is also known as a "NY Rangers hangout."

Automatic Slim's   19 | 11 | 14 | $8

733 Washington St. (Bank St.), A/C/E/L to 14th St./8th Ave., 212-645-8660

"Wall-to-wall people" jammed into a space "smaller than some dorm rooms" makes for "sweaty" times at this Village watering hole that's a "drunk preppy meat market" on weekends; expect "inappropriate" behavior from the "easy bachelorettes" and "unnecessarily forward men" in attendance, all with "nothing to lose except their inhibitions."

Avalon   17 | 19 | 14 | $12

662 Sixth Ave. (20th St.), F/V to 23rd St., 212-807-7780; www.avalonnewyorkcity.com

A "good old-fashioned thumping dance club", this "cavernous" Chelsea venue is carved out of a former church and was previously home to Limelight, the notorious "'80s club kid" hangout; some say this "poor imitation" has "lost its spark", citing "overpriced drinks", "airport-lounge" looks and a "mostly B&T" following, but idolizers adore the "outdoor smoking patio" and "less crowded" VIP space, Spider Club.

Ava Lounge
23 | 21 | 17 | $11

Dream Hotel, 210 W. 55th St., 14th fl. (B'way), N/Q/R/W to 57th St./7th Ave., 212-956-7020; www.avaloungenyc.com
It's "all about indulgence" at this "way cool" "sky-high" Midtown lounge that draws huzzahs for its "penthouse" airs and "fabulous" rooftop bar equipped with an "outdoor bed"; inside, picture a "*Bright Lights, Big City*" scene with "young Uptown execs" "forking over a fortune for drinks" and the inevitable "stinky service" from "models pretending to be waitresses."

Azaza
∇ 14 | 18 | 16 | $10

891 First Ave. (50th St.), 6 to 51st St./Lexington Ave., 212-751-0700; www.azazanyc.com
Parked in a "not too popular area" off Sutton Place is this "low-key" bar/lounge offering different terraced levels for your drinking enjoyment; even though "service is friendly" and the digs "nicely decorated", some shrug "wannabe."

Babel Lounge
– | – | – | M

131 Ave. C (8th St.), L to 1st Ave., 212-505-3468; www.babellounge.com
Take a trip to Morocco on Avenue C via this new bar/eatery where hookahs, belly dancers and live Middle Eastern music supply the authenticity; for best results, bring a group as this far-out stretch of Alphabet City is usually underpopulated.

Back Fence
18 | 9 | 14 | $7

155 Bleecker St. (Thompson St.), A/B/C/D/E/F/V to W. 4th St., 212-475-9221; www.thebackfenceonline.com
"Semi-talented musicians" "perpetually playing Eagles" covers take the stage at this longtime "Village landmark", an "old-school bar" known for its "cheap beer", "peanut shells on the ground" and overall "rollicking" mood; the "dingy" digs don't faze the mix of "NYU students and aging boomers" in the crowd.

Back Page
18 | 15 | 16 | $6

1472 Third Ave. (bet. 83rd & 84th Sts.), 4/5/6 to 86th St., 212-570-5800; www.backpagebar.com
There are "TVs everywhere you look" (enough of them to "ensure that your game will be on") at this "basic" East Side sports bar; its "meat-and-potatoes" following shows up to "view sports, and not for anything else", though the "top-notch" buffalo wings are a secondary draw.

Baggot Inn
18 | 11 | 19 | $7

82 W. Third St. (bet. Sullivan & Thompson Sts.), A/B/C/D/E/F/V to W. 4th St., 212-477-0622; www.baggotinn.com
It may be "dark as a dungeon", but this Village Irish pub lightens up with nightly live music running the gamut from "great to decent" (it also hosts one of the city's "best bluegrass nights" on Wednesdays); a "down-to-earth" vibe, "friendly" barkeeps and "reasonably priced drinks" compensate for the "bare-bones" decor.

Baker Street Pub
18 | 15 | 20 | $7

1152 First Ave. (63rd St.), 4/5/6/N/R/W to 59th St./Lexington Ave., 212-688-9663; www.bakerstreetnyc.com
This "solid Irish pub" may be famed as the location for the "Tom Cruise movie *Cocktail*" (and the site of NY's very first TGI Fridays in '65), but today it's just a "casual" joint with a "friendly, playful" vibe; despite "not much atmosphere", it's hard to beat for "down-to-earth" drinking.

BALTHAZAR
24 | 24 | 20 | $12

80 Spring St. (bet. B'way & Crosby St.), 6 to Spring St., 212-965-1414; www.balthazarny.com

"Cheek kissing" is the preferred mode of greeting at this "so *français*" SoHo "institution" where "interesting characters" and "beautiful women looking for a second husband" hold court at the bar; a "vibrant", "spirited" atmosphere charged by random "star sightings" and "*très cher*" cocktails makes for "lots of energy" at this "very NY" – albeit "mock Parisian" – scene.

BAMcafé
23 | 22 | 20 | $10

Brooklyn Academy of Music, 30 Lafayette Ave. (Ashland Pl.), Brooklyn, 2/3/4/5/B/Q to Atlantic Ave., 718-636-4100; www.bam.org

"Savor a drink before a performance" at the Brooklyn Academy of Music at this "cool cafe" offering equal parts of "culture and serenity"; even if its hours of operation are "sort of unpredictable", it's always an "interesting" evening with "live music sometimes" as a bonus.

Banc Cafe
17 | 19 | 18 | $9

431 Third Ave. (30th St.), 6 to 33rd St., 212-252-0146; www.banccafe.com

Murray Hill's longtime Bank Cafe has "just reopened" and is "worthy of a deposit" after its "great redo" and slight name tweak; look for the "same crowd" in "ever so chic", faux-Parisian environs, and even if spoilers "miss the pool table", at least the "bathrooms are nicer."

Bandol
17 | 16 | 17 | $11

181 E. 78th St. (bet. Lexington & 3rd Aves.), 6 to 77th St., 212-744-1800; www.bandolbistro.com

"Tucked away" on the Upper East Side, this "quietish little" wine bar/eatery offers a "broad", "comprehensive" selection of vinos dispensed with "French flair"; indeed, with 50-plus varieties available by the glass (and over 100 by the bottle), it's no wonder that it can sometimes feel "cramped."

Baraonda
20 | 20 | 17 | $11

1439 Second Ave. (75th St.), 6 to 77th St., 212-288-8555; www.baraondany.com

"Everyone's out to have a good time" at this Upper East Side bar/ restaurant where "Euro-trendies" turn up to "dance on tabletops" on Sunday and Wednesday nights; sure, the "tight space" can get "slightly chaotic" with all the "cologne and perfume" and "plastic surgery" on display, but the payoff is a scene that's "perpetually *en fuego*."

Bar @ Etats-Unis
22 | 17 | 22 | $11

247 E. 81st St. (bet. 2nd & 3rd Aves.), 4/5/6 to 86th St., 212-396-9928

"Low-key" says it all about this East Side wine bar, a "secret escape" parked opposite its "more serious mother restaurant", Etats-Unis; even though it's "too small for comfort" (26 seats) and no rezzies makes getting in "a gamble", it's still "one of the hippest places" in the area.

Baraza ⊄
23 | 16 | 18 | $8

133 Ave. C (bet. 8th & 9th Sts.), L to 1st Ave., 212-539-0811

"Hot 'n' sweaty" times await at this Latin-themed East Village bar that's usually "cramped and crowded" with amiable folks "out to have fun"; the "extremely affordable" mojitos and caipirinhas may come in plastic cups, but "no one cares at those prices"; P.S. "check out the bathroom covered in pennies."

Barbalùc
21 | 25 | 22 | $12

135 E. 65th St. (bet. Lexington & Park Aves.), 6 to 68th St., 212-774-1999; www.barbaluc.com

"Older sophisticates" and "stylish Euros" are drawn to this "lovely" if "underpopulated" wine bar near Bloomie's perched above a more formal dining room below; its minimalist, "eye-catching" design sets the "calm" tone here, and the staff is "welcoming even if you're not dressed in Gucci or Armani."

Bar Below ⌐   16 | 19 | 18 | $8
209 Smith St., downstairs (bet. Baltic & Butler Sts.), Brooklyn, F/G to Carroll St., 718-694-2277
Featuring a design that looks like a cross between a "swimming pool", a "sauna" and a "suburban YMCA", this white-tiled Cobble Hill "bar below the restaurant Faan" earns kudos for being "quite the singles scene"; but foes say its "strange mix of people" and "claustrophobia-inducing lack of windows" just "doesn't cut it."

Barbès   ▽ 22 | 16 | 21 | $7
376 Ninth St. (6th Ave.), Brooklyn, F to 7th Ave., 718-965-9177;
www.barbesbrooklyn.com
For "Manhattan quality entertainment without leaving the nabe", Park Slopers head to this "cozy" bar for an "eclectic array" of "free live music", readings, movies and other "intellectual" pursuits; while it oozes *beaucoup de* "Parisian cool", fans still "wish it were bigger."

Barcade   – | – | – | M
388 Union Ave. (bet. Ainslie & Powers Sts.), Brooklyn, G/L to Metropolitan Ave./ Lorimer St., 718-302-6464; www.barcadebrooklyn.com
As the name implies, this new Williamsburg barroom sports a wide array of vintage arcade games (at equally vintage prices, 25 cents a play), all lined up in a gritty warehouse space that comes complete with its own resident dog; drinkingwise, there's an impressive list of tap and bottled brews as well as the hard stuff.

Bar Coastal   16 | 12 | 18 | $6
1495 First Ave. (78th St.), 6 to 77th St., 212-288-6635; www.barcoastal.com
"Much like the rest on this strip" – "hello, fraternity row!" – this Upper East Side sports bar–cum–"sausagefest" may be "nothing special", but at least it's "not too crowded"; just be careful not to get so drunk that the "wings look more appetizing than the women."

Bar East   14 | 8 | 18 | $5
1733 First Ave. (90th St.), 4/5/6 to 86th St., 212-876-0203
Granted, it's a "little out of the way", so this "huge" Yorkville Irish pub can be pretty "dead in the middle of the week", but things pick up on weekends when the new downstairs music space, the Underscore, gets going; critics find "no personality", but fans say the "friendly neighborhood" mood makes for "relaxing good times."

Bar 89   22 | 24 | 19 | $12
89 Mercer St. (bet. Broome & Spring Sts.), B/D/F/V to B'way/Lafayette St., 212-274-0989
It's all about the "peekaboo" bathrooms at this "old reliable" SoHo lounge where the "ultracool" see-thru doors "frost over after the lock is latched"; the rest of the "chic", bi-level space is equally eye-opening, from the "cute bartenders" to the "super-high ceilings" to "how quick the bar tab rises."

Bar 515   16 | 15 | 15 | $8
515 Third Ave. (bet. 34th & 35th Sts.), 6 to 33rd St., 212-532-3300;
www.bar515.com
A "kick-back crowd" of "totally wasted" "twentysomethings just out of college" converges on this "fratty" sports bar parked on the "Murray Hill strip"; while some say this "Joshua Tree clone" has "nothing to distinguish itself" from the competition, others call it a "good-for-everything place", citing "after-work happy-hour" appeal.

Barfly

16	14	18	$7

244 Third Ave. (20th St.), 6 to 23rd St., 212-473-9660

Home to "many loyal locals", this "decent" enough Gramercy sports bar sports the usual ton of TVs ogled by "frat" boys guzzling cheap "pitchers of beer"; maybe it's "just your average hole-in-the-wall" to some, but for athletic supporters it's still a "good place to catch a game."

Bar 41

∇ 21	21	20	$9

Hotel 41 at Times Square, 206 W. 41st St. (7th Ave.), 1/2/3/7/N/Q/R/S/W to 42nd St./Times Sq., 212-703-8600; www.hotel41.com

On a secluded Theater District block "next to *Rent*" lies this "classy" little hotel bar that's particularly "well-located" for Port Authority commuters; it also attracts suits from "nearby Ernst & Young", who like the "intimacy" and don't mind that it's a "bit on the pricey side."

Bar 4

∇ 14	18	18	$8

444 Seventh Ave. (15th St.), Brooklyn, F to 7th Ave., 718-832-9800; www.bar4.net

The "trendy", the "artistic" and the "young" go for this "laid-back" lounge that imparts the feeling of "Manhattan transported to Park Slope"; even better, it offers a long list of specialty martinis and is "open later than other things on the block."

Bar Jamón

24	20	22	$11

125 E. 17th St. (Irving Pl.), 4/5/6/L/N/Q/R/W to 14th St./Union Sq., 212-253-2773

Those "nostalgic for Barcelona" tout this "little Spanish wine bar" in Gramercy Park that's a satellite of Casa Mono around the corner; given the beyond-"minuscule" setting ("bring your thin friends"), it's frequently "impossible to get in", but the "excellent choice" of vinos and "tasty snacks" make the "elbow-to-elbow" scene more bearable.

Bar Masa

∇ 21	23	22	$15

Time Warner Ctr., 10 Columbus Circle, 4th fl. (60th St. at B'way), 1/A/B/C/D to 59th St./Columbus Circle, 212-823-9800

"Hidden in the Time Warner Center", this "oh-so-chic" adjunct of Masa (NY's most expensive restaurant) may not be as "ridiculously priced", but is still pretty darn "expensive"; high maintenance types say the overall "experience is nowhere near" that of its sire, yet the "fab" ambiance and smooth service still seduces some of the "upper crust."

Bar Nine

16	13	18	$7

807 Ninth Ave. (bet. 53rd & 54th Sts.), C/E to 50th St., 212-399-9336; www.barnine.com

There's "lots of space" at this "loud" Hell's Kitchen venue where the "best area is the back room" stocked with "loungey" (albeit "grungy") couches; some say it's "kinda stale" and could use a redo, but at least there's no problem "getting a drink here in prompt fashion."

Bar None

11	8	13	$7

98 Third Ave. (bet. 12th & 13th Sts.), L to 3rd Ave., 212-777-6663; www.barnonenyc.com

For "binge drinking in a no-frills atmosphere", look no further than this "skanky" East Village "dive" just "around the corner from the NYU dorms"; while there's nothing wrong with the "can't-be-beat" 11 PM power hour (featuring $2 drinks), the "permanent stale beer smell" and "massive crowds" of "frat boys gone wild" are another story.

Bar on A

∇ 22	20	23	$7

170 Ave. A (bet. 10th & 11th Sts.), L to 1st Ave., 212-353-8231; www.baronanyc.com

Folks who "wish it were bigger" will be pleased to hear that this East Village watering hole is "newly expanded" to almost double its size;

it's "never overly crowded (especially for this neighborhood)", and the "friendly" barkeeps contribute to the "nice", relaxed vibe.

Barracuda ⬆ | 19 | 14 | 17 | $8 |

275 W. 22nd St. (bet. 7th & 8th Aves.), C/E to 23rd St., 212-645-8613
It's the "un-Chelsea-like", "boy-next-door" crowd that's the real draw at this "funky" Chelsea gay bar that's been "renovated more times than Joan Rivers"; some of "NY's hottest transvestites" appear in its "frequent drag performances", and like everywhere else, the "crowd gets better looking as the night wears on."

Barrage ⬆ | 20 | 15 | 18 | $9 |

401 W. 47th St. (bet. 9th & 10th Aves.), C/E to 50th St., 212-586-9390
Further evidence that "Chelsea's moving north" is this "cool" Hell's Kitchen gay bar frequented by a "nice mix" of "casual drinkers and serious cruisers"; while some say it's "lost its luster" since rival Therapy appeared on the scene, a "great 11 PM–12 AM happy hour" still "draws crowds."

Barramundi ⬆ | 20 | 18 | 18 | $7 |

67 Clinton St. (bet. Rivington & Stanton Sts.), F/J/M/Z to Delancey/ Essex Sts., 212-529-6900; www.barramundinyc.com
This Lower East Side "old standard" has relocated several blocks east to Clinton Street but remains just as "low-priced", "low-key" and "laid-back" as ever; expect an "interesting" "young hipster" following, "friendly" barkeeps and "funky" digs that so far are "not ridiculously crowded."

Bar Reis | 17 | 17 | 20 | $6 |

375 Fifth Ave. (bet. 5th & 6th Sts.), Brooklyn, F/M/R to 4th Ave./9th St., 718-832-5716
This "nice neighborhood spot" in Park Slope "feels much bigger than it actually is" owing to a nooks-and-crannies setup that includes a "totally cute downstairs bar and garden" as well as a "spiral staircase" leading up to a little loft space; since it can be "empty on weeknights", it's an ideal choice for a "group of friends to meet up" and spread out.

Barrio Chino | ∇ 22 | 16 | 18 | $12 |

253 Broome St. (bet. Ludlow & Orchard Sts.), B/D to Grand St., 212-228-6710; www.barriochinonyc.com
Part of the "boom on Broome", this "small" but "sexy" Lower Eastsider is known for its "extensive selection of tequilas" and "delicious" tapas menu of "Mexican street food"; the "understated, sophisticated" design (with some "Chinese motifs" thrown in to provide the chino) is one reason why it's "jam-packed on weekends."

Bar Room | 17 | 18 | 18 | $8 |

986 Second Ave. (bet. 52nd & 53rd Sts.), E/V to Lexington Ave./53rd St., 212-207-8877; www.barroomnyc.com
A location "in the middle of all the action" on the Second Avenue strip makes it "hard to move anywhere" in this "long, narrow" barroom that attracts "young single professionals" in droves; insiders report "a lot more room upstairs", but no matter where you wind up, there's a "total meat market vibe."

Barrow Street Ale House | 17 | 11 | 19 | $6 |

15 Barrow St. (bet. 7th Ave. S. & W. 4th St.), 1 to Christopher St., 212-691-6127
"Former frat dudes" and "silly drunk girls" hook up at this "two-years-out-of-college" Greenwich Village "staple" that's both "old-school" and "affordable"; despite "bathrooms right out of *Animal House*", it's

a "decent" enough joint for "sports-watching" along with all the other "meatheads" wearing "backward baseball caps."

Bar 6
18 | 18 | 17 | $9

502 Sixth Ave. (bet. 12th & 13th Sts.), 1/2/3 to 14th St., 212-691-1363
For a "Euro feel without the Euro attitude", try this French-Moroccan bar/eatery in the Village that used to be "too cool for school" but is now regarded as a reliable "old standby"; an ever-"beautiful" crowd (plus some "Page Six wannabes") supplies excellent "people-watching" opportunities and overall "stylish fun."

BarTabac
22 | 21 | 17 | $9

128 Smith St. (Dean St.), Brooklyn, F/G to Bergen St., 718-923-0918
There are "actual French people all over the place" at this Boerum Hill "hipster bistro"–cum–watering hole that's cool for a "late-night chill"; though "slow service" and "Parisian prices" come with the territory, aesthetes say it's one of "Brooklyn's best in terms of ambiance."

Bartini's Lounge
19 | 18 | 19 | $10

1 Station Sq. (71st Ave.), Queens, E/F/G/R/V to Forest Hills/71st Ave., 718-896-5445
"Much nicer than you'd expect from a Queens hangout", this Forest Hills martini specialist comes equipped with a "block of ice built into the bar so your drink will stay cold"; but those who complain about "wasted potential" cite "Manhattan prices" and "lounge-lizard" patrons poured into "tight spandex."

BAR VELOCE
24 | 23 | 22 | $10

175 Second Ave. (bet. 11th & 12th Sts.), L to 3rd Ave., 212-260-3200
176 Seventh Ave. (bet. 20th & 21st Sts.), 1 to 23rd St., 212-629-5300
www.barveloce.com
"Suave" is the word for this pair of "true Italian wine bars" offering an "extensive selection" of vinos decanted by a staff with a "wealth of knowledge" on the subject; while the "streamlined" East Village version is "teeny-tiny" and its Chelsea sibling bigger but "blander", both "hit maximum velocity" in the wee hours.

Bateaux New York
▽ 22 | 23 | 20 | $11

Chelsea Piers, Pier 61, W. 23rd St. & Hudson River, C/E to 23rd St., 212-352-2022; www.bateauxnewyork.com
Setting sail from Chelsea Piers, this NY version of a "Parisian *bateau-mouche*" is an "all-glass cruise ship" offering dinner along with a live band as you sail along the Hudson; of course, its real raisons d'être are the "great sunsets" and "phenomenal views" of the city and harbor.

Bayard's Blue Bar
▽ 22 | 19 | 22 | $13

1 Hanover Sq. (bet. Pearl & Stone Sts.), 2/3/4/5 to Wall St., 212-514-9454; www.bayards.com
Blue-chip "business execs" unwind at this "excellent" barroom set in the historic India House that oozes men's-club appeal; "cozy" and "serene", it's just the place to take "new clients" or to have a quiet drink and "watch the goings-on in Hanover Square."

B Bar
19 | 18 | 14 | $9

40 E. Fourth St. (bet. Bowery & Lafayette St.), 6 to Astor Pl., 212-475-2220; www.bbarandgrill.com
"Way less trendy" than it used to be, this NoHo bar/lounge may be long past its "mid-'90s glory days" but some find the scene more "comfortable" now – despite the "inattentive staff" and "annoying door"; its "unrivalled outdoor terrace", however, will never go out of fashion, ditto Tuesday night's Beige party, an "infamous" gay gathering that's "still pumping."

B. B. King Blues Club   21 | 19 | 17 | $11

237 W. 42nd St. (bet. 7th & 8th Aves.), A/C/E to 42nd St./Port Authority, 212-997-4555; www.bbkingblues.com

"Get your blues on" at this "spacious" Times Square music venue that boasts "unmatched talent", "amazing acoustics" and "not a bad seat in the house"; while some find the "touristy" setup too "Disneyesque" and the "underquality" nibbles "overpriced" ("stick to the fluids"), in the end the "good bookings" make it worthwhile.

Beacon Theatre ⊭   22 | 19 | 16 | $9

2124 Broadway (74th St.), 1/2/3 to 72nd St., 212-496-7070

"Just the right size", this "vintage" 1928 West Side concert hall is "not too big, not too small" but might be beginning to "show some wear and tear"; even if the "service is average" and the drink prices a "rip-off" ("six bucks for a can of Bud"), the "top-notch shows" and "energetic" audiences more than compensate.

Beauty Bar   19 | 21 | 17 | $7

231 E. 14th St. (bet. 2nd & 3rd Aves.), L to 3rd Ave., 212-539-1389; www.beautybar.com

Set in a former "1960s beauty salon", this "kitschy little" East Village theme bar offers the chance to "get a manicure and get drunk at the same time" as you relax under "old-style hair dryers"; expect a "quirky", "semi-subversive" crowd, and don't mind that "dizzy feeling caused by the nail polish fumes."

Becky's   14 | 12 | 16 | $7

1156 First Ave. (bet. 63rd & 64th Sts.), 4/5/6/N/R/W to 59th St./ Lexington Ave., 212-317-8929

"Foreign-born soccer fans" and "local drunks" like this East Side sports bar that's rated somewhere between "nothing special" and "decent at best"; an "out-of-hand" Internet jukebox and "many beers on tap" help blot out its "low-budget" looks.

BED NEW YORK   – | – | – | VE

530 W. 27th St., 6th fl. (bet. 10th & 11th Aves.), C/E to 23rd St., 212-594-4109; www.bedny.com

On a funky block of West Chelsea above the nightclub Spirit rests this new restaurant/lounge, a descendent of the original Miami model that first introduced the dining-in-bed trend; drinking options include a mod, mattress-free bar as well as a rooftop deck, and if things go well, you can always book a table instead of getting a room.

Beer Bar at Cafe Centro   18 | 13 | 17 | $9

200 Park Ave. (45th St. & Vanderbilt Ave.), 4/5/6/7/S to 42nd St./Grand Central, 212-818-1222; www.restaurantassociates.com

For a "quickie beer before catching the train to the 'burbs", this "commuter happy-hour" magnet is conveniently located right above Grand Central; the indoor bar is "small", but a bigger outdoor adjunct "under the Park Avenue overpass" can be a "mob scene" in the summer, provided you don't mind a few "taxi fumes" with your suds.

Bellevue Bar ⊭   20 | 13 | 20 | $5

540 Ninth Ave. (bet. 39th & 40th Sts.), A/C/E to 42nd St./Port Authority, 212-760-0660

"Even if you're only minimally pierced, you'll feel at home" at this "dingy, dirty" Hell's Kitchen "hole" that's moved to the building next door but still remains one of the "best dive bars in the entire city"; "soft-core porn" on the tube and a "killer jukebox" stocked with "music you don't hear anywhere else" cement its reputation as the "perfect balance of fun and scum."

Belly
23 | 21 | 21 | $8

155 Rivington St. (bet. Clinton & Suffolk Sts.), F/J/M/Z to Delancey/ Essex Sts., 212-533-1810
An "uncanny sense of kewl" prevails at this "groovy little" beer, wine and sake dispenser, a "red"-lit Lower East Side den done up in "half-tiki, half-Buddha" style; its "excellent" long-running happy hour and "tasty snacks" draw applause, but what's "cute and cozy" for some equals "not enough room" for others.

Belmont Lounge
18 | 16 | 15 | $8

117 E. 15th St. (bet. Irving Pl. & Park Ave. S.), 4/5/6/L/N/Q/R/W to 14th St./ Union Sq., 212-533-0009; www.belmontloungenyc.com
This "perfect pre–Irving Plaza show destination" always seems to be "busy" with "college-age" types who head for the back rooms to "make out by candlelight" or smoke on the "outdoor patio"; despite an erratic but "annoying cover charge", it exudes enough "high energy" to remain a "top destination in the Union Square area."

Bembe ⌀
▽ 20 | 20 | 21 | $6

81 S. Sixth St. (Berry St.), Brooklyn, L to Bedford Ave., 718-387-5389; www.bembe.us
"Superfine bartenders" concoct "lip-smacking" tropical drinks at this "smoking hot" spot that may be near the Williamsburg Bridge but feels more like the "South Seas"; when the DJs spin "Brazilian beats" backed by "block-rockin' live percussion", lots of "booty-shaking" and "smoochie eye"–making ensue.

BEMELMANS BAR
27 | 27 | 26 | $15

Carlyle Hotel, 35 E. 76th St. (Madison Ave.), 6 to 77th St., 212-744-1600; www.thecarlyle.com
"Old-fashioned sophistication" is alive and well at this Upper East Side "upper-crust" "bar to end all bars" where "fantastic" libations, smart repartee, live piano music and Ludwig Bemelmans' "famous murals" add up to one "timeless classic"; as for the cost, "if you have to ask . . ."

Bereket ⌀
19 | 5 | 17 | $6

187 E. Houston St. (Orchard St.), F/V to Lower East Side/2nd Ave., 212-475-7700
"After a drunken night on Orchard Street", this 24/7 Turkish kebab joint supplies "awesome late-night eats" at "incredible deal" prices (but no liquor); the tradeoffs are "zero decor" and a self-serve cafeteria setup.

Bice
21 | 20 | 21 | $13

7 E. 54th St. (bet. 5th & Madison Aves.), E/V to 5th Ave./53rd St., 212-688-1999; www.bicenewyork.com
"Slightly older" "Euro chic" types turn up at this "sophisticated", "oh-so-Italian" bar/restaurant that's at its best "when the windows are open and you can people-watch" the passing Midtown parade; granted, it's "expensive", unless of course "you are coming from work – and work is paying."

Biddy's Pub
▽ 18 | 15 | 21 | $6

301 E. 91st St. (bet. 1st & 2nd Aves.), 4/5/6 to 86th St., 212-534-4785
This "basic" Upper East Side Irish pub is "really tiny" ("you can take over the whole place with about a dozen people"), but makes up for it with some of the "friendliest bartenders" in town; "great pints of Guinness" and a "loud jukebox" are other distractions.

Big Bar ⌀
– | – | – | M

75 E. Seventh St. (bet. 1st & 2nd Aves.), 6 to Astor Pl., 212-777-6969
"Not big" at all, this East Village salute to irony has a capacity of 35 and thus "can't accommodate large groups"; still, its "neighborhoody",

"utterly unpretentious" vibe "lets you do your own thing", and since it's rather undiscovered, there's almost "always a seat, even on Saturdays."

Big City

16 | 14 | 17 | $7

1600 Third Ave. (90th St.), 4/5/6 to 86th St., 212-369-0808; www.bigcitybarandgrill.com

There's more than enough "room to move around" at this "huge" Upper East Side sports bar/grill where "convenience to Normandy Court" is the "biggest draw"; a "family hangout by day", it morphs into a "predictable" frat scene after dark, with "plenty of beer, but not many girls."

Big Easy

12 | 8 | 13 | $6

1768 Second Ave. (bet. 92nd & 93rd Sts.), 6 to 96th St., 212-348-0879; www.bigeasynyc.com

"Binge drinkers and beer pong" addicts toast this "Mardi Gras–themed" Eastsider as a "crazy, let-loose" kind of joint fueled by "cheap beer" and "Jell-O shots"; but party-poopers say the "sleazy", "*Animal House*"– like "fratmosphere" makes for "hazy nights" and "rough mornings"-after.

Big Nose Kate's

15 | 15 | 17 | $8

2484 Arthur Kill Rd. (St. Luke's Pl.), Staten Island, 718-227-3282

"Originally a church", this "unique" Staten Island spot on the south shore is named after gunslinger Doc Holliday's mistress and feels like a "small-town bar somewhere in Oklahoma"; "inexpensive" pours, a countrified jukebox and a "townie" vibe are all part of its charm.

Bill's Gay 90's

18 | 17 | 19 | $9

57 E. 54th St. (bet. Madison & Park Aves.), E/V to 5th Ave./53rd St., 212-355-0243

"Named after the time period, not the patrons", this longtime Midtown "diamond in the rough" began life as a speakeasy in 1924 and might be the city's best-preserved example, still festooned with its original "photos of boxers" and opera singers; its "mixed-aged" hetero crowd (mostly "over-40" types) shows up mainly to "sing along with the piano man."

BILTMORE ROOM

24 | 26 | 22 | $13

290 Eighth Ave. (bet. 24th & 25th Sts.), C/E to 23rd St., 212-807-0111; www.thebiltmoreroom.com

In a part of Chelsea "where you'd least expect it" comes this "absolutely beautiful" spot reminiscent of "NY's golden past", with "elegant" decor salvaged from the old Biltmore Hotel; while more of a restaurant than a watering hole, it still draws a "pretty, witty" crowd to its separate barroom thanks to "perfectly composed" libations, a "cell-phone booth" and overall "grown-up" aura.

BINY

∇ 17 | 14 | 17 | $10

8 Thompson St., 2nd fl. (bet. Canal & Grand Sts.), A/C/E to Canal St., 212-334-5490; www.biny.com

"Go ahead, make a fool of yourself" at this SoHo karaoke bar boasting such an "awesome selection of songs" that you can "sing till you drop"; the "mainly Chinese" crowd discounts the hefty tabs and somewhat "watered-down drinks" so long as the "techno noise machine" keeps "thump-thump-thumping."

Birdland

25 | 19 | 21 | $11

315 W. 44th St. (bet. 8th & 9th Aves.), A/C/E to 42nd St./Port Authority, 212-581-3080; www.birdlandjazz.com

"Top talent", "good sightlines" and "great sound" make for a "first-rate" experience at this "spacious" Theater District "jazz-and-gin" joint that's "civilized, not down and dirty"; given the "large tabs", a "table will cost you", so economizers opt to catch the show from a barstool.

Bitter End
18 11 15 $8

147 Bleecker St. (bet. La Guardia Pl. & Thompson St.), A/B/C/D/E/F/V to W. 4th St., 212-673-7030; www.bitterend.com
"Despite its rich history", this longtime Bleecker Street music club remains "unpretentious" and has showcased everyone from Bob Dylan to Norah Jones to countless "unknowns"; it "still brings in the crowds" despite a "funky", red-brick ambiance that "hasn't changed" in over 40 years – and fans "hope it never does."

Black & White
19 14 20 $8

86 E. 10th St. (bet. 3rd & 4th Aves.), 6 to Astor Pl., 212-253-0246
A "rock 'n' roll dive" with plenty of "hip appeal", this East Villager can be "oddly fun", with "cheap beer" and "indie rocker" sightings as inducements; "excellent DJs" and "decent upscale bar food" keep its "casual crowd" content.

Black Bear Lodge
20 20 21 $6

274 Third Ave. (bet. 21st & 22nd Sts.), 6 to 23rd St., 212-253-2178; www.bblnyc.com
Like "drinking in the Berkshires", this "ski lodge"–themed Gramercy tavern comes equipped with "antler lamps, snowshoes, a roaring fire" and an "addictive Buck Hunter game"; fans find all the "kitsch" trappings "totally funny", but admit it's the cheap pricing that "keeps you coming back."

Black Betty
∇ 19 13 17 $6

366 Metropolitan Ave. (Havemeyer St.), Brooklyn, G/L to Metropolitan Ave./Lorimer St., 718-599-0243; www.blackbetty.net
"Get your groove on" at this Billyburg bar/restaurant where a "small dance floor" lures everyone from "poseurs to ethnic locals"; some say the Mideastern grub is "better than the drink", but when the "kickin' DJs" start cooking, there's a whole lot of shaking going on.

Black Door
20 17 20 $8

127 W. 26th St. (bet. 6th & 7th Aves.), 1 to 28th St., 212-645-0215
From the minds behind Park Bar comes this "more spacious" Chelsea entry that's a popular drop-in for the "tenants of the new luxury buildings" on nearby Sixth Avenue; "dark and intimate", with a vintage speakeasy vibe, it's a "quiet, civilized environment" in which to unwind, with a bonus back room for private parties.

BlackFinn
17 17 16 $7
(fka Tammany Hall)

218 E. 53rd St. (bet. 2nd & 3rd Aves.), E/V to Lexington Ave./53rd St., 212-355-6607; www.blackfinnnyc.com
A "great improvement over their old place" on Second Avenue, this East Side sports bar has been transplanted into the former Tammany Hall digs and the verdict is "so far, so good"; expect "lots of TVs", a "friendly, casual" ambiance and a "fantastic" albeit "crowded happy hour."

Black Sheep
17 13 20 $6

583 Third Ave. (bet. 38th & 39th Sts.), 4/5/6/7/S to 42nd St./Grand Central, 212-599-3476
"They know how to treat their regulars" at this Murray Hill Irish pub where the owner is "hands on" and the "quick" bartenders "always remember your name"; though some scenesters yawn "generic" and "forgettable", this "local hangout" remains more than "comfortable" enough for most.

Blarney Stone
12 | 10 | 15 | $7

410 Eighth Ave. (bet. 30th & 31st Sts.), A/C/E to 34th St./Penn Station, 212-465-1790
340 Ninth Ave. (bet. 29th & 30th Sts.), A/C/E to 34th St./Penn Station, 212-502-4656 ☞
710 Third Ave. (bet. 44th & 45th Sts.), 4/5/6/7/S to 42nd St./Grand Central, 212-490-0457 ☞
11 Trinity Pl. (Morris St.), 1 to Rector St., 212-269-4988
307 W. 47th St. (bet. 8th & 9th Aves.), C/E to 50th St., 212-245-3438
106 W. 32nd St. (bet. 6th & 7th Aves.), 1/2/3 to 34th St./Penn Station, 212-502-5139

"Men who want to get drunk fast" like these "cheap 'n' dreary" Irish pubs where the "old-time Bowery" feel is supplied by the "grease stains" and "giant steam tables"; aside from the "scary", semi-"derelict" clientele, they may be "nothing special", but still many say "long may they survive."

Bleecker Street Bar
19 | 14 | 18 | $7

56-58 Bleecker St. (bet. B'way & Lafayette St.), 6 to Bleecker St., 212-334-0244

"Regress to college" at this "dependable" Village taproom, a "typical, no-frills pub" made "for frat boys, and only frat boys"; despite a "ton of dartboards, pool tables" and "great draft specials", "it's either dead or packed – no one knows why."

Bleu Evolution
20 | 19 | 15 | $9

808 W. 187th St. (bet. Ft. Washington & Pinehurst Aves.), A to 181st St., 212-928-6006; www.metrobase.com/bleu

"One of the few good places Uptown", this Washington Heights lair with "flair" offers a "funky bohemian" setting that's one part "red velvet bordello", one part "mad hatter tea party"; P.S. since the bar area here is so "tiny", the owners have opened Monkey Room, a new lounge just across the patio.

Blind Tiger Ale House
21 | 11 | 20 | $6

518 Hudson St. (10th St.), 1 to Christopher St., 212-675-3848

A "thoughtfully chosen, always-changing list" of brews on tap "from around the world" awaits this "down-to-earth" Village "guy bar" that's all about "beer, beer and more beer" (with backup from a stellar list of single malts); sure, it "could use a spruce-up" and it sure "smells funky sometimes", but after a few pints, "who cares?"

Bliss
16 | 16 | 16 | $8

256 E. 49th St. (bet. 2nd & 3rd Aves.), 6 to 51st St./Lexington Ave., 212-644-8750; www.blissnyc.com

"Frat boys entering the land of careers and suits" are part of the "loyal following" of this "major pickup scene" in Turtle Bay that's mainly frequented by "younger twentysomethings"; the double-decker setup is "loud" downstairs and more mellow above, but either way the "*Miami Vice* look is alive and well here."

Blondies
19 | 14 | 19 | $7

1770 Second Ave. (bet. 92nd & 93rd Sts.), 6 to 96th St., 212-410-3300
212 W. 79th St. (bet. Amsterdam Ave. & B'way), 1 to 79th St., 212-362-4360

"Televisions as far as the eye can see" serve as decor at these crosstown "sports lovers' dreams" where "rowdy crowds" munch on "wings to die for" and get "unbelievably loud"; insiders say remember the unofficial "dress code" ("ratty T-shirt", "baseball cap turned backwards") and "get there early" as there can be "lines down the block" for big games.

Blue and Gold Tavern 🍴
18 | 8 | 14 | $5

79 E. Seventh St. (bet. 1st & 2nd Aves.), 6 to Astor Pl., 212-473-8918
An East Village "grunge classic", this "rough-tumble" barroom
blends "no pretenses", "cheapo prices" and "gross bathrooms" into
one "tried-and-true" package; its "NYU college crowd" reports many
"close encounters of the frat kind" here and vows it's "impossible
to leave sober."

Blue Fin
22 | 24 | 19 | $11

*W Times Square Hotel, 1567 Broadway (47th St.), R/W to 49th St.,
212-918-1400; www.brguestrestaurants.com*
"Right smack in the middle" of Times Square lies this "splashy" Steve
Hanson seafooder with two bars – a ground-floor, "fishbowl-esque"
model made for "watching the world go by" through "walls of glass"
or a "dark and brooding" upstairs alternate that's an "escape from
the tourists"; either way, "everyone feels sexy" here, especially after
the "pricey" pops take effect.

Blue Mill
∇ 21 | 21 | 17 | $9

(fka Grange Hall)
50 Commerce St. (Barrow St.), 1 to Christopher St., 212-352-0009
"Old-time Greenwich Village" is alive and well at this new bar and
grill set in the slightly remodeled "old Grange Hall space" (fka Blue
Mill in the 1940s); fans think it's "charm personified" thanks to "classic
drinks" and a "fantastic atmosphere", and just the ticket "pre–Cherry
Lane Theater" or for "mellowing out after a hectic day."

Blue Note
23 | 16 | 15 | $13

*131 W. Third St. (6th Ave.), A/B/C/D/E/F/V to W. 4th St., 212-475-8592;
www.bluenotejazz.com*
"Big-name live jazz" is the lure at this longtime Village lair, a "cool,
cultured" cubbyhole where "top-notch talent" performs in cozy
(verging on "tight") digs; sure, the "steep covers" and "drink minimums"
can add up to a "very expensive night out" – wags tag it the "C-note" –
but let's face it, "you won't get this close to the performers at MSG."

Blue Ribbon
23 | 19 | 23 | $12

*97 Sullivan St. (bet. Prince & Spring Sts.), C/E to Spring St.,
212-274-0404*
There's "real glamour in the faded velvet" of this "intimate" SoHo
"scene" where "exotic" types resort to cocktail sipping and oyster
shucking at the bar while they "wait for a table"; it's much more "fun"
late night when it morphs into an "industry hangout" after all the off-
duty "waiters and chefs" toddle in.

BLUE RIBBON BROOKLYN
25 | 21 | 25 | $12

*280 Fifth Ave. (bet. 1st St. & Garfield Pl.), Brooklyn, M/R to Union St.,
718-840-0404*
Park Slope stay-at-homes declare there's "no more need to go to
Manhattan" thanks to this "lively" bar/eatery that's more than
"comparable to its SoHo sibling", with the same "knowledgeable
drink masters" but "more space" to move about; in short, it's a "safe
bet" for Brooklyn "trendsetters", though "less wealthy" folk might
have trouble "stomaching the cost."

Blue Room
∇ 20 | 18 | 22 | $7

*1140 Second Ave. (60th St.), 4/5/6/N/R/W to 59th St./Lexington Ave.,
212-688-4344*
"Just starting to pick up", this "new little place" in the shadow of the
Roosevelt Island tram is a "welcome addition" to an arid stretch of
Midtown, with "friendly" barkeeps, sports on the tube and "frat party

music" in the air; it's also convenient for a couple of "cheap" pops "on your way to Scores" down the street.

Blue Smoke   22 | 19 | 20 | $9
116 E. 27th St. (bet. Lexington Ave. & Park Ave. S.), 6 to 28th St., 212-447-7733; www.bluesmoke.com
"Come dressy or messy" to this "down-to-earth" Gramercy BBQ palace, a "highbrow/lowbrow" hybrid from Danny Meyer done up in "Southern twang"–style; while the "food might surpass the bar scene", "so many beers to choose from" and a "mellow" downstairs music venue (the Jazz Standard) compensate.

BLUE WATER GRILL   24 | 23 | 21 | $12
31 Union Sq. W. (16th St.), 4/5/6/L/N/Q/R/W to 14th St./Union Sq., 212-675-9500; www.brguestrestaurants.com
"Forever chill", this "busy, bustling" Union Square seafood specialist exudes a "big city" aura that attracts "cool" customers; set in an "old bank" space, it encompasses an "always happening" bar (with "limited seating") as well as "outdoor tables" for primo "people-watching" and "jazz downstairs" in a former vault; don't forget your "expense account", and if you're dining, "book in advance."

Blu Lounge ⊭   ▽ 22 | 20 | 20 | $6
197 N. Eighth St. (Driggs Ave.), Brooklyn, L to Bedford Ave., 718-782-8005; www.theblulounge.com
"Mellow" fellows like this Williamsburg lounge that has the "vibe of a basement make-out party" with low lights, "comfy", funky furnishings and "great happy-hour deals"; it's more than "decent" enough for drinks, though some report a "strange mix of people later at night."

Boat   20 | 12 | 20 | $5
175 Smith St. (bet. Warren & Wyckoff Sts.), Brooklyn, F/G to Bergen St., 718-254-0607
Made for "low-key hanging out", this Boerum Hill barroom may have "no sign" and "minimal decor" (read: "hole-in-the-wall"), but the "cheap drinks" and "well-stocked" "treasure trove" of a jukebox keep things "hopping" here; news flash: they recently "painted the facade."

BOAT BASIN CAFE   24 | 17 | 15 | $8
W. 79th St. (Hudson River), 1 to 79th St., 212-496-5542; www.boatbasincafe.com
Experience "Key West" on the Upper West Side at this "picturesque" "escape from NY", a seasonal, "open-air" venue replete with "priceless views of the Hudson" and some mighty "cool breezes"; sure, it's "crowded", service skews toward "inattentive" and it's a "long walk back to Broadway", but after one "beautiful sunset", you'll think it's one of the "best uses of space in the city."

Boat House   26 | 24 | 17 | $11
Central Park, Central Park Lake, enter on E. 72nd St. (Central Park Dr. N.), 6 to 68th St., 212-517-2233; www.thecentralparkboathouse.com
"Smack dab in the middle of Central Park" overlooking a lake lies this "idyllic" indoor/outdoor "total getaway" where "you can't ask for a prettier view"; the restaurant's open year-round, the outdoor bars only "when the weather is kind", but no matter what the season, it's got extreme "pop-the-question" potential.

Bob   19 | 13 | 16 | $7
235 Eldridge St. (bet. Houston & Stanton Sts.), F/V to Lower East Side/ 2nd Ave., 212-529-1807
"If you don't mind being pressed up against sweaty strangers", you'll enjoy this ultra-"small", ultra-"crowded" Lower Eastsider where

"awesome hip-hop" is spun by some of the "finest DJs around"; naturally, the "tight, hot" setup can turn the "diverse young crowd" a "little rowdy."

BOGART'S
18 | 20 | 17 | $9

99 Park Ave. (39th St.), 4/5/6/7/S to 42nd St./Grand Central, 212-922-9244
"Everyone you know from college" turns up at this "spacious" yet "crowded" Murray Hill "up-and-comer", a "happening hot spot" by default in a "lacking" part of town; though some find it a "typical after-work" joint "dominated by males", at least there's "no cover, so it's good if you're indecisive."

Bohemian Hall
26 | 14 | 16 | $6

29-19 24th Ave. (31st St.), Queens, N/W to Astoria Blvd., 718-274-4925
Somewhere between a "block party" and "Oktoberfest", this alfresco Astoria "king of the beer gardens" draws hopsheads with "cheap", "hard-to-find" brews served in a vast, "picnic table"–bedecked backyard; expect a "mixed-age" crowd comprised of "two types of bohemians" – "old expats from Czechoslovakia" and "funky young" hipsters from all over.

Boiler Room ⇗
12 | 7 | 16 | $6

86 E. Fourth St. (bet. 1st & 2nd Aves.), F/V to Lower East Side/2nd Ave., 212-254-7536
"Guys ready to get drunk and have fun" let it all hang out at this "dark", "grungy" East Village gay bar where there's "no attitude" and it's "never crowded"; but soberer sorts say this dive's "over", a "mere shadow of its former self."

Bond Street
25 | 24 | 22 | $12

6 Bond St. (bet. B'way & Lafayette St.), 6 to Bleecker St., 212-777-2500
"Home of the beautiful people", this still "happening" NoHo nightspot "hasn't lost its appeal", drawing "cool" Downtowners to its upstairs sushi restaurant and "dark and sexy" subterranean lounge; of course, the "expensive look and expensive drinks" will cost you, so "bring your sugar daddy" or, better yet, "pick one up while you're there."

B1 Drink Club
– | – | – | M

139 E. 45th St., 2nd fl. (bet. Lexington & 3rd Aves.), 4/5/6/7/S to 42nd St./ Grand Central, 212-370-0080; www.b1drinkclub.com
The atmosphere's "elegant yet laid-back" at this "chill" new Grand Central–area arrival, a long, multilevel affair where "drinks priced just right" can be accompanied by Pan-Asian nibbles; given its hopping after-work scene, some say it's a "place to start off, not end up", though the rear outdoor deck works as a "smoker's haven" all night long.

Bongo
21 | 20 | 21 | $10

299 10th Ave. (bet. 27th & 28th Sts.), C/E to 23rd St., 212-947-3654
A "'50s Rat Pack" mood infuses this Way West Chelsea lounge with "style to spare", starting with its "midcentury-modern-meets-*Brady-Bunch*" decor (and "glassware straight from grandma's cupboard"); after the "frosty martinis" and "insanely delicious lobster rolls" kick in, it's very "easy to be here."

Boogaloo
– | – | – | M

168 Marcy Ave. (bet. B'way & S. 5th St.), Brooklyn, J/M/Z to Marcy Ave., 718-599-8900
"Sixties bachelor pad" by way of "*2001: A Space Odyssey*" sums up the look of this "mod", white-on-white club that draws everyone from "punks" to "mild-mannered Clark Kent" types; despite an "out-of-the-way" Billyburg location, regulars keep returning for its "experimental" DJs, expansive selection of rum and warm-weather rooftop bar.

Boss Tweed's Saloon   – | – | – | M

*115 Essex St. (bet. Delancey & Rivington Sts.), F/J/M/Z to Delancey/
Essex Sts., 212-475-9997; www.bosstweeds.com*
"Formerly Smithfield", this new Lower East Side Irish pub looks much
the same as before, and a few are disappointed by the "uninspired
remodel"; on the other hand, the mood's unpretentious, the price right
and there's a "cool backyard" for nature lovers.

Boston Comedy Club   14 | 11 | 13 | $8

*82 W. Third St. (bet. Sullivan & Thompson Sts.), A/B/C/D/E/F/V to
W. 4th St., 212-477-1000; www.bostoncomedyclub.com*
"Every so often you see comics you wouldn't expect" at this Village
laugheteria that usually books "up-and-comers" – although "famous"
folk occasionally take the stage; a low cover makes it just right "when
you're on a budget", yet purists rate it in the "lower tier" of the genre.

Botanica   ▽ 17 | 12 | 15 | $8

*47 E. Houston St. (bet. Mott & Mulberry Sts.), B/D/F/V to B'way/
Lafayette St., 212-343-7251*
For "cheap underground fun", get down at this NoLita basement dive
frequented by "rock 'n' roll boys" and other "Downtown" types; look
for "friendly" staffers, a "laid-back", "old-school" vibe and plenty of
"PBR" – "what more could you want?"

Bottega del Vino   – | – | – | E

*7 E. 59th St. (bet. 5th & Madison Aves.), 4/5/6/N/R/W to 59th St./
Lexington Ave., 212-223-3028; www.bottegadelvinonyc.com*
Cloned from the famed original in Verona, this new Midtown wine bar/
restaurant offers over 60 pours by the glass at its cozy front bar (with
dining in the rear and a vaulted downstairs cellar for private parties);
it's a serious destination for oenophiles, with equally serious pricing.

Bouche Bar   ▽ 21 | 20 | 21 | $8

*540 E. Fifth St. (bet. Aves. A & B), F/V to Lower East Side/2nd Ave.,
212-420-9265; www.bouchebar.com*
A "cute little stop-in", this "snug" East Village boîte is "calm, chill" and
"surprisingly not crowded", though a "weekend DJ" makes it swing;
"friendly service" and "good drinks" are givens, while the "Catherine
Deneuve photo" over the bar provides "a certain je ne sais quoi."

Boudoir Bar ⌐   ▽ 15 | 14 | 15 | $7

*273 Smith St. (bet. Degraw & Sackett Sts.), Brooklyn, F/G to Carroll St.,
718-624-8878; www.boudoirbar.com*
Entertainment ranging from "burlesque" to "comedy" provides some
variety at this Carroll Gardens wine bar where the staff is clad either
in nighties or PJs; foes yawn it's a "wannabe sexy place", citing an
"unorganized staff" and a vaguely "chaotic" air.

Bounce   21 | 19 | 19 | $10

1403 Second Ave. (73rd St.), 6 to 77th St., 212-535-2183; www.bounceny.com
The "only place there isn't a television is the ceiling" at this "upscale"
Upper East Side sports bar/lounge combo where "ladies sip martinis
while men chug beers"; it's nice and "airy" when the floor-to-ceiling
windows are opened up, but you should expect the "same crowd" that
patronized "the old Trilogy" (a former longtime incarnation).

Bourbon St.   13 | 11 | 16 | $6

*407 Amsterdam Ave. (bet. 79th & 80th Sts.), 1 to 79th St., 212-721-1332;
www.bourbonstreetnyc.com*
"Frat boys and beads" abound at this Upper West Side "guilty pleasure
palace", a tribute to N'Awlins that wants to be something out of a

44   subscribe to zagat.com

"*Girls Gone Wild* video" but is usually more "hit-or-miss"; "there are a lot worse places to end up", so give up and pop a "cheap, strong drink" – but "beware the Hurricanes", or you might wind up "throwing off pieces of clothing."

Bowery Ballroom   24 | 19 | 18 | $8
6 Delancey St. (bet. Bowery & Chrystie St.), F/V to Lower East Side/ 2nd Ave., 212-533-2111; www.boweryballroom.com
A Lower East Side concert hall with "grit", featuring "all the best aspects of Irving Plaza in miniature": an "excellent sound system" and "perfect sightlines" in an "intimate" setting with "no long trek from the stage to the bar"; maybe the "drink quality" could use some work, but "who cares?" given the chance to see bands "on the cusp of greatness" at a "fraction of the price of larger venues."

Bowery Poetry Club   22 | 15 | 21 | $6
308 Bowery (bet. Bleecker & Houston Sts.), F/V to Lower East Side/ 2nd Ave., 212-614-0505; www.bowerypoetry.com
"Anything can happen" at this slice of "shabby bohemia", offering a "broad variety of entertainment" from "poetry slams" to "performance art" and beyond; many call it a "totally cool" example of the "way the East Village used to be", "full of adventure" and patronized by "all ages and types."

Bowlmor Lanes   22 | 17 | 15 | $9
110 University Pl. (bet. 12th & 13th Sts.), 4/5/6/L/N/Q/R/W to 14th St./ Union Sq., 212-255-8188; www.bowlmor.com
The "best of Manhattan's limited bowling options", this longtime Villager adds a "stylish" spin to the sport with "club lighting", a "large bar" area and drinks "strong enough that you won't notice how bad a bowler you are"; though the "expensive" tabs, "looong waits" and "ugly shoes" roll "gutter balls", it's still hard to beat for "good cheesy fun."

Boxcar Lounge   21 | 17 | 21 | $7
168 Ave. B (bet. 10th & 11th Sts.), L to 1st Ave., 212-473-2830; www.boxcarlounge.com
Maybe most "studio apartments are larger" than this "narrow" East Village "hideaway"–cum–"interior of a train car", yet the "cramped" feel actually works to "bring people together"; a "secret", "spacious" back garden and a "long happy hour" keep it chugging along.

Boxers   15 | 15 | 15 | $8
190 W. Fourth St. (Barrow St.), 1 to Christopher St., 212-206-7526
When it comes to "local hangouts", this Village bar and grill is a "decent" enough destination with a "relaxing, at-home" vibe and "tasty" pub grub; some find this "little piece of New Jersey" way too "suburban", although they admit it's a good choice for "out-of-town guests" – at least "you won't frighten them" here.

BOYS ROOM ∅   23 | 16 | 19 | $7
9 Ave. A (bet. 1st & 2nd Sts.), F/V to Lower East Side/2nd Ave., 212-995-8684; www.tripwithus.com
"Happy, horny" gay blades are wilde about this "naughty" new East Village "sleazeathon", "two levels of fun" whirling with "gyrating go-go" dancers, "seedy movies" and "boys aplenty"; "almost anything goes" at this "playful" joint, but it could be a tad too "trashy" for timid types.

Branch   19 | 19 | 15 | $10
226 E. 54th St. (bet. 2nd & 3rd Aves.), E/V to Lexington Ave./53rd St., 212-688-5577; www.branchny.com
"Young professionals" on the prowl for an "after-work" Midtown playground tout this "untypical" club/lounge replete with a "sunken

dance floor" and "great sound system"; sure, it's "pricey" and the
service "so-so", but they must be doing something right – "everyone's
always partying" at this "crowded" spot.

Brandy Library
- – – E

*25 N. Moore St. (bet. Hudson & Varick Sts.), 1 to Franklin St., 212-226-5545;
www.brandylibrary.com*
"F. Scott Fitzgerald couldn't have dreamed up a jazzier place" than
this "seductive", amber-hued new TriBeCa lounge that feels like it
belongs in a swank hotel; offering an "extensive", "unparalleled menu
of scotches, brandies" and cocktails served by a "knowledgeable,
top-shelf" staff, it's a coolly "classy" operation designed for grown-
ups, with a bonus outdoor smoking porch for cigar aficionados.

Brandy's Piano Bar ∌
25 | 13 | 20 | $8

*235 E. 84th St. (bet. 2nd & 3rd Aves.), 4/5/6 to 86th St., 212-650-1944;
www.brandyspianobarnyc.com*
"Cocktails and torch songs" says it all about this Upper East Side piano
bar where a "flamboyant", "good-humored" staff oversees nightly
"sing-alongs" and open mike sessions; be prepared for a "music-
loving" crowd of all stripes, everyone from "Broadway babies" to
"football players", "gay and straight alike", all having "lots of fun."

Brasserie
21 | 22 | 20 | $12

*100 E. 53rd St. (bet. Lexington & Park Aves.), E/V to Lexington Ave./
53rd St., 212-751-4840; www.thebrasserieny.com*
Midtown goes "über-cool" at this "sleek 'n' sexy" restaurant/watering
hole exuding the kind of "NY sophistication" that appeals to a very
"low-key" high-powered set; "video monitors above the bar" broadcast
who's coming and going, while a long, catwalklike ramp is made
for "grand entrances."

Brasserie 8½
22 | 25 | 21 | $12

*9 W. 57th St. (bet. 5th & 6th Aves.), N/R/W to 5th Ave./59th St., 212-829-0812;
www.brasserie8andahalf.com*
"One of those places where you should only order a martini", this
"super-swank" underground lair is frequented by "hedge-fund"-
manager types who appreciate the "low noise level" and tolerate the
"pricey" libations; the "glamorous", "retro-chic" interior (think '60s
airport lounge by way of "*Austin Powers*") is accessed via a "sweeping
spiral staircase" right out of *Sunset Boulevard.*

BRASS MONKEY
22 | 19 | 21 | $8

*55 Little W. 12th St. (bet. 10th Ave. & Washington St.), A/C/E/L to 14th St./
8th Ave., 212-675-6686; www.brassmonkeybar.com*
For the Meatpacking District "without the posing", try this "simple"
new pub, a big, "warehouselike" affair featuring a "lot of wood" and
"rustic", brick-lined walls; its "unpretentious" crowd says it's a "real
bar in a land where there are none", with a bonus call-out to its
"excellent beer selection."

Brazen Head
15 | 12 | 19 | $5

*228 Atlantic Ave. (bet. Boerum Pl. & Court St.), Brooklyn, M/R to Court St.,
718-488-0430; www.brazenheadbrooklyn.com*
"Relatively cheap" beer from an "excellent selection" draws "regular"
Joes to this "basic" Boerum Hill taproom; trendoids yawn "predictable",
but admit there's nothing wrong with its "cozy backyard."

Brewsky's
- – – M

41 E. Seventh St. (bet. 2nd & 3rd Aves.), 6 to Astor Pl., 212-420-0671
The "beer list looks like a manuscript" at this East Village shrine to
suds that vends over 600 bottled varieties; the "tiny" setup may be

strictly "hole-in-the-wall", but if you're in a "loud mood", it's a fine Plan B for its next-door sibling, Burp Castle, where shouting is forbidden.

Bridge Cafe | 22 | 19 | 21 | $10 |

279 Water St. (Dover St.), 4/5/6/J/M/Z to Brooklyn Bridge/City Hall, 212-227-3344

Way "off the beaten track" beneath the Brooklyn Bridge lies this "historic, very special" cafe that's been dispensing spirits since 1794; "comfy" and "intimate", it's got that "classic old NY" thing down pat, and fans feel everyone "should stop there at least once" – just "not too late at night", as they usually close around 11 PM.

Brite Bar | 19 | 16 | 20 | $9 |

297 10th Ave. (27th St.), C/E to 23rd St., 212-279-9706;
www.britebar.com

"Take a break" from West Chelsea's "megaclub nonsense" at this more "casual" bar/lounge that's a refuge for a "diverse mix of lifestyles"; even if some use it as a "pre-Marquee, pre–Bungalow 8" pit stop, others argue it "could be the main event" under the right circumstances.

Broadway Dive | ∇ 16 | 9 | 16 | $7 |

2662 Broadway (bet. 101st & 102nd Sts.), 1 to 103rd St., 212-865-2662;
www.divebarnyc.com

"True to its name", this Upper West Side "real dive" is good for "watching a game" or "kibitzing with a crony" alongside "loyal neighborhood" folk; landlubbers lament it's "not worth a trip", no matter how much "they clean it up."

Broadway Lounge | 20 | 19 | 19 | $11 |

Marriott Marquis Hotel, 1535 Broadway, 8th fl. (bet. 45th & 46th Sts.), 1/2/3/7/N/Q/R/S/W to 42nd St./Times Sq., 212-398-1900;
www.nymarriottmarquis.com

"Above the fray of Times Square", this eighth-floor perch in the Marriott Marquis "impresses out-of-towners" with its "unbeatable view" of the Great White Way – "provided you get a window seat", that is; otherwise, the atrium setting is "roomy" and service "accommodating", though blasé types feel it's "strictly for tourists afraid to leave the hotel."

Brooklyn Ale House | 23 | 17 | 23 | $6 |

103 Berry St. (N. 8th St.), Brooklyn, L to Bedford Ave., 718-302-9811

A "steady stream of regulars" streams into this Williamsburg taproom, a "tried-and-true" destination that just might be the "platonic ideal of a neighborhood bar"; it's also known as a "dog lover's heaven", so feel free to let Fido tag along.

Brooklyn Brewery | 22 | 16 | 20 | $6 |

79 N. 11th St. (bet. Berry St. & Wythe Ave.), Brooklyn, L to Bedford Ave., 718-486-7422; www.brooklynbrewery.com

"No-frills fresh beer" on the "cheap" sums up the scene at this "authentic" Williamsburg brewery that's "not open to the public very much" (only Friday evenings and Saturday afternoons), but is quite the "experience" when it is; weekly "tours of the facilities" and occasional "special events" add to its allure.

BROOKLYN INN ⌿ | 27 | 25 | 21 | $5 |

148 Hoyt St. (Bergen St.), Brooklyn, F/G to Bergen St., 718-625-9741

"Harkening back to Brooklyn's yesteryears" is this "woodwork-laden" Boerum Hill watering hole, an "old-school classic" featuring a "killer jukebox", "jocular" staff and "back room pool table"; its "eccentric" crowd of regulars (everyone from "city bus drivers to Pulitzer Prize winners") shows up for its "credibility" and happily report "nothing trendy" going on.

BROOKLYN SOCIAL ⌐   25 | 23 | 23 | $6
335 Smith St. (bet. Carroll & President Sts.), Brooklyn, F/G to Carroll St., 718-858-7758
Set in a "former Smith Street Sicilian social club", this "approachable" remake exudes a "speakeasy vibe" via vintage sepia-toned photos and "perfectly made classic cocktails"; targeting "adult hipsters" with equal parts of "charm and whimsy", it's "nostalgic without being self-conscious" and acknowledges present-day needs with a rock-stocked jukebox and outdoor smoking patio.

Broome Street Bar   19 | 15 | 19 | $8
363 W. Broadway (Broome St.), C/E to Spring St., 212-925-2086
There's "no need to dress up" since this "longtime" bar and grill is the "closest thing to a real pub that you'll find in SoHo", with "affordable" pricing and "no attitude"; even though it's a bit "dumpy", it still attracts "laid-back" locals grooving on its faint air of "'60s hippiedom."

BROTHER JIMMY'S BBQ   16 | 13 | 17 | $7
428 Amsterdam Ave. (bet. 80th & 81st Sts.), B/C to 81st St., 212-501-7515
1485 Second Ave. (bet. 77th & 78th Sts.), 6 to 77th St., 212-288-0999
1644 Third Ave. (92nd St.), 6 to 96th St., 212-426-2020
www.brotherjimmys.com
Bring your "Southern drawl" to fit in at these "sweaty, drunken" stabs at "College Part II", where the crowd's "young", the look's "white trash" and the "waitresses are as hot as the wings"; brace yourself for "loud frat boys" eyeballing "ACC games" on the tube as they slurp down "huge fishbowls of blue liquid" and boogie to "classic rock" – "Bon Jovi never gets old" here.

Bryant Park Cafe/Grill   22 | 19 | 16 | $11
25 W. 40th St. (behind NY Public Library), 7/B/D/F/V to 42nd St./6th Ave., 212-840-6500; www.arkrestaurants.com
Upscale "hook-up opportunities" abound at this alfresco cafe opposite Bryant Park, a warm-weather after-work magnet for "rich-husband" hunters and other "upwardly mobile" folk; "pricey" cocktails, so-so service and "killer ladies'-room lines" are the downsides, so those not in the mood for a "super-crowded" "total scene" opt for the "quieter", adjoining indoor grill.

B-Side   ∇ 17 | 14 | 16 | $7
204 Avenue B (bet. 12th & 13th Sts.), L to 1st Ave., 212-475-4600; www.b-sidenyc.com
An "awesome jukebox" stocked with "cool" tunes draws "cool" dudes and dudettes to this otherwise "average" East Village barroom renowned for its $5 Rheingold-and-a-shot "deal"; on the flip side, there's video gaming and a "pool table in the back."

B61 ⌐   – | – | – | M
187 Columbia St. (Degraw St.), Brooklyn, F/G to Carroll St., 718-643-5400; www.almarestaurant.com
Named after the Brooklyn bus line that stops nearby, this far-out Carroll Gardens bar beneath the restaurant Alma exudes a "feel-good vibe" via a "cool crowd", long "dark-wood" bar and "diverse music" from a "great juke"; front windows featuring drop-dead "Manhattan skyline views" ice the cake.

B3   20 | 16 | 21 | $8
33 Ave. B (3rd St.), F/V to Lower East Side/2nd Ave., 212-614-9755
"Key outside seating" complete with wacky East Village "people-watching" adds some zip to this "solid" bar/eatery that's also home to a "hidden" downstairs lounge offering varied entertainments including

"open mike" nights; still, aesthetes think its "basic Alphabet City atmosphere" "needs a face-lift."

Bua
`– | – | – | M`
(fka Noa)
122-126 St. Marks Pl. (bet. Ave. A & 1st Ave.), 6 to Astor Pl., 212-979-6276; www.buany.com
The name is Gaelic for "victory", and it seems at hand at this new East Village Irish lounge that picks up where former tenant Noa left off; exposed-brick walls studded with candles bathe the room in a warm glow, while large windows provide an open-air feel in the summertime.

BUBBLE LOUNGE
`22 | 22 | 19 | $13`
228 W. Broadway (bet. Franklin & White Sts.), 1 to Franklin St., 212-431-3433; www.bubblelounge.com
"Woo a date" or "celebrate your bonus" at this "upscale" TriBeCa champagne lounge, a "confident, stylish" site to "meet up with your sugar daddy" or pick up "bankers and traders galore"; some say it's a "throwback to the boom days when money grew on trees" (and thus better "on someone else's expense account"), yet it still "exudes decadence" and "panache" for many.

Buddha Lounge
`– | – | – | M`
29 E. Third St. (2nd Ave.), F/V to Lower East Side/2nd Ave., 212-505-7344; www.buddhaloungenyc.com
Following a light revamp, the former Opium Den is reincarnated as this new lounge, a candlelit, brick-walled affair tricked up with mirrors, leather couches and random Buddhas; while the ambiance may be a bit glitzy for the gritty East Village, its modest size and laid-back air are more neighborhood appropriate.

Bull & Bear
`20 | 21 | 21 | $13`
Waldorf-Astoria Hotel, 570 Lexington Ave. (49th St.), 6 to 51st St./ Lexington Ave., 212-872-4900; www.waldorf.com
For an "honest drink" in "sturdy" digs, try this "impressive", "old boys' club" bar in the Waldorf that "feels like money" (and comes complete with its very own stock ticker); sure, it's "stodgy" with "lots of jackets" and "suspenders" in evidence, but it does the trick for "post-work power meetings" or "picking up divorcées."

Bull McCabe's
`17 | 15 | 18 | $6`
29 St. Marks Pl. (bet. 2nd & 3rd Aves.), 6 to Astor Pl., 212-982-9895; www.ryansnyc.com
"NYU kids, tattooed folks" and "maybe even your dad" turn up at this East Village "neighborhood" Irish pub offering all the standard amenities – a "great jukebox", "bar games", "beer sludge coating the ground" – along with something different: a conversation-starting "crashed Cesna" in the backyard garden.

Bull Moose Saloon
`17 | 11 | 19 | $6`
354 W. 44th St. (bet. 8th & 9th Aves.), A/C/E to 42nd St./Port Authority, 212-956-5625
"Aspiring actors" and "sports fans" populate this Hell's Kitchen Irish pub, a "low-key" affair that's "never too crowded" so you can bring "your entire cast and crew"; maybe the decor's "uninspired", but its "loyal" following says "regular" bars with a "real neighborhood feel" like this one are hard to find.

Bull's Head Tavern
`16 | 14 | 19 | $6`
295 Third Ave. (bet. 22nd & 23rd Sts.), 6 to 23rd St., 212-685-2589
With "just enough grunginess for character", this Gramercy bar is a "friendly, easygoing" hangout where "newly legal drinkers" shoot

pool, throw darts and play Golden Tee; while it's essentially a "guy's night out" spot that's a real "sausagefest on weekends", Thursday's "Dave Matthews cover band attracts crowds" of both genders.

BUNGALOW 8
22 | 22 | 16 | $14

515 W. 27th St. (bet. 10th & 11th Aves.), C/E to 23rd St., 212-629-3333

"Harder to get into than Harvard", this Way West Chelsea "fortress" of cool from club queen Amy Sacco "hasn't gotten stale yet", drawing a late-night mix of "the rich, the pretty" and the "who's who of the celebrity scene"; those who "only see it from the outside" moan about its "snobby door policy", but smug insiders call it the "last bastion for avoiding the B&T" and report it's "still the place to be no matter what night it is."

Burp Castle
21 | 19 | 21 | $8

41 E. Seventh St. (bet. 2nd & 3rd Aves.), 6 to Astor Pl., 212-982-4576

"Silence is golden" at this "curious", "medieval"-themed East Village taproom where "bartenders in brown monk's robes" pour a "fine selection" of brew ("especially the Belgians") and "shush you if you speak too loudly"; the "Gregorian chant" and "classical music" soundtrack makes it a bit "weird" for some, yet most concur it's "interesting" and "worth checking out."

Burton Pub/Kama Lounge
_ | _ | _ | M

(fka Evelyn Lounge)

380 Columbus Ave., 2nd fl. (78th St.), 1/2/3 to 79th St., 212-724-9888
380 Columbus Ave., downstairs (78th St.), 1/2/3 to 79th St., 212-724-2363

What was once the Evelyn Lounge has been lightly reworked into these two newcomers; early visitors report "not much going on" in the upstairs Burton Pub except for the fireplace, so they "head downstairs" to the "livelier" Kama Lounge, a sprawling space that's "cool" if "loud."

Buster's Garage
19 | 14 | 16 | $7

180 W. Broadway (bet. Leonard & Worth Sts.), 1 to Franklin St., 212-226-6811; www.bustersgarage.com

"So different from everything else" in the area, this "laid-back" "quintessential sports bar" brings a taste of the "Jersey shore" to TriBeCa via "nothing-fancy", vaguely "beachy" design, a "large outdoor deck" and intense "beer pong tournaments"; it's "no longer a secret", so be prepared for "loud and rowdy" crowds running the gamut from "firemen" to "NY law school" types.

Butta' Cup Lounge
21 | 20 | 19 | $12

271 Adelphi St. (DeKalb Ave.), Brooklyn, C to Lafayette Ave., 718-522-1669

"Attractive buppies" patronize this Fort Greene bar/eatery, a "nice 'n' cozy" nexus that blooms on weekends when the "DJ gets the crowd grooving"; maybe the drinks are too "pricey for Brooklyn", but the Asian-inflected soul food menu leads some to report the grub's "better than the nightlife" here.

BUTTER
21 | 24 | 18 | $11

415 Lafayette St. (bet. Astor Pl. & E. 4th St.), 6 to Astor Pl., 212-253-2828; www.butterrestaurant.com

"If you can get in", the "celeb-watching" can be "mind-bending" at this "swanky" spot near the Public Theater that's become "more popular now that Pangaea has closed"; a "soaring", cedar-and-birch-lined upstairs dining room is eclipsed by a sleek bar below that "churns out the hottest Monday night party in town."

Buttermilk Bar
∇ 26 | 18 | 23 | $5

577 Fifth Ave. (16th St.), Brooklyn, M/R to Prospect Ave., 718-788-6297
"Only locals" know about this "under-the-radar hipster bar" on the
"far side of Park Slope", where "indie rock dominates the jukebox"
and the crowd's "cool without being pretentious"; it also hosts some of
the "best board-game tournaments in town" with lots of "Candyland
champions" and "Trivial Pursuit players" in attendance.

Byzantio
16 | 15 | 13 | $9

45-30 Bell Blvd. (Northern Blvd.), Queens, LIRR to Bayside,
718-279-7200 ⊄
28-31 31st St. (Newtown Ave.), Queens, N/W to 30th Ave., 718-956-5600
These Greek cafes in Astoria and Bayside patronized by "lots of
young people" are "nice for a few drinks" (though many use them as
a warm-up "before hitting the real bars"); some find them "nothing
special", but all agree they're "neighborhoody" and "European."

CABANAS
24 | 23 | 16 | $12

Maritime Hotel, 88 Ninth Ave. (enter at 16th or 17th St.), A/C/E/L to 14th St./
8th Ave., 212-835-5537; www.themaritimehotel.com
That "already overcrowded scene at the Maritime Hotel" gets a
little tighter with the arrival of this pair of "beautiful" rooftop lounges
right out of "Miami Beach" and right above the La Bottega bar and
restaurant; despite a "stringent door" and "snooty" service, it's one
of the "few worthy outdoor spots" in the area where "you can smoke"
and maybe even "spot Paris Hilton – but don't let that deter you."

Cabin Fever
– | – | – | I

(fka Raccoon Lodge)
1439 York Ave. (bet. 76th & 77th Sts.), 6 to 77th St., 212-650-1775;
www.cabinfeverbar.com
An all-purpose venue, this wide-open new Upper Eastsider "off the
beaten path" offers a "nice" long bartop, an ATM for those short on
dough and just about every bar game imaginable: pool, darts, Golden
Tee and Buck Hunter; weekend DJs and karaoke complete the picture.

Cafe Bar ⊄
24 | 24 | 14 | $9

32-90 36th St. (34th Ave.), Queens, G/R/V to Steinway St., 718-204-5273;
www.cafebar-lic.com
"Arty" Astorians mix it up in this "laid-back" "hipster hangout" that
feels like a "1970s kitchen"; though the "dull name", "slacking" service
and no-credit-card policy lower the bar a bit, modern touches like
"wireless Internet" and "big-screen" TVs compensate.

CAFE CARLYLE
27 | 24 | 25 | $15

Carlyle Hotel, 35 E. 76th St. (Madison Ave.), 6 to 77th St., 212-744-1600;
www.thecarlyle.com
Epitomizing "old-money" "cafe society", this 50-year-old cabaret in the
Upper East Side's "elegant" Carlyle Hotel is the kind of "expensive",
"oh-so-civilized" place to "bring your mistress – or rediscover your
wife"; of course, the late "Bobby Short will be missed", but in his
place are some "legendary musicians" performing for the Waspy
"gin-and-scotch" sippers in the audience.

Café Charbon
24 | 22 | 18 | $9

168-170 Orchard St. (Stanton St.), F/V to Lower East Side/2nd Ave.,
212-420-7520
This atmospheric Lower East Side bar/cafe masquerades as moody
Montmartre with a "faux" facade that "out-McNally's McNally" in terms
of "French/Disney" decor; inside, it's "hip" with occasional live music,
Thursday–Saturday DJs and all-around "great atmosphere."

Cafe de Bruxelles
23 | 19 | 22 | $10

118 Greenwich Ave. (13th St.), A/C/E/L to 14th St./8th Ave., 212-206-1830

"Belgian beers abound" at this venerable Village *moules-friterie*, a "classic boho hangout" that makes many "feel like they're in Europe" (or maybe even "heaven"); "cute and quiet" with "lots of atmosphere", it's a natural for "people-watching on Greenwich Avenue" along with a "terrific ale."

Café des Artistes/The Parlor
24 | 24 | 23 | $14

1 W. 67th St. (bet. Columbus Ave. & CPW), 1 to 66th St., 212-877-3500; www.cafenyc.com

This "elegant lounge" opposite the "charming" restaurant is a "perfect" complement or precedent to an "evening at Lincoln Center"; it also works for "sipping incredible wines", "discussing inspiring art" (like the H. C. Christy drawings on the wall) or for just "feeling all grown up – except when the bill comes and you wish dad was around to pay it."

Cafe Deville/Bar Bleu
17 | 19 | 15 | $9

103 Third Ave. (13th St.), L to 3rd Ave., 212-477-4500

Take a quick "trip to France" via this "cute" East Village bistro with a downstairs lounge that may be a bit "narrow" compared to the "large brasserie" upstairs, but is requisitely "dark and sexy"; $1 oysters and "great drinks" at happy hour keep things "kinda fun."

Cafe Gitane ⊄
23 | 18 | 15 | $10

242 Mott St. (bet. Houston & Prince Sts.), 6 to Spring St., 212-334-9552

"Beautiful ladies" in "skimpy clothes" are par for the course at this "terrific" NoLita cafe that emits enough "French-Moroccan" flair to draw "throngs of Eurotrash"; despite the "cooler-than-thou" staff and "waiting around forever" to get in, payoffs include an "incredibly convenient" location and truly "bohemian feel."

Café Gray Brasserie
– | – | – | E

Time Warner Ctr., 10 Columbus Circle, 3rd fl. (60th St.), 1/A/B/C/D to 59th St./Columbus Circle, 212-823-6338; www.cafegray.com

A "chic" anteroom to Gray Kunz's adjacent restaurant, this new bar in the Time Warner Center is designed like a Viennese brasserie, with warm lighting reflected in a bevy of beveled mirrors; whether just for a drink or as a prelude to dinner, it's a "pleasing" if pricey destination, tended by a "friendly" staff.

Cafe Lalo ⊄
23 | 21 | 17 | $10

201 W. 83rd St. (bet. Amsterdam Ave. & B'way), 1 to 86th St., 212-496-6031; www.cafelalo.com

"Don't expect tranquil tea-sipping" at this "bustling" Upper West Side coffee bar, a "sweet place" famed for its "decadent, mile-high desserts" and appearance in *You've Got Mail*; sure, it may be a "bit too bright" and the noise can reach a "concert-level pitch", but it's always a "great resource" so long as you "pick an off time to go"; P.S. sorry, they still "don't accept credit cards."

Cafe Luxembourg
22 | 21 | 21 | $13

200 W. 70th St. (bet. Amsterdam & West End Aves.), 1/2/3 to 72nd St., 212-873-7411

"Always entertaining", this "very French" West Side bistro is also "quietly upscale" enough for "fortysomething" types to feel at home (the "flattering lighting" helps); admirers say this "pioneer" exudes "incredible character", and even if the "tiny" bar area is "cramped", "you won't mind if there's a celeb standing next to you."

Cafe Noir 21 | 17 | 17 | $9
32 Grand St. (Thompson St.), A/C/E to Canal St., 212-431-7910
"After-work drinks turn into dinner that turns into more drinks" at this "always banging" SoHo cafe that's "passed the test of time" thanks to "long-term cool" and a "good mix of people"; spoilers say the "sultry" servers are too busy "trying to hook up with the clientele", but in such an "electric atmosphere", who can blame them?

CAFÉ PIERRE 24 | 25 | 26 | $15
Pierre Hotel, 2 E. 61st St. (5th Ave.), N/R/W to 5th Ave./59th St., 212-940-8195; www.fourseasons.com
So "civilized" it will "make you want to order a Manhattan", this "sophisticated" "standard" in the Pierre Hotel remains "as old world as ever" and is a "sure thing" for the "old-money" set; whether for a "quiet drink" with "someone's grandmother" or just to enjoy the nightly piano music with other "adults", this one's a "must."

Cafeteria 19 | 18 | 17 | $11
119 Seventh Ave. (17th St.), 1 to 18th St., 212-414-1717
Nothing like your high-school cafeteria, this 24/7 "Chelsea mainstay" has the "minimal chic" thing down to a science, ditto the "decent" comfort chow that might be the "only thing standing between you and tomorrow's hangover"; everyone agrees the late-night "hours are what makes it great" – not the "slow service" from "aspiring actors."

Cafe Wha? 20 | 14 | 18 | $10
115 MacDougal St., downstairs (bet. Bleecker & W. 3rd Sts.), A/B/C/D/E/F/V to W. 4th St., 212-254-3706; www.cafewha.com
Get "down and dirty" at this Village basement music venue, a "'60s throwback" where a "rockin'" house band makes for "mosh pit–like dancing"; foes say it's a "cramped" "tourist trap" aggravated by "forget-about-you" service and a "onetime experience."

Caffe Dante ⊄ 21 | 15 | 15 | $8
79-81 MacDougal St. (bet. Bleecker & Houston Sts.), 1 to Houston St., 212-982-5275
This "old-school Italian coffeehouse" brings a "Little Italy feel to the Village" with "fine java" and "to-die-for desserts" served alfresco on sidewalk seats; it's even good for "eat-and-run" types, since "making room for other customers" seems like "what they want you to do."

Caffe Rafaella 24 | 21 | 17 | $8
134 Seventh Ave. S. (bet. Charles & W. 10th Sts.), 1 to Christopher St., 212-929-7247
Chatterboxes "sit and talk forever" at this Village java hut where "taking your time can be enjoyable" (and necessary, since service can be on the leisurely side); in addition to coffee, beer, wine and "yummy desserts", it also offers a daily "street show" from its "inviting" sidewalk seats.

Caffe Reggio ⊄ 21 | 19 | 16 | $7
119 MacDougal St. (bet. Bleecker & W. 3rd Sts.), A/B/C/D/E/F/V to W. 4th St., 212-475-9557; www.caffereggio.com
Things "never change" at this "true Italian cafe", a circa-1927 bohemian "favorite" famed for its "aged atmosphere", "literary" following and overall Village-y verve; sure, there's no alcohol, no credit cards and "unconventional" service, but that's part of its "timeless hipness."

CAIN 24 | 24 | 19 | $13
544 W. 27th St. (bet. 10th & 11th Aves.), R/W to 28th St., 212-947-8000; www.cainnyc.com
Among the latest "über-hot" spots in über-hot West Chelsea is this "super-trendy" new arrival done up like an African game lodge that

lends a "cocktailing on safari" air to the proceedings (à la the late Pangaea); since many feel it's the city's coolest club, expect a "tough door" admitting a "select" few of "NY's most eligible" who are more than accustomed to bottle-service pricing.

Cajun
20 | 16 | 18 | $10

129 Eighth Ave. (bet. 16th & 17th Sts.), A/C/E/L to 14th St./8th Ave., 212-691-6174; www.jazzatthecajun.com
A "touch of the Big Easy in the Big Apple", this longtime Chelsea bar/eatery offers "hot and sassy" live jazz and Dixieland; while the "bar area is accommodating", it's a long way from the bandstand, so aficionados spring for dinner and "sit in the dining room."

Calico Jack's Cantina
15 | 14 | 16 | $8

800 Second Ave. (bet. 42nd & 43rd Sts.), 4/5/6/7/S to 42nd St./Grand Central, 212-557-4300; www.calicojacksnyc.com
A "pickup bar, pure and simple", this "fun", "festive" Midtowner lures "frat boys hitting on everything that walks" and those who love them; picky drinkers shrug "no great shakes" and move on "before the one-night-stand crowd gets drunk and desperate."

Caliente Cab Co.
13 | 13 | 14 | $9

61 Seventh Ave. S. (Bleecker St.), 1 to Christopher St., 212-243-8517
21 Waverly Pl. (Greene St.), A/B/C/D/E/F/V to W. 4th St., 212-529-1500
"Accessible" Village locations and "outdoor people-watching" lure "tourists" and "local student bodies" to these "McMexican" bars; foes find them "*muy* tired", citing "lackluster margaritas", "indifferent service" and "cheesy" setups more appropriate to "Times Square."

Calle Ocho
24 | 25 | 21 | $11

446 Columbus Ave. (bet. 81st & 82nd Sts.), B/C to 81st St., 212-873-5025; www.calleochonyc.com
The "mojitos are *bueno*" at this "super-swanky" Nuevo Latino, ditto the "stunning bar" jammed with "beautiful" folk; it's as close to "Miami" that the Upper West Side gets, and even if it can be "noisy", "pricey" and "cramped", it's still a "great place to take a date", with "wonderfully inventive food" as a bonus.

CAMPBELL APARTMENT
25 | 27 | 21 | $13

Grand Central Terminal, 15 Vanderbilt Ave. (bet. 42nd & 43rd Sts.), 4/5/6/7/S to 42nd St./Grand Central, 212-953-0409; www.hospitalityholdings.com
Savor a "Manhattan moment" at this "civilized" Grand Central "time warp" set in a former "railroad baron's drawing room" and specializing in "serious drinks for sophisticated drinkers"; despite a "hard-to-find" location and "hefty" tabs, it's "extremely crowded after work", so insiders suggest you "show up after seven to avoid the commuters"; P.S. a "top hat and monocle" isn't mandatory, but "dress appropriately" (i.e. no sneakers, caps or T-shirts).

CANAL ROOM
18 | 20 | 17 | $10

285 W. Broadway (Canal St.), A/C/E to Canal St., 212-941-8100; www.canalroom.com
A "credit reference and a mink" might help you wiggle past the "hard door" at this "swanky" TriBeCa club, primarily known as a music-industry showcase thanks to its "hot" sound system; still, what's "interesting" and "bumping" for some is "ridiculously trendy" and "overhyped" for others.

Candle Bar ⌂
– | – | – | M

309 Amsterdam Ave. (bet. 74th & 75th Sts.), 1/2/3 to 72nd St., 212-874-9155
"Serving a purpose" as one of the few gay bars on the Upper West Side, this "divey" den "could use some sprucing up" but that doesn't

matter much to its "cliquish neighborhood" crowd; just be prepared to "teach the young bartenders how to mix your favorite drink."

Canyon Road
20 | 18 | 19 | $9

1470 First Ave. (bet. 76th & 77th Sts.), 6 to 77th St., 212-734-1600; www.arkrestaurants.com

Margaritas so "powerful" you might "forget your name" are the draw at this Yorkville "neighborhood singles" magnet that attracts "older" folks as well as the "young and the restless"; though the "small bar area" can get "crowded", the "friendly service" and "ski lodge in New Mexico" ambiance compensate.

Capital Grille
– | – | – | E

155 E. 42nd St. (bet. Lexington & 3rd Aves.), 4/5/6/7/S to 42nd St./ Grand Central, 212-953-2000; www.thecapitalgrille.com

Grand Central users have a new place to wet their whistles at this chain chophouse installed in the glass pyramids adjoining the Chrysler Building; despite the way-out exterior, inside things are very clubby, all mahogany and brass, and set off by oil paintings of noted New Yorkers (Fiorello LaGuardia, Billie Holiday); P.S. word's out, so brace yourself for a tight squeeze after work.

Capone's ⊅
– | – | – | M

221 N. Ninth St. (bet. Driggs Ave. & Roebling St.), Brooklyn, L to Bedford Ave., 718-599-4044

Inside an unmarked door lies this red-lit new Williamsburg watering hole trading on godfather lore and furnished with random gangster photos and an impressive turn-of-the-century bar imported from Chicago; while the pool table and glassed-in smoker's patio are nice touches, the pièce de résistance is a free pizza with every drink.

Cargo
21 | 19 | 21 | $8

120 Bay St. (Slosson Terrace), Staten Island, 718-876-0539

A "mellow, friendly" vibe and occasional "live music" keep the trade brisk at this "funky" Staten Island bar/eatery "just a short walk from the ferry"; it attracts "older, bohemian" types by changing the decor "pretty often", and as a bonus, there's "outside seating" with views of the Verrazano Bridge.

Carnegie Club
∇ 22 | 21 | 22 | $13

156 W. 56th St. (bet. 6th & 7th Aves.), N/Q/R/W to 57th St./7th Ave., 212-957-9676; www.hospitalityholdings.com

Oozing "old-boy" charm (with a crowd to match), this "vibrant" bar/ lounge near Carnegie Hall makes you "nostalgic for the good old pre-Bloomberg days of yore" since you can legally light up a stogie on its mezzanine; it also provides "enjoyable live music", especially those crooners channeling "Frank Sinatra."

Carolines
22 | 16 | 17 | $12

1626 Broadway (bet. 49th & 50th Sts.), R/W to 49th St., 212-757-4100; www.carolines.com

"Laugh till you cry" at this "legendary" Times Square comedy club where the "top acts" range from "major headliners" to "superb" though "relatively unknown" newcomers; their "R-rated-and-beyond" material is funny, but the "pricey" cover charges and two-drink minimums are no joke.

Casa La Femme North
22 | 24 | 18 | $12

1076 First Ave. (bet. 58th & 59th Sts.), 4/5/6/N/R/W to 59th St./ Lexington Ave., 212-505-0005; www.casalafemme.com

Romeos seeking a "sexy" "third date" pitch their tents at this "dreamy" Egyptian "oasis" set in the "boring" East Side; "great sangria" and "delicious" mezes set bellies in blissful motion (mimicking the live dancing), and the staff will "leave you alone" for "private" bon temps.

Casimir
21 | 21 | 18 | $9

103-105 Ave. B (bet. 6th & 7th Sts.), F/V to Lower East Side/2nd Ave., 212-358-9683
It's like "Casablanca in Alphabet City" at this "candlelit" bistro/lounge that's "always busy" with "good-lookers" soaking up the authentic "Mediterranean vibe"; though the "jam-packed weekend" scene might not "encourage you to linger", a "lovely shabby-chic garden" helps ease the squeeze.

Cávo
25 | 26 | 20 | $12

42-18 31st Ave. (bet. 42nd & 43rd Sts.), Queens, G/R/V to Steinway St., 718-721-1001; www.cavocafelounge.com
Dionysian revelers proclaim it's "like partying in Athens" at this "hip" Astoria bar/restaurant, a "classy" "hot spot" so "spacious" that there's "a room for any preference"; on warm weather nights "pretty people" cávort in the "huge" outdoor garden where you definitely "won't feel like you're in Queens anymore."

CBGB's ⌀
22 | 12 | 14 | $7

315 Bowery (Bleecker St.), 6 to Bleecker St., 212-982-4052; www.cbgb.com
"Still gritty, still sleazy" and "still about the music", this Bowery rock 'n' roll "institution" is a "classic rat hole" that's so "loud" the "windows are usually shaking"; punkers pining for its former "glory days" contend it "lives off its reputation", but optimists insist it will "never go out of style" so long as it can hold onto its lease; P.S. "yes, the bathrooms are that disgusting."

CB's 313 Gallery
23 | 15 | 17 | $7

313 Bowery (Bleecker St.), 6 to Bleecker St., 212-677-0455; www.cbgb.com
The "less rowdy" younger sister of punk "granddaddy" CBGB's next door, this "comfortable" East Villager is an art gallery by day and an "independent" music site by night; given the "toned-down" mood, it's possible to spot "suits" sipping "Courvoisier" among the mohawks.

Cedar Tavern
21 | 18 | 18 | $7

82 University Pl. (bet. 11th & 12th Sts.), 4/5/6/L/N/Q/R/W to 14th St./ Union Sq., 212-741-9754
"You can feel the beatniks", at least in spirit, at this "old-school" Village tavern where "wannabe writers" and artists gather to guzzle suds and "plot revolutions"; if the "historic charm" emanating from its "exquisite" eponymous wood bar fails to inspire your inner "Jackson Pollock", at the very least it's a decent "way station on a pub crawl."

Cellar, The
- | - | - | M

325 E. 14th St. (bet. 1st & 2nd Aves.), L to 1st Ave., 212-477-7747
"Your parents' 1970s den" ("plastic-covered" furniture and "board games" included) is reincarnated at this "comfortable" East Village newcomer that's "worth stopping in" for its "silly" mix of brew and "déjà vu"; if the idea of playing "Battleship" leaves a sinking feeling, "free WiFi" will remind you which decade this is.

Cellar Bar
22 | 23 | 18 | $12

Bryant Park Hotel, 40 W. 40th St., downstairs (bet. 5th & 6th Aves.), 7/B/D/F/V to 42nd St/6th Ave., 212-642-2211; www.bryantparkhotel.com
Go "underground" and get high with "large, potent martinis" at this "slick" cavern opposite Bryant Park that exudes "retro" appeal via a dramatic arched ceiling and sex appeal thanks to "pretty" patrons; "pricey" tabs turn off some, while variable "cell service" draws mixed reactions.

Central
24 | 22 | 18 | $9

20-30 Steinway St. (bet. 20th Ave. & 20th Rd.), Queens, G/R/V to Steinway St., 718-726-1600; www.centrallounge.com
There's no shortage of space for downing "specialty drinks" and grooving to a "modern European" soundtrack at this "ultramodern" Astoria lounge/restaurant that comes complete with a seasonal courtyard; Queensbound clubbers say it "tries hard" to emulate its Manhattan counterparts, and "kind of gets close."

Central Bar
20 | 17 | 18 | $7

109 E. Ninth St. (bet. 3rd & 4th Aves.), 6 to Astor Pl., 212-529-5333; www.centralbarnyc.com
"Flat screens aplenty" and pints "priced right" attract lots of athletic supporters to the first floor of this wide "open" East Village Irish pub, while the "neat" upstairs lounge offers "more intimate" environs; for some, the vibe's more "Murray Hill" than Downtown, but fans feel this joint is "nicer than most."

'Cesca
24 | 22 | 22 | $12

164 W. 75th St. (Amsterdam Ave.), 1/2/3 to 72nd St., 212-787-6300; www.cescanyc.com
Fans "wish they'd enlarge" the bar top of super-chef Tom Valenti's Upper West Side "hot spot", where the Italian eats are so "damn good" that much of the drinking area resembles a "restaurant arrivals lounge"; still, the "attentive" service and "smart" surroundings make it "one of the classier places" in the 'hood.

Chango
19 | 18 | 19 | $9

239 Park Ave. S. (bet. 19th & 20th Sts.), 6 to 23rd St., 212-477-1500; www.changonyc.com
"Another Park Avenue South spot", this "loud" cantina purveys "decent" margaritas and "surprisingly fresh" Mexican fare in "cute", "Disney"-esque digs; despite a "franchise feel" and a "tight" bar area, most feel that this "casual spot" is a "good chango from the ordinary thango."

Channel 4
– | – | – | M

58 W. 48th St. (bet. 5th & 6th Aves.), B/D/F/V to 47-50th Sts./Rockefeller Ctr., 212-819-0095; www.channel4barnyc.com
This new Midtown bar near Rockefeller Center takes its name from the local NBC TV station that broadcasts nearby; otherwise, it's a pretty standard Irish pub, with a bi-level format featuring drinking downstairs and dining above.

Cheap Shots ⊘
– | – | – | I

140 First Ave. (bet. 9th St. & St. Marks Pl.), 6 to Astor Pl., 212-254-6631
Like the name says, this no-frills East Village dive vends cheap swill in tiny, dim digs where picnic tables sub for banquettes and flat screens sub for conversation; other amusements include games like darts and Monopoly as well as one of the few air hockey tables in the city, but ultimately the rock-bottom prices are what keep people coming back here.

Chelsea Brewing Co.
18 | 15 | 15 | $8

Chelsea Piers, Pier 59 (W. 18th St. & Hudson River), A/C/E/L to 14th St./8th Ave., 212-336-6440; www.chelseabrewingco.com
In warm weather, the "excellent view of the Hudson" and the "sunset" from the "outdoor deck" of this Chelsea Piers microbrewery is "worth the trek" to its "off-the-beaten-path" locale; but off-season, the "only reason to go" to this "mainstream" joint is the "home brews."

Chelsea Piers Bowling Alley   18 | 15 | 15 | $9

*Chelsea Piers, Pier 60 (W. 18th St. & Hudson River), A/C/E/L to 14th St./
8th Ave., 212-835-2695; www.chelseapierslanes.amfcenters.com*
As an "alternative to going to a bar", this "upscale" Chelsea Piers
bowling alley rolls out "hilarious good times", especially for a "group"
outing; although "not cheap", it's "hard to get lanes" on weekends
(when "all of Jersey shows up"), so either go early or "reserve a
lane" in advance.

Cherry   21 | 23 | 17 | $11

*W Tuscany Hotel, 120 E. 39th St. (bet. Lexington & Park Aves.), 4/5/6/7/S to
42nd St./Grand Central, 212-519-8508; www.mocbars.com*
"Everyone looks better in the dark" at this "red-lit", "votive-candled"
Murray Hill lounge where the "waitresses look like working girls" and
the bartenders are "almost as beautiful as the clientele"; opinion
splits on its trendiness: "way cool" versus "yet another W Hotel bar."

Cherry Tavern ⊯   16 | 9 | 16 | $5

*441 E. Sixth St. (bet. Ave. A & 1st Ave.), F/V to Lower East Side/2nd Ave.,
212-777-1448*
"Bored 21-year-olds looking to get plowed" frequent this East Village
"dive" for its incredibly "cheap" "Tecate-and-tequila-shot special";
there may be "no atmosphere" in this "dimly lit" "rec room", but the
"kick-ass jukebox" and "good crowd" compensate.

Chetty Red   12 | 12 | 14 | $9

*28 E. 23rd St. (bet. Madison Ave. & Park Ave. S.), 6 to 23rd St., 212-254-6727;
www.chettyred.com*
Although this Flatiron club/lounge has "good music" and a "red theme
going for it", some of its "just-graduated-from-college" crowd feels it
"doesn't distinguish itself" from the pack, citing a "poor location",
"tame atmosphere" and "rude bartenders."

Chez Josephine   23 | 24 | 20 | $12

*414 W. 42nd St. (bet. 9th & 10th Aves.), A/C/E to 42nd St./Port Authority,
212-594-1925; www.chezjosephine.com*
A "show of its own" in the Theater District, this "dark", "bordello"-
like bar/restaurant is "basically a Josephine Baker museum" curated
by her adopted son, Jean-Claude (a host with the most who treats
everyone "like family"); a piano player helps keep things "lively."

Chibi's Sake Bar   25 | 20 | 24 | $10

*238 Mott St. (bet. Prince & Spring Sts.), 6 to Spring St., 212-274-0054;
www.chibisbar.com*

Chibitini

*63 Clinton St. (bet. Rivington & Stanton Sts.), F/J/M/Z to Delancey/
Essex Sts., 212-674-7300; www.chibitini.com*
A "fussy French bulldog" with an affinity for "leopard print scarves"
is the namesake and sometime "host" of these "adorable" little
sake bars where the rice wine offerings are mighty "good" (if "a bit
costly") and the "charming" human hospitality "will make you feel
like an old friend."

China Club   18 | 18 | 16 | $11

*268 W. 47th St. (bet. B'way & 8th Ave.), C/E to 50th St., 212-398-3800;
www.chinaclubnyc.com*
"All walks of life" walk into this Theater District "hook-up club", a
"spacious" three-floor affair long known for its "Monday night"
parties; once "legendary", now "a bit past its prime", it draws both
the "young and old at heart" despite "steep" pricing and too much
"waiting in line."

Chow Bar
21 | 21 | 20 | $10

230 W. Fourth St. (10th St.), 1 to Christopher St., 212-633-2212
Potent, "tasty" drinks and a "fun atmosphere" are a winning combination at this "cute" West Villager that also dishes out "delicious" Pan-Asian vittles; the "cool" vibe attracts the "young" and hip, but even fans wish the bar area was a tad less "cramped."

CHUMLEY'S ⊘
24 | 19 | 18 | $7

86 Bedford St. (bet. Barrow & Grove Sts.), 1 to Christopher St., 212-675-4449
"Don't blink or you might miss" the "unmarked door" to this former speakeasy, a "charming", circa-1922 Village "hideaway" with a "roaring" fireplace and a beatnik "literary" feel via framed, "first edition" book jackets; it can't be beat for a "little history with your beer" ("Fitzgerald and Kerouac kicked a few back" here), even if it's patronized by "too many college kids" today.

Church Lounge
23 | 24 | 19 | $12

Tribeca Grand Hotel, 2 Sixth Ave. (White St.), A/C/E to Canal St., 212-519-6600; www.tribecagrand.com
Everybody "feels grand" in this "dramatic" TriBeCa hotel lobby lounge set beneath a "soaring" eight-story atrium that draws some very "cool" customers; maybe the staff is "more beautiful than professional", but it's "great if you have an endless expense account" and want to "see and be seen."

CIBAR
24 | 23 | 20 | $11

Inn at Irving Place, 56 Irving Pl. (bet. 17th & 18th Sts.), 4/5/6/L/N/Q/R/ W to 14th St./Union Sq., 212-460-5656; www.cibarlounge.com
"Win over" that special someone at this "sophisticated", "boudoir pink" lounge in a Gramercy townhouse, where "amazing" martinis from a "girl-friendly" cocktail list "help move the conversation along"; "dark", "smooch"-worthy corners and a "lovely" bamboo garden embellish its "romantic" allure.

CIELO
22 | 22 | 16 | $12

18 Little W. 12th St. (bet. 9th Ave. & Washington St.), A/C/E/L to 14th St./8th Ave., 212-645-5700; www.cieloclub.com
Banquettes ring the petite "sunken dance floor" at this "minimalistic", "smaller scale" Meatpacking District "jewel" where "exceptional music", "full-bodied sound" and a "great DJ lineup" enthrall a "crowd that just wants to dance"; outsiders gripe about the "snobby door scene" overseen by "strict", "power-drunk" bouncers.

Cipriani Downtown
24 | 21 | 20 | $14

376 W. Broadway (bet. Broome & Spring Sts.), C/E to Spring St., 212-343-0999; www.cipriani.com
"The famous, the pretty, the rich and the thin" squeeze into this "snooty", "sassy", "star-studded" bar/restaurant that's SoHo's version of "Biarritz"; a "sugar daddy" or a "Brinks truck" might help settle the tab, and "good luck" getting into the "exclusive", members-only club upstairs.

Circa Tabac
23 | 19 | 18 | $10

32 Watts St. (bet. 6th Ave. & Thompson St.), A/C/E to Canal St., 212-941-1781; www.circatabac.com
"Smoke indoors while drinking" is the novel concept at this SoHo den "spared by Bloomberg" that's "one of the few bars" in town where it's "legal" to light up; nicotine fiends like the "upscale" deco decor and "great selection of booze", and don't care "what the prices are" – it's "worth every penny" to inhale inside.

Cité Grill   22 | 21 | 23 | $11

120 W. 51st St. (bet. 6th & 7th Aves.), B/D/F/V to 47-50th Sts./
Rockefeller Ctr., 212-956-7262; www.citerestaurant.com
A convenient Midtown location makes this "after-work" bar and grill
a "favorite" for the Time Inc. crowd and other "networkers" in the
Rock Center area; "huge bowls of wine" and "martinis you could do
the backstroke in" might result in "trouble getting up for work" the
next day, however.

Citrus Bar & Grill   21 | 21 | 19 | $10

320 Amsterdam Ave. (75th St.), 1/2/3 to 72nd St., 212-595-0500;
www.citrusnyc.com
"Worth their weight in Cuervo Gold", the "amazing margaritas"
are the calling cards of this Latin-Asian eatery that's "as cool as the
Upper West Side gets"; its "youngish" followers fret about the "too
crowded", "zoo"-like bar scene and "early closing" hours, but still
get "decked out" to see and be seen from its popular sidewalk seats.

City Hall   19 | 21 | 22 | $11

131 Duane St. (bet. Church St. & W. B'way), 1/2/3 to Chambers St.,
212-227-7777
Reeking of "old NY", this "not too crowded" TriBeCa surf 'n' turf
specialist boasts a "sexy bar area" that's "completely isolated from
the dining room"; after a couple of "happy-hour cocktails" dispensed
by "friendly bartenders", it's "hard not to order dinner", especially when
you see a "gorgeous seafood platter" passing by.

Clem's   ▽ 17 | 15 | 20 | $5

264 Grand St. (Roebling St.), Brooklyn, L to Bedford Ave., 718-387-9617
A little slice of "Middle America", this "low-key" Williamsburg bar
offers some of the "best deals in the nabe", i.e. the "Patriot (shot of
bourbon + can of Bud") and the "Federale (shot of tequila + can of
Tecate")"; otherwise, some find "no personality" here, save for its
"chatty, affable owner."

Cleopatra's Needle   18 | 15 | 15 | $10

2485 Broadway (bet. 92nd & 93rd Sts.), 1/2/3 to 96th St., 212-769-6969;
www.cleopatrasneedleny.com
"No cover" and a "low minimum" earn kudos at this "low-key" bar/
eatery featuring "straight-ahead" live jazz; alright, it's "not a destination
spot" since some acts are "nothing to write home about", but it is one
of the "few places offering nightly music" on the Upper West Side.

Cloister Cafe   18 | 21 | 15 | $8

238 E. Ninth St. (bet. 2nd & 3rd Aves.), 6 to Astor Pl., 212-777-9128
"Wonderful in the summer" when its "awesome garden" is in full
bloom, this "charming" East Village cafe feels more cloistered in
winter months, with a stained glass–lined interior that's "not bad
either"; "iffy service", however, seems to be a year-round feature.

Clubhouse   – | – | – | M

700 E. Ninth St. (Ave. C), L to 1st Ave., 212-260-7970; www.clubhousenyc.com
The "new Avenue C" could be summed up by this "sexy little" lounge
featuring a "unique" meandering bar and "terrific music" spun by
"some of the best DJs around"; it may be "high priced" for the nabe,
but that's not fazing its "chic" mixed crowd of gay and nongay folk.

Club Macanudo   24 | 25 | 23 | $13

26 E. 63rd St. (bet. Madison & Park Aves.), 4/5/6/N/R/W to 59th St./
Lexington Ave., 212-752-8200
Like "walking into a men's club from the 1920s", this "mahogany"-laden
East Side cigar lounge features a copper-topped bar populated by

the "pinstripe-suit-and-suspenders" set ("females are few and far between"); "one of the few establishments" where you can legally puff indoors, it's a "great place to smoke a stogie" – or at least "smell like you did."

C-Note ⊅

20 | **12** | **19** | **$7**

157 Ave. C (bet. 9th & 10th Sts.), L to 1st Ave., 212-677-8142; www.thecnote.com
"Wax nostalgic" about the "old days of the East Village" at this "cheap" purveyor of "live local music", both "good and bad"; lookswise, it's "nothing special" and the location is undoubtedly "out of the way", but it's "worth it" if you happen to stumble in for one of those "rare singer-songwriter finds."

Cock, The ⊅

19 | **7** | **14** | **$7**

188 Ave. A (12th St.), L to 1st Ave., 212-946-1871
Just "as sleazy as it sounds", this "dark and dingy" East Village "vice palace" is the kind of gay dive where "anything can happen (and usually does)"; it's best "after 2 AM" when it's "always crowded" with "horny" men shooting for a "happy ending"; P.S. it's set to move to the former Hole space (29 Second Avenue) in late summer 2005.

Cocktail Room

20 | **21** | **20** | **$10**

334 E. 73rd St. (bet. 1st & 2nd Aves.), 6 to 77th St., 212-988-6100; www.cocktailroom.com
Starting with their "delicious" chocolate martinis, the masters of mixology at this Upper East Side bar/lounge oversee a cocktail list with more varieties than a certain ketchup brand; stats aside, this "hidden" side-street spot with a "Miami" feel is a "nice change of pace" from the less flavorful offerings in the area.

Coda

17 | **20** | **16** | **$9**

34 E. 34th St. (bet. 5th & Madison Aves.), B/D/F/N/Q/R/V/W to 34th St./ Herald Sq., 212-685-3434; www.coda34.com
By some accounts, the "old bank" space (complete with the "actual vault" downstairs) inhabited by this Murray Hill lounge/music venue is a "welcome change" in an area hardly known for diversity; on balance, however, critics say if it's "as high class as it thinks it is", it should hire "more bartenders."

COFFEE SHOP

19 | **15** | **14** | **$9**

29 Union Sq. W. (16th St.), 4/5/6/L/N/Q/R/W to 14th St./Union Sq., 212-243-7969
"Too-cool-for-school" types are all over this double-decker Union Square "late-night staple", a "club that thinks it's a diner" (and vice versa), where the pastime of "being seen" still "reigns supreme"; as for the service, just be patient: the "sashaying" "pseudo-model" staff will get to you as soon as the "beautiful people have been served."

Coliseum Bar

▽ **13** | **12** | **16** | **$7**

312 W. 58th St. (bet. 8th & 9th Aves.), 1/A/B/C/D to 59th St./Columbus Circle, 212-977-3523
It may be "less of a dive" since it was "recently remodeled", but this "no-frills" Midtown bar still sticks to the "cheap-pitchers-and-dartboards" formula of old; while a "choice" hangout for "locals" and "Hudson Hotel" personnel, most yawn "boring."

Collins Bar

▽ **18** | **12** | **21** | **$6**

735 Eighth Ave. (bet. 46th & 47th Sts.), A/C/E to 42nd St./Port Authority, 212-541-4206
"Free popcorn" and a "fairly priced" tap list keep this "tiny" Theater District watering hole filled with "Local 1 guys" and even the occasional "shady" type; "no pretension", "no tourists" and "sweet" bartenders are additional draws.

Comedy Cellar   25 14 16 $9
117 MacDougal St. (bet. Bleecker & W. 3rd Sts.), A/B/C/D/E/F/V to W. 4th St., 212-254-3480; www.comedycellar.com
"Quinn", "Chappelle" and "Attell" are just a few of the "big-time" headliners dropping one-liners at this West Village comedy club, voted the "best" of the genre in this *Survey* despite its "cramped", "dungeon"-like setting; just "don't expect great service", and as for eating, its "attempts at food can be funnier than some of the comics."

Comic Strip   20 11 15 $10
1568 Second Ave. (bet. 81st & 82nd Sts.), 6 to 77th St., 212-861-9386; www.comicstriplive.com
When it comes to "side-splitting" entertainment, few can top this Upper East Side house of mirth where "quality" jokesters roam the same stage that once showcased "Romano" and "Seinfeld"; annoying "drink minimums" and "poor service" to the contrary, it's "worth the hassle" for "a night away from the typical."

Commonwealth   – – – M
497 Fifth Ave. (12th St.), Brooklyn, F to 4th Ave., 718-768-2040
Park Slope thirtysomethings cluster on decrepit vinyl-and-chrome couches and around Eames-inspired tables in this high-ceilinged, brick-lined bar; audiophiles study the CD juke's homemade mixes for the latest Guided by Voices tunes while ironists add to the corkboard's file-card fodder in the 'brutally honest personals' corner.

Company   – – – M
242 E. 10th St. (bet. 1st & 2nd Aves.), L to 1st Ave., 212-420-7101; www.company-bar.com
Savor the "unpretentious" vibe and "great drink specials" at this East Village taproom that draws an "eclectic" mix of "neighborhood" types; while its *Twin Peaks*–esque decor may be a tad "fancy" for this part of town, it's still a "secret" given the side-street address.

Connolly's Pub   17 14 20 $7
150 E. 47th St. (bet. Lexington & 3rd Aves.), 6 to 51st St./Lexington Ave., 212-692-9342
14 E. 47th St. (bet. 5th & Madison Aves.), E/V to 5th Ave./53rd St., 212-867-3767
121 W. 45th St. (bet. 6th & 7th Aves.), 1/2/3/7/N/Q/R/S/W to 42nd St./ Times Sq., 212-597-5126
www.connollyspubandrestaurant.com
"Truly traditional", this "typical" Irish trio "gets the job done" with "relaxed atmospheres" and an "always welcoming staff"; they're usually "packed to the rafters after work", and the 45th Street branch is SRO on Saturdays when the band "Black 47" takes the stage.

Continental   14 9 16 $6
25 Third Ave. (bet. 9th St. & St. Marks Pl.), 6 to Astor Pl., 212-529-6924; www.continentalnyc.com
A "reminder of how it used to be", this "raw" East Villager dolled up like a "classic dive" is one of the "few rock venues left in the increasingly gentrified St. Marks Place area"; it's so "small" that it's "impossible to get any closer to the band", which is "nice if a good act is playing", otherwise "don't bother."

Coogan's Parrot Bay   – – – M
(fka Lounge 68)
1668 Third Ave. (bet. 93rd & 94th Sts.), 6 to 96th St., 212-426-1416; www.coogans.com
A gaudy tropical paint job has transformed the Upper East Side's former Lounge 68 into this more relaxed barroom offering reasonably priced

pops to the usual frat boy suspects; still, islands-esque specialty drinks can't disguise what's really an Irish sports bar.

COPACABANA
23 | 20 | 18 | $12

560 W. 34th St. (11th Ave.), A/C/E to 34th St./Penn Station, 212-239-2672;
www.copacabanany.com
So "huge" you should "bring a map", this "lively" double-decker club with "two dance floors" features "big-name" Latin bands upstairs and a "cool hip-hop room" below; sure, it's on the "expensive" side and the way-out location near the Javits Center "could be better", but the "salsa-loving", "ready-to-party" crowd sporting their "finest threads" is having too much "fun" to care.

Coral Room
18 | 21 | 15 | $10

512 W. 29th St. (bet. 10th & 11th Aves.), 1 to 28th St., 212-244-1965;
www.coralroomnyc.com
Well, it "sounds like a cool concept" – a "kitschy" bar/lounge featuring a "huge fish tank" stocked with "real live mermaids" – but surveyors split on this West Chelsea nightspot: fans applaud its "creative" ambitions and recommend it for "out-of-towners", but sinkers say the "novelty" aspect of this "bottom feeder" "gets old fast": "came, swam, went."

Cornelia Street Cafe
21 | 16 | 18 | $9

29 Cornelia St. (bet. Bleecker & W. 4th Sts.), 1 to Christopher St.,
212-989-9319; www.corneliastreetcafe.com
"Brunch is great", the "atmosphere pleasant" and the "drinks well mixed" at this "Village institution" renowned for its "hidden downstairs" cabaret showcasing everything from "live jazz" to "poetry readings"; an "intellectual" yet "down-to-earth" vibe draws a "warm 'n' fuzzy" mix of "hippies" and "yuppies."

Corner Billiards
▽ 17 | 12 | 15 | $7

85 Fourth Ave. (bet. 10th & 11th Sts.), 6 to Astor Pl., 212-995-1314;
www.cornerbilliards.com
This "large" East Village billiard parlor is usually crowded with "NYU students", so expect a "wait" for one of its 28 "coveted tables"; though connoisseurs claim it "looks like a pool table factory" and "leaves much to be desired", realists reply there "aren't that many places to play" to begin with.

Corner Bistro ⊭
23 | 11 | 17 | $5

331 W. Fourth St. (Horatio St.), A/C/E/L to 14th St./8th Ave., 212-242-9502
NY's "worst-kept secret" is this "overdiscovered" Village "institution", a bona fide "dump" renowned for "sensational burgers" served with "some of the cheapest mugs of McSorley's in town"; don't let the "looong lines" discourage you: it's run like a "well-oiled machine" and ultimately the "prices are worth the wait."

Cosmo
▽ 18 | 18 | 25 | $8

359 W. 54th St. (bet. 8th & 9th Aves.), C/E to 50th St., 212-582-2200;
www.cosmo-bar.com
Some of the "cheapest martinis in NYC" are poured at this "small but serviceable" Hell's Kitchen boîte that's so "intimate" you shouldn't "expect much privacy"; on the other hand, it's frequented by "friendly people who know each other" and "want to know you."

Cotton
– | – | – | E

(fka Wye Bar)
105 W. 27th St. (bet. 6th & 7th Aves.), 1 to 28th St., 212-627-1444
The former Wye Bar has been remade into this new Chelsea lounge, a "narrow" affair bracketed by two bars and festooned with textiles to

justify its name; a "cool bottom level" that "not everyone knows about" comes equipped with a cotton candy machine and the inevitable beds, while an in-house limo service is available for VIPs sans wheels.

Cowgirl
20 | 20 | 20 | $8

519 Hudson St. (10th St.), A/C/E/L to 14th St./8th Ave., 212-633-1133
"Kitsch is taken to a whole new level" at this "home-on-the-range"-themed Villager with a "barbed-wire collection" on the walls and "killer margaritas" served in "Mason jars"; though they might want to "rustle up some better grub", the "drinks are tasty enough" and have the "desired effect."

Coyote Ugly Saloon
12 | 9 | 13 | $7

153 First Ave. (9th St.), L to 1st Ave., 212-477-4431;
www.coyoteuglysaloon.com
Ok, it "doesn't live up to the movie hype", but this East Village "white-trash" dive does display "barely clothed bartendresses" "grinding on the bar" in front of a bunch of "horny males"; locals find it "overdone" and "getting old", but at least the "tourists seem to have fun" here.

Crash Mansion/BLVD
∇ 21 | 21 | 17 | $9

199 Bowery (Spring St.), J/M/Z to Bowery, 212-982-7767;
www.crashmansionnyc.com
This "brick-walled" Bowery music venue below the restaurant BLVD shows "great potential", boasting state-of-the-art equipment and an eclectic roster of talent; though the cover and minimum charges may be "pricey", it's worth it for the overall "easygoing" vibe; P.S. they've raised the stage so you don't "have to stand" anymore to see.

Crif Dogs
– | – | – | I

113 St. Marks Pl. (bet. Ave. A & 1st Ave.), 6 to Astor Pl., 212-614-2728
This hole-in-the-wall hot dog hawker in the heart of St. Marks Place is renowned for its sloppy specialty franks and eye-grabbing 'Eat Me' sign; catering to the post–pub crawl crowd with cheap beer, old-school video games and a recently acquired liquor license, it can be more packed at 3 AM than most bars.

Crime Scene
– | – | – | M

310 Bowery (bet. Bleecker & Houston Sts.), F/V to Lower East Side/2nd Ave., 212-477-1166; www.crimescenebar.com
The Bowery's latest upstart is this arresting new crime themer put together by former NYPD officers who've painted handcuffs on the wall and handprints above the urinals, and named the cocktails appropriately (the Mugshot, etc.); a pool table, two projection screens and welcoming barkeeps complete the lineup.

CROBAR
20 | 22 | 17 | $12

530 W. 28th St. (bet. 10th & 11th Aves.), C/E to 23rd St., 212-629-9000;
www.crobar.com
As "explosive dance clubs" go, this Way West Chelsea "behemoth" takes the cake, hosting the "most popular DJs on the world circuit" in a "cavernous", "Ibiza-size" space where the "sweaty, cruising crowd" ranges from "suits to sweatsuits"; there's also a "tight" hip-hop room and a "mellow" VIP area for "lower-stress high times", but wherever you wind up, it's a guaranteed "wild night" – and proof that "big clubs are back."

Croton Reservoir Tavern
20 | 17 | 17 | $7

108 W. 40th St. (bet. B'way & 6th Ave.), 1/2/3/7/N/Q/R/S/W to 42nd St./Times Sq., 212-997-6835; www.crotonreservoirtavern.com
The Garment District gets some "energy" from this "friendly" bi-level bar/eatery named for the 19th-century reservoir that once stood in

Bryant Park; expect a "big after-work crowd" weeknights given the convenient location between Grand Central and Port Authority, and a pretty "dead" scene on weekends.

Croxley Ales

22 | 18 | 17 | $7

28 Ave. B (bet. 2nd & 3rd Sts.), F/V to Lower East Side/2nd Ave., 212-253-6140; www.croxley.com

An "epic beer list", "ginormous projection screens" and a "great selection of frat boys" sum up the scene at this "loud" East Village sports bar where the "big draw" is its "amazing" tented outdoor space; "spacey" service leads some to order their brews "three at a time" to sidestep the inevitable "wait."

Cubby Hole ⊅

18 | 15 | 18 | $8

281 W. 12th St. (W. 4th St.), A/C/E/L to 14th St./8th Ave., 212-243-9041

From the "knickknack-packed ceiling" to the "hilarious bartenders", this Village lesbian bar is "always fun" with a "townie" vibe ("everyone seems to know everyone else"); though you can expect a fair number of "softball coaches and field hockey goalies" in the crowd, whether you're "gay, straight or undecided", all are "welcome."

Cub Room

19 | 19 | 19 | $11

131 Sullivan St. (Prince St.), C/E to Spring St., 212-677-4100; www.cubroom.com

SoHo's corner "living room hangout" on the scene since the mid-'90s, this "somewhat upscale" couches-and-cocktails spot has its paw on the "thirtysomething" pulse; it still can be pretty "romantic", but been-there-done-that types call it "more of a standby than a go-to."

Culture Club

17 | 15 | 14 | $9

179 Varick St. (bet. Charlton & King Sts.), 1 to Houston St., 212-414-2882; www.cultureclub.com

"As fun and as cheesy as ever", this SoHo double-decker dance club features a "tacky homage to the '80s" on the ground floor as well as a revamped upstairs (Nerveana) saluting the '90s; one cover charge provides admission to both, but either way expect about "90 percent women", most of them attending "New Jersey bachelorette parties."

Cupping Room Café

18 | 17 | 17 | $9

359 W. Broadway (bet. Broome & Grand Sts.), C/E to Spring St., 212-925-2898; www.cuppingroomcafe.com

Whether as a "launching pad" for the evening's festivities or for a post-prandial "nightcap", this SoHo cafe is a "quiet, comfortable refuge" with a "warm", rustic design complete with a potbellied stove; despite occasional live music and belly dancers, analysts say it's "too preppy for the Downtown crowd."

Cutting Room

19 | 17 | 18 | $9

19 W. 24th St. (bet. B'way & 6th Ave.), R/W to 23rd St., 212-691-1900; www.thecuttingroomnyc.com

It's always "fun to pop into" this Flatiron lounge, a "nice chill option" where "you never know who you're going to see"; up front, the "mellow" bar is "sceney without being intimidating", while the back room houses a performance space showcasing everything from "great jazz" to postmodern "burlesque shows."

Daddy-O

▽ 22 | 15 | 23 | $8

44 Bedford St. (Leroy St.), 1 to Houston St., 212-414-8884

"Simple yet appealing", this "underrated" Villager can "serve PBR in a can" yet also "mixes a mean martini" according to its "cool-cat" crowd; the overall "relaxed" vibe owes a lot to barkeeps "who treat customers like family" and encourage an overall "chatty" air.

Dakota Roadhouse ⊄   ▽ 17 14 19 $6
43 Park Pl. (bet. Church St. & W. B'way), 2/3 to Park Pl., 212-962-9800
"Cheap after-work drinks" keep things cheerful at this Financial District roadhouse that's a "great place to watch a game" along with other "low-key" dudes; a yank-the-lobster-from-the-tank game and "rodeo on the tube" contribute to the down-home doings.

Daltons   – – – M
(fka Revolution)
611 Ninth Ave. (bet. 43rd & 44th Sts.), A/C/E to 42nd St./Port Authority, 212-245-5511
The latest arrival on Hell's Kitchen's Ninth Avenue strip is this new bar and grill, a vast blond wood space dominated by a long bar and the inevitable big-screen TVs; although a tad too suburban for city slickers, it's a hit with locals looking for drinks and tidbits without attitude.

Dangerfield's   19 13 15 $12
1118 First Ave. (61st St.), 4/5/6/N/R/W to 59th St./Lexington Ave., 212-593-1650; www.dangerfields.com
"Gone but not forgotten", the late Rodney Dangerfield "lives on" at this East Side comedy club that still "packs a crowd" looking for a "good laugh"; what with the "overpriced drinks", there's fortunately no table minimum (only a cover charge) and ironists like the "elegantly shabby" digs reminiscent of "'50s Las Vegas."

DANIEL   26 27 28 $16
60 E. 65th St. (bet. Madison & Park Aves.), 6 to 68th St., 212-288-0033; www.danielnyc.com
"Have a drink and dream of the dinner to come" (or eat at the bar if you don't have reservations) in this "posh" lounge at Daniel Boulud's "epicurean heaven", frequented by "older sophisticates" used to "impeccable service" and "luxurious" trappings; *bien sur*, it's *très* "expensive", but what else would you expect for something so "elegant" and "classy"?

Danny's Skylight Room   ▽ 19 13 18 $9
346 W. 46th St. (bet. 8th & 9th Aves.), A/C/E to 42nd St./Port Authority, 212-265-8130; www.dannysgsp.com
Danny's Broadway Piano Bar
346 W. 46th St. (bet. 8th & 9th Aves.), A/C/E to 42nd St./Port Authority, 212-265-8130; www.dannysgsp.com
A "continual changeover" of songbirds take flight at this Restaurant Row cabaret that can be "hit-or-miss" (with the exception of frequent performer Blossom Dearie, who "always steals the show"); maybe the decor's a "bit ragged", but the adjacent piano bar provides distraction.

DARK ROOM   ▽ 22 18 18 $6
(fka Ludlow Bar)
165 Ludlow St. (bet. Houston & Stanton Sts.), F/V to Lower East Side/ 2nd Ave., 212-353-0536
Enjoying "instant street cred", this new Lower East Side "hipster haven" has become "*the* place for bands to hold after-parties" thanks to its "perfect location", "awesome jukebox" and parallel bars in "two separate rooms"; party-poopers say it's "really fun until the weekend" hordes invade – "but isn't that the case everywhere?"

David Copperfield's   19 15 21 $7
1394 York Ave. (74th St.), 6 to 77th St., 212-734-6152; www.davidcopperfields.com
"Hidden" away on "desolate" York Avenue, this Yorkville "brewski-lover's paradise" offers a "solid" selection of suds that "changes and

keeps up with the season"; it might "feel like a chain", but no one's complaining as it's one of the "few decent places to go this far east."

D.B.A.
21 | 14 | 17 | $7

41 First Ave. (bet. 2nd & 3rd Sts.), F/V to Lower East Side/2nd Ave., 212-475-5097; www.drinkgoodstuff.com

"Fine-spirits freaks" and hard-core hopsheads head for this "male-dominated" East Village bar, drawn by "dozens of single-malts" and an "incredible rotating selection" of beer, all "fairly priced" and "listed on chalkboards"; frosting the cake is an "open-air patio" that "transports you to Europe" – or at least "Brooklyn."

Dead Poet
19 | 16 | 22 | $6

450 Amsterdam Ave. (bet. 81st & 82nd Sts.), B/C to 81st St., 212-595-5670; www.thedeadpoet.com

"Escape the college bars" lining Amsterdam Avenue at this "calm" Irish pub, a "narrow", "couldn't-be-smaller" affair that could be the "skinniest bar on the West Side"; its "down-to-earth" denizens dig the poet portraits lining the walls ("you feel smarter just walking in") and vow there's "nothing dead about it."

Decibel
24 | 18 | 18 | $9

240 E. Ninth St. (bet. 2nd & 3rd Aves.), 6 to Astor Pl., 212-979-2733

As if "pulled out of central Tokyo", this "tiny" East Village sake bar "feels like a secret underground cave", right down to a "buzzer for entrance to add to the adventure"; once inside, it's "so dark you can barely see your drink", but no one minds given the "astounding selection" of rice wine and "authentic snacks" that take you on a "journey to Japan."

Deep
21 | 19 | 15 | $10

16 W. 22nd St. (bet. 5th & 6th Aves.), R/W to 23rd St., 212-229-2000; www.deepny.com

"Deep indeed", this great "big" Flatiron dance club features a "hot loud" sound system that may make you "wake up the next morning with the bass still beating in your head"; it's "never too packed" with "plenty of seating", though sinkers say it's "falling off the deep end", citing "pricey" cocktails and a "has-been" scene.

Dekk
– | – | – | M

134 Reade St. (bet. Greenwich & Hudson Sts.), 1/2/3 to Chambers St., 212-941-9401; www.thedekk.com

A combination bar, restaurant and screening room, this new TriBeCan does it all in a cozy, brick-walled space where movies are projected both in the dining area and in a separate private room; a downstairs lounge (dubbed Below Dekk) offers everything from live music to a reading series.

DELANCEY, THE
23 | 21 | 17 | $8

168 Delancey St. (bet. Attorney & Clinton Sts.), F/J/M/Z to Delancey/Essex Sts., 212-254-9920; www.thedelancey.com

"So many hipsters, so little time" says it all about this "new kid on the block", a triple-decker "down-to-earth destination" featuring a "comfy cool" main bar bracketed by a basement performance space and a "fun", faux-"tropical" roof deck; it's especially moving to Brooklynites given its "endearing view" of the "Williamsburg Bridge off-ramp."

Del Frisco's
24 | 24 | 23 | $12

1221 Sixth Ave. (49th St.), B/D/F/V to 47-50th Sts./Rockefeller Ctr., 212-575-5129; www.lonestarsteakhouse.com

"Fast-paced" folks "not looking to slow down" relish the "power happy hour" at this "high-energy" Midtown chain chophouse popular with "alpha males" and their "beautiful" dates; sure, it can be "brutally expensive", but the "jaw-dropping" bi-level setting with "totally fab" drinks and huge windows overlooking Sixth Avenue compensate.

Delia's Lounge
21 | 24 | 19 | $10

9224 Third Ave. (93rd St.), Brooklyn, R to 95th St., 718-745-7999; www.deliaslounge.com

"As good as it gets in Bay Ridge", this "sweet" lounge shows how "Brooklyn meets the big city" via "candles, couches" and "fabulous martinis"; despite a lot of "gold pinkie rings" in evidence, there are definitely "decent pickings" to be found at this "seductive" spot.

Delta Grill
20 | 17 | 21 | $7

700 Ninth Ave. (48th St.), C/E to 50th St., 212-956-0934

Spend some time "on the bayou without leaving the comforts of Manhattan" at this Hell's Kitchen Cajun number, a "little piece of Bourbon Street" offering a "not-too-loud bar" and "wonderful bands" on the weekends; in addition to "all of the basics", it's one of the "few places in town to get Abita on tap."

Desmond's
– | – | – | M

433 Park Ave. S. (bet. 29th & 30th Sts.), 6 to 33rd St., 212-684-9472; www.desmondstavern.com

"If you don't mind the scent of stale beer", this "dingy drinking hole" on otherwise tony Park Avenue South is just the ticket; despite the "boiler-room atmosphere", its "college crowd" digs the "easygoing" air and cheap prices.

Detour
▽ 23 | 14 | 19 | $7

349 E. 13th St. (bet. 1st & 2nd Aves.), L to 1st Ave., 212-533-6212; www.jazzatdetour.com

There's "never any cover" (only a "reasonably priced" two-drink minimum) at this "relaxed" East Village jazz joint where the nightly performers range from the "talented" to the "strange"; exuding "character without trying" too hard – "it feels dark and smoky even without smoke" – it's a "perfect place" to get "on the lowdown."

Dewey's Flatiron
15 | 13 | 17 | $7

210 Fifth Ave. (bet. 25th & 26th Sts.), R/W to 23rd St., 212-696-2337; www.deweysflatiron.com

"Decent" enough "after work", this "unpretentious" Chelsea watering hole is good for "getting loud with friends" in "airy", "dark-wooded" environs; foes call it "just like every other bar in the city" with a "not very compelling crowd", but if you like "cheap beer and no atmosphere, this is your place."

Dick's ⌀
– | – | – | M

192 Second Ave. (12th St.), L to 3rd Ave., 212-475-2071

"Low-key, low-maintenance" gay blades get together at this East Village "neighborhood" dive with a "great jukebox" and sketchy decor that lies somewhere between "seedy" and "scary"; the "crowd seems to know each other very well" here, though outsiders report "strangers are ignored."

Diner 24
18 | 18 | 18 | $11

102 Eighth Ave. (15th St.), A/C/E/L to 14th St./8th Ave., 212-242-7773; www.diner24.com

Maybe "more restaurant than nightlife" what with its small bar area, this Chelsea diner is "open 24 hours" and is thus an "after-the-clubs-close" destination; fans say its "appealingly simple" grub "without grease" satisfies "late-night cravings", even if it's "slightly overpriced" and the room itself on the "loud" side.

Ding Dong Lounge ⊄

∇ | 24 | 19 | 21 | $6

929 Columbus Ave. (bet. 105th & 106th Sts.), 1 to 103rd St., 212-663-2600; www.dingdonglounge.com

Whether a "CBGB's for Morningside Heights" or a "heavy metal version of the Abbey Pub", this "dark, dank" punk bar is "cooler than you think", especially for those intent on "picking up indie rock girls"; bell ringers say that it's similar to "what the East Village used to be" and definitely helping to change a neighborhood that's "going through a transition."

Dip

21 | 19 | 18 | $10

416 Third Ave. (bet. 29th & 30th Sts.), 6 to 28th St., 212-481-1712; www.dipcafe.com

Take a "change of pace from beer and wings" and have "fondue and martinis" at this "atypical" Murray Hill bar/lounge popular with the "just-graduated" set; a "candlelit", bi-level setup and table configurations "made for socializing" make this one stand apart from the other "generic" joints along Third Avenue.

Discothèque

14 | 17 | 13 | $10

17 W. 19th St. (bet. 5th & 6th Aves.), R/W to 23rd St., 212-352-9999; www.discothequenyc.com

"Remember the old days" at this Flatiron dance club that brings back "all the excitement of the '80s" for a crowd that's "looking to have fun"; unfun types say its "smaller" setup makes for a "cramped" scene that's as "overpriced" as it is "overcrowded."

'disiac

24 | 23 | 20 | $10

402 W. 54th St. (bet. 9th & 10th Aves.), C/E to 50th St., 212-586-9880; www.disiacnyc.net

"Off the beaten path" on a Hell's Kitchen side street lies this "pretty" little lounge that gives the nabe some zip with "colorful" Moroccan decor and an underlit bar reminiscent of *Saturday Night Fever*; a "cute garden in back" with "charm" to spare makes dreamers imagine they're "lounging on the Mediterranean."

Diva

20 | 17 | 17 | $11

341 W. Broadway (bet. Broome & Grand Sts.), 6/J/M/N/Q/R/W/Z to Canal St., 212-941-9024

"Very sexy" decor – all crimson walls and candlelight – sets the "cool, calm" tone at this SoHo bar/restaurant popular with Euro types and staffed by "good-lookers dressed in black"; floor-to-ceiling windows that open in warm weather are just the ticket when you want "to be seen."

Dive Bar

16 | 12 | 18 | $7

732 Amsterdam Ave. (bet. 95th & 96th Sts.), 1/2/3 to 96th St., 212-749-4358; www.divebarnyc.com

As "frayed around the edges as a dive should be", this "aptly named" Upper Westsider "does the job as advertised" (and at "dirt-cheap" tabs) according to its "Columbia grad school" fan base; pool, darts and a "very cool fish tank" provide extra amusements.

Dive 75

19 | 13 | 19 | $6

101 W. 75th St. (bet. Amsterdam & Columbus Aves.), 1/2/3 to 72nd St., 212-362-7518; www.divebarnyc.com

"More upscale than the name implies", this West Side "swillery" is "like going out and being home at the same time" thanks to "reasonable prices", "board games galore" and a "huge fish tank" to "lower your blood pressure"; as for the crowd, expect a group that "still remembers college clearly, but is too old to relive it nightly."

DIVINE BAR
21 | 19 | 19 | $10

244 E. 51st St. (bet. 2nd & 3rd Aves.), 6 to 51st St./Lexington Ave., 212-319-9463
236 W. 54th St. (bet. B'way & 8th Ave.), C/E to 50th St., 212-265-9463
"Wines by the glass" is this dynamic duo's "claim to fame" and given the "tremendous selection", they're a "safe call" whether for a "romantic rendezvous" or a "girls' night out"; expect a "nice mix of people" (from "all age groups and personality types") "drinking and fondueing" to a "mostly '80s" soundtrack; P.S. the newer, larger West Side outpost is becoming a particular favorite "before theater."

DIZZY'S CLUB COCA-COLA
– | – | – | M

Jazz at Lincoln Center, 10 Columbus Circle, 5th fl. (60th St.), 1/A/B/C/D to 59th St./Columbus Circle, 212-258-9595; www.jalc.org
Named after bebop legend Dizzy Gillespie, this "quietly classy" new boîte is the most intimate of the three performance spaces at Jazz at Lincoln Center, offering 140 seats arranged around a bandstand with "great views" of Central Park as the backdrop; a down-home soul food menu and fairly reasonable pricing ($30 admission and a $10 table minimum) have younger types licking their chops.

Django
20 | 22 | 18 | $11

480 Lexington Ave. (46th St.), 4/5/6/7/S to 42nd St./Grand Central, 212-871-6600
The "Midtown East work crew" likes the "classy" scene at this "convenient" lounge/restaurant near Grand Central, citing its "airy", "casbah"-ish looks, "exotic drinks" and fellow "investment banker" following; granted, it's "expensive", but what else would you expect for something so "impressively upscale"?

Doc Holliday's
16 | 9 | 15 | $5

141 Ave. A (bet. 8th & 9th Sts.), L to 1st Ave., 212-979-0312;
www.docholidaybar.com
There are "no pretenders" at this "low-brow" East Village "hole-in-the-wall", just "drunken frat boys" and "random icky old guys" trying to hit on the "rocking" barmaids; no surprise, it's "divey to the nth degree", but there's "so much soul" in the air that fans "can't get enough of it."

Docks Oyster Bar
19 | 18 | 19 | $11

2427 Broadway (bet. 89th & 90th Sts.), 1 to 86th St., 212-724-5588
633 Third Ave. (40th St.), 4/5/6/7/S to 42nd St./Grand Central, 212-986-8080
www.docksoysterbar.com
"Over-40" types hoping to "get in the mood" comprise the "after-work scene" at these "old-school" seafooders that get so "lively" you may have to "scream over the din"; maybe they're "not the most exciting places in town", but the "decent-size cocktails" and "great NY atmosphere" just might make you want to "stay for the food."

Doc Watson's
19 | 15 | 20 | $7

1490 Second Ave. (bet. 77th & 78th Sts.), 6 to 77th St., 212-988-5300;
www.docwatsons.com
A "local's bar every night of the week", this "laid-back" Upper East Side Hibernian pub pays "tribute to the Emerald Isle" with "Irish music on Sundays" and one of the "best pours of Guinness" around; the finicky who find it "ordinary but still appealing" says it stays "lively" thanks to "spillover from Brother Jimmy's across the street."

D.O.C. Wine Bar ⊄
∇ 26 | 25 | 24 | $10

83 N. Seventh St. (bet. Kent & Wythe Aves.), Brooklyn, L to Bedford Ave., 718-963-1925
"You're in Italy" in Williamsburg at this "cozy wine bar" with an "unbeatable selection" of vinos accompanied by some mighty "great

tapas"; it's naturally a "nice place for a date" (albeit a "little pricey") and maybe just "charming" enough to be "worth the trip" from Manhattan.

Don Hill's
16 | 7 | 11 | $7

511 Greenwich St. (Spring St.), C/E to Spring St., 212-219-2850; www.donhills.com

"Rough around the edges" and proud of it, this black-walled SoHo music club/"total dive" can be "really loud" and "sweaty" but remains a "no-nonsense" place for younger types to "see up-and-coming bands" for "cheap covers"; "stinky bathrooms" and "inconvenience to public transportation" to the contrary, it works well whether you want to "rock out or chase the ladies."

Donovan's ∌
19 | 16 | 21 | $7

214-16 41st Ave. (Bell Blvd.), Queens, LIRR to Bayside, 718-423-5178
57-24 Roosevelt Ave. (58th St.), Queens, 7 to 52nd St., 718-429-9339

Bayside and Woodside "old reliables" exuding a "classic neighborhood pub feel" that "can't be beat with an Irish walking stick"; ok, they're "not much in the way of hot spots" and you "don't go here for women" – you "go to see double and hear the Pogues" on the jukebox.

Don't Tell Mama ∌
23 | 15 | 21 | $10

343 W. 46th St. (bet. 8th & 9th Aves.), A/C/E to 42nd St./Port Authority, 212-757-0788; www.donttellmama.com

"Deliciously camp" yet "always fun", this Restaurant Row cabaret–cum–piano bar draws "musical comedy buffs", "local theater" folk and plenty of "tourists" with an ever-changing repertoire of "great performers"; though it's a bit "clichéd" to some, Broadway hopefuls hope to "catch a rising star" here.

Door, The
– | – | – | M

508 Ninth Ave. (bet. 38th & 39th Sts.), A/C/E to 42nd St./Port Authority, 212-594-6095; www.thedoornyc.com

Way off the beaten path in the Garment District behind Port Authority lies this Moroccan lounge offering hookahs, belly dancers and plenty of room in which to enjoy them; given the quiet, anonymous vibe, this one's got illicit tryst written all over it.

Dorrian's Red Hand
15 | 11 | 15 | $7

1616 Second Ave. (84th St.), 4/5/6 to 86th St., 212-772-6660

"Just-out-of-college preppies" with "trust funds" frequent this "late-night" Upper Eastsider that "never seems to get old" for each new generation of "Buckley boys"; remember the unofficial dress code ("pleated khakis", "polo shirts with the collar turned up") and be prepared to "run into people you didn't like in boarding school."

DOS CAMINOS
23 | 22 | 19 | $11

373 Park Ave. S. (bet. 26th & 27th Sts.), 6 to 28th St., 212-294-1000
475 W. Broadway (Houston St.), 1 to Houston St., 212-277-4300
www.brguestrestaurants.com

"More types of tequila than one can imagine" line the shelves of these "swanky, sexy" cantinas where the "only danger comes the next morning" ("how do you say 'hangover' in Spanish?"); granted, the "small bar areas" can make it "difficult to move around", yet "no matter how crowded they get, service stays on point."

Double Happiness
22 | 19 | 17 | $9

173 Mott St. (bet. Broome & Grand Sts.), J/M/Z to Bowery, 212-941-1282

A "subterranean speakeasy with style", this "hidden" Little Italy lounge is made for those who want "the hot without the trendy", offering a number of "cozy private nooks" and "Chinatown-inspired cocktails" like the much-beloved "green tea martini"; it may be "impossible to find", but conversely it's a good "place to be when you don't want to be found."

Dove, The ▽ 22 | 25 | 23 | $8
228 Thompson St. (bet. Bleecker & W. 3rd Sts.), A/B/C/D/E/F/V to W. 4th St., 212-254-1435
For an "adult find" in the otherwise "collegiate Village", this "down-to-earth" underground newcomer mixes "Victorian furniture", flocked wallpaper and "dim lights" into one "classy package"; "reasonable prices" and "friendly" barkeeps have fans already calling it a "keeper."

Down the Hatch 17 | 10 | 17 | $6
179 W. Fourth St. (bet. 6th Ave. & 7th Ave. S.), A/B/C/D/E/F/V to W. 4th St., 212-627-9747; www.nycbestbars.com
Take "refuge from real life" at this "cheap" Village "hole-in-the-ground", a "subterranean sardine can" known for "mass consumption of beer, wings and football" by "rowdy" collegians; "low ceilings", "elbow-to-elbow" conditions and an unmistakable "frat house smell" make no difference to a crowd bent on going "down the drain."

Dream Lounge – | – | – | E
Dream Hotel, 210 W. 55th St. (bet. B'way & 7th Ave.), N/Q/R/W to 57th St./ 7th Ave., 212-246-2211
"Colorful" is the word for this new lounge parked in a Midtown boutique hotel lobby that channels the '70s with a mirrored ceiling, multihued tiled bar and vividly striped wallpaper and carpeting; so far, it's frequented by intrepid trendsters and international tourists, but things might pick up when its downstairs sibling, a club dubbed Subconscious, opens up.

Druids 20 | 16 | 20 | $7
736 10th Ave. (bet. 50th & 51st Sts.), C/E to 50th St., 212-307-6410
Livening up a stretch of Tenth Avenue "without much life" is this "quaint" "neighborhood Irish pub" that's "very much a local" hangout but always "welcomes new faces"; a "lovely" outdoor patio and some "surprisingly delicious food" distinguish it from the competition.

DT.UT 23 | 19 | 18 | $7
1626 Second Ave. (bet. 84th & 85th Sts.), 4/5/6 to 86th St., 212-327-1327; www.dtut.com
"Hipper than Starbucks", this "earthy" coffeehouse/bar "stays busy day and night", with an AM "laptop crowd" ceding to "daters eating s'mores" after dark; whenever you go, it's a "cozy, cuddly" site, even if scoring one of their "shabby-chic" couches is like "finding a parking place in Times Square."

Dublin House ⊄ 19 | 9 | 20 | $6
225 W. 79th St. (bet. Amsterdam Ave. & B'way), 1 to 79th St., 212-874-9528
The "epitome of an Irish pub", this circa-1927 Westsider is "what a bar should be": "cheap", open early (8 AM) and with "no pretension whatsoever"; a vintage neon sign adds to the "time warp" appeal, but regulars avoid the nights when "frat boys take it over thinking they're back at Lehigh."

Dublin 6 ▽ 21 | 18 | 22 | $7
575 Hudson St. (bet. Bank & W. 11th Sts.), A/C/E/L to 14th St./8th Ave., 646-638-2900; www.dublin6nyc.com
"Pleasant even when it's not hopping", this "warm" Village Irish pub may not be trendy, but sure is "friendly" (maybe because the "owner works there all day every day"); "strong drinks", "really good bar food" and a "nice fireplace" add to its charm.

Duff's ⊘
                                                        – | – | – | M
N. 3rd St. (Kent Ave.), Brooklyn, L to Bedford Ave., 718-302-0411
From a former owner of Manhattan's Bellevue Bar comes this new
Williamsburg rocker saloon where the walls and ceiling are plastered
with metal/horror/biker memorabilia and the patrons are just plain
plastered; the studio apartment–size space expands in warm weather,
when a gritty outdoor smokers/drinkers patio opens up.

Dugout ⊘
                                                   ▽ 16 | 9 | 18 | $7
*185 Christopher St. (bet. Washington & West Sts.), 1 to Christopher St.,
212-242-9113*
NY's "premier" bear and cub hangout, this longtime Village gay bar is
frequented by "real guys" looking for "woofy" hookups; Sunday's
"laid-back beer blast" attracts a "hot crowd from all over the world",
mainly because "there aren't many other alternatives" around.

Duke's
                                                       20 | 16 | 19 | $7
99 E. 19th St. (Park Ave. S.), 6 to 23rd St., 212-260-2922
"Do the roadhouse thing" and "get drunk cheap" at this "energetic"
Gramercy tavern, a "kitschy" ode to "trailer trash" known for its "free-
flowing PBR" and "belly-filling grub"; needless to say, there's "no
need to dress up" for the "down 'n' dirty" doings – "it is what it is."

Duke's
                                                   ▽ 21 | 14 | 17 | $6
129 Ave. C (bet. 8th & 9th Sts.), L to 1st Ave., 212-982-5563
Despite its way-off-the-beaten-path location, this "neighborhood
dive" is considered an "East Village staple" by regulars out to "grab
a quick drink, watch the game" or "play pool"; it's usually "packed
with hot, sweaty men" who cool off on the funky rear patio.

Duplex, The
                                                       19 | 13 | 17 | $8
*61 Christopher St. (7th Ave. S.), 1 to Christopher St., 212-255-5438;
www.theduplex.com*
"Even breeders" patronize this "mostly gay" Village cabaret/piano
bar where "Broadway aficionados" "sing along to Carpenters songs"
on the ground floor or go upstairs for theatrical performances; sure,
the talent can be "spotty" and the decor might need "dusting", but the
mood's always "friendly" and more than a little "campy."

Dusk
                                                   ▽ 18 | 16 | 21 | $7
147 W. 24th St. (bet. 6th & 7th Aves.), F/V to 23rd St., 212-924-4490
"Only locals know about" this "best-kept secret" in Chelsea, a "dark",
"low-key" locus with a pool table in front and "see-through mirrors"
in the loo so you can "spy on people at the bar"; although "never very
crowded", the "lack of revelers" makes for "attentive service."

DUVET
                                                        – | – | – | E
(fka Centro-Fly)
*45 W. 21st St. (bet. 5th & 6th Aves.), F/V to 23rd St., 212-989-2121;
www.duvetny.com*
An aquarium stocked with jellyfish stands opposite a frosted glass
bar meant to look like melting ice at this too-cool-for-school Flatiron
restaurant/lounge, with chill white walls that act as a backdrop for a
night-long light show; while better known for its bed-equipped dining
room (and see-thru bathroom doors), its soul is nightlife all the way.

Dylan Prime
                                                       25 | 25 | 21 | $12
*62 Laight St. (Greenwich St.), 1 to Canal St., 212-334-4783;
www.dylanprime.com*
"Wow a date" at this "sublime" TriBeCa steakhouse, featuring a
"super-duper romantic" lounge that's never too packed "since most

people won't make the trip" to its out-of-the-way locale; its "well-heeled" clientele says the food's well done, and suggests you "drink your dessert" by ordering an "irresistible pie-flavored martini."

Eagle, The ⊘ | 21 | 13 | 20 | $7

554 W. 28th St. (bet. 10th & 11th Aves.), C/E to 23rd St., 646-473-1866; www.eagle-ny.com

"NY's only leather bar", this West Chelsea gay "pit" lures "hairy, masculine" dudes who "look like the construction worker from the Village People" and are definitely "into the scene"; still, it's "a bit scary" for khaki-pants wearers lured by an "awesome" roof deck that "brings all sorts of hot men out to play."

Eamonn's | 13 | 14 | 20 | $6

174 Montague St. (bet. Clinton & Court Sts.), Brooklyn, M/R to Court St., 718-596-4969; www.eamonns.net

"Everyone knows your name, your drink and your business" at this very "local" Irish pub in Brooklyn Heights that attracts all types from "noisy civil servants" to wheezy "old geezers"; even those who say it's "not my cup of gin" report "getting happier with each well-poured Guinness."

Ear Inn | 22 | 17 | 19 | $7

326 Spring St. (bet. Greenwich & Washington Sts.), 1 to Houston St., 212-226-9060

This "classic longshoreman's bar" on the SoHo scene since 1817 is a "required stop" on any tour of historic city watering holes, and appeals in that "been-around-forever kind of way" with decor that "puts the 'old' in 'old school'"; P.S. "ride your hog" over on Tuesdays, when local bikers assemble to kick up some dust.

EARTH | – | – | – | E

116A Tenth Ave. (bet. 17th & 18th Sts.), A/C/E/L to 14th St./8th Ave., 212-337-0016; www.earth-nyc.com

Bollywood comes to West Chelsea via this new Indian lounge, an airy double-decker featuring a loftlike upstairs level and a tapas menu of Bombay street food; it might be best remembered for its stunning wall of votive candles (that owe more to fiber optics than to wax and flame).

East 4th Street Bar | ∇ 19 | 11 | 21 | $5

78-80 E. Fourth St. (bet. Bowery & 2nd Ave.), F/V to Lower East Side/ 2nd Ave., 212-253-2237

"Always reliable", this "traditional" dive is a "surprisingly decent" destination for "cheap" pops, a "great jukebox" and "key outdoor seating"; given its proximity to several East Village theaters, it's become known as an "actor's bar", especially on Monday nights.

East of Eighth | 19 | 16 | 19 | $8

254 W. 23rd St. (bet. 7th & 8th Aves.), C/E to 23rd St., 212-352-0075

For a "better show than at the movie theater next door", try this Chelsea double-decker home to a "colorful cast" of "gay and straight folks" alike peppered with some "trannies and cross-dressers"; a "phenomenal garden" out back "never disappoints", nor do the "flirty boys" behind the bar.

East River | – | – | – | I

97 S. Sixth St. (bet. Bedford Ave. & Berry St.), Brooklyn, J/M/Z to Marcy Ave., 718-302-0511; www.eastriverbar.com

Off the beaten path and a "long walk from the subway", this funky new South Billyburger is worth the effort given a sprawling yet "comfortable" setup, "cheap drinks", pool and foosball tables and a "friendly local crowd"; P.S. an "awesome" patio hosts BYO BBQ in warm weather.

EAST SIDE COMPANY BAR   _ _ _ E

49 Essex St. (Grand St.), F/J/M/Z to Delancey/Essex Sts., 212-614-7408
Master mixologist Sasha Petraske's latest opus, this new Lower East
Side bar/lounge is a more democratic version of his smash hit Milk
and Honey, with no secret phone number for admission; here, the
narrow, tin-lined space recalls a train with swell cocktails that will
certainly take you for a ride.

Eden   15 18 15 $9

2728 Broadway (bet. 104th & 105th Sts.), 1 to 103rd St., 212-865-5565
Even though the "neighborhood is aching for better meet-up-for-drinks"
spots, Upper Upper Westsiders split on this semi-swanky bar/lounge:
fans say it's "relaxing" and shows "great potential", but critics cite
"slow service" and "expensive" cocktails (it "tries too hard to be hip");
in sum, "don't expect much and you won't be disappointed."

Edgar's Cafe ⊅   19 18 16 $10

255 W. 84th St. (bet. B'way & West End Ave.), 1 to 86th St., 212-496-6126
"Quieter and less crowded" than its archrival, Cafe Lalo, this Upper
West Side coffeehouse is a "good place to end up if a first date's going
well"; "desserts are the true attraction here", not the "inattentive
service" or the "ho-hum" ambiance that's a vague tribute to its
namesake, Edgar Allan Poe.

Edge, The ⊅   ∇ 20 13 20 $6

*95 E. Third St. (bet. 1st & 2nd Aves.), F/V to Lower East Side/2nd Ave.,
212-477-2940*
Some mighty "fun slumming" can be had at this East Village barroom,
a "no-frills neighborhood" joint right down to the "original linoleum
flooring"; although it's a "dart thrower's haven", the "easygoing" vibe
makes everyone feel welcome.

1849   17 17 17 $8

*183 Bleecker St. (bet. MacDougal & Sullivan Sts.), A/B/C/D/E/F/V to W. 4th St.,
212-505-3200*
Gold Rush decor with some "country-western bordello" flourishes leads
some to wonder if there's an "identity crisis" at this Village bar that's
"not quite a college dive, but not an adult hangout" either; still, fans
tout its "central location", "good drink deals" and "plenty of seating."

Eight Mile Creek   18 14 21 $7

*240 Mulberry St., downstairs (bet. Prince & Spring Sts.), 6 to Spring St.,
212-431-4635; www.eightmilecreek.com*
"Aussie charm" prevails at this "relaxed" NoLita barroom parked
"down under an Australian eatery" that's "perfect for casual but hip
get-togethers"; "nothing-special" decor is overruled by a particularly
"friendly" mood, though it helps to "have an understanding of soccer
to fully appreciate this place."

Eight of Clubs ⊅   _ _ _ M

230 W. 75th St. (bet. B'way & West End Ave.), 1/2/3 to 72nd St., 212-580-7389
This longtime Upper West Side gay bar might not be the most happening
thing around, but it's got some new life thanks to a totally revamped
backyard, an ultra-funky, conversation-starting space decorated in
everything-but-the-kitchen-sink style; the clientele is equally funky,
consisting primarily of confirmed bachelors of a certain age.

Eleven   ∇ 23 21 18 $8

*152 Orchard St. (bet. Stanton & Rivington Sts.), F/V to Lower East Side/
2nd Ave., 212-979-2240*
"Hip and happening", this new "club-esque" bar on the Lower East
Side pairs "high ceilings" with a "low-key" vibe on its main floor, with

a bonus *Scarface* tribute (the "Tony Montana Room") below; it's "just being discovered" and getting "popular", despite its velvet-rope-and-bottle-service aspirations.

ELEVEN MADISON PARK
26 | 27 | 25 | $14

11 Madison Ave. (24th St.), R/W to 23rd St., 212-889-0905;
www.elevenmadisonpark.com
The bar at Danny Meyer's "snazzy" Madison Square Parker is "just as good as the restaurant" with "gourmet nibbles" and "classic cocktails" appropriately served in a "classic NYC setting"; its "successful clientele" applauds the "awesome wine list" and dismisses the "upscale prices."

Eleventh St. Bar
∇ 22 | 17 | 21 | $6

510 E. 11th St. (bet. Aves. A & B), L to 1st Ave., 212-982-3929
"Live Irish music on Sundays" is a highlight of this East Village Hibernian pub that daily delivers "good drinks", a "friendly" air and easy-on-the-wallet prices; its "expat" following finds it especially "nice for soccer games" on the telly.

El Flamingo
18 | 15 | 15 | $9

547 W. 21st St. (bet. 10th & 11th Aves.), C/E to 23rd St., 212-243-2121;
www.thedonkeyshow.com
This "big" West Chelsea dance club hosts one of the "longest running Latin music nights" on Mondays, but is better known for its weekend performances of *The Donkey Show* (a disco take on *A Midsummer Night's Dream*) and *The Karaoke Show* (just like it sounds); a "bachelorette party" staple, it's "great fun for the young."

elmo
19 | 20 | 16 | $10

156 Seventh Ave. (bet. 19th & 20th Sts.), 1 to 18th St., 212-337-8000
"Good if you're straight, great if you're gay", this "glossy" Chelsea bauble is an excellent "default" with plenty of "eye-candy boys" at the smallish bar or in the casual restaurant; its "retro-chic" downstairs lounge may be weekends-only, but upstairs is "reliably trendy" at any time.

El Quijote
17 | 16 | 20 | $9

226 W. 23rd St. (bet. 7th & 8th Aves.), 1 to 23rd St., 212-929-1855
"Seedy in the best way", this "longtime Spanish doyenne" under the Chelsea Hotel mixes "worn", "take-you-back-in-time" decor with "excellent sangria" for "stupor-inducing" results; though the scene's "busy" and "noisy", and you'll leave "smelling like garlic", that's all part of the "appeal."

El Rio Grande
18 | 15 | 16 | $9

160 E. 38th St. (3rd Ave.), 4/5/6/7/S to 42nd St./Grand Central, 212-867-0922;
www.arkrestaurants.com
"Blackout boulevard is right around the corner" after more than two of the "knock-you-on-your-ass" margaritas at this "popular" Murray Hiller that's happening at "happy hour"; few "have any idea if the food's any good" or not, though some report hazy memories of a "nice outdoor patio."

EMPLOYEES ONLY
∇ 23 | 20 | 23 | $11

510 Hudson St. (bet. Christopher & W. 10th Sts.), 1 to Christopher St., 212-242-3021; www.employeesonlynyc.com
Dress for a "1920s atmosphere" at this speakeasy-ish Village newcomer created by seasoned nightlife vets with a knack for "genius" specialty cocktails and "enthusiastic" service; the expansive bar area comes complete with a "welcome" fireplace making for romantic imbibing, and you can make an evening of it in the skylit dining room or rear

garden; P.S. the tarot card reader at the door suggests they're not taking themselves too seriously.

English Is Italian

_| _| _| E

(fka Tuscan)

622 Third Ave. (40th St.), 4/5/6/7/S to 42nd St./Grand Central, 212-404-1700; www.chinagrillmanagement.com

Physically not much different from Tuscan, its last incarnation, this airy Midtown restaurant has been reinvented foodwise as an all-you-can-eat Italian from star chef Todd English, but its nightlife raison d'être remains intact: a spectacular balcony bar overlooking the dining room with a view that will make you swoon.

Enid's ⊘

21 | 19 | 16 | $6

560 Manhattan Ave. (Driggs Ave.), Brooklyn, L to Bedford Ave., 718-349-3859; www.enids.net

"Hepcat hangouts" don't get much hepper than this Greenpoint "institution" that's "hipster central" in an otherwise "nowhere 'hood"; an "open", "high-ceilinged" affair, it comes complete with video games, pinball and a photo booth machine.

EN Japanese Brasserie

_| _| _| E

435 Hudson St. (Leroy St.), 1 to Houston St., 212-647-9196; www.enjb.com

Joining the ranks of über-designed Asian eateries, this Village Japanese boasts an epic, eye-popping main dining room where the chefs holler greetings to incoming patrons; the separate barroom, lined by sake and shochu bottles, is more conventional and laid-back, however.

Enoteca I Trulli

23 | 20 | 22 | $12

124 E. 27th St. (bet. Lexington & Park Aves.), 6 to 28th St., 212-481-7372; www.itrulli.com

"Romantic and quiet", this "heavenly" Gramercy wine bar is an "escape" from the norm offering "superb Italian" vintages and "fun flight samplers", paired with "tasty" cheeses; since it's a "bit pricey", economists taste first then "head across the street" to their retail outlet to buy full bottles.

Epstein's Bar ⊘

_| _| _| M

82 Stanton St. (Allen St.), F/V to Lower East Side/2nd Ave., 212-477-2232

Maybe the name sounds like chronic fatigue, but this new Lower East Side barroom is anything but, drawing energetic crowds from the get-go; credit the cool whitewashed setting, big windows overlooking Allen Street and fair-weather sidewalk seating for its success.

Escuelita

_| _| _| E

301 W. 39th St. (bet. 8th & 9th Aves.), A/C/E to 42nd St./Port Authority, 212-631-0588; www.enyclub.com

Think Latin "gay frat party meets _La Cage Aux Folles_" to get the gist of this Garment District dance club with a notorious "late-night drag show" that's "really well done"; it's "tons of fun" so long as you're "open-minded about your dance partners" – not everyone is what they seem here.

ESPN Zone

19 | 18 | 14 | $9

1472 Broadway (42nd St.), 1/2/3/7/N/Q/R/S/W to 42nd St./Times Sq., 212-921-3776; www.espnzone.com

"Sports junkies" call this Times Square theme bar "on steroids" just the ticket for "watching a high-profile game" – even "in the bathroom" – on one of its "many, many, many TVs"; despite catcalls for its "vanilla" ambiance and "families-and-tourists" following (bring your "Midwest slang dictionary"), it's always "crowded" for a reason.

Essex
18 | 18 | 16 | $9

120 Essex St. (Rivington St.), F/J/M/Z to Delancey/Essex Sts., 212-533-9616;
www.essexnyc.com

It's all about the "upstairs balconies" at this Lower East Side bar/
eatery, a "big", "lofty" thing with "super-high ceilings" and "minimalist"
furnishings; while it's "gone through all the phases of popularity"
during its five-year run, it's now settled into an "unpretentious" yet
"sophisticated" stop for "slightly older, well-dressed" types.

Eugene
18 | 20 | 15 | $11

27 W. 24th St. (bet. 5th & 6th Aves.), R/W to 23rd St., 212-462-0999;
www.eugenenyc.com

The "door policy is easier than in the past" at this "lively" Flatiron club
that was once "cool, then lame and now back to cool again"; foes cite
a "B&T" following and "arm-and-a-leg" pricing, but allow that the
"small dance floor" "always makes for a good time."

Excelsior ⊅
▽ 23 | 22 | 24 | $8

390 Fifth Ave. (bet. 6th & 7th Sts.), Brooklyn, F/M/R to 4th Ave./9th St.,
718-832-1599

Those "Brooklyn boys sure know how to dress" at this "way gay" Park
Slope barroom that somehow manages to attract "mixed crowds" of
all persuasions; a "nice outdoor patio" works for "smokers" or folks
just "looking to enjoy a summer night."

Exit
– | – | – | E

610 W. 56th St. (12th Ave.), 1/A/B/C/D to 59th St./Columbus Circle,
212-582-8282; www.exit2nightclub.com

Back to its original name after brief stints as Black and Ikon, this old-
school Hell's Kitchen dance club remains as sprawling as ever, a
multilevel behemoth with plenty of space to shake your groove thing;
don't expect pretension or bottle-service VIPs here: its youngish crowd
shows up to strut their stuff and have a good time.

Faces & Names
17 | 16 | 19 | $8

161 W. 54th St. (bet. 6th & 7th Aves.), C/E to 50th St., 212-586-9311;
www.facesandnames.com

"Well located" for a Midtown "happy hour", this "neighborhoody"
bar offers an intoxicating mix of "strong drinks" and "reasonable"
tabs; maybe the crowd leans toward "tourists" and "accountants in
Dockers", but at least the barkeeps are "engaging and humorous."

Failte
20 | 16 | 21 | $7

531 Second Ave. (bet. 29th & 30th Sts.), 6 to 28th St., 212-725-9440

An "authentic slice of the Auld Sod" planted in Gramercy Park, this
"cozy" Irish pub is "never too crowded, never too young" and there's
"always a smile with your pint"; geographically, it's conveniently
"across the street from the movie theater" and blessedly far away
from the "Third Avenue frat-boy" scene.

Falls, The
▽ 22 | 16 | 23 | $9

218 Lafayette St. (bet. Kenmare & Spring Sts.), 6 to Spring St., 212-226-5233

"Just waiting to be discovered", this new SoHo tavern "doesn't try too
hard", nonchalantly offering an airy, wood-lined setting and "friendly"
folks behind the bar; early visitors say the "lounge area in the back is
the place to go" when in the mood for "relaxing with a few beers."

Falucka
▽ 17 | 18 | 15 | $10

162 Bleecker St. (bet. Sullivan & Thompson Sts.), A/B/C/D/E/F/V to W. 4th St.,
212-777-4555; www.falucka.com

"Middle Eastern music with hip-hop beats" is spun at this Village
"hookah bar"/lounge done up Moroccan style with the occasional

belly dancer to shake things up; although romeos call it a "sure bet", critics say it's "too crowded" and "loud."

Fanelli's Cafe
20 | 15 | 16 | $8

94 Prince St. (Mercer St.), R/W to Prince St., 212-431-5744

For "zero pretension", try this "gritty, grubby" SoHo "stalwart"; one of the few "down-to-earth" joints in the area, it's a "red-and-white-checkered-tablecloth kind of place" decorated with "old boxing photos" and populated by "drunk regulars" and "artists who still have rent-controlled lofts" – not the "slavish fashionista" set.

Fashion 40
▽ 19 | 18 | 18 | $9

202 W. 40th St. (bet. 7th & 8th Aves.), A/C/E to 42nd St./Port Authority, 212-221-3628; www.fashion40lounge.com

Despite the Garment District address and "cheesy" moniker, this "upscale" lounge "doesn't feel garmento" thanks to "pretty" decor, flattering lights and fashionably "expensive" libations; while there's "enough room to mingle" downstairs, insiders head upstairs when they "want to let their hair down."

Fat Black Pussy Cat
18 | 15 | 17 | $7

130 W. Third St. (bet. MacDougal St. & 6th Ave.), A/B/C/D/E/F/V to W. 4th St., 212-533-4790; www.thefatblackpussycat.com

"Something for everyone" could be the motto of this Village venue, a "schizo" joint featuring a "sticky frat house" scene up front and an "emo velvet lounge" in back (it's the "one bar where all your friends can find their niche"); no matter where you wind up, however, be prepared for "college students galore."

Fat Cat
– | – | – | M

75 Christopher St. (bet. Bleecker St. & 7th Ave. S.), 1 to Christopher St., 212-675-6056; www.fatcatjazz.com

Whether for a "game of billiards" or a "set of jazz" at a "reasonable price", this Village pool hall/music venue "can't be beat", though the trade-off is an ultra-funky underground setup; from the same minds behind the reborn Smalls, this cool cat is planning to refurbish and embellish its stage, and may offer more varied music in the future.

Feinstein's at the Regency
23 | 22 | 23 | $15

Regency Hotel, 540 Park Ave. (61st St.), 4/5/6/N/R/W to 59th St./ Lexington Ave., 212-339-4095; www.feinsteinsattheregency.com

Many consider this "sophisticated" East Side hotel room the "ultimate NYC cabaret experience" thanks to a "top-of-the-line" talent roster presented by Michael Feinstein; all right, it's geared toward the "silver-haired set" and the prices are "extraordinary", but for "amazing" musicians and an "over-the-top" evening, look no further.

Fez
– | – | – | M

2330 Broadway, 2nd fl. (85th St.), 1 to 86th St., 212-579-5100; www.feznyc.com

Though the Downtown branch is now closed (and much missed), its "relaxing", "candlelit" Upper West Side sibling remains a "world of its own" with "Moroccan decor" and an overall "exotic ambiance"; drinks may be on the "pricey" side, but it's still a "quality choice" in an underserved neighborhood.

Fiamma Osteria
24 | 25 | 24 | $12

206 Spring St. (bet. 6th Ave. & Sullivan St.), C/E to Spring St., 212-653-0100; www.brguestrestaurants.com

For a "swanky night out in SoHo", this Steve Hanson opus is a "home run", a "beautiful" site for "civilized" albeit "pricey" cocktailing; those who insist it's a "restaurant, not a place for drinks" haven't discovered the "stylish" second-floor lounge that's considerably larger than the cramped street-level version (and accessed by a "trendy elevator").

Fiddlesticks
| 19 | 13 | 17 | $7 |

54-58 Greenwich Ave. (bet. 6th & 7th Aves.), 1/2/3 to 14th St., 212-463-0516; www.fiddlestickspub.com
Take a "great trip across the pond" in the Village via this "big, noisy" Irish pub that still manages to seem "cozy"; a spread-out, multi-chambered affair with "furniture and decorations at every turn", it's a particular favorite of "sweaty" frat boys and "English soccer" fans.

58
| – | – | – | VE |

(aka Au Bar)
41 E. 58th St. (bet. Madison & Park Aves.), 4/5/6/N/R/W to 59th St./ Lexington Ave., 212-308-9455; www.58newyork.com
Late night, after Le Jazz Au Bar shuts down, this subterranean Midtown club gears up and morphs into a party promoter–driven lounge; a longtime presence on the scene (from the days when it was known as Au Bar), it's been rejiggered with some African game lodge touches and offers a very modern banquettes-and-bottle-service experience.

55 Bar ⌿
| ▽ 22 | 13 | 15 | $7 |

55 Christopher St. (bet. 6th Ave. & 7th Ave. S.), 1 to Christopher St., 212-929-9883; www.55bar.com
A "true jazz dive bar", this Village basement around since the "prohibition era" offers "non-mainstream" music performed by "under-the-radar" acts for a reasonable cover and drink minimum; the decor may be "practically nonexistent", but its "diverse" following says when it comes to authenticity, this one "feels just right."

FIFTY SEVEN FIFTY SEVEN
| 24 | 25 | 23 | $15 |

Four Seasons Hotel, 57 E. 57th St. (bet. Madison & Park Aves.), 4/5/6/N/R/W to 59th St./Lexington Ave., 212-758-5757; www.fourseasons.com
Oozing "money and power", this "elegant" Midtown hotel bar is a perfect "people-watching" perch to ogle "A-list" characters ranging from "titans of industry" to "Hollywood" swingers to "professional" gals hoping to "meet Mr. Rich"; of course, the tabs are "*très cher*" and the "attitude can be *très* much", but it's always "happening" and "man, can they mix a cocktail."

Film Center Cafe
| 17 | 15 | 17 | $8 |

635 Ninth Ave. (bet. 44th & 45th Sts.), A/C/E to 42nd St./Port Authority, 212-262-2525; www.filmcentercafe.com
There's "no pretense" in evidence at this "cool but not too cool" Hell's Kitchen shrine to the movies, where the TVs are permanently tuned to AMC and the "film-lover" following is a "smiling" mix of "tourists" and Broadway babies; critics who find "nothing to rave about" cite "cheesy" cinematic decor and "not much happening" overall.

Finnegans Wake
| 17 | 13 | 19 | $6 |

1361 First Ave. (73rd St.), 6 to 77th St., 212-737-3664
This "solid" East Side Irish pub caters to an "older crowd" during the day and gets "younger and louder" at night; "boring" say those who advise "keep walking", but lingerers claim it's "consistently good."

Fiona's
| 21 | 19 | 21 | $7 |

1664 First Ave. (bet. 86th & 87th Sts.), 4/5/6 to 86th St., 212-348-3783
"Witty" Irish folk and "extremely friendly" barkeeps "right off the boat" make "everyone feel like part of the family" at this "step-up-from-the-typical" Yorkville pub; whether to "practice your brogue" or catch a "rugby match" on the tube, this one's a "welcome break" in an underserved nabe.

Firehouse

17 13 17 $7

522 Columbus Ave. (bet. 85th & 86th Sts.), 1 to 86th St., 212-787-3473;
www.firehousenyc.com

"Firehouse paraphernalia dangling from the rafters" makes this
Upper West Side "utility player sports bar" a good place to get hosed
and munch on "awesome wings"; it may be "nothing to blow you
away", but it still attracts random "college" Joes as well as post-
game "office softball teams."

First Edition

16 14 17 $8

41-08 Bell Blvd. (41st Ave.), Queens, LIRR to Bayside, 718-428-8522

"Sports fans gather" at this Bayside watering hole what with the
"plethora of TVs" broadcasting "every possible game you can
imagine" and "no meat market pressure"; it might be a "less than
stellar" scene, but at least it's a "good starting point for a night out
on Bell Boulevard."

Fitzgerald's Pub

∇ 20 13 22 $6

336 Third Ave. (25th St.), 6 to 23rd St., 212-679-6931;
www.fitzgeraldspubnyc.com

"Authentic Irish bartenders" deliver a "big-accented hello" at
this "local" Gramercy watering hole where "everyone feels like a
regular" after a drink or three; maybe the decor could use some work,
but the "bar area is kept clean, if not the language – just the way
we like it."

5 NINTH

23 23 18 $12

5 Ninth Ave. (bet. Gansevoort & Little W. 12th Sts.), A/C/E/L to 14th St./
8th Ave., 212-929-9460; www.5ninth.com

"Like visiting your incredibly wealthy friend's home", this "trendy"
new Meatpacking District "hot spot" set in a "gorgeous townhouse"
triplex is popular with the "hip and beautiful"; since the bar area's
so "tiny" ("what time do the crowds die down?"), a better drinking
alternative is its "enchanting garden" – or else "squeeze" upstairs
for a "delicious dinner" in the dining room.

FIVE POINTS

24 22 25 $10

31 Great Jones St. (bet. Bowery & Lafayette St.), 6 to Bleecker St.,
212-253-5700; www.fivepointsrestaurant.com

Perhaps "more restaurant than bar", this "elegant" NoHo destination
dispenses equal parts of "food, drink and Zen" in ultra-"cool" environs;
a "happy, helpful" staff pours a particularly "good happy-hour martini"
for those more keen on drinking than dining.

Five Spot

∇ 14 20 15 $9

459 Myrtle Ave. (bet. Washington & Waverly Aves.), Brooklyn, G to
Clinton/Washington, 718-852-0202; www.fivespotsoulfood.com

Both "neighborhood hip-hoppers and Pratt students" go for this "very
chill" Fort Greene soul food supper club featuring both DJs and live
performers; downsides include "sometimey service" and dudes who
become "a little too much in the evening" – it's "not a place for a girls'
night out, unless you want some play."

Fizz

– – – VE

137 E. 55th St. (bet. Lexington & 3rd Aves.), E/V to Lexington Ave./53rd
St., 212-755-7055

A "plush setting" draws "beautiful" folk to this members-only East
Side private club with both a ground-floor restaurant and a "swanky"
downstairs lounge that's all about "younger ladies and the older men
who love them"; foes find "no buzz" in the air, and caution you may
"feel out of place – unless you just came off the boat from France."

Flannery's Bar
14 | 12 | 17 | $6

205 W. 14th St. (bet. 7th & 8th Aves.), 1/2/3 to 14th St., 212-929-9589;
www.flannerysny.com
"Old-fashioned" and proud of it, this "typical NYC Irish joint" on the
Chelsea/West Village border draws "crusty", "rough-around-the-
edges" types accustomed to "gruff but quick" service; "not a place to
add to your evening itinerary", it's more a first stop to "meet up with
friends before heading to something better."

Flashdancers
18 | 12 | 15 | $11

1674 Broadway (bet. 52nd & 53rd Sts.), 1 to 50th St., 212-315-5107;
www.flashdancersnyc.com
"High-priced drinks and very naked women" collide at this Midtown
stripteaser, a "typical booty scene" where the "European-accented",
"silicone"-enhanced dancers "think you're an ATM machine";
connoisseurs say "this place is like school in the summer: no class."

FLATIRON LOUNGE
23 | 23 | 21 | $11

37 W. 19th St. (bet. 5th & 6th Aves.), 1 to 18th St., 212-727-7741;
www.flatironlounge.com
Return to the "days of the sidecar" at this "real deal" Flatiron lounge,
a "solid class act" seemingly "from another era" given its "elegant
deco styling" and "finely crafted cocktails" ("who knew gin could be
so versatile?"); its "white-collar crowd" digs the "ultracool vibe" and
shrugs off the "splurge"-worthy tabs.

Flight 151
15 | 11 | 18 | $7

151 Eighth Ave. (bet. 17th & 18th Sts.), A/C/E/L to 14th St./8th Ave.,
212-229-1868
For "urban blue-collar appeal" aplenty, check out this "local dive", one
of the few "str8" places in the "land of Chelsea boys"; besides "trivia
nights", "inexpensive" pops and "sports" on the tube, it's "nothing
special", though its low-tech aeronautics theme is "a bit odd."

Flor de Sol
22 | 22 | 20 | $10

361 Greenwich St. (bet. Franklin & Harrison Sts.), 1 to Franklin St.,
212-366-1640; www.flordesolnyc.com
"Close the deal with your lady" at this "sultry" TriBeCa exercise in
"cushiony luxury", lit by "Gothic candles" and lubricated by "excellent"
tapas and sangria so "intoxicating" that fans wouldn't mind "bathing
in it"; despite an ample bartop, "space is at a premium" in the "narrow"
setting, yet even the squeeze strikes some as "romantic."

Florent ⌀
22 | 15 | 17 | $10

69 Gansevoort St. (bet. Greenwich & Washington Sts.), A/C/E/L to 14th St./
8th Ave., 212-989-5779; www.restaurantflorent.com
Ever an "original" in the "oh-so-trendy Meatpacking District", this
"oldie but moldie" diner is "open 24 hours" and thus is a "classic
backup" for "pre-hangover breakfasts"; there may be "fewer trannies
and more yuppies" than in the past, but the waiters and waitresses
("hard to tell them apart") are just as "fun and cranky" as ever;
P.S. cash only.

Flow
16 | 19 | 15 | $11

150 Varick St. (bet. Spring & Vandam Sts.), 1 to Houston St., 212-929-9444;
www.flownewyork.com
A "nice", waterfall-equipped space arranged over two floors is the
lure at this "sleek" SoHo nightspot that otherwise can be a "hit-or-
miss" proposition; trendoids snipe it's "sooo last year", citing
"slow bartenders" pouring drinks for a crowd straight from the
nearby "Holland Tunnel."

FLOYD
26 24 21 $6

131 Atlantic Ave. (bet. Clinton & Henry Sts.), Brooklyn, F/G to Bergen St., 718-858-5810

The funky name nails the funky mood at this "cozy" new barroom that's part of the "proliferating" scene on Atlantic Avenue; picture a sprawling den decorated with "hodgepodge" furniture and stuffed animal heads, topped off by an incongruous "indoor bocce ball" court; add "reasonably priced" draft brews and Kentucky beer cheese snacks to complete the relaxed, low-rent mood.

Flûte
22 21 18 $12

40 E. 20th St. (bet. B'way & Park Ave. S.), 6 to 23rd St., 212-529-7870
205 W. 54th St. (bet. B'way & 7th Ave.), N/Q/R/W to 57th St./7th Ave., 212-265-5169
www.flutebar.com

"In the tradition of Bubble Lounge", these "champagne-focused" spots offer a wide variety of bubbly at "blow-your-entire-paycheck" prices; opinion splits over which one is more "snog"-worthy: some like the speakeasy-ish northern outpost (aka the "make-out capital of Midtown"), while others prefer the airier double-decker Flatiron branch.

Fondue
– – – M

303 E. 80th St. (bet. 1st & 2nd Aves.), 6 to 77th St., 212-772-2390;
www.fonduelounge.com

Hidden on a Yorkville side street lies this fondue-and-drinks dispenser, a narrow lounge featuring a sliver of a bar up front and a pillowy back den with its own projection screen; usually quiet, it's just the thing for intimate tête-à-têtes or for letting your hair down with the girls.

Forbidden City
20 19 18 $10

212 Ave. A (bet. 13th & 14th Sts.), L to 1st Ave., 212-598-0500;
www.forbiddennyc.com

One of the East Village's "best-kept secrets", this "Asian fusion lounge" "seethes with Eastern appeal" ("kung-fu movies" projected on the wall) as well as multiculti allure (a "hip-hop" soundtrack); its horseshoe-shaped bar allows one to "check out the other patrons instead of staring at your own reflection."

40/40
21 23 18 $12

6 W. 25th St. (bet. B'way & 6th Ave.), F/V to 23rd St., 212-989-0040;
www.the4040club.com

"ESPN Zone meets Bungalow 8" at this "hotter than hot" Chelsea "sports bar with a DJ", where "sightings of owner Jay-Z" give "groupies and Lil' Kim wannabes" a thrill; recently expanded to nearly double its size, it features "floating orb chairs", "weird unisex bathrooms" and a new Cigar Room; "high prices", "intimidating lines" and "door guys in need of a chill pill" are the downsides.

49 Grove
– – – VE

(fka Play, Halo)

49 Grove St. (Bleecker St.), 1 to Christopher St., 212-727-4949;
www.49grove.com

This vintage Village basement once renowned as Halo is now home to a velvety lounge reminiscent of a private library in the Playboy Mansion; so long as money is no object, concierge services, a full-time sommelier and an on-call limousine fleet are all at your disposal.

46 Grand
17 14 17 $9

46 Grand St. (bet. Thompson St. & W. B'way), A/C/E to Canal St., 212-219-9311

"Small but not too small", this "chill", mirror-lined SoHo lounge is known for its "loud", DJ-spun soundtrack and "cool owner"; still, some find "nothing hot" to be found in the "bare-bones" space, outside of the "occasional bartender."

Four-Faced Liar ⌿   – | – | – | M

165 W. Fourth St. (bet. 6th Ave. & 7th Ave. S.), A/B/C/D/E/F/V to W. 4th St., 212-366-0608

Its "great location" in the heart of the Village is the strong card of this "cozy" Irish pub, a no-frills item done up with rough-hewn furniture and vintage photos of the neighborhood; occasional live bands and poetry readings (at no cover) keep its "grown-up" crowd content.

FOUR SEASONS BAR   26 | 26 | 26 | $15

99 E. 52nd St. (bet. Lexington & Park Aves.), 6 to 51st St./Lexington Ave., 212-754-9494; www.fourseasonsrestaurant.com

"Watch masters of the universe" and other "big wigs" in action at this "high-powered" Midtowner where you should keep your Blackberry handy "in case you overhear any stock tips"; "everything a NY bar should be", it reeks of "high style and high fashion", but don't forget to bring "wads of cash" as all this "ego building" doesn't come cheap.

4₂O   16 | 16 | 15 | $8

420 Amsterdam Ave. (80th St.), 1 to 79th St., 212-579-8450; www.420barandlounge.com

"Low-key local bars" don't get more "casual" than this double-decked Upper Westsider where canoodlers are convinced that the "cozy" downstairs lounge is "far superior to upstairs"; "nothing special" and "played out" to some, it's "convenient" and "laid-back" to others; your call.

Frank's Cocktail Lounge ⌿   ▽ 13 | 12 | 15 | $8

660 Fulton St. (bet. Lafayette Ave. & S. Elliott Pl.), Brooklyn, G to Fulton St., 718-625-9339; www.frankscocktaillounge.com

"Step back in time" to "'70s Memphis" at this Fort Greene "dive", a "fun reminder of the neighborhood's roots" that's been "discovered by young hipsters"; it's a "nice escape from the trendy" complete with a downstairs "wiggle room" for dancing to "Stevie Wonder cover bands", and usually "packed on any given night."

Freddy's Bar & Backroom ⌿   ▽ 25 | 19 | 23 | $5

485 Dean St. (6th Ave.), Brooklyn, 2/3 to Bergen St., 718-622-7035; www.freddysbackroom.com

There's "loads of atmosphere" at this "nice dive" in Prospect Heights, where locals and hipsters coexist and "expand each other's horizons"; the "scruffy" front bar ("cheap drinks", sports on the tube) yields to a back room featuring "free live music", arty videos and "quirky acts", but wherever you wind up, this place "oozes Brooklyn pride."

FREDERICK'S   19 | 18 | 19 | $16

8 W. 58th St. (bet. 5th & 6th Aves.), N/Q/R/W to 57th St./7th Ave., 212-752-6200; www.fredericksnyc.com

"Impress a date" at this new, semi-private club opposite the Plaza Hotel, a "well-appointed" lounge with a front room for commoners leading to a "members-only back room" accessed by a fingerprint scanner; either way, it's the same "suit-and-tie/Euro crowd" that frequented the original '90s incarnation on Madison Avenue, and so far, "Part II" is just as "fabulous."

FREEMANS   24 | 22 | 17 | $9

end of Freeman Alley (off Rivington St., bet. Bowery & Chrystie St.), F/V to Lower East Side/2nd Ave., 212-420-0012; www.freemansrestaurant.com

"Getting hipper by the day", this Lower East Side hot spot parked "way out of the way" on an alley off Rivington Street may be more restaurant than bar, but is a bona fide scene nonetheless; inside the shabby-chic, hunting lodge–esque digs (replete with stuffed animal heads), "cool" customers sip specialty cocktails, graze on reasonably priced grub and enjoy some of the city's "best people-watching."

French Roast   17 | 17 | 15 | $9

2340 Broadway (85th St.), 1 to 86th St., 212-799-1533
458 Sixth Ave. (11th St.), F/L/V to 14th St./6th Ave., 212-533-2233
www.frenchroastnyc.com
"Wind the night down" at this "trusty", "open-'round-the-clock" duo renowned for "good after-midnight menus" that help you "sober up"; though some roast the "clueless" staff and occasional cup of "*cafe froid*", others warm to their "Parisian" atmosphere and "giant lattes."

Frying Pan   20 | 17 | 16 | $8

Chelsea Piers, Pier 63 (23rd St. at the W. Side Hwy.), C/E to 23rd St., 212-989-6363; www.fryingpan.com
"Amazing" outdoor fun awaits at this "unique scenario", a "rusty old" lightship moored just above Chelsea Piers that's only accessible for private parties; sure, it's "rickety" and "smells like it's been sitting at the bottom of the ocean for years", but fans say "nothing beats it" for "spooky" good times.

Fubar   16 | 11 | 18 | $7

305 E. 50th St. (bet. 1st & 2nd Aves.), 6 to 51st St./Lexington Ave., 212-872-1325; www.fubar-nyc.com
A "great place to meet a woman . . . with a drinking problem", this Midtown dive lures "serious" imbibers intent on getting, um, messed up "beyond all recognition"; it "looks and smells like a basement even though it's above ground", perhaps due to its "down-to-earth crowd."

Fuelray   21 | 22 | 19 | $8

68 W. Third St. (bet. La Guardia Pl. & Thompson St.), A/B/C/D/E/F/V to W. 4th St., 212-995-1900; www.fuelray.com
Follow the narrow "tunnel" from the "great coffeehouse" in front to the "velvety" space in back to access this "secret" Village lounge, a "seductive" spot serving "delicious cocktails" and "romantic date food" (i.e. "fondue and s'mores"); it's "chic without the attitude", with a "nice garden" as a bonus.

Fujiyama Mama   19 | 18 | 21 | $10

467 Columbus Ave. (bet. 82nd & 83rd Sts.), B/C to 81st St., 212-769-1144
There's always a "birthday party" going on (sometimes "way too many") at this Upper West Side Japanese "oldie but goodie" vending cocktails and "techno sushi" in a loud, strobe-lit setup; too "cheesy" for some, it's a "mainstay" for others, particularly when "out-of-town guests" need entertaining.

Full Shilling   19 | 17 | 18 | $8

160 Pearl St. (bet. Pine & Wall Sts.), 2/3/4/5 to Wall St., 212-422-3855; www.thefullshilling.com
"Lots of suits" with limited options in the "barren Financial District" turn up at this "roomy", "rustic" Irish pub that's an "excellent after-work" choice; fans praise its "authenticity", citing the "bartenders' brogues" and "beautiful bar" brought from Belfast.

Fun House   – | – | – | M

160 N. Fourth St. (bet. Bedford & Driggs Aves.), Brooklyn, L to Bedford Ave., 718-302-4300
Adding some variety to the Williamsburg scene is this wacky new lounge that's one part circus (clown heads, fun house mirrors) and one part art bar (pyramid sculptures, wall projections), with a Ping-

Pong table thrown in for good measure; it's all served up in a cavernous, cement-floored space that's pure Billyburg.

Fusion
∇ 17 | 15 | 18 | $8

818 10th Ave. (bet. 54th & 55th Sts.), C/E to 50th St., 212-397-1133
A pretty "dead" location on a "far-out" stretch of 10th Avenue houses this "rare find" serving "quick drinks" either inside or outdoors on its all-seasons patio; while some say "nothing special", boosters respond "nice enough."

G ⊄
21 | 21 | 17 | $9

225 W. 19th St. (bet. 7th & 8th Aves.), 1 to 18th St., 212-929-1085;
www.glounge.com
Gay blades "dressed to kill and buffed to thrill" chill at this "glossy" Chelsea lounge that's been "recently renovated" (but "nothing too drastic"); same as before are the "circular bar", "shirtless, eye-candy bartenders" and some of the "best frozen Cosmos in the city", but the "attitude central" vibe makes some wonder "can you be too trendy?"

Gaf Bar
20 | 14 | 22 | $6

1715 First Ave. (89th St.), 4/5/6 to 86th St., 212-427-6482
401 W. 48th St. (bet. 9th & 10th Aves.), C/E to 50th St., 212-307-7536
www.thegafnyc.com
"Simple", "no-frills" neighborhood bars, this Irish twosome draws "eclectic crowds" with ultra-"relaxed" atmospheres and "perfect pints"; while some prefer the "dark" Hell's Kitchen outpost over its "roomier" East Side cousin, either way the "friendly" staff will "make you feel like a regular even if it's your first time."

Galapagos
21 | 23 | 16 | $7

70 N. Sixth St. (bet. Kent & Wythe Aves.), Brooklyn, L to Bedford Ave.,
718-782-5188; www.galapagosartspace.com
"Bohemian NY" blossoms in Williamsburg at this "off-the-wall" "hipster" magnet set in a "cavernous" former mayo factory tricked up with a "reflecting pool" in front and "funky candlelight" everywhere else; its "transporting" acts include an "eclectic mix of dance, rock, burlesque and performance art", most of which is "genuinely original."

Galaxy Global Eatery
∇ 21 | 21 | 17 | $9

15 Irving Pl. (15th St.), 4/5/6/L/N/Q/R/W to 14th St./Union Sq., 212-777-3631;
www.galaxyglobaleatery.com
"Tasty signature cocktails" from a "far-out" drink list and a "diverse", hemp-heavy menu provide the lift-off at this Gramercy bar/eatery "conveniently" next door to Irving Plaza; fans say the "food's out of this world", but unfortunately the "servers' heads are too."

Gallery
∇ 21 | 22 | 15 | $11

Gershwin Hotel, 7 E. 27th St. (bet. 5th & Madison Aves.), 6 to 28th St.,
212-447-5700; www.gallerynyc.com
Gramercy's Gershwin Hotel is home to this "interesting" bar/lounge done up with colorful, multimedia pop art; while cynics nix the "rude service" and sometimes "cheesy" crowd, supporters say it's a "great scene on a good night."

Garage
20 | 18 | 19 | $9

99 Seventh Ave. S. (bet. Barrow & Grove Sts.), 1 to Christopher St.,
212-645-0600; www.garagerest.com
For a "bit of sophistication" in otherwise "harried" Sheridan Square, park yourself at this "cute 'n' cozy" bar/restaurant offering nightly "live jazz" with "no cover" or minimum; maybe it's "where the tourists go" since it looks a little like "Applebee's", but there's no argument about the "convivial" mood and "summertime sidewalk seating."

Gaslight
16 | 15 | 15 | $9

400 W. 14th St. (9th Ave.), A/C/E/L to 14th St./8th Ave., 212-807-8444; www.gaslightnyc.com

G2
39 Ninth Ave. (14th St.), A/C/E/L to 14th St./8th Ave., 212-807-8444

"When you can't get in anywhere else in the Meatpacking District", there's always this "last resort", a "no-brainer" bar with a "college vibe", "decently priced drinks" and "nice" French doors that let in summer breezes; since it's "always crowded" ("can't figure out why"), claustrophobes hide out in its "roomier" next-door sibling, G2.

Gate, The
24 | 17 | 21 | $6

321 Fifth Ave. (3rd St.), Brooklyn, M/R to Union St., 718-768-4329

An "excellent beer selection" at "reasonable prices" lures locals into this "laid-back" Brooklyn taproom where both "strollers" and "dogs are welcome"; regulars have "food delivered", then head for the "outdoor deck" where they while away the evening "watching the Slopers lope along."

Gatsby's
12 | 12 | 15 | $8

53 Spring St. (bet. Lafayette & Mulberry Sts.), 6 to Spring St., 212-334-4430; www.gatsbysnyc.com

A "frat bar plopped in the middle of trendy NoLita", this "cheesy" Irish pub "belongs Uptown" since it doesn't "fit the neighborhood it's in", but at least service is "attentive" and the drinks "pretty inexpensive."

Geisha
24 | 25 | 20 | $14

33 E. 61st St. (bet. Madison & Park Aves.), 4/5/6/N/R/W to 59th St./ Lexington Ave., 212-813-1113; www.geisharestaurant.com

"Pretty drinks" and "pretty faces" make for a "sexy" scene at this "chic" East Side Japanese duplex where the downstairs bar may be "a little small for comfort" but that doesn't stop its Euro-and-"Hamptons crowd" from "packing in like sardines"; "it may have lost some of its steam", but fans feel it's ever "fashionable" and fashionably "pricey."

George Keeley's
21 | 18 | 21 | $6

485 Amsterdam Ave. (bet. 83rd & 84th Sts.), 1 to 86th St., 212-873-0251; www.georgekeeley.com

Everything a "neighborhood bar should be", this Upper West Side Irish pub is "clean and spacious", with "cordial service", a "genial" air and a cool roster of tap brews; it's a "little less fratty" than its neighbors thanks to a "slightly more mature crowd" that congregates to catch "Premiership football" on the tube.

GINGER MAN
21 | 18 | 19 | $8

11 E. 36th St. (bet. 5th & Madison Aves.), B/D/F/N/Q/R/V/W to 34th St./ Herald Sq., 212-532-3740; www.gingerman-ny.com

It seems like "every beer under the sun" is on tap at this Murray Hill watering hole where "blue-shirted", "wing-tipped" dudes congregate to wet their whistles; while the "huge", "wide-open space" is "comfortable" off-peak, it's so "nuts at happy hour" that regulars advise "making friends with someone sitting at the bar – you may not get a drink otherwise."

Ginger's ∉
∇ 23 | 18 | 24 | $8

363 Fifth Ave. (bet. 5th & 6th Sts.), Brooklyn, F/M/R to 4th Ave./9th St., 718-788-0924

A "fixture in the Park Slope scene", this "great lesbian hangout" attracts "girls who like girls and cheap beer" along with the "mom-and-mom" set; whether "chilling at the bar", "listening to ABBA" on the jukebox or unwinding in the back garden, "everything's mellow" here.

Gin Mill
14 | 11 | 18 | $6

442 Amsterdam Ave. (bet. 81st & 82nd Sts.), 1 to 79th St., 212-580-9080; www.nycbestbars.com
The crowd's "more concerned with getting drunk than posing" at this Upper West Side "mainstay" that's "overrun with former frat boys" who want college life to "continue for a few more years"; ok, it's "dumpy" and "rowdy" and "crowded", but "if you're a Florida Gators fan", it's a guaranteed "fun night out."

GIRLS ROOM
– | – | – | M

(fka Infrared Lounge)
210 Rivington St. (Pitt St.), F/J/M/Z to Delancey/Essex Sts., 212-995-8684; www.girlsroomnyc.com
The latest entry in the underserved lesbian bar scene, this new Lower Eastsider hopes to fill the hole left by the departed Meow Mix by offering an equally funky setting but a much more edgy address on the far reaches of Rivington Street; DJs, karaoke and go-go dancers are among its varied attractions.

Glass
19 | 22 | 17 | $11

287 10th Ave. (bet. 26th & 27th Sts.), C/E to 23rd St., 212-904-1580; www.glassloungenyc.com
"When you can't get into Marquee", there's always this "cool" next-door neighbor, a "slick", "*Wallpaper*-like" affair with curved walls and a minimalist bamboo garden–cum–smoker's lounge out back; it's also famed for its "must-see" unisex bathroom featuring "two-way mirrors" that "allow people on the street to watch you fix your makeup."

GLO
– | – | – | VE

431 W. 16th St. (bet. 9th & 10th Aves.), A/C/E/L to 14th St./8th Ave., 212-229-9119
In the ginormous space that housed the ill-fated Powder (come and gone in a matter of months) lies this new West Chelsea megaclub, a South Beach–esque spot with whitewashed walls lit in ever-changing hues; the ground level sports a dance floor and a number of bars for plebes, who aspire to make the leap to its balcony VIP room.

Gonzalez y Gonzalez
20 | 19 | 16 | $9

625 Broadway (bet. Bleecker & Houston Sts.), 6 to Bleecker St., 212-473-8787; www.arkrestaurants.com
"Get your salsa fix" at this "pumpin'" NoHo Latino featuring a "long bar" in front and "live bands" and dancing in the rear; although "less than stellar service" hinders that "search for a perfect margarita", the "hyper atmosphere" and swell "people-watching" opportunities are ample distractions.

Good World Bar & Grill
23 | 17 | 19 | $8

3 Orchard St. (bet. Canal & Division Sts.), F/V to Lower East Side/2nd Ave., 212-925-9975; www.goodworldbar.com
"Under the radar" because of a "tucked-away" location on the fringes of the Lower East Side, this "fun little find" offers "cool" specialty cocktails and "authentic Swedish" grub to a "hip international" crowd; its "tiny garden is a haven for smokers" and for claustrophobes when the "small bar area gets filled up."

Gotham Bar & Grill
24 | 24 | 23 | $12

12 E. 12th St. (bet. 5th Ave. & University Pl.), 4/5/6/L/N/Q/R/W to 14th St./ Union Sq., 212-620-4020; www.gothambarandgrill.com
For "occasions that need a little class", sip a "nice cold martini in style" at this "luxe" Village "landmark" where "you'll feel glamorous as soon as you walk in"; despite "expensive" pricing and a "bar scene

largely confined to pre-dinner patrons", the "cost fits the crowd" and is "worth it" for a "classic NY" experience.

Gotham Comedy Club   23 | 14 | 18 | $11 |
34 W. 22nd St. (bet. 5th & 6th Aves.), R/W to 23rd St., 212-367-9000; www.gothamcomedyclub.com
"Start the night off with a good laugh" at this Flatiron comedy club with a "usually excellent" roster of both big names ("Seinfeld", "Larry David") as well as "hidden talent waiting to be discovered"; the unamused find the cover and "two-drink minimum" a "bit excessive", but more say the "laughs are well worth it."

Gowanus Yacht Club ⊘   23 | 16 | 17 | $4 |
323 Smith St. (President St.), Brooklyn, F/G to Carroll St., 718-246-1321
The "highlight of summertime in Brooklyn" is this seasonal beer garden serving "budget-conscious brews" and weenies in a "really crowded", "stand-on-each-other's-shoulders" kind of setting; its fancy name is wholly "tongue-in-cheek", what with the "total lack of atmosphere", "no-pretensions" patrons and very "scary bathroom."

Grace   23 | 21 | 22 | $10 |
114 Franklin St. (bet. Church St. & W. B'way), 1 to Franklin St., 212-343-4200
An "excellent selection of specialty cocktails" that will "numb your brain quickly" lures imbibers to this "classy" TriBeCa known for its "looong", "sweet mahogany bar" and "friendly" staff of "hotties"; as a bonus, the "kitchen's open late", offering "upscale" noshing "till the wee hours."

GRAMERCY TAVERN   26 | 25 | 27 | $13 |
42 E. 20th St. (bet. B'way & Park Ave. S.), 4/5/6/L/N/Q/R/W to 14th St./ Union Sq., 212-477-0777; www.gramercytavern.com
"Everything's appealing" at Danny Meyer's "one-and-only" Flatiron "class act" that manages to be both "relaxed and sophisticated at the same time"; regulars say "if you're only here for drinks, you're missing the best part", but others plant themselves at the bar, "eat great little plates", sip "lovely wines" and watch a fascinating "cross-section of people come and go."

Grand Bar   23 | 23 | 20 | $12 |
SoHo Grand Hotel, 310 W. Broadway, 2nd fl. (bet. Canal & Grand Sts.), A/C/E to Canal St., 212-965-3000; www.sohogrand.com
"Not your mother's hotel bar", this "fabulous" SoHo number is the kind of place where "everyone wears Prada" and the "ooh-la-la" "waitresses are part of the decor"; while the crowd splits between "hip young things" and "freaked-out out-of-towners", prices are uniformly "steep" but "worth it" for the "fantastic atmosphere" alone.

Grand Press   – | – | – | I |
284 Grand St. (bet. Havemeyer & Roebling Sts.), Brooklyn, L to Bedford Ave., 718-218-6955
There's "no b.s." in evidence at this "traditional" Williamsburg taproom, a spacious, brick-walled joint that takes its name from the printing company that formerly inhabited the space; a "nice staff", "cute little garden" and pool and foosball tables are all part of its low-key charm.

Grassroots Tavern ⊘   17 | 10 | 18 | $5 |
20 St. Marks Pl. (bet. 2nd & 3rd Aves.), 6 to Astor Pl., 212-475-9443
Few East Village "holes-in-the-wall" are more "old-school" than this longtime "St. Marks staple", a "'70s dive that won't close" largely due to its winning formula of "cheap stiff drinks" and "free popcorn"; "random animals" milling around ("dogs and cats", that is) add to its "antifabulous" appeal.

Great Jones Cafe ▽ 23 | 13 | 16 | $7

54 Great Jones St. (bet. Bowery & Lafayette St.), 6 to Bleecker St., 212-674-9304; www.greatjonescafe.com

"Rustic" is putting it mildly at this funky NoHo "shack" serving "basic but good" Cajun grub washed down with refreshingly "inexpensive" pops (including a famed Bloody Mary); a "neighborhood fave" for over 20 years, it's still a "rare find" for many.

Great Lakes 21 | 15 | 21 | $6

284 Fifth Ave. (1st St.), Brooklyn, M/R to Union St., 718-499-3710

Everything a "neighborhood bar should be", this "good old-fashioned" dive is renowned for a "jukebox chock-full of indie rock" that's "one of the best in Park Slope"; oddly enough, it's "miles from any lake (great or otherwise)" yet still "smells like an ancient frigate."

Green Room – | – | – | VE
(fka Blur, Groovejet)

286 Spring St. (bet. Hudson & Varick Sts.), A/C/E to Canal St., 212-929-8560; www.greenroomnyc.com

This West SoHo lounge is named after the celeb holding pens used before TV appearances and offers such over-the-top perks as private butlers, masseuses and even French maid service; it might seem a bit much for a simple night out, but if you're game, "plan to spend a lot."

Greenwich Brewing Co. 16 | 13 | 18 | $7

418 Sixth Ave. (9th St.), A/B/C/D/E/F/V to W. 4th St., 212-477-8744; www.greenwichbrew.com

There's a "myriad of beers to choose from" (including some "good house brews") at this Village microbrewery set in a "faux old-world saloon"; those who find it "unremarkable" amuse themselves by getting a window seat and "watching people walk by on Sixth Avenue."

Grey Dog's Coffee 25 | 20 | 21 | $7

33 Carmine St. (bet. Bedford & Bleecker Sts.), 1 to Christopher St., 212-462-0041; www.thegreydog.com

This "NYU coffeehouse fave" exudes a "laid-back" "college town" vibe (with a hint of "San Francisco") and offers "strong" cups of Joe as well as beer and wine; fans call it the "anti-Starbucks" and think it's just the spot to "write the next great indie screenplay."

Groove ▽ 17 | 14 | 17 | $9

125 MacDougal St. (W. 3rd St.), A/B/C/D/E/F/V to W. 4th St., 212-254-9393; www.clubgroovenyc.com

"Live music" for "no cover" is the claim to fame of this "grungy" Village dive (though there is a "two-drink minimum"); foes dis the "extremely tight" digs and say the performers are "seriously out of touch", citing a "'70s throwback" band lineup.

Gstaad 20 | 22 | 21 | $9

43 W. 26th St. (bet. B'way & 6th Ave.), F/V to 23rd St., 212-683-1440; www.gstaadnyc.com

"Named after a Swiss resort", this "ski-lodgey" Chelsea bar is set in a "sleek" "wood-lined" space featuring "snowboard movies" projected on the wall; "too much open space" and too few patrons make it feel "as cold as ice" to those who diagnose an "identity crisis."

Guastavino's 22 | 25 | 18 | $12

409 E. 59th St. (bet. 1st & York Aves.), 4/5/6/N/R/W to 59th St./Lexington Ave., 212-421-6644; www.guastavinos.com

"Built to hold a crowd (and it does)", this "breathtaking" room beneath the Queensboro Bridge may be "out of the way" but is "still going strong" thanks to a "gorgeous", "high-energy" following and a "great long bar" serving "every cocktail imaginable"; sure, it would be nice if the "service aspired to the height of the ceiling", but the overall "oh-so-cool" mood certainly "impresses out-of-towners."

GYM Sportsbar
`–  –  –  M`

167 Eighth Ave. (bet. 18th & 19th Sts.), A/C/E/L to 14th St./8th Ave., 212-337-2439; www.gymsportsbar.com

Athletic supporters and those who love them are all over this Chelsea newcomer that's the city's first gay sports bar, a handsome, brick-walled thing with a pool table and a semi-impressive assortment of TVs (a downstairs expansion is in the works); it's already drawing droves of local dudes thrilled to find something new on the Eighth Avenue runway.

GYPSY TEA
`–  –  –  VE`

33 W. 24th St. (bet. 5th & 6th Aves.), R/W to 23rd St., 212-645-0003; www.gypsyteanyc.com

One of the Flatiron's latest scenes is this duplex lounge, an ultra-slick club featuring a sleek bar/lounge upstairs and a labyrinthine lower level complete with fish tanks, VIP nooks and "great hip-hop DJs"; early visitors report it's "large", and thus "not so tough to get into", so long as you're prepared to shell out big bottle-service bucks for the privilege.

Hairy Monk
`18  13  22  $7`

337 Third Ave. (25th St.), 6 to 23rd St., 212-532-2929

"Home sweet home" to "locals" and "Bo-Sox fans", this "decent" Murray Hill Irish pub is a "welcome retreat" for "happy hour or game-watching"; fans say it's a "bit less hectic" than the neighborhood competition, and thus "more fun", complete with "authentic barkeeps" who transport you "back to the old country."

Half King
`19  15  18  $8`

505 W. 23rd St. (bet. 10th & 11th Aves.), C/E to 23rd St., 212-462-4300; www.thehalfking.com

"Interesting" "bookish" types turn up for the "Monday night readings" at this West Chelsea "lit bar"/Irish pub where the drinks come "with a side of thinking"; on a "lazy summer night" the "secret back garden" is a "great enclave", even if some critics sense a hint of "highbrow pretense" in the air.

Half Wine Bar Lounge
`∇ 22  22  19  $8`

626 Vanderbilt Ave. (bet. Park & Prospect Pls.), Brooklyn, 2/3 to Bergen St., 718-783-4100

"Up-and-coming" Prospect Heights is home to this newish wine bar offering an "excellent selection" of vino and, as the name suggests, specializing in half bottles; the "cozy" space meandering over several rooms (including a roomy patio) draws an "eclectic crowd."

Hammerstein Ballroom
`19  15  14  $9`

311 W. 34th St. (bet. 8th & 9th Aves.), A/C/E to 34th St./Penn Station, 212-279-7740; www.mcstudios.com

"Catch local acts that made it big" at this "decent midsize" concert hall near Penn Station that was formerly an opera house, hence the "good acoustics"; "zoolike crowds" and "unorganized bar lines" come with the territory, but at the very least it "serves its purpose."

Hangar, The ⊅
`11  9  17  $8`

115 Christopher St. (bet. Bleecker & Hudson Sts.), 1 to Christopher St., 212-627-2044; www.hangarbar.us

There are "no hang-ups" and "no gym boys" in sight at this West Village gay dive featuring a "more ethnic crowd" and a lot "less attitude than in Chelsea"; yet those who find things too "dark and depressing" want to know if "any of the Christopher Street bars are fun anymore."

Hanger, The

— | — | — | I

(fka Plant)

217 E. Third St. (bet. Aves. B & C), F/J/M/Z to Delancey/Essex Sts., 212-228-1030

Ok, it's "not Plant" (its former incarnation), but "it's not trying to be" either: this schizo new East Villager is a "cool" vintage clothing store by day that morphs into a barroom after dark; the already cheap drinks are further discounted if you buy something off the rack, which is not that hard to do given the "nice shoe collection."

Hank's Saloon

∇ 14 | 8 | 15 | $4

46 Third Ave. (Atlantic Ave.), Brooklyn, 2/3/4/5/B/Q to Atlantic Ave., 718-625-8003

"Not as scary inside as the outside would make you think", this Boerum Hill "grunge palace" supplies "cheap beer", "seedy regulars" and "free honky-tonk barbecue on Sunday nights"; there's also "gritty live music" so "don't expect to leave with your eardrums intact."

Happy Ending

19 | 19 | 16 | $9

302 Broome St. (bet. Eldridge & Forsyth Sts.), J/M/Z to Bowery, 212-334-9676; www.happyendinglounge.com

A "former massage parlor" lightly remodeled into a bi-level bar/ lounge, this Lower Eastsider still showcases "remnants" of its past with waist-high showerheads and steam rooms remade into private alcoves; despite the "seedy" nabe and "hit-or-miss" crowd ("filled with models one night, completely dead the next"), it's a "guaranteed thing" for hard-core followers.

Harbour Lights

17 | 19 | 14 | $11

Pier 17, South Street Seaport, 3rd fl. (bet. Fulton & South Sts.), 2/3/4/5/ A/C/J/M/Z to Fulton St./B'way/Nassau, 212-227-2800; www.harbourlightsrestaurant.com

Alright already, "it's touristy" (whaddya expect given the South Street Seaport address?), but the exhilarating "twilight view" of the Brooklyn Bridge is the payoff at this Financial District bar/eatery; natives sigh "unexciting", but pragmatists label it a "staple" in an underserved nabe.

Hard Rock Cafe

14 | 18 | 13 | $10

221 W. 57th St. (bet. B'way & 7th Ave.), N/Q/R/W to 57th St./7th Ave., 212-489-6565; www.hardrock.com

"Been there, done that, got the T-shirt" sums up reactions to this music-themed Midtown "tourist attraction" that will move to Times Square in the fall of 2005; while it's cool with those "intrigued by rock 'n' roll paraphernalia", most put it down as "way too commercial" – and ubiquitous ("same thing, different city").

Harrison, The

24 | 23 | 23 | $12

355 Greenwich St. (Harrison St.), 1 to Franklin St., 212-274-9310; www.theharrison.com

"Top-of-the-line all the way", this "high-end" TriBeCan reeks of "sophistication" from its "cozy yet roomy" dining room to its very "knowledgeable" staff; sure, many at the bar are "waiting for a table", but it also works for "classy" cocktails as a prelude to "romance."

Harrison's Tavern

19 | 14 | 16 | $6

355 Amsterdam Ave. (77th St.), 1 to 79th St., 212-724-3600; www.harrisonstavern.com

"New England sports fans" get together at this "solid" Upper West Side "Boston bar" that's "perfect" for guzzling beer and cheering on the

Red Sox and Patriots; needless to say, it sure was "fun during the World Series", even if spoilers grouse it's "average" verging on "ho-hum."

Harry Cipriani
25 | 23 | 23 | $15
Sherry Netherland Hotel, 781 Fifth Ave. (bet. 59th & 60th Sts.), N/R/W to 5th Ave./59th St., 212-753-5566; www.cipriani.com

"Order a Bellini and pretend you're rich and famous" at this "fancy" Midtown bar/restaurant favored by "money men" and their "trophy wives"; it's a "real experience – if they know you" – and if they don't, make sure you're earning "at least a quarter of a mil a year" to cover the "break-the-bank" tabs.

HEARTLAND BREWERY
16 | 15 | 17 | $8
Empire State Bldg., 350 Fifth Ave. (34th St.), B/D/F/N/Q/R/V/W to 34th St./ Herald Sq., 212-563-3433
1285 Sixth Ave. (51st St.), B/D/F/V to 47-50th Sts./Rockefeller Ctr., 212-582-8244
93 South St. (Fulton St.), 2/3/4/5/A/C/J/M/Z to Fulton St./B'way/ Nassau, 646-572-2337
35 Union Sq. W. (bet. 16th & 17th Sts.), 4/5/6/L/N/Q/R/W to 14th St./ Union Sq., 212-645-3400
127 W. 43rd St. (bet. B'way & 6th Ave.), 1/2/3/7/N/Q/R/S/W to 42nd St./ Times Sq., 646-366-0235
www.heartlandbrewery.com

"Original microbrews you won't find anywhere else" (especially a "superb oatmeal stout") are the calling cards of these "boys'-night-out" magnets that get particularly "loud" after work; but those who think they're "heroically average" cite "suburban", "Disney-like" scenes comparable to a "glorified TGI Friday's."

Heaven ⌿
13 | 10 | 13 | $8
579 Sixth Ave. (16th St.), 1 to 18th St., 212-243-6100

The crowd varies "depending on the night" at this "very young", "very gay" Chelsea "dump", a "trashy" triplex that gets "crazy cramped" on weekends; regulars report "sleaze" with ease, especially if you enjoy "brushing up against hot strangers."

Heights Bar & Grill
21 | 16 | 17 | $7
2867 Broadway, 2nd fl. (bet. 111th & 112th Sts.), 1 to Cathedral Pkwy./ 110th St., 212-866-7035; www.heightsnyc.com

"Columbians of all ages" – everyone from the "swim team to the director of admissions" – tip their hats to this Morningside Heights bar and grill whose "real draw" is its summertime roof deck, a "perennial favorite"; maybe the staff's "only moderately alive", but "reasonable prices" and "nightly drink specials" are ample distractions.

Helen's
21 | 20 | 22 | $9
169 Eighth Ave. (bet. 18th & 19th Sts.), A/C/E/L to 14th St./8th Ave., 212-206-0609; www.helensnyc.com

For a "different night out", try this "classy new" Chelsea cabaret, a "cozy little" boîte with a piano bar up front and a supper club behind; true, it's campy and "old-fashioned" ("Judy Garland" medleys), but there's some "surprising talent" showcased, and for those in need of a laugh, the "owner's a hoot."

Henrietta Hudson
16 | 11 | 16 | $7
438 Hudson St. (Morton St.), 1 to Christopher St., 212-924-3347; www.henriettahudsons.com

"Chicks meet chicks" at this "dependable" Village lesboteria, an infamous "hole-in-the-wall" that attracts everyone from "young grungettes" to "NJ softball players" to "celebs"; while it's a "tough" door for guys at any time (unless you "bring a girl"), it's "insanely packed" with all genders on weekends.

Hi-Fi
18 | 14 | 19 | $6

169 Ave. A (bet. 10th & 11th Sts.), L to 1st Ave., 212-420-8392;
www.hifi169.com
The "hipster cred" at this East Villager is provided by what might be
the "best jukebox in the city" – and "possibly the world" – loaded
with "tens of thousands of tunes"; though it's "no longer a secret"
("forget weekends"), if you "get there early enough, the evening
could be all about you."

Highline
22 | 25 | 18 | $11

835 Washington St. (Little W. 12th St.), A/C/E/L to 14th St./8th Ave.,
212-243-3339; www.nychighline.com
"Another trendy Meatpacking District place", this "fab" new triple-
decker bar/lounge/restaurant is all about design, featuring an eye-
popping mix of "South Beach", "*Austin Powers*" and the "*Jetsons*",
with some beds and a waterfall thrown in for good measure; maybe
it "looks best when drunk" (especially the "all-white" downstairs den
that's part "swimming pool", part "cave"), but overall it's "fun" – and
there's "no cover and no line."

Hi-Life
16 | 13 | 17 | $9

477 Amsterdam Ave. (83rd St.), 1 to 86th St., 212-787-7199
1340 First Ave. (72nd St.), 6 to 68th St., 212-249-3600
www.hi-life.com
"When you feel like going to a bar that's nothing fancy", this crosstown
"diner" duo "does the trick" with retro "padded-booth" settings and
"relatively inexpensive" food and drink; maybe it has "seen better
days" and "needs a face-lift", but it's still a "good choice" for "catching
up with old buddies."

HIRO
23 | 24 | 17 | $12

Maritime Hotel, 369 W. 16th St. (9th Ave.), A/C/E/L to 14th St./8th Ave.,
212-242-4300; www.themaritimehotel.com
There's "sightseeing galore" at this "scenester haven" in Chelsea's
Maritime Hotel, a "dark and mysterious" lair reminiscent of the "set from
Kill Bill" and popular with "trust fund" babies, "beautiful models" and
"Keith Richards' spawn"; of course, the "impossible door scene"
makes access a challenge, although now that they've "opened the
adjacent ballroom", there's "more space" to be "fabulously trendy" at
this "consistently solid" place.

Hog Pit
18 | 10 | 16 | $7

22 Ninth Ave. (13th St.), A/C/E/L to 14th St./8th Ave., 212-604-0092;
www.hogpit.com
"Your brand of jeans doesn't matter" at this "raw" barroom, a "perfect
antidote" to the "newly ruined Meatpacking District" that "hasn't
lost its soul" and "lives down to all expectations" – if anything, the
"name's too fancy for this dump"; its "sassy", "biker chick barmaids"
may be the only women in sight, but there's plenty of "PBR, foosball"
and "tasty ribs" for distraction.

Hogs & Heifers ⊄
16 | 11 | 13 | $8

859 Washington St. (13th St.), A/C/E/L to 14th St./8th Ave., 212-929-0655;
www.hogsandheifers.com
"Have bra, will shimmy" could be the motto of this "skuzzy" biker
bar in the Meatpacking District, the "original Coyote Ugly" given
the combustible mix of "dingy" digs, "rowdy" dudes, "floozy"
bachelorettes and "raunchy" barkeeps with "trailer-trash" mouths;
don't forget to "leave a tip" and "drink like a man" (i.e. "no 'girl'
cocktails") or risk being the "subject of public ridicule"; P.S. "make
sure to use the bathroom before you go in."

Holiday Cocktail Lounge ⌖   15 | 8 | 14 | $5

75 St. Marks Pl. (bet. 1st & 2nd Aves.), 6 to Astor Pl., 212-777-9637
The "dive of all dives", this way grungy East Villager might have
the "grumpiest bartender" ever but neighborhood types "keep
coming back for more punishment" – with drinks so "dirt-cheap",
"people will put up with anything" here; a "scratchy jukebox",
"strange hours" and just plain "ugly" decor are all part of this
"original boulevard of broken dreams."

Hook, The ⌖   – | – | – | M

*18 Commerce St. (bet. Columbia & Richards Sts.), Brooklyn, F/G to
Carroll St., 718-797-3007; www.thehookmusic.com*
It may be "a pain to get to", but this "fantastic" music venue in remote
Red Hook reels 'em in with a "big" space showcasing everything from
"Southern rock to New York hard-core" bands; a horseshoe-shaped
bar, "great" sound system and cheap pops lead fans to say "this
place just rocks."

Hook and Ladder   17 | 11 | 21 | $6

611 Second Ave. (bet. 33rd & 34th Sts.), 6 to 33rd St., 212-213-5034
A heated "outdoor deck with a pool table" is the most "amazing"
thing about this otherwise "typical" Murray Hill pub owned by
firemen and decorated with firefighting memorabilia; fans like its
"cheap and easy" ways, especially Thursday night's $10 "all-you-
can-drink" beerathon.

Hooters   14 | 9 | 16 | $8

*211 W. 56th St. (bet. B'way & 7th Ave.), N/Q/R/W to 57th St./7th Ave.,
212-581-5656; www.originalhooters.com*
This "wonderfully tacky guilty pleasure" lures Midtowners with
waitresses clad in "tight tops" and "little orange shorts" – not its
"cheesy" decor and "love-'em-or-hate-'em wings"; some say it's the
"Howard Johnson's of nightlife", while others "can't put their finger
on its appeal" – though they'd like to.

Hop Devil Grill ⌖   – | – | – | M
(fka Stingy Lulu's)
*129 St. Marks Pl. (bet. Ave. A & 1st Ave.), L to 1st Ave.,
212-533-4467*
From the owners of David Copperfield's comes this new East Village
ale house boasting an impressive selection of suds both on tap and in
the bottle; set in the old Stingy Lulu space, it has undergone a slight
renovation with more bar space, fewer tables and lots of brewerania
on the walls.

HOUSE OF BREWS   25 | 23 | 25 | $7

*363 W. 46th St. (bet. 8th & 9th Aves.), 1/2/3/7/N/Q/R/S/W to 42nd St./
Times Sq., 212-245-0551; www.houseofbrewsny.com*
"Beers from all over the world" are the calling cards of this "solid"
Restaurant Row newcomer, a "laid-back", "big screen TV"–laden
joint that gets a "full thumbs-up"; it's also "home of the 96-ounce beer
bong", a gimmicky glass that looks just like it sounds and "can't
be found elsewhere."

Houston's   20 | 19 | 20 | $10

*Citicorp Bldg., 153 E. 53rd St. (enter at 54th St. & 3rd Ave.), E/V to
Lexington Ave./53rd St., 212-888-3828*
378 Park Ave. S. (27th St.), 6 to 28th St., 212-689-1090
www.houstons.com
"Packed with professional" types after work, these "upscale" bar/
eateries are "loud", "fun" and "so dark" they could be sets in a "Philip

Marlowe movie"; some say they're "more food places" (given that "must-try" spinach dip), but overall they're "one of the only chains Manhattanites aren't ashamed of frequenting."

Hudson Bar & Books   21 | 23 | 21 | $11
636 Hudson St. (bet. Horatio & Jane Sts.), A/C/E/L to 14th St./8th Ave., 212-229-2642; www.barandbooksnet.com
Folks "feel smarter drinking" at this "library"-like Village bar, a "sophisticated, worldly" spot with "James Bond" on the telly to add to its "old-school" "British appeal"; not incidentally, it's "one of the few places" where you can "legally smoke" indoors – a "blessing or a curse", depending on one's point of view.

HUDSON HOTEL BAR   25 | 25 | 17 | $12
Hudson Hotel, 356 W. 58th St. (bet. 8th & 9th Aves.), 1/A/B/C/D to 59th St./Columbus Circle, 212-554-6000; www.morganshotelgroup.com
Always "in style", this Hell's Kitchen hotel bar "lives on" for a "new breed of wannabes", even if most of its "genetically superior" original crowd has moved on; you'll still "need patience" for the "snooty service" and "big-bucks" tabs, but in return there's "smashing", "space-age design", lots of "attractive Euro" tourists and a "gorgeous" outdoor patio that's a "welcome reprieve" from the din within.

HUDSON HOTEL LIBRARY   24 | 26 | 18 | $12
Hudson Hotel, 356 W. 58th St. (bet. 8th & 9th Aves.), 1/A/B/C/D to 59th St./Columbus Circle, 212-554-6000; www.morganshotelgroup.com
"You can actually have a conversation" in this "intimate" alternative to the Hudson Hotel Bar, where the decor's right out of an "ivy league fraternity" house with a fireplace and purple felt pool table; some imagine "cobwebs forming on the glassware as you wait for service", but for the majority it's "perennially sexy" and "sophisticated."

Hue   19 | 23 | 14 | $12
91 Charles St. (Bleecker St.), 1 to Christopher St., 212-691-4170; www.huenyc.com
An "average bar upstairs" gives hue to a "great lounge downstairs" at this "swank", "larger-than-it-looks" Village Vietnamese; while drawbacks include a "hard" door, "major moolah" pricing and a "huge side of attitude" from the "rude" staff, at least it's good for "avoiding the frat boys" – the "style keeps them away."

Hunk Mania   14 | 8 | 14 | $11
2i's, 248 W. 14th St. (bet. 7th & 8th Aves.), A/C/E/L to 14th St./8th Ave., 800-800-6067; www.hunkmania.com
"Legions of screaming ladies" tout the "onetime novelty value" of this Village male strip revue where "horny bachelorettes" get frisky with "hands-on" dudes who "all look like Fabio"; some, however, find the sight of "men dry humping anything in sight" too "sleazy" and "yearn for the days when Chippendales was open."

Hustler Club   ∇ 18 | 16 | 16 | $12
641 W. 51st St. (12th Ave.), C/E to 50th St., 212-247-2460; www.hustlerny.com
As the "girls shake", "you get shaken down for pricey drinks" (and a "hefty cover") at this "middle-of-nowhere" Hell's Kitchen strip club; connoisseurs say this "jiggle joint" is the "high end" of a "low kind" of entertainment, but those "disappointed" say the "name is not ironic."

I.C.U. ⊭   – | – | – | M
(fka Finally Fred's)
765 Washington St. (12th St.), A/C/E/L to 14th St./8th Ave., 646-279-3703
What was formerly Finally Fred's has been lightly doctored up into this far West Village Intensive Care Unit; so far, both the street-level bar

and underground performance space are cool, calm and collected, in direct contrast to its out-of-control next-door neighbor, Tortilla Flats.

Ideya
23 | 21 | 20 | $10

349 W. Broadway (bet. Broome & Grand Sts.), C/E to Spring St., 212-625-1441; www.ideya.net

"Fab mojitos" turn up the "tropical heat" at this "flirty" SoHo Caribbean eatery that's "fun, festive" and "full of energy" after a couple of "lethal" drinks; maybe it was "once more popular", but adherents say it's "certainly not past its prime."

Iggy's
13 | 9 | 16 | $7

132 Ludlow St. (bet. Rivington & Stanton Sts.), F/J/M/Z to Delancey/ Essex Sts., 212-529-2731
1452 Second Ave. (bet. 75th & 76th Sts.), 6 to 77th St., 212-327-3043
www.iggysnewyork.com

With the "same appeal as a beaten-up couch", this Irish dive duo are "neighborhood" spots drawing everyone "from prepsters to punks"; Downtown is "dark and murky" with "cozy little nooks", while Uptown features nightly karaoke for a crowd "too drunk to notice."

Iguana
19 | 19 | 18 | $9

240 W. 54th St. (bet. B'way & 8th Ave.), C/E to 50th St., 212-765-5454; www.Iguananyc.com

"Packed after work", this Midtown bar/restaurant is a "decent" enough "meat market", and on weekends there's a "nice little dance space" in its downstairs lounge; critics hedge that the scene "depends on the night", though in general it "has potential."

Il Posto Accanto
– | – | – | M

190 E. Second St. (bet. Aves. A & B), F/V to Lower East Side/2nd Ave., 212-228-3562

Connected to the much-loved restaurant Il Bagatto, this East Village adjunct is the "perfect wine bar" with lots of vinos to choose from and a cozy, "romantic" air; you'll "feel like you're in Italy because of all the expats" in attendance, and you'll probably get to know them given the small setup.

Improv ⌦
– | – | – | E

318 W. 53rd St. (bet. 8th & 9th Aves.), C/E to 50th St., 212-757-2323; www.nyimprov.com

This longtime comedy club, recently "relocated to Hell's Kitchen", is "good after theater" providing "random star sightings" and "great laughs – depending on who's performing" – but there's nothing funny about the "grandma's basement" setting; P.S. the improvisational Chicago City Limits troupe has taken up residence here.

Indochine
23 | 23 | 18 | $12

430 Lafayette St. (bet. Astor Pl. & E. 4th St.), 6 to Astor Pl., 212-505-5111

"Still lovely" and "still hanging in there", this "classy" 22-year-old French-Vietnamese bar/restaurant near the Public Theater keeps on keeping on serving "ample, well-made drinks" in a chic, neo-Colonial setting; service may skew toward "spotty", but there's "no shortage of beauty" among its "always-cool" followers.

'inoteca
24 | 20 | 22 | $10

98 Rivington St. (Ludlow St.), F/J/M/Z to Delancey/Essex Sts., 212-614-0473; www.inotecanyc.com

"It's all about the wine" at this "stellar" Lower East Side enoteca (the "big brother of 'ino"), where an "unpretentious, knowledgeable" staff offers "generous pours" and "crave-worthy panini" at "easy-on-the-wallet" prices; its "massive windows" make it plain to see that it's "always crowded" ("*always!*"), though an underground wine cellar helps ease the squeeze.

International Bar ∌
—|—|—| I

120½ First Ave. (bet. 7th St. & St. Marks Pl.), 6 to Astor Pl., 212-777-9244

"Grungy" is the word for this prototypical "East Village dive bar" where "cheap drinks", year-round Christmas tree lights and a "fantastic jukebox" make for rollicking good times; "Ramones, anyone?"

In Vino
∇ 26 | 21 | 23 | $9

215 E. Fourth St. (bet. Aves. A & B), F/V to Lower East Side/2nd Ave., 212-539-1011

A "rustic", "cave"-like ambiance adds an authentic air to this East Village enoteca featuring an "offbeat, eclectic" list of Southern Italian wines decanted by a "helpful" staff; a small menu of "comforting" edibles enhances this "overall great package."

Iona ∌
∇ 23 | 16 | 21 | $6

180 Grand St. (bet. Bedford & Driggs Aves.), Brooklyn, L to Bedford Ave., 718-384-5008

This "small" Irish pub in Williamsburg "does the basics well" with "plenty of beers on tap" and a "comfy" vibe; out back, one of the "prettiest gardens in the five boroughs" seals the deal.

Iridium
21 | 17 | 17 | $12

1650 Broadway, downstairs (bet. 50th & 51st Sts.), 1 to 50th St., 212-582-2121; www.iridiumjazzclub.com

"All the big names in jazz" at "big prices" sums up the scene at this "quite cool" Theater District music club that may "lack the mystique of the Village Vanguard" but compensates with a "low-lit", "clean, crisp" ambiance; "not to be missed" are "guitar legend" Les Paul's Monday night sets.

Irish Rogue
—|—|—| M

356 W. 44th St. (bet. 8th & 9th Aves.), A/C/E to 42nd St./Port Authority, 212-445-0131; www.theirishrogue.com

This new Hell's Kitchen barroom is a cavernous, brick-walled affair where flat-screen TVs and old-fashioned light fixtures serve as the decor; supporters say it's a "good addition" for either "starting the night, or finishing it off", while economists reserve it for "cheap happy-hour drinks."

Irving Plaza
22 | 12 | 15 | $8

17 Irving Pl. (15th St.), 4/5/6/L/N/Q/R/W to 14th St./Union Sq., 212-777-6817; www.irvingplaza.com

"Major rock acts" as well as "bands just breaking through" "play to the devoted" at this "packed tight" Gramercy music hall, a "terrific" "virtual mosh pit" with "almost no seats" ("bring a lawn chair"); the drinks may come in "cans" or "plastic cups", but no one cares as the focus is on the "electrifying" performers.

Isis @ Union Bar
—|—|—| E
(fka Union Bar)

204 Park Ave. S. (bet. 17th & 18th Sts.), 4/5/6/L/N/Q/R/W to 14th St./Union Sq., 212-674-2105; www.isisny.com

With a more relaxed ambiance than its predecessor, Union Bar, this revamped watering hole right off Union Square now has bigger windows as well as a brand-new DJ booth, though you can expect the same after-work crowds – along with the overflow from the W Hotel across the street.

I Tre Merli
21 | 19 | 19 | $11

463 W. Broadway (bet. Houston & Prince Sts.), C/E to Spring St., 212-254-8699
183 W. 10th St. (W. 4th St.), 1 to Christopher St., 212-929-2221
www.itremerli.com
"Very inviting" is the long bar and high-ceilinged, "exposed-brick" interior of this "congenial" SoHo stalwart that's "been around for a while" and is still a fun place to "run into someone from the old days in the '90s"; its newer Village sibling may not be as large, but is just as "cute" for a "quick drink."

Jade Island
▽ 17 | 18 | 19 | $9

2845 Richmond Ave. (Yukon Ave.), Staten Island, 718-761-8080
It's all about the mai tais (served in hollowed-out coconuts) at this "friendly" Staten Island tiki lounge that might be a "better restaurant than bar"; either way, it's essential that you "like plastic flowers" and kitschy bamboo knickknacks.

Jade Terrace
21 | 20 | 17 | $11

268 W. 47th St. (bet. B'way & 8th Ave.), C/E to 50th St., 212-398-3800;
www.chinaclubnyc.com
For a "night under the stars" against a "skyscrapers-of-NY" backdrop, check out this Midtown rooftop lounge above China Club done up with exotic, "crouching tiger" decor; the jaded show up "really late" ("it's a bore before 10 PM"), but boosters insist it's a guaranteed "good time" whenever owing to that "nice view."

Jake's Dilemma
16 | 11 | 17 | $6

430 Amsterdam Ave. (bet. 80th & 81st Sts.), 1 to 79th St., 212-580-0556;
www.nycbestbars.com
"Calling all frat boys": "throw back a few" "without breaking the bank" at this "run-down" Upper Westsider where "cheap and fast describes everything about it"; ok, there are "way too many guys" intent on "extreme inebriation", but "no dilemma" about the weekend happy hour when the "whole bar is half price."

Jake's Saloon
▽ 16 | 13 | 18 | $6

875 10th Ave. (57th St.), 1/A/B/C/D to 59th St./Columbus Circle, 212-333-3100
206 W. 23rd St. (bet. 7th & 8th Aves.), 1 to 23rd St., 212-337-3100
www.jakessaloonnyc.com
Everything's jake at this "great neighborhood" Irish pub on the far western stretches of Hell's Kitchen that draws a mix of "workers from nearby TV studios" and "hospital" types from St. Luke's; some say it's "struggling to find an identity", but most identify with the "excellent happy hour"; P.S. the Chelsea branch is new and unrated.

Jameson's Pub
16 | 13 | 20 | $7

975 Second Ave. (bet. 51st & 52nd Sts.), 6 to 51st St./Lexington Ave., 212-980-4465
"No frills" says it all about this "average" Irish pub parked in the "heart of Midtown" and populated by everyone from suits to frat boys; its "dark, moody" decor contrasts with the "fun, casual mood", while a "friendly staff" and "good prices" seal the deal.

Jazz Gallery ⌀
_ | _ | _ | _

290 Hudson St. (Spring St.), 1 to Houston St., 212-242-1063;
www.jazzgallery.org
There's "great jazz" to be heard at this "bare-bones" SoHo cultural center, a "nonprofit venue" where cover charges are low and the energy level high; no liquor is served, so drink up before heading over, and call ahead for performance schedules – it's not open every night.

Jazz Standard
24 | 19 | 21 | $11

116 E. 27th St., downstairs (bet. Lexington & Park Aves.), 6 to 28th St., 212-576-2232; www.jazzstandard.com
"Younger and hipper than more established jazz clubs", this "low-key" Gramercy venue serves up a "perfect combination" of music, "beer and ribs"; a "varied" roster of acts featuring "musicians actually interested in giving you a good time" compensate for the "expensive" pricing.

JEAN GEORGES
25 | 25 | 26 | $15

Trump Int'l Hotel, 1 Central Park W. (bet. 60th & 61st Sts.), 1/A/B/C/D to 59th St./Columbus Circle, 212-299-3900; www.jean-georges.com
"Everything's outstanding" at this "upscale" bar nestled in the Nougatine Room of Jean-Georges Vongerichten's "extraordinary" flagship restaurant; the "stunning space", "glitzy crowd" and "make-you-feel-like-royalty" service all contribute to the "simply priceless" mood, but you'll pay for the privilege ("winning the lottery" helps).

Jean-Luc
∇ 18 | 18 | 16 | $12

507 Columbus Ave. (bet. 84th & 85th Sts.), B/C to 86th St., 212-712-1700; www.jeanlucrestaurant.com
"Upscale but worth it", this "cool" bar/eatery is "much needed" on the Upper West Side, providing "beautiful people"–watching and "'girlie' drink" guzzling in a faux Parisian setting; maybe service skews a little "snotty", but overall, it's a "fun scene."

Jekyll & Hyde
18 | 23 | 16 | $10

91 Seventh Ave. S. (bet. Barrow & W. 4th Sts.), 1 to Christopher St., 212-989-7701; www.jekyllpub.com
"Spooky" looks and "creative atmospherics" supply the cheap thrills at this "Halloween"-esque Village bar where "locating the hidden bathroom can be fun – unless you really have to go"; those who find it "frightfully dull" say it's "essentially a tourist trap."

Jeremy's Ale House
19 | 12 | 16 | $7

228 Front St. (bet. Beekman St. & Peck Slip), 2/3/4/5/A/C/J/M/Z to Fulton St./B'way/Nassau, 212-964-3537; www.jeremysalehouse.com
"Wall-Streeters" and the "dregs of humanity" coexist at this Financial District bar famed for "cheap" "big beers" served in "Styrofoam cups"; a recent relocation distresses diehards who "liked the old spot better" and hope they'll find some "new bras" to dangle from the rafters.

J.G. Melon ∅
19 | 14 | 17 | $7

1291 Third Ave. (74th St.), 6 to 77th St., 212-744-0585
The East Side "preppy HQ", this longtime "beer-and-burger institution" is where "Brad and Muffy" model their "L.L. Bean" apparel and chat up "everyone they went to school with"; the "comfortably worn" digs feature a lot of "exposed brick" and "watermelon memorabilia."

Jimmy's Corner
∇ 21 | 16 | 19 | $6

140 W. 44th St. (bet. B'way & 6th Ave.), 1/2/3/7/N/Q/R/S/W to 42nd St./Times Sq., 212-221-9510
A "real knockout" in the midst of "corporate Times Square", this "dive bar for boxing enthusiasts" is a "beer-and-a-shot" kind of joint untrammeled by tourists; it's run by former pugilist Jimmy Glenn, who will "sit with you and watch the game on TV."

Jimmy Walker's
17 | 11 | 21 | $7

245 E. 55th St. (bet. 2nd & 3rd Aves.), E/V to Lexington Ave./53rd St., 212-319-6650
This "typical" Midtown Irish pub is the "opposite of a scene", with the obligatory "sticky floors", "wisecracking bar maids" and "pool, darts

and Golden Tee"; regulars call it a "great neighborhood bar" even if "no one there lives in the neighborhood."

Joe Allen
22 | 20 | 20 | $11

326 W. 46th St. (bet. 8th & 9th Aves.), A/C/E to 42nd St./Port Authority, 212-581-6464; www.joeallenrestaurant.com
"Broadway regulars" and "tourists" collide at this Restaurant Row "landmark", a longtime "perpetual favorite" for a "brew and a burger" spiced up by some "old celebrity sightings"; famed as a "classic pre-show/after-show" meeting place, insiders whisper it's "best after the theater rush."

Joe's Bar ⊄
– | – | – | M

520 E. Sixth St. (bet. Aves. A & B), L to 1st Ave., 212-473-9093
"Neighborhoody and friendly", this longtime East Village dive draws a mix of old folks and "rock 'n' roll" types with "cheap beers" and a "small pool table"; a "great jukebox" stocked with "country tunes" ices the cake.

Joe's Pub
23 | 21 | 18 | $11

Public Theater, 425 Lafayette St. (bet. Astor Pl. & E. 4th St.), 6 to Astor Pl., 212-539-8770; www.joespub.com
"You can't beat the intimate setting" of this "cutting-edge" Village cabaret adjunct to the Public Theater where the "wide array" of "eclectic entertainment" runs the gamut from "insiders' favorites" to the "next big thing"; its "diverse" following "gets in a groove" and ignores the "pricey" drinks and "spotty" service.

Joey's
▽ 18 | 20 | 18 | $9

186 Ave. B (bet. 11th & 12th Sts.), L to 1st Ave., 212-353-9090
It's all about the "back porch" furnished with "comfy, slouchy couches" at this East Village "neighborhood" watering hole; inside, "Scrabble" and a variety of other "board games" keep its low-key crowd occupied.

Johnny's Bar
– | – | – | I

90 Greenwich Ave. (bet. 12th & 13th Sts.), A/C/E/L to 14th St./8th Ave., 212-741-5279
About "as small as your first studio apartment", this Village "dive of all dives" is the kind of joint where "you lose all track of time"; its "interesting" regulars (an "only-in-NY" crew of "characters") can always be counted on for "good conversation – until they pass out", that is.

John Street Bar & Grill
14 | 8 | 16 | $6

17 John St. (bet. B'way & Nassau St.), 2/3/4/5/A/C/J/M/Z to Fulton St./B'way/Nassau, 212-349-3278; www.johnstreet.com
"UPS workers", "local bums" and "traders after a bad day" assemble at this "roomy", "dumpy" basement dive that's as "unassuming" as the Financial District gets; part "biker bar", part "sports bar", there's "no rational explanation for the popularity of certain nights", but the dirt "cheap" pops probably have something to do with it.

Joshua Tree
16 | 14 | 16 | $8

513 Third Ave. (bet. 34th & 35th Sts.), 6 to 33rd St., 212-689-0058
366 W. 46th St. (bet. 8th & 9th Aves.), A/C/E to 42nd St./Port Authority, 212-489-1920
The "perfect transition bars for recent grads" just landed in the big city, these "frat-party flashbacks" feature plenty of "sports on tap" via "über-large flat screens" plus "hook up" potential galore (they're definitely "not date places"); count on "always seeing someone you know" – "whether or not that's a good thing is debatable."

Josie Wood's   14 | 10 | 18 | $6

11 Waverly Pl. (bet. Greene & Mercer Sts.), R/W to 8th St., 212-228-6806
"Hit on (or be hit on)" by NYU types at this "semi-divey" Village bar
boasting a "fantastic Internet jukebox" and "cheap" suds; given the
"underground" setting, don't expect "consistent cell phone service",
and if you're "not a college kid", you may "feel a little old."

Joya ⊅   21 | 20 | 20 | $9

215 Court St. (Warren St.), Brooklyn, F/G to Bergen St., 718-222-3484
Maybe "more restaurant than bar", this Cobble Hill Thai still "turns up
the volume in the later hours" drawing "hip singles" with "affordable"
libations and a "stylish", "Manhattan-like" vibe; since it can be a
"mob scene" on weekends, regulars "go early" to sidestep the
"typically long lines."

Jules   24 | 20 | 15 | $9

65 St. Marks Pl. (bet. 1st & 2nd Aves.), 6 to Astor Pl., 212-477-5560
"Live jazz at no cover" is the hook at this East Village "Francophile's
haven", a "sexy little" Gallic bistro that channels a "back alley
Parisian cafe"; "typical French service" comes with the territory, but
after a "bottle of Sancerre and some moules frites", who cares?

Julius ⊅   – | – | – | M

159 W. 10th St. (Waverly Pl.), 1 to Christopher St., 212-929-9672
"NY's oldest gay bar", this "historic Village landmark" (a former
speakeasy) attracts an "oddball crowd" that looks as aged as the
establishment; while far from a happening scene, it does pair "good
burgers" with "strong drinks."

Juniper Suite   – | – | – | VE

*44 W. 56th St. (bet. 5th & 6th Aves.), N/Q/R/W to 57th St./7th Ave.,
212-586-4737; www.thejunipersuite.com*
This posh new duplex in the heart of Midtown features a coolly
modern downstairs bar/lounge dispensing fancy specialty cocktails
topped by an upstairs dining room with a small-plates menu (both food
and drink are adjusted seasonally); the swank looks are reflected in
the swanky pricing.

Justin's   18 | 17 | 13 | $12

*31 W. 21st St. (bet. 5th & 6th Aves.), F/V to 23rd St., 212-352-0599;
www.justinsrestaurant.com*
"Hip-hop and R&B stars" dripping with the "obligatory bling" are the
target audience of this Flatiron bar/eatery best known because of its
owner, the one-and-only P. Diddy; but there's bad news for the "single
African-American" gals sipping "pricey drinks" and "hoping Puffy
will pop in and miraculously choose them" – "he's rarely there."

Kabin   ∇ 16 | 14 | 21 | $7
(fka Black Star Bar)

*92 Second Ave. (bet. 5th & 6th Sts.), F/V to Lower East Side/2nd Ave.,
212-254-0204*
This new East Villager with vague log-cabin trappings sports a "simple
bar" in front, a "pool table" room in the middle and a lounge with
"couches in the back"; pragmatists say it's "good enough" for "no-
fuss drinks" while "waiting for a table at the Mermaid Inn next door."

Kaña   ∇ 24 | 16 | 20 | $8

*324 Spring St. (bet. Greenwich & Washington Sts.), C/E to Spring St.,
212-343-8180; www.kanatapasbar.com*
Lovers of "Latin music and Latin people" love this "hot little" SoHo
tapas lounge for its "spicy rhythms" and "infectiously happy" "expat"

crowds; the music's similar to "what you'd hear in a club in Spain", and after they remove the tables, late-night revelers report one heck of a "good party."

Kanvas
17 | 18 | 17 | $9

219 Ninth Ave. (bet. 23rd & 24th Sts.), C/E to 23rd St., 212-727-2616; www.kanvasnyc.com
Thanks to "interesting cocktails", "reasonable prices" and a "good location", this Chelsea "standby" is "prone to many birthday parties"; while the rotating art on the walls is a matter of debate – "pretty cool" versus "awful" – many critics claim it's "underrated."

Karma
21 | 19 | 18 | $8

51 First Ave. (bet. 3rd & 4th Sts.), F/V to Lower East Side/2nd Ave., 212-677-3160; www.karmanyc.com
"Get lit" at this "friendly", "unpretentious" East Village bar where "you can smoke" cigarettes or "puff on a hookah" and "enjoy NYC the way it was in the past"; despite "shaggy decor", "so-so music" and waking up the next morning "smelling like apricot tobacco", inhalers confess they feel "special and loved again" here.

Katwalk
∇ 17 | 14 | 16 | $8

2 W. 35th St. (bet. 5th & 6th Aves.), B/D/F/N/Q/R/V/W to 34th St./Herald Sq., 212-594-9343; www.katwalknyc.com
Along with a slight name tweaking (from Catwalk to Katwalk), this Garment District lounge has been remodeled with "softer chairs" and "larger projection TVs"; while the "dimly lit upstairs" balcony has kewl kats "really purring", foes hiss it's "pitched to the fashion set" but is really a "stereotypical sports bar."

Kavehaz
∇ 21 | 18 | 21 | $9

37 W. 26th St. (bet. B'way & 6th Ave.), R/W to 28th St., 212-343-0612; www.kavehaz.com
"Appealing and comfortable", this Chelsea bar/restaurant/jazz joint is a "great loungey place to end the night" even if the "loud" acoustics "make intimate conversations virtually impossible"; "good coffees" are available in addition to harder stuff, but the "worn-out sofas" could use some perking up.

Keens Steakhouse
23 | 23 | 23 | $12

72 W. 36th St. (bet. 5th & 6th Aves.), B/D/F/N/Q/R/V/W to 34th St./Herald Sq., 212-947-3636; www.keenssteakhouse.com
You're "surrounded by history" (starting with the "hundreds of clay pipes" hanging from the ceiling) at this circa-1885 Garment District steakhouse, a "dark-wood", "old-fashioned" magnet for "guys going to the Garden"; a "great selection of single malts" keeps its "older" regulars in their cups.

Kemia Bar
22 | 25 | 20 | $10

630 Ninth Ave., downstairs (enter on 44th St.), A/C/E to 42nd St./Port Authority, 212-582-3200; www.kemiabarnyc.com
"As yet undiscovered by the masses", this "transporting" Hell's Kitchen French-Moroccan lounge is like something out of a "movie", starting with its "semi-hidden" underground location (down a "rose petal–strewn staircase" beneath the restaurant Marseilles); the "outrageous prices" are muted by its "intriguing" aura and "mysterious corners."

Kennedy's
17 | 14 | 18 | $8

327 W. 57th St. (bet. 8th & 9th Aves.), 1/A/B/C/D to 59th St./Columbus Circle, 212-307-1722
A "respite from the intense Manhattan bar scene", this "local" Midtown Irish pub lures a "clientele getting on in years" with a cozy fireplace

and a "great back room"; it's a "feel-at-home-and-drink-a-Guinness" kind of place – and the way they treat regulars "makes you wish you were one."

Kenny's Castaways
13 | 10 | 15 | $7

157 Bleecker St. (bet. Sullivan & Thompson Sts.), A/B/C/D/E/F/V to W. 4th St., 212-979-9762
"If only the walls could talk" at this venerable Village venue, a "relatively spacious" joint that's been showcasing "up-and-coming bands" for the last 40 years; foes dis the "tacky" scene and "quirky crowd", a bunch of "kids holding on to their dads' old rock 'n' roll dreams."

Kettle of Fish
18 | 14 | 19 | $7

59 Christopher St. (bet. 7th Ave. S. & Waverly Pl.), 1 to Christopher St., 212-414-2278
Thankfully "not shoulder-to-shoulder", this "classic old" Village taproom feels like "hanging out with friends in your parents' basement"; "playing darts is its mainstay", though "sports TV" attracts "Green Bay Packers" fans.

Kevin St. James
15 | 13 | 19 | $7

741 Eighth Ave. (46th St.), A/C/E to 42nd St./Port Authority, 212-977-5984; www.kevinstjames.com
"Always lively", this "basic" Theater District Irish pub/sports bar is popular with "young" twentysomethings and "tourists looking for a good time"; but picky drinkers dis this "frat party gone wrong" as "no great shakes", except for a "beer after work."

Keybar
21 | 20 | 18 | $8

432 E. 13th St. (bet. Ave. A & 1st Ave.), L to 1st Ave., 212-478-3021; www.keybar.com
There's nothing "better in the winter than the fireplace" at this "small", red-lit East Villager, an unusually "comfy and cozy" spot; later in the evening, "spunky" house DJs "get everyone moving", even if the bar's "signature Rolo shots" "prevent everyone from moving the next day."

KGB Bar ⌒
19 | 16 | 16 | $7

85 E. Fourth St., 2nd fl. (bet. 2nd & 3rd Aves.), F/V to Lower East Side/ 2nd Ave., 212-505-3360; www.kgbbar.com
"For communist propaganda and a drink", where else but this second-floor East Village "literary bar" where "disheveled academics", "political leftists" and "annoying hipsters" assemble for "interesting readings" and other "intellectual" pursuits; "Cold War" decor and prole prices add to its "funky appeal."

Kili
▽ 19 | 21 | 16 | $7

81 Hoyt St. (bet. Atlantic Ave. & State St.), Brooklyn, A/C/G to Hoyt/ Schermerhorn St., 718-855-5574
A "fireplace" and "tasty, amnesia-inducing apple martinis" make things mellow at this Downtown Brooklyn watering hole, a "comfortable neighborhood" spot with a ski-lodgey feel; expect a "varied" crowd, particularly "as the evening progresses."

Killmeyer's
23 | 20 | 23 | $8

4254 Arthur Kill Rd. (Sharrotts Rd.), Staten Island, 718-984-1202; www.killmeyers.com
"Imported beer" (and lots of it) seduces suds lovers at this Staten Island German restaurant that's particularly "great on warm days" what with its spacious biergarten; the crowd may skew older, but the "excellent" old-NY atmosphere (especially that stunning, circa-1890 mahogany bar) is ageless.

KING COLE BAR
27 | 27 | 24 | $15

St. Regis Hotel, 2 E. 55th St. (5th Ave.), E/V to 5th Ave./53rd St., 212-339-6721;
www.starwood.com

"Class and cool" blend seamlessly at this "timeless" Midtown hotel bar that harkens back to a "more genteel era", starting with its "focal point", a vintage Maxfield Parrish mural of the merry old soul himself; since the cocktails come with "money-is-no-object" price tags, consider "bringing a date who only drinks water."

King's Head Tavern
18 | 18 | 18 | $6

222 E. 14th St. (bet. 2nd & 3rd Aves.), L to 3rd Ave., 212-473-6590

The "post-college" crowd is "laid-back and not trendy" at this big, "dark" East Village barroom that reels them in with an "awesome selection" of "cheap" brews; its "medieval look" includes "suits of armor", though critics say that "Beyoncé on the jukebox" and "UPN on TV" "kill the mood."

Kinsale Tavern
22 | 17 | 22 | $7

1672 Third Ave. (bet. 93rd & 94th Sts.), 6 to 96th St., 212-348-4370

"Half the fun" at this "rousing" Upper East Side Irish pub is supplied by its "friendly" staff that knows how to pour a "great pint of Guinness" and is "funny" to boot; "plenty of TVs" tuned to every "major sporting event" and "better-than-average" grub make it a more than "reliable" stop.

K Lounge
19 | 23 | 22 | $11

(aka Kama Sutra Lounge)

30 W. 52nd St., 2nd fl. (bet. 5th & 6th Aves.), B/D/F/V to 47-50th Sts./
Rockefeller Ctr., 212-265-6665; www.kloungenyc.com

This "very exotic" Midtown lounge with a gimmick – a "Kama Sutra theme" – features "Indian/Persian decor" and "velvety sofas", all infused with the "scent of incense"; given its second-floor address, the stairs may be "difficult to navigate" after an "evening of heavy partying", so let the "attractive staff" help you.

Knickerbocker Bar & Grill
21 | 19 | 21 | $9

33 University Pl. (9th St.), R/W to 8th St., 212-228-8490;
www.knickerbockerbarandgrill.com

You might want to wear a "mink coat" to this venerable Village chophouse, an "old-school" hangout frequented by "older" types hungry for some "old-world class"; "antique posters", original "Hirschfeld drawings" and "live weekend jazz" all contribute to its "throwback" appeal.

Knitting Factory
22 | 14 | 16 | $10

74 Leonard St. (bet. B'way & Church St.), 1 to Franklin St., 212-219-3006;
www.knittingfactory.com

Expect a "funky mix" of music that usually "defies categorization" at this "gritty" TriBeCa performance space, an "amusement park for the alternative set"; three different rooms showcase "non-corporate", "non-mainstream" acts, and even if the digs are "not pretty", it's certainly "worthwhile."

Koi
– | – | – | VE

Bryant Park Hotel, 40 W. 40th St. (bet. 5th & 6th Aves.), 7/B/D/F/V to
42nd St./6th Ave., 212-921-3330; www.koirestaurant.com

Abutting the sceney Japanese restaurant of the same name, this rollicking new bar/lounge in the Bryant Park Hotel is usually jammed with trendy types vying for a coveted table for dinner; cloned from the much-hyped original in LA, it's most tolerable (i.e. less frantic) either very early or very late.

Korova Milk Bar

19 | 22 | 18 | $8

200 Ave. A (bet. 12th & 13th Sts.), L to 1st Ave., 212-254-8838;
www.korovamilkbar.com

The "alcoholic milkshakes" and black-and-white color scheme "pay homage to *A Clockwork Orange*" at this "kitschy" East Village theme bar that's a "must-see for Kubrick fans"; but some droogs say this "gimmicky", "oddball place" is "so yesterday" and usually "empty" as a result.

Kos

— | — | — | VE

264 Bowery (bet. Houston & Prince Sts.), 6 to Bleecker St.,
212-343-9722

Famed for its famed "owners, Lenny Kravitz and Denzel Washington", this Bowery lounge is a self-styled "hideaway for supermodels and rock stars" with a "Miami-meets-NY" vibe; but foes call it nothing more than a "wannabe bar" that's "too cool for itself" and frequented by "snotty patrons."

Koze Lounge

— | — | — | I

676 Fifth Ave. (bet. 20th & 21st Sts.), Brooklyn, M/R to Prospect Ave.,
718-832-8282

Sunset Park's multiethnic twentysomethings finally have their own lounge to chill in; this green-walled storefront sports low banquettes and tables, local pop art, a flat-panel TV, a DJ laying down hip-hop and house, and a tidy, mirrored bar putting out a chartreuse glow and cheap cocktails; the vibe is mellow and friendly.

Kush

— | — | — | M

191 Chrystie St. (bet. Rivington & Stanton Sts.), F/V to Lower East Side/
2nd Ave., 212-677-7328; www.kushlounge.com

Formerly on hopping Orchard Street, this romantic Moroccan lounge has relocated to roomier digs on up-and-coming Chrystie Street, with even more canoodle-worthy nooks and kush-y, candlelit crannies than before; the hookahs have made the trip as well, along with global DJs adding to the sultry scene.

La Bottega Caffé

23 | 22 | 16 | $12

Maritime Hotel, 88 Ninth Ave. (16th St.), A/C/E/L to 14th St./8th Ave.,
212-243-8400; www.themaritimehotel.com

"Look cool even if you're not" at this West Chelsea bar, a wine bottle–lined bistro that's "especially good in summer" when a vast, "Miami"-esque outdoor patio attracts standing-room-only business; despite "overpriced drinks", servers "more interested in being discovered" than on waiting tables and a crowd "hoping to be noticed by someone . . . anyone", it still shows lots of "potential."

La Caverna

20 | 19 | 15 | $8

122-124 Rivington St., downstairs (bet. Essex & Norfolk Sts.), F/J/M/Z
to Delancey/Essex Sts., 212-475-2126; www.lacavernanyc.com

Done up to look like an "underground cavern", this Lower Eastsider can be "cool" – "if you manage to find it" down a long flight of stairs (the big new sign helps); still, some sense "something isn't right", blaming "lame looks" and "spotty music" for the "sparse crowds."

Laila Lounge ⊅

— | — | — | M

113 N. Seventh St. (bet. Berry St. & Wythe Ave.), Brooklyn, L to
Bedford Ave., 718-486-6791; www.lailalounge.com

"Lots of events" – "art shows, live bands, nightly DJs" – are the draws at this "excellent neighborhood bar" that comes without any "Williamsburg pretension"; inquiring minds want to know "why this place isn't busier."

Lakeside Lounge
18 | 13 | 16 | $6

162 Ave. B (bet. 10th & 11th Sts.), L to 1st Ave., 212-529-8463;
www.lakesidelounge.com
"Perfect for trouble", this "dark and dirty" East Village barroom is an
"old-school dive" with a "totally hipster" following thanks to the
winning combo of "beer in cans", "rockers on the stage" and a
"jukebox full of lost hits"; a "fun photo booth" completes the picture.

La Lanterna Next Door
▽ 25 | 25 | 21 | $10

131 MacDougal St. (bet. W. 3rd & 4th Sts.), A/B/C/D/E/F/V to W. 4th St.,
212-529-5945
"Great lighting" and an "awesome fireplace" set the ultra-"romantic"
mood at this "simply magical", somewhat "secret" Village adjunct to
the restaurant La Lanterna di Vittorio; occasional "live jazz" and
"desserts brought from next door" are sweet diversions while you're
getting "cozy with someone special."

La Linea
▽ 14 | 11 | 14 | $7

15 First Ave. (bet. 1st & 2nd Sts.), F/V to Lower East Side/2nd Ave.,
212-777-1571; www.lalinealounge.com
Convenient for "grabbing a drink before eating at Boca Chica next
door", this very dark East Villager is a "true NYC neighborhood bar"
with "no tourists" in sight; still, critics caution "don't expect much
from the decor or service."

Larry Lawrence
_ | _ | _ | M

295 Grand St. (bet. Havemeyer & Roebling Sts.), Brooklyn, L to
Bedford Ave., 718-218-7866
This "never-too-crowded" Williamsburg bar radiates "mystique",
starting with its off-the-beaten-path address, "unmarked entrance"
and unpromising long hallway; but inside the "vast", double-height
space is a blend of exposed brick and "warm" wood, plus an "unusual",
"fishbowl"-esque outdoor smoking mezzanine.

Last Exit
20 | 17 | 21 | $6

136 Atlantic Ave. (bet. Clinton & Henry Sts.), Brooklyn, 2/3/4/5/M/R to
Borough Hall, 718-222-9198; www.lastexitbar.com
Away from the "crowded Smith Street mess", this "funky, friendly"
Cobble Hill taproom (named after Hubert Selby's infamous novel) is a
"hipster bar without the city attitude" and might even "make you
forget you're in yuppie central"; the ever-changing collection of
"locals' art hanging on the walls" is a "good conversation sparker."

LATITUDE
_ | _ | _ | M

783 Eighth Ave. (bet. 47th & 48th Sts.), C/E to 50th St., 212-245-3034;
www.latitudebarnyc.com
Among the latest arrivals in the Theater District is this mega-triplex
that manages to sandwich together six bars, three lounges, two
outdoor rooftops, a billiards room and a fireplace for your drinking
pleasure; it's the latest chapter from the owners of Social, a similarly
large extravaganza a block away, and further evidence of the rise of
Hell's Kitchen as a destination neighborhood.

Laugh Factory
▽ 15 | 11 | 13 | $11

669 Eighth Ave. (42nd St.), A/C/E to 42nd St./Port Authority, 212-586-7829;
www.laughfactory.com
Forget the former Times Square "strip club" setting with "skeevy"
street life still milling around on the sidewalk: this new "laughfest"
hosts "fun comics" and a "pretty good bar scene", though the
enjoyment level "totally depends on who's playing"; but so long as the
"alcohol keeps flowing", most keep laughing.

Laugh Lounge

– | – | – | E

151 Essex St. (bet. Rivington & Stanton Sts.), F/J/M/Z to Delancey/ Essex Sts., 212-614-2500; www.laughloungenyc.com

The only "comedy lounge on the Lower East Side", this double-decker house of mirth offers standup routines on its "cozy" lower level and a posh lounge above; maybe the drinks are "overpriced", but it's "worth it if the comics are good."

Lava Gina

∇ 21 | 22 | 21 | $9

116 Ave. C (bet. 7th & 8th Sts.), L to 1st Ave., 212-477-9319; www.lavagina.com

Alright, the "sophomoric name" can be a "challenge after a few drinks", but this "out-of-the-way" East Village lounge works its "gimmick" well, right down to the "red walls" and "bold", V-shaped bar; it's also renowned for its DJ-spun world music and "relaxed" vibe.

Lea

∇ 21 | 21 | 21 | $10

230 Park Ave. (Helmsley Bldg. East Walkway, bet. 45th & 46th Sts.), 4/5/6/7/S to 42nd St./Grand Central, 212-922-1546; www.leanyc.com

The "waitresses are hot" and the "drinks cold" at this "undiscovered hideaway" secreted near Grand Central in the Helmsley Building East Walkway; while it's "more appealing after the commuter rush" and an "expense account" doesn't hurt, it's an overall "upscale experience" with a "casual feel"; P.S. closed Saturday and Sunday.

Le Bateau Ivre

23 | 19 | 20 | $11

Pickwick Arms Hotel, 230 E. 51st St. (bet. 2nd & 3rd Aves.), 6 to 51st St./ Lexington Ave., 212-583-0579; www.lebateauivrenyc.com

"Feel like an expat living in France" at this "easy" East Side wine bar that channels "Paris in the '50s" with a "seductively romantic" bistro setting frequented by folks who actually "speak French"; an "amazing list" of vinos by the glass or the bottle comes with "pricey" price tags, but is "worth every cent."

Le Colonial

23 | 24 | 20 | $11

149 E. 57th St. (bet. Lexington & 3rd Aves.), 4/5/6/N/R/W to 59th St./ Lexington Ave., 212-752-0808; www.lecolonialnyc.com

"Stylish, exotic" and "a little snooty", this "posh", bamboo-laden Midtown restaurant features a "happening upstairs bar" recalling "what Vietnam was like in the 1930s" under French rule; sure, it's "pricey", but in return it's "classy" enough to work as a "perfect first date spot."

Le Figaro Cafe

18 | 15 | 14 | $7

184 Bleecker St. (MacDougal St.), A/B/C/D/E/F/V to W. 4th St., 212-677-1100

"Grab a streetside table" and "watch the world go by" at this "landmark" coffeehouse that's a "little piece of Paris in the Village" ("wear your beret"); ever reminiscent of the area's onetime "folkie scene", it "feels touristy" though locals claim it's more "relaxed" during the week than on the "busy weekends."

Legacy

16 | 15 | 16 | $11

437 88th St. (bet. 4th & 5th Aves.), Brooklyn, R to 86th St., 718-748-1002

A real "Brooklyn crowd" boogies at this Bay Ridge disco, an "ok dance club" that does the job when you're "bored on a Saturday night"; but others say the "'80s are over", adding "if the fumes from the hairspray don't kill you, the fumes from the cologne might."

Leisure Time Bowling

∇ 15 | 9 | 12 | $5

Port Authority Bus Terminal, 625 Eighth Ave., 2nd fl. (42nd St.), A/C/E to 42nd St./Port Authority, 212-268-3539; www.leisuretimebowl.com

Somewhat "cheaper" than the competition, this Hell's Kitchen bowling alley parked in Port Authority may skew toward "divey", but it's "good for what it is", offering "arcade games" and pub grub; "poor service" makes it "hard to get a drink on Saturday night."

Le Jazz Au Bar   21 | 25 | 20 | $12
(aka 58)
41 E. 58th St. (bet. Madison & Park Aves.), 4/5/6/N/R/W to 59th St./ Lexington Ave., 212-308-9455; www.lejazzaubar.com
"Good sightlines" and a "stunning" setting make this "intimate" albeit "hidden" Midtown boîte a "fine place to hear jazz"; early in the evening, it attracts "grown-ups" who can afford the "high prices", but later on Thursday–Sunday it gets younger (and "livelier") when it morphs into a dance club dubbed '58.'

Lemon, The   15 | 16 | 15 | $10
230 Park Ave. S. (bet. 18th & 19th Sts.), 6 to 23rd St., 212-614-1200; www.lemonnyc.com
One of the few Park Avenue South spots that have "gone the distance", this 10-year-old duplex is particularly "nice on a warm evening" when they "open the doors to the street"; but sourpusses say it has "no soul" and dis the "expensive drinks", "passé scene" and "pushy" crowd ("attitude will get you everywhere" here).

Lenox Lounge   18 | 14 | 18 | $10
288 Lenox Ave. (125th St.), 2/3 to 125th St., 212-427-0253; www.lenoxlounge.com
"Like going back in time", this "legendary" Harlem jazz boîte on the scene since 1939 was once home to the likes of Billie Holiday and Miles Davis, and now showcases "old-school" acts in its deco Zebra Room; the "friendly" upfront barroom is equally "interesting" for its "great atmosphere" alone.

Lenox Room   23 | 22 | 19 | $11
1278 Third Ave. (bet. 73rd & 74th Sts.), 6 to 77th St., 212-772-0404; www.lenoxroom.com
"For those who have outgrown Dorrian's", there's this "sophisticated" Upper East Side bar/restaurant where the "grown-up" "preppy" regulars all "know each other" and show up for "late-night" revelry; "lovely" decor and a "classy" vibe makes up for the "high-end" pricing.

Les Enfants Terribles   ▽ 25 | 23 | 17 | $8
37 Canal St. (Ludlow St.), F/J/M/Z to Delancey/Essex Sts., 212-777-7518; www.lesenfantsterriblesnyc.com
"Very out of the way" on the Lower East Side/Chinatown border lies this "hip" French-African bar/eatery, a "noisy, happening" joint that can be a "tight squeeze" at prime times; service scores suggest they "could do with more bar staff", but otherwise, it's "ooh-la-la."

Le Singe Vert   21 | 19 | 19 | $10
160 Seventh Ave. (bet. 19th & 20th Sts.), 1 to 18th St., 212-366-4100
A "real little piece of Paris" planted in Chelsea, this "poor man's Pastis" is "big on atmosphere and easy on the budget"; admirers say it's "more authentically French" than the competition – "with slow service to prove it" – but, *zut alors,* when it gets crowded it feels more like "sardineville."

Le Souk   23 | 22 | 15 | $9
47 Ave. B (bet. 3rd & 4th Sts.), F/V to Lower East Side/2nd Ave., 212-777-5454; www.lesoukny.com
Experience "Morocco" in the East Village at this North African–themed restaurant/lounge, a mazelike, "multilevel" affair that's always perennially "packed" thanks to the intoxicating blend of "hookahs", "Middle Eastern melodies" and belly dancer "navel-watching"; "slow

service" distracts high-maintenance types, but the majority is having too much "fun" to notice.

Le 26 ⊄
(fka Chazal)

▽ 20 | 17 | 14 | $10

41 Madison Ave. (26th St.), 6 to 23rd St., 212-545-8555; www.le26.com
This "very Euro" Flatiron spot (fka Chazal) can be a "serious pickup place" for "Rolex-wearing" dudes chasing after "$200 jeans–wearing" gals; despite "expensive" prices and "too much attitude for what it is", the "redeeming quality" is that terrific summertime "sidewalk seating."

Levee, The ⊄
(fka Antique Lounge)

– | – | – | M

212 Berry St. (Metropolitan Ave.), Brooklyn, L to Bedford Ave., 718-218-8787; www.theleveenyc.com
Set in the former Antique Lounge space, this new Williamsburger is a two-part affair, with a standard-issue bar at the entrance abutted by a canoodle-worthy lounge; early visitors report it's much the same as before with some subtle tweaks, mainly less flea-market furniture.

LEVEL V

23 | 22 | 17 | $12

675 Hudson St., downstairs (14th St.), A/C/E/L to 14th St./8th Ave., 212-699-2410
"If you can get past the tough door", a "sweet" scene awaits at this "sexy", "sultry" new Meatpacking District lounge parked in the basement beneath the restaurant Vento; its "eye-candy" crew gets cozy in one of the "little private alcoves" (formerly turn-of-the-century horse stalls), and tolerates the inevitable "attitude" and "hefty bottle service tabs."

Lexington Bar & Books

20 | 23 | 18 | $12

1020 Lexington Ave. (73rd St.), 6 to 77th St., 212-717-3902
An "intellectual's idea of a perfect bar", this "very old-money" Upper East Side cigar bar is one of the "last refuges" for stogie-smoking masters of the universe, starting with its "gentlemen's club" setting; it may be too "highbrow" for some, but ultimately the "best thing about it is that you can smoke"; P.S. jacket required.

L'Express

20 | 16 | 16 | $9

249 Park Ave. S. (20th St.), 6 to 23rd St., 212-254-5858; www.lexpressnyc.com
"24-hour party people" gravitate to this "always open", "always busy" Flatiron French bistro for "bacon and eggs after a night of clubbing"; ok, "service can be spotty" and the seating "cramped", but for those who "don't want to go home" yet, it's a perfect "wee-hours" way station.

Le Zinc

21 | 19 | 20 | $11

139 Duane St. (bet. Church St. & W. B'way), A/C/E to Canal St., 212-513-0001; www.lezincnyc.com
Seemingly transplanted from the "Marais" in Paris, this "cool" French bistro brings a "warm feeling" to TriBeCa via "delicious cocktails" made by "bartenders who know what they're doing"; it may be more restaurant than bar, so if you're waiting for a table, "all the posters on the wall" will give you "something to talk about."

LIBATION
(fka Torch)

– | – | – | E

137 Ludlow St. (bet. Rivington & Stanton Sts.), F/V to Lower East Side/ 2nd Ave., 212-529-2153; www.libationnyc.com
"Just trendy enough", this "massive" new triplex on Ludlow Street features a ground-floor bar and a mezzanine bottle-service lounge,

crowned by a private party space; it's already attracting "fun" folks who say it reflects the Lower East Side's "up-and-coming" status, but old-timers see a portent of "the way things are heading down here."

Library
20 | 18 | 17 | $6

7 Ave. A (bet. Houston & 2nd Sts.), F/V to Lower East Side/2nd Ave., 212-375-1352; www.librarybarnyc.com

"If you plan on reading, bring a flashlight" to this "dark", "no-frills" East Village bar that's best known for its "amazing jukebox" and "hot" barmaids, not its book-lined setting; "cheap" beverages and "old Japanese monster flicks" on the back wall keep things "festive" here.

Life
∇ 16 | 19 | 13 | $9

30-07 Newtown Ave. (30th St.), Queens, N/W to 30th Ave., 718-626-9100; www.life-nyc.com

This "very Manhattanish" Astoria club is a sleek, all-white spot that gets "very crowded" with "lively", "trendy" locals out to have fun; only open weekends, it features a "don't-miss" Brazilian party on Fridays and a Greek bash on Saturdays.

Life Cafe
17 | 14 | 20 | $6

343 E. 10th St. (Ave. B), L to 1st Ave., 212-477-8791
983 Flushing Ave. (bet. Bogart & Central Sts.), Brooklyn, L to Morgan Ave., 718-386-1133
www.lifecafenyc.com

An "easy spot to grab drinks and snacks", this longtime East Villager (and its newer Bushwick sibling) is appropriately "laid-back", though a tad "touristy" thanks to its appearance in *Rent*; still, critics claim what was "formerly hip and cool" is now a "little dated" and just "like any other place" in the nabe.

Light
18 | 20 | 16 | $11

125 E. 54th St., downstairs (bet. Lexington & Park Aves.), E/V to Lexington Ave./53rd St., 212-583-1333; www.lightnyc.com

"All you could ask for in a lounge", this "below-ground" Midtowner is "spacious", "swanky" and so "dimly lit" that "you'll feel like a bat"; trendoids say "its time has passed", but it's always a "safe bet" to get up close and personal with "Lehman Brothers boys" and other "young twentysomething professionals."

Lighthouse Tavern
∇ 16 | 13 | 19 | $7

243 Fifth Ave. (bet. Carroll St. & Garfield Pl.), Brooklyn, M/R to Union St., 718-788-8070; www.lighthousetavern.net

"Basic" drinking in Park Slope is yours at this "typical" watering hole enhanced by "warm and cozy" appeal; some find "nothing out of the ordinary" here, save the all-seasons backyard that's a "great place for a beer and a burger."

Lillie's ∌
– | – | – | M

46 Beard St. (Dwight St.), Brooklyn, F/G to Smith/9th Sts., 718-858-9822

There's "grungy glamour" galore at this far-out waterfront saloon, starting with owner Lillie Haws, "Red Hook's answer to Mae West"; its "interesting crowd" digs the "offbeat" vibe, "Sunday BBQ" and most of all, a "wondrous garden" that seems like an "urban fantasy jungle" after a few drinks.

Link
16 | 17 | 17 | $10

120 E. 15th St. (Irving Pl.), 4/5/6/L/N/Q/R/W to 14th St./Union Sq., 212-995-1010

Much "warmer than the modern decor suggests", this Gramercy spot near Irving Plaza is the "ultimate multitasker", a bar, lounge and restaurant all rolled into one slick, glass-walled package; maybe there's "not much going on here" ("when is it finally going to get popular?"), but at least it's "harmless" and "not offensive."

Lion's Den ⊄
15 | 9 | 14 | $6

214 Sullivan St. (bet. Bleecker & W. 3rd Sts.), A/B/C/D/E/F/V to W. 4th St., 212-477-2782; www.cegmusic.com/lionsden/
"Grungy good times" await at this "decent-size" Village music club showcasing a "fairly reliable" talent roster; although the setting is "not much to look at", its "random", "rowdy" crowds say the "hole-in-the-wall" feel adds to the "authentic concert" experience.

Lips
22 | 19 | 20 | $10

2 Bank St. (Greenwich Ave.), 1/2/3 to 14th St., 212-675-7710; www.lipsnyc.com
"Everyone know your name" ('cause "everyone's name is honey") at this "raucous", "tacky" Village cabaret where "amazing looking" "waitresses in drag" crack wise and "perform numbers" when they're not slinging "mean cocktails"; given all the "opportunities to be embarrassed in front of a room of strangers", it's naturally a "bachelorette party" magnet.

Lit
18 | 13 | 16 | $7

93 Second Ave. (bet. 5th & 6th Sts.), 6 to Astor Pl., 212-777-7987; www.litloungenyc.com
The "prototype of the unpretentious hipster bar", this "dingy" East Village "den of iniquity" draws "indie girls" and "rocker boys" by "booking solid DJs" and displaying "underground art" in its rear gallery; a "dank", "musty" basement "dungeon" showcases live music and random "suspicious activities."

Live Bait
13 | 11 | 15 | $7

14 E. 23rd St. (bet. 5th & Madison Aves.), R/W to 23rd St., 212-353-2400
"Like going to the South without the accents", this "downmarket-on-purpose" Flatiron dive is a "great old standby" parked on a "way lame block"; some yawn it's "so over, even the underage models are in their 40s", but fans retort there's "nothing bait-er" for "pounding shots and shooters."

Living Room ⊄
23 | 18 | 17 | $7

154 Ludlow St. (bet. Rivington & Stanton Sts.), F/V to Lower East Side/ 2nd Ave., 212-533-7235; www.livingroomny.com
"Any night of the week" there's "something worthwhile" going on at this "intimate" Lower East Side music venue, a "singer/songwriter scene" that "focuses on quieter, acoustic bands"; even better, there's usually no cover and only a "one-drink minimum" in exchange for some mighty "interesting entertainment."

Lobby
∇ 21 | 19 | 15 | $10

330 W. 38th St. (bet. 8th & 9th Aves.), A/C/E to 42nd St./Port Authority, 212-465-2200; www.lobbynyc.com
The "crowd is mixed" and the "space is huge" at this bi-level Garment District lounge that's a "decent" enough destination, particularly if you can worm your way up to the mezzanine VIP area overlooking the bar below; while trendsters feel it "could be better", others claim it has enough "potential for a fun evening."

Local
16 | 14 | 17 | $7

1 Penn Plaza (33rd St., bet. 7th & 8th Aves.), A/C/E to 34th St./Penn Station, 212-629-7070
1004 Second Ave. (53rd St.), E/V to Lexington Ave./53rd St., 212-755-7020
www.localcafenyc.com
Despite its "tiny" dimensions, this Upper Eastsider attracts a "good happy-hour crowd" comprised of "just-out-of-college-and-in-the-

big-city" types; while "generic" and sometimes "too packed to move" inside, at least it keeps prices "relatively low"; P.S. the much larger Penn Station offshoot is new and unrated.

Local 138   ▽ 22 | 18 | 19 | $6

138 Ludlow St. (bet. Rivington & Stanton Sts.), F/J/M/Z to Delancey/ Essex Sts., 212-477-0280

There's "nothing fancy" about this "simple" Lower East Side Irish pub that's a "safe bet" for low-key imbibing in "dark", divey digs; "people-watchers" aim for the "window booths", the best seats in the house.

Loki   18 | 19 | 20 | $6

304 Fifth Ave. (2nd St.), Brooklyn, M/R to Union St., 718-965-9600; www.lokilounge.com

With a vibe "somewhere between a frat house and an Elks club", this "split-personality" Park Sloper features a "low-key" barroom as well as an "extensive lounge area" that works for "mushy dates"; a fireplace, pool table, darts and an "outdoor patio" cement its something-for-everyone approach.

Lolita   20 | 18 | 19 | $7

266 Broome St. (bet. Allen & Orchard Sts.), F/J/M/Z to Delancey/Essex Sts., 212-966-7223; www.lolitabar.net

"Far from the unwashed hipster masses", this "undiscovered" Lower East Side bar is "never crowded" (but "not in a creepy way") and exhibits "zip" via "interesting art" that changes monthly and been-around-forever flea-market furniture; it "meets your basic drinking/socializing needs" with "reasonable prices" and "no attitude."

Long Tan   20 | 19 | 19 | $9

196 Fifth Ave. (bet. Berkeley Pl. & Union St.), Brooklyn, M/R to Union St., 718-622-8444; www.long-tan.com

"Neighborhoody and low-key", this "hip" Park Slope Thai features its own "cozy" bar area and "draws a good crowd" with "fun froufrou drinks", notably its blood orange Cosmo; though prices skew "high", the mood's "down-to-earth" and the bartenders "interesting characters."

L'Orange Bleue   22 | 16 | 17 | $9

430 Broome St. (Crosby St.), R/W to Prince St., 212-226-4999; www.lorangebleue.com

Always "festive" ("is it everyone's birthday tonight?"), this SoHo French-Moroccan is "like a night in Marrakech", particularly on Mondays when a belly dancer gyrates; it's "not so noisy" during the rest of the week but come the weekend it can get "crowded and uncomfortable quickly."

Loreley   22 | 17 | 19 | $7

7 Rivington St. (bet. Bowery & Chrystie St.), J/M/Z to Bowery, 212-253-7077; www.loreleynyc.com

It's "Oktoberfest all year long" at this "authentic" German "hideaway" hidden on the fringes of the Lower East Side, offering "tasty beers" from the Cologne region and a "real Bavarian beer garden" in which to sample them; fence-sitters say it's "no Zum Schneider, but close enough" – and "less crowded" to boot.

Lot 61   18 | 18 | 15 | $12

550 W. 21st St. (bet. 10th & 11th Aves.), C/E to 23rd St., 212-243-6555; www.lot61.com

"Trendy back in the day" – "not sure what it is now" – this "arty" West Chelsea lounge from club queen Amy Sacco draws mixed reviews: some say it's "going fairly strong" thanks to "aesthetically pleasing patrons" and an encyclopedic "martini list", but foes fret this "has-been" "used to be perfect . . . not anymore."

LOTUS

21 | 22 | 15 | $13 |

409 W. 14th St. (bet. 9th Ave. & Washington St.), A/C/E/L to 14th St./8th Ave., 212-243-4420; www.lotusnewyork.com

The "Meatpacking District spot that started it all", this "posh" pioneer has seen "some of its shine wear off" and stalwarts report they've thankfully "lost the attitude" as a result; but more say they've also "lost their edge" ("everyone can get in now") and besides "putting a dent in your wallet", it will only "thrill those from Milwaukee."

Lotus Lounge

20 | 20 | 18 | $9 |

35 Clinton St. (Stanton St.), F/J/M/Z to Delancey/Essex Sts., 212-253-1144

This "true neighborhood hangout" has a dual personality, vending coffee and sandwiches by day and morphing into a "bar by night"; it's everything you'd "expect from a Lower East Side place": "small", "funky" and "arty."

Louis

– | – | – | M |

649 E. Ninth St. (bet. Aves. B & C), L to 1st Ave., 212-673-1190

"Soothing" is the word for this "small", no-frills East Village bar, a "wonderful date place" given its out-of-the-way address and "great service"; but some say a "change in management has made it less appealing", particularly now that the former owner's "dog is gone."

LQ

19 | 21 | 16 | $11 |

Radisson Lexington Hotel, 511 Lexington Ave. (bet. 47th & 48th Sts.), 6 to 51st St./Lexington Ave., 212-593-7575; www.lqny.com

"Music with a Latin tinge" provides *la vida loca* at this "flashy" Midtown club, a "huge" underground space centered around a "unique sunken dance floor" outfitted with "bars along the perimeter"; invariably "buzzing with energy", it draws mainly "B&T teenyboppers", not that there's anything wrong with that.

Luca Lounge ∌

20 | 19 | 16 | $9 |

220 Ave. B (bet. 13th & 14th Sts.), L to 1st Ave., 212-674-9400; www.lucaloungenyc.com

Luca Bar

119 St. Marks Pl. (bet. Ave. A & 1st Ave.), L to 1st Ave., 212-254-1511; www.lucaloungenyc.com

It's all about the "amazing back garden" – "one of the best in the East Village" – at this "fun" lounge that's decorated inside with "*Friends*-like" "old comfy couches"; while it has a "different vibe during the week" (i.e. more "relaxed"), all around it's a "very chill hang"; P.S. the more basic St. Marks Place satellite is new and unrated.

Lucky Cat ∌

– | – | – | M |

245 Grand St. (bet. Driggs Ave. & Roebling St.), Brooklyn, J/M/Z to Marcy Ave., 718-782-0437; www.theluckycat.com

'Something for everyone' could be the motto of this Williamsburg combination of coffeehouse, lounge and performance space set on rapidly gentrifying Grand Street; the mood's "relaxed", the crowd's equally "laid-back" and there's even a backyard complete with a "koi pond" for alfresco imbibing.

Lucky Jack's

– | – | – | M |

129 Orchard St. (bet. Delancey & Rivington Sts.), F/J/M/Z to Delancey/ Essex Sts., 212-477-6555; www.luckyjacksnyc.com

A looong bar that extends all the way from Orchard Street to Allen Street is the key element of this brick-walled Lower East Side Irish newcomer that thus offers two entrances made for quick getaways; if that's not roomy enough for you, a downstairs lounge opens at peak times to absorb the overflow.

Lucky Strike
18 | 16 | 17 | $9

*59 Grand St. (bet. W. B'way & Wooster St.), A/C/E to Canal St., 212-941-0479;
www.luckystrikeny.com*
One of Keith McNally's first eateries, this "reliable" SoHo French bistro
is like a "quieter, less hip version of Pastis" – and "that's not a bad
thing"; "since the smoking ban, it's become less of a scene" and more
of a restaurant, though some bon vivants say it "still has its moments."

Lucky 13 Saloon ⌐
– | – | – | M

*273 13th St. (bet. 5th & 6th Aves.), Brooklyn, F/M/R to 4th Ave./9th St.,
718-499-7553; www.lucky13saloon.com*
Still Brooklyn's only 'full-time punk metal death rock alternative bar',
this "wild ride" in Park Slope is decorated with lots of Goth doodads
beneath a ceiling wallpapered with concert posters; while its crowd
can be both "scary and fun", the "owners are the nicest people."

Lucy's
∇ 26 | 13 | 22 | $5

135 Ave. A (bet. 9th St. & St. Marks Pl.), 6 to Astor Pl., 212-673-3824
A "perfect total dump", this "old favorite" East Village dive is a strictly
"no-frills", "impromptu" kind of place jazzed up by a couple of pool
tables and a "killer jukebox"; the "drinks are strong" (and "cheap"),
and owner "Lucy's hair is always fun to look at."

Luke & Leroy
∇ 17 | 12 | 17 | $8

*21 Seventh Ave. S. (Leroy St.), 1 to Houston St., 212-645-0004;
www.lukeandleroy.com*
"Great parties" take place upstairs on the "spacious" dance floor of
this bi-level Village bar/lounge that's renowned for booking "dope DJs";
fans say it stays cooking "till the wee hours" when "lots of bar and
restaurant people" toddle in.

Luke's Bar & Grill ⌐
16 | 13 | 18 | $8

1394 Third Ave. (bet. 79th & 80th Sts.), 6 to 77th St., 212-249-7070
"Everyone knows everyone" at this longtime Upper East Side bar and
grill that lures a "preppy", "somewhat older crowd" ("especially when
Mike Wallace is there"); even if it's "not the most glamorous place in
town", it's "particularly well run" since the "owner's always around."

LUNA PARK
23 | 17 | 13 | $9

*Union Sq. Pavilion, 50 E. 17th St. (bet. B'way & Park Ave. S.), 4/5/6/L/N/Q/R/W
to 14th St./Union Sq., 212-475-8464*
"Wind down after work" with "young investment bankers and their
interns" at this alfresco Union Square spot, a seasonal offering that's
"great if you're 22 and just out of college"; maybe it's "expensive" and
you can "brew a beer faster than order one", but ultimately there's
nothing "better than drinking outdoors on a sunny day."

Lunasa
∇ 21 | 19 | 24 | $7

*126 First Ave. (bet. 7th St. & St. Marks Pl.), L to 1st Ave., 212-228-8580;
www.lunasabar.com*
For an "easygoing" night out, look no further than this East Village
Irish pub offering lots of "exposed brick" inside as well as a "nice
space out back" for "smoking and chilling"; even better, its "friendly"
staff knows how to "pour a great Guinness."

Lure Fishbar
– | – | – | E

(fka Canteen)

*142 Mercer St., downstairs (Prince St.), R/W to Prince St., 212-431-7676;
www.lurefishbar.com*
Set in the old Canteen space, this new SoHo seafooder is a "surprisingly
desirable haunt" thanks to a luxurious, private-yacht feel via portholes,

chrome handrails and white leather upholstery; a rocking "see-and-be-seen" scene at the bar keeps things lively after the dinner hour.

Lush
20 | 19 | 18 | $10

110 Duane St. (bet. B'way & Church St.), 1/2/3 to Chambers St., 212-766-1275; www.lush-lounge.com
The "off-the-beaten-path" address makes this TriBeCa lounge a "well-kept secret" and diehards "hope it will remain that way"; although a "solid backup spot" with a dark, "chic" setting, some say this "once-happening" place is "struggling to attract" a following.

MacDougal Street Ale House
16 | 12 | 16 | $7

122 MacDougal St. (bet. Bleecker & W. 3rd Sts.), A/B/C/D/E/F/V to W. 4th St., 212-254-8569
In the midst of the "touristy heart of the Village" lies this "dingy hole-in-the-wall" that draws plenty of "college kids" with "cheap drinks", darts, pool and sports on the tube; patrons who have "no concept of what time of day it is" are part of the package.

Madame X
19 | 19 | 17 | $9

94 W. Houston St. (bet. La Guardia Pl. & Thompson St.), A/B/C/D/E/F/V to W. 4th St., 212-539-0808; www.madamexnyc.com
Tricked out like a "belle epoque" brothel, this "racy" Village lounge is part "*Moulin Rouge*", part "*Rocky Horror Show*", and so "red" that some "feel like they're on Mars"; the "dark, dark, dark" back room and "cuddly" rear garden/smokers' heaven are "sufficiently sexy and sultry" enough to lead to "wicked" ideas.

Mad River
15 | 12 | 15 | $7

1442 Third Ave. (bet. 81st & 82nd Sts.), 4/5/6 to 86th St., 212-988-1832; www.madrivergrille.com
Brace yourself for a "full-on frat party" at this Yorkville bar and grill where folks can to "relive their college days" with cheap "tap beer and bottom-shelf booze"; it's "usually packed to the gills" on weekends with "rowdy" dudes shooting for a "one-night hookup", and so long as you don't mind "drinks being spilled on you", it can be a great "de-stresser."

Maggie's Place
15 | 14 | 17 | $7

21 E. 47th St. (bet. 5th & Madison Aves.), B/D/F/V to 47-50th Sts./ Rockefeller Ctr., 212-753-5757
For "reliable after-work" drinking in Midtown, fans tout this "family-owned" Irish bar offering "efficient service" and "good weekday happy hours"; despite "not bad" pub grub and a "comfortable" mood, some find it "not especially remarkable."

Magician ∅
15 | 13 | 17 | $6

118 Rivington St. (Essex St.), F/J/M/Z to Delancey/Essex Sts., 212-673-7851
The "only place on Rivington where you can actually get a seat on weekends", this underemployed spot comes through with a "fantabulous jukebox" and "no attitude" whatsoever; still, a few call it the "least magical bar on the Lower East Side" owing to plain Jane decor and "rude" bartenders.

Magnetic Field
20 | 18 | 20 | $6

97 Atlantic Ave. (bet. Henry & Hicks Sts.), Brooklyn, 2/3/4/5/M/R to Borough Hall, 718-834-0069; www.magneticbrooklyn.com
There's "no hipper-than-thou 'tude" at this "laid-back" "alternative" bar on the Brooklyn Heights/Carroll Gardens rim offering everything from "Ms. Pac-Man" to "poetry readings" to "wacky" live band karaoke; if all that's not enough, an "old-fashioned photo booth" comes to the rescue if "conversation gets a little dull."

Maison
∇ 16 | 20 | 10 | $9

1700 Broadway (bet. 53rd & 54th Sts.), B/D/E to 7th Ave./53rd St., 212-757-2233; www.maisonnyc.com
An "oasis in the madness" of the Theater District, this "oh-so-French" bistro may not be known for its bar scene, but is worth remembering for its 24/7 open-door policy and "huge" outdoor patio; still, foes bemoan the "intolerably slow service" and "flock-of-tourists" crowd.

Makor
21 | 17 | 20 | $8

35 W. 67th St. (bet. Columbus Ave. & CPW), 1 to 66th St., 212-601-1000
"Something for everyone" could be the motto of this Upper West Side bar/cultural center that pairs a "Jewish singles scene" with an "eclectic mix of venues and events" drawing "culture vultures" of all ages; it works "whether you're spiritually minded or not", and the "crowd varies depending on the music that evening."

Malachy's
15 | 6 | 16 | $5

103 W. 72nd St. (bet. B'way & Columbus Ave.), 1/2/3 to 72nd St., 212-874-4268
Best known as the "last bar before the express subway train", this Upper West Side Irish dive is home to an "interesting mix" of rowdy "young collegians" just blown in and "old men who have been there all day"; given the "over-the-hill" bartenders and pervasive scent of "stale beer", this one's "for serious drinkers only."

Mama's Bar
– | – | – | M

200 E. Third St. (Ave. B), F/V to Lower East Side/2nd Ave., 212-777-4425; www.mamasfoodshop.com
Next door to the much loved Mama's Food Shop lies this funky East Village barroom, a down-home destination with unfinished concrete walls and a country-western jukebox; the only signage is a green awning still advertising its former incarnation as a deli, but big windows facing Avenue B make its business plain to passersby.

Mambi Lounge
– | – | – | M

933 Second Ave. (bet. 49th & 50th Sts.), 6 to 51st St./Lexington Ave., 212-832-3500; www.mambilounge.com
This new Midtown bar/lounge brings some Latin zing to the Second Avenue corridor via mojitos and sangria served with Cuban sandwiches on the side; velvet banquettes supply a cushy air to the otherwise standard-issue setup.

Manhattan Lounge
22 | 22 | 21 | $9

1720 Second Ave. (bet. 89th & 90th Sts.), 4/5/6 to 86th St., 212-987-5555
Not your typical Upper East Side fratfest, this "dark and sexy" number features some of the "best blue drinks" in town at its front bar and a "quiet" back lounge for those yearning for "romance"; still, the slick, "big city look" to the contrary, locals report it's "kind of empty."

Manitoba's
20 | 17 | 19 | $6

99 Ave. B (bet. 6th & 7th Sts.), F/V to Lower East Side/2nd Ave., 212-982-2511; www.manitobas.com
"Rub leather-clad elbows" with "retired hard-core musicians" at this "no-frills" punk bar owned (and occasionally bartended) by Dictators front man, 'Handsome Dick' Manitoba; fans who come to "pay homage" to "how the East Village should be" say it's "like walking into history."

Mannahatta
18 | 19 | 15 | $10

316 Bowery (Bleecker St.), 6 to Bleecker St., 212-253-8644; www.mannahatta.us
"Usually packed", this "happening" NoHo lounge arranged on "two levels" has "two vibes": "laid-back and classy" in the living room–ish upstairs, and "slamming" in the basement dance club (that's "so dark

no one can see your bad moves"); downsides include "pricey" pops and management that "wouldn't last one week on *The Apprentice*."

Margarita & Murphy's
– | – | – | M

(fka P.J. Carney's)

591 Third Ave. (bet. 38th & 39th Sts.), 4/5/6/7/S to 42nd St./Grand Central, 212-684-4421

Despite the name, this Murray Hill barroom is more Irish pub than south-of-the-border cantina, populated by the usual frat-centric crowd that you've come to expect on the Third Avenue strip.

Marie's Crisis ⊄
21 | 9 | 16 | $7

59 Grove St. (bet. Bleecker St. & 7th Ave. S.), 1 to Christopher St., 212-243-9323

"Old chorus boys reminisce about their glory days" and "sing along" at this Village piano bar "blast" where "show tune aficionados abound", both gay and straight alike; regulars advise "if you don't know the words to *The Sound of Music*", "just keep drinking."

Marion's Continental
▽ 25 | 23 | 22 | $10

354 Bowery (bet. 4th & Great Jones Sts.), 6 to Astor Pl., 212-475-7621; www.marionsnyc.com

A shot of "pure kitschy fun", this "entertaining" NoHo eatery/"retro cocktail" dispenser features an "ultracool", "let's-do-the-time-warp-again" setting enhanced by a swell martini list and a few random "drag queens"; fans say "if you're not having fun here", you either "need medication or are on the wagon."

MARK'S BAR
24 | 25 | 24 | $13

Mark Hotel, 25 E. 77th St. (bet. 5th & Madison Aves.), 6 to 77th St., 212-744-4300; www.markhotel.com

"Impress your in-laws" at this Upper East Side "class act" in the Mark Hotel, a "discreet" den "away from the rat race" with "knowledgeable bartenders" and "English country manor" decor; while "secluded" and "expensive" enough to wow a "special one", it may be "a bit stuffy" for younger types.

MARKT
19 | 19 | 18 | $10

401 W. 14th St. (9th Ave.), A/C/E/L to 14th St./8th Ave., 212-727-3314

The "looong bar" might soak up the "overflow from more popular" Meatpacking District spots, but this "huge" brasserie–cum–"Belgian beer candy store" holds its own thanks to a "European feel" and lots of "outdoor seating"; the "meat markt" vibe and "noisy" "carnival atmosphere" turn off some, but ultimately it's one of the more "approachable" in the nabe.

MARQUEE
23 | 21 | 17 | $13

289 10th Ave. (bet. 26th & 27th Sts.), C/E to 23rd St., 646-473-0202; www.marqueeny.com

It's "models and bottles" galore at this West Chelsea lounge from Jason Strauss and Noah Tepperberg where "skinny" "A-listers" "sail past the guards" at one of the "most impenetrable doors" in town; inside, the upstairs "celeb"-friendly VIP area is the place to be, but wherever you wind up, "money talks" – so be ready to "shell out some serious cash" for a seat or "be left standing with the peons"; word to the wise: "don't show up with a pack of guys."

Mars Bar ⊄
14 | 12 | 13 | $5

25 E. First St. (2nd Ave.), F/V to Lower East Side/2nd Ave., 212-473-9842

A "right of passage" for "derelicts only", this "skanky", "smelly", "dingy", "dirty" East Village dive is made for folks who like "feisty" service and "get a kick out of slumming"; but those "scared out of their wits" advise, "watch your purse", "don't use the bathroom" and only "order beer in cans or bottles."

Marseille

20 21 20 $10

630 Ninth Ave. (44th St.), A/C/E to 42nd St./Port Authority, 212-333-3410; www.marseillenyc.com

"Escape the fratty crowds" on Ninth Avenue at this "classy" French-Moroccan bar/eatery that draws "older" types with a "wonderful wine list" served by "bartenders who really know their stuff"; the Hell's Kitchen address makes it a natural for "post-theater drinks", even if it's a "little high-priced."

Mars 2112

18 22 16 $10

1633 Broadway (51st St.), 1 to 50th St., 212-582-2112; www.mars2112.com

"Great for having drinks when you can't get a babysitter", this Midtown outer-space themer offers "spacey cocktails" and a "silly", "kitschy" setting, starting with a "motion ride" at the entrance; but alienated types call it a "onetime" only affair what with the "totally tourist" crowd and "big bar bills."

Martell's

16 13 18 $7

200 E. 83rd St. (3rd Ave.), 4/5/6 to 86th St., 212-879-1717; www.martellsnyc.com

The "next step after the college bar scene", this East Side "yuppie prepster" magnet is where "Buffy, Binky and Sloane" show up "before or after Dorrian's"; nothing about it has "changed in 20 years", including the "generic classic rock" soundtrack.

Martignetti Liquors

– – – M

(fka Carnaval)

159 E. Houston St. (bet. Allen & Eldridge Sts.), F/J/M/Z to Delancey/ Essex Sts., 212-995-0330

A light reworking of the former Carnaval space, this Lower East Side duplex is now a self described 'dive nightclub', with a vaguely tropical upstairs lounge and a darker, dance floor–equipped den below; famed for its 'white trash bottle service' (a $120 case of beer on ice), it also boasts the cheapest bottle service in town, with top-shelf labels topping off at $200.

Martini Red ⊅

– – – M

372 Van Duzer St. (Beach St.), Staten Island, 718-442-9362; www.martini-red.com

Downtown comes to Staten Island via this "fun" bar/lounge, a red-lit den offering a variety of entertainment, everything from DJs to live performances to film screenings to open mike nights; no surprise, it's considered one of the "best" in an underserved nightlife area.

Matchless ⊅

▽ 20 19 25 $5

557 Manhattan Ave. (Driggs Ave.), Brooklyn, G to Nassau Ave., 718-383-5333; www.barmatchless.com

"Young arty" locals are drawn to this Greenpoint tavern housed in a former garage and affording "lots of different areas to sit and have a conversation"; it's "quieter and chiller" than nearby Enid's, with an "excellent jukebox" and a "rarely used foosball table."

MATSURI

24 27 20 $13

Maritime Hotel, 369 W. 16th St. (9th Ave.), A/C/E/L to 14th St./8th Ave., 212-243-6400; www.themaritimehotel.com

A "majestic", soaring underground space (one of the "most stylish" in town) is the setting for this "sooo trendy" Japanese restaurant/bar in the Maritime Hotel, where "Asian-inspired cocktails" and an "incredible sake" list lure everyone from "bankers" to "rock stars" to "Eurotrash";

even if "prices are steep", after a few drinks, many are tempted to "upgrade to dinner."

Matt's Grill
19 | 14 | 21 | $7

932 Eighth Ave. (bet. 55th & 56th Sts.), 1/A/B/C/D to 59th St./Columbus Circle, 212-307-5109

"Neighborhood places" don't get much more "friendly" than this "unpretentious" Hell's Kitchen pub where the grub is as "homey" as the mood; city slickers find "nothing special" going on at this "generic" place, but more rate it "great all-around."

Max Fish ⊅
19 | 16 | 17 | $7

178 Ludlow St. (bet. Houston & Stanton Sts.), F/V to Lower East Side/ 2nd Ave., 212-529-3959; www.maxfish.com

"Catch professional skateboarders in their natural environment" at this Lower East Side "institution", a "come-as-you-are", "no-frills" bar that's "resisted the steady gentrification around it"; maybe the "lights are too bright" and the crowd "infrequently bathed", but at least the "beer's cheap and cold."

M Bar
– | – | – | E

Mansfield Hotel, 12 W. 44th St. (bet. 5th & 6th Aves.), 7/B/D/F/V to 42nd St./ 6th Ave., 212-277-8888; www.mansfieldhotel.com

"Small" and "elegant", this hotel lobby bar near Times Square is a sweet spot in which to "unwind with a Cosmo or two" after work; set in what was a former reading room, the book-lined space is both "classy" and "romantic", and far enough off the beaten track to have clandestine affair written all over it.

M Bar
21 | 20 | 21 | $11

(aka Masat)

349 Broome St. (bet. Bowery & Elizabeth St.), J/M/Z to Bowery, 212-274-0667

The 'M' stands for "mmm" at this "terrific" Little Italy barroom with a "speakeasy" vibe and "kick-ass bartenders"; even though on the "small" side, it "doesn't feel too crowded" and a "DJ willing to listen to your requests" keeps the party hopping.

McAleer's Pub
15 | 10 | 19 | $6

425 Amsterdam Ave. (bet. 80th & 81st Sts.), 1 to 79th St., 212-874-8037; www.mcaleerspub.com

"Why go all the way to Ireland" for a "good pint" when there's this "old-school" Upper West Side Irish pub, an "unassuming" slice of Eire parked on a "street of college bars"; ok, it may be "stereotypical" and a bit "down at the heels", but it's a "decent" enough joint to "catch a game."

McCormack's
∇ 20 | 15 | 21 | $8

365 Third Ave. (26th St.), 6 to 28th St., 212-683-0911; www.mccormacks.net

Televised "rugby and soccer matches" are the draws at this Gramercy Irish pub that's the "real deal" when it comes to "hanging out and having fun"; admirers admit it "always seems to lift their spirits", citing a particularly "spot-on Guinness pour."

McCormick & Schmick's
18 | 17 | 20 | $11

1285 Sixth Ave. (52nd St., bet. 6th & 7th Aves.), N/Q/R/W to 57th St./7th Ave., 212-459-1222; www.mccormickandschmicks.com

"Schmooze with business folks" as you slurp down "martinis and oysters" at this Midtown link of the national seafood chain; while some find it too "generic" ("you could just as well be in Cleveland"), it works well for those "over the hill but still in denial" about it.

McFadden's
16 | 13 | 17 | $7

800 Second Ave. (42nd St.), 4/5/6/7/S to 42nd St./Grand Central, 212-986-1515; www.mcfaddens42.com

Aka "McFratten's", this Irish pub near the UN gets "packed to the gills" on Thursday nights with "preppy professionals in blue striped shirts" and "sorority girls" who "flirt their way through the evening and end up dancing on the bar"; despite "slow" service and "typical" pub looks, stalwarts swear it's a "safe bet."

McGee's
20 | 16 | 22 | $6

240 W. 55th St. (bet. B'way & 8th Ave.), 1/A/B/C/D to 59th St./Columbus Circle, 212-957-3536; www.mcgeespub.com

"Fast and friendly service" is the hallmark of this "fun" Midtown Irishman, a "relaxing" double-decker that's a magnet for local nine-to-fivers; a fireplace and "great jukebox" make it a "solid" favorite.

McHales ⌿
19 | 13 | 19 | $6

750 Eighth Ave. (46th St.), A/C/E to 42nd St./Port Authority, 212-997-8885

There's "no need to dress up" for this "incognito", "dark 'n' dingy" joint that's "been around forever" and is equally renowned for "hockey on the TV" and "huge", juicy burgers on the plate; in fact, this "escape from the tourists" is one of the "few places in the Theater District where you feel like you're among fellow New Yorkers."

MCSORLEY'S ⌿
22 | 16 | 17 | $6

15 E. Seventh St. (bet. 2nd & 3rd Aves.), 6 to Astor Pl., 212-254-2570

"Not for the faint of heart", this "manly", "noisy" Irish bar offers a basic choice of "light or dark" ale served by "uncouth" waiters who appear to "have been there since it opened" in 1854; a "last outpost" of a "long bygone NY", it's become a "right of passage" for "beer-chugging" young "meatheads."

McSwiggan's
14 | 7 | 13 | $6

393 Second Ave. (bet. 22nd & 23rd Sts.), 6 to 23rd St., 212-725-8740

"Get in touch with your inner frat boy" at this Gramercy Irish dive, a "homey dump" with "basic" amenities like darts, pool and video games; while harmlessly "typical" to some, others say the "only reason to go is if you live within a two-block radius."

Meet
18 | 20 | 17 | $11

71-73 Gansevoort St. (Washington St.), A/C/E/L to 14th St./8th Ave., 212-242-0990; www.the-meet.com

"Chic appointments" and a "beautiful crowd" lend a "night-on-the-town feel" to this Meatpacking District bar/eatery that's "mellowed out since it first opened"; some wonder why it "never seems to get crowded anymore", though diehards insist this "underrated" joint is "still hot."

MEGU
25 | 28 | 22 | $15

62 Thomas St. (bet. Church St. & W. B'way), 1/2/3 to Chambers St., 212-964-7777; www.megunyc.com

"Drop-dead beautiful" describes both the setting and those seated at this "over-the-top" TriBeCa Japanese extravaganza, a renowned restaurant topped by an equally "happening" upstairs lounge known for its "extensive selection of sake"; of course, you'll need megu-bucks when the check comes, but even if you "break the bank, you'll do it in style" here.

Mehanata 416 B.C. ⌿
– | – | – | M

416 Broadway (Canal St.), 6/J/M/N/Q/R/W/Z to Canal St., 212-625-0981; www.mehanata.com

"Nothing is better than jumping up and down to Eastern European techno" at this "fun" Bulgarian bar on the TriBeCa/SoHo border; since it's a "rowdy" space with "dancing on every available surface", ladies are advised to "wear sneakers and a sports bra."

Mercantile Grill   17 14 20 $9

126 Pearl St. (bet. Hanover Sq. & Wall St.), 2/3/4/5 to Wall St., 212-482-1221
"Engineers, bankers and people waiting for the ferry" populate this Financial District bar/eatery where the "burgers are terrific" but the "selection of tap beers could be improved"; ignore the "boring" decor and focus on the "friendly Irish" staff instead.

Merc Bar   21 21 18 $10

151 Mercer St. (bet. Houston & Prince Sts.), R/W to Prince St., 212-966-2727; www.mercbar.com
"Well-made cocktails" stir surveyors at this "chill" SoHo lounge, an Adirondacks lodge–like affair that's been around so long that there's "no bottle policy for table seating"; "quiet" these days (but ever "hip"), it's "never tough to get into", so why not "hang out and catch up with old friends"?

Mercer Bar   23 23 19 $13

Mercer Hotel, 99 Prince St. (Mercer St.), R/W to Prince St., 212-966-5454; www.jean-georges.com
"Live like a rock star – and pay like a rock star" – at this "chic" SoHo hotel bar where the "decor's minimal, but the crowd's anything but", comprised of "black-clad urbanites" and a few "show biz hip types"; there may be a whiff of "attitude" in the air, but overall it remains a "good scene after all these years."

Merchants, N.Y.   18 18 17 $10

1125 First Ave. (62nd St.), 4/5/6/N/R/W to 59th St./Lexington Ave., 212-832-1551
112 Seventh Ave. (bet. 16th & 17th Sts.), 1 to 18th St., 212-366-7267
www.merchantsny.com
"You know what you'll get" at these "reliable" restaurant/bar "staples" with "cozy fireplaces", "comfy couches" and legal smoking (in the First Avenue branch's downstairs cigar lounge); though foes say they've got "no distinct personality" and are getting "dated", at least they're fairly "easy on the wallet."

Mercury Bar   16 14 16 $8

659 Ninth Ave. (46th St.), C/E to 50th St., 212-262-7755
493 Third Ave. (bet. 33rd & 34th Sts.), 6 to 33rd St., 212-683-2645
www.mercurybarnyc.com
"Suck down some beers and yell at the TVs" at these "busy" "frat central" satellites where the "women are looking for husbands" and the men are looking to "hook up"; though the Hell's Kitchen branch is "more low-key than its Murray Hill sibling", both are "basically clones of Joshua Tree."

Mercury Lounge   20 14 16 $7

217 E. Houston St. (bet. Essex & Ludlow Sts.), F/V to Lower East Side/2nd Ave., 212-260-4700; www.mercuryloungenyc.com
Maybe the "bar scene isn't that great" given the "way narrow" layout, but "everyone comes for the music anyway" at this Lower Eastsider known for showcasing "generally unsigned bands"; despite "snide bouncers", it's "smaller than the average rock joint", and thus offers a "better, closer" view of the stage.

Mesa Grill   21 21 22 $12

102 Fifth Ave. (bet. 15th & 16th Sts.), 4/5/6/L/N/Q/R/W to 14th St./Union Sq., 212-807-7400; www.mesagrill.com
A "quick drink after work" could lead to "staying for dinner" at celeb chef Bobby Flay's Flatiron Southwesterner where most of the "people

at the bar are waiting to be seated"; an "excellent variety of tequila" is the basis for some of the "best margaritas in the city", served by a "crisp, professional" staff.

Métrazur   20 | 22 | 18 | $12

Grand Central Terminal, East Balcony (bet. 42nd St. & Park Ave.), 4/5/6/7/S to 42nd St./Grand Central, 212-687-4600; www.metrazur.com

"Watch the world rush by" from the balcony of Grand Central Station at this "classy little" American brasserie that burnishes the "magnificent view" with "delicious" cocktails; sure, it's "noisy" and "pricey", and the crowd "commuter"-centric, but some enjoy it so much they're willing to "miss one or two more trains."

Metro 53   16 | 15 | 17 | $8

307 E. 53rd St. (bet. 1st & 2nd Aves.), E/V to Lexington Ave./53rd St., 212-838-0007; www.metro53.com

Metro Loft

305 E. 53rd St., 2nd fl. (bet. 1st & 2nd Aves.), E/V to Lexington Ave./53rd St., 212-838-0007

It may be "roomy", but this "popular" East Side bar sure "gets crowded", especially during the "loud, packed happy hour" where there's "no place" to move; while the "aircraft hangar ambiance" has "no character", most are too focused on "hook-up" possibilities to notice; P.S. the lesser known Metro Loft next door is a better option for the claustrophobic.

Metro Grill Roof Garden ⌐∀   ▽ 22 | 17 | 16 | $10

Metro Hotel, 45 W. 35th St. (bet. 5th & 6th Aves.), B/D/F/N/Q/R/V/W to 34th St./Herald Sq., 212-279-3535; www.hotelmetronyc.com

Take in the "great outdoors" at this seasonal Garment District rooftop bar boasting "phenomenal views" of Midtown and the Empire State Building; but high-maintenance types cite drinks served in "plastic cups" and claim the bare-bones setup is "hardly worth mentioning."

Metropolitan ⌐∀   ▽ 21 | 16 | 19 | $6

559 Lorimer St. (bet. Devoe St. & Metropolitan Ave.), Brooklyn, G/L to Metropolitan Ave./Lorimer St., 718-599-4444

"Cheap, fun" and "local", this Williamsburg gay/lesbian bar features a "popular pool table", "two roaring fireplaces" and a "huge backyard" for "neighborhood hipsters" to get lost in; it may be somewhat of a "hole-in-the-wall", but at least its "experienced" crowd is very "friendly."

METROPOLITAN MUSEUM ROOF GARDEN   27 | 27 | 15 | $10

Metropolitan Museum, 1000 Fifth Ave. (bet. 81st & 82nd Sts.), 4/5/6 to 86th St., 212-879-5500

It's "too bad it's only open a few months of the year", as this "must-see" seasonal rooftop above the Met offers "spectacular" views of Central Park and attracts a crowd of "fine young things"; sure, it "closes way too early", the "drinks are overpriced" and "seating options are sparse", but no one cares given the "New Yorkiness of it all."

Mexican Radio   19 | 16 | 19 | $8

19 Cleveland Pl. (bet. Kenmare & Spring Sts.), 6 to Spring St., 212-343-0140; www.mexrad.com

"Sweetly prepared margaritas" take center stage at this "cool little" NoLita cantina, but be wary as "more than one might knock you out"; it's "mainly a locals' hangout" thanks to a somewhat obscure address, though once inside both the bartenders and the crowd are "friendly."

Mica Bar
18 | 18 | 17 | $9

252 E. 51st St. (bet. 2nd & 3rd Aves.), 6 to 51st St./Lexington Ave., 212-888-2453
587 Third Ave. (bet. 38th & 39th Sts.), 4/5/6/7/S to 42nd St./Grand Central,
212-661-3181
www.micabar.com
These "comfortable" watering holes cater to "lively after-work" types, though many say the 51st Street "original is better", given its split-level layout and "cool" outdoor deck (complete with retractable roof); the newer Murray Hill offspring, by contrast, "still has a way to go in bringing in the crowds."

Michael Jordan's
The Steak House
18 | 20 | 18 | $13

Grand Central Terminal, West Balcony (42nd St. & Vanderbilt Ave.), 4/5/6/7/S to
42nd St./Grand Central, 212-655-2300; www.theglaziergroup.com
"Grand Central Concourse is the backdrop" for this Midtown chop shop/wine bar that's most "relaxing" compared to the jaw-dropping view of "frenzied commuters" below; its "right-in-the-middle-of-everything" location makes it just the ticket "for a quickie", but have a "gold Amex" handy when the bill comes.

Mickey Mantle's
17 | 18 | 16 | $10

42 Central Park S. (bet. 5th & 6th Aves.), N/R/W to 5th Ave./59th St.,
212-688-7777
"Baseball nuts" congregate to "talk sports" at this Central Park South shrine to No. 7, offering "good stuff on tap" and lots of souvenirs to commemorate your visit; diehards deem it an out-of-the-park "hit", but natives protest this "tourist trap" is "nothing special besides the name."

Micky's Blue Room
– | – | – | M

171 Ave. C (bet. 10th & 11th Sts.), L to 1st Ave., 212-375-0723;
www.mickysblueroom.com
A "comfortable neighborhood" dive, this "real" East Village joint hidden way out of the way on Avenue C has no cover, "no attitude" and "no wannabe trendy Upper Eastsiders" present; instead, look for pool, darts, video games and occasional live music, all overseen by a "friendly" staff.

Milady's
16 | 7 | 16 | $6

162 Prince St. (Thompson St.), R/W to Prince St., 212-226-9340
"Walking the line" between "down and dirty" dive and "quirky alternative bar", this SoHo spot stands out in an "otherwise trendy" area; an "interesting cross section of humanity" (mostly "lowbrows") shows up to get "sloppy drunk", play pool and cope with the "barely functioning bathroom."

MILK AND HONEY
27 | 24 | 25 | $12

134 Eldridge St. (bet. Broome & Delancey Sts.), J/M/Z to Bowery,
unlisted phone
Imagine "you're living during Prohibition" at this "famously discreet", "speakeasy"-esque Lower Eastsider accessed only by calling a "secret phone number" and "reserving a booth" in advance (it's the "Rao's of bars"); insiders say the "to-die-for cocktails" are "expensive but worth it", and are afraid that this "calm, cool oasis" is becoming "a bit too known."

miniBar ⊽
– | – | – | M

482 Court St. (bet. 4th & Luquer Sts.), Brooklyn, F to Carroll St., 718-874-6579
A lot of personalities are packed into a square, brick Carroll Gardens space as diminutive as the name implies: low banquettes line one wall and high stools and tables take up another, while 20-year-old

ports share the drink menu with kitschy Girl Scout martinis; still, the attitude is well-integrated, Brooklyn palsy-walsy.

Miracle Grill
22 19 20 $9

415 Bleecker St. (bet. Bank & W. 11th Sts.), 1 to Christopher St., 212-924-1900
112 First Ave. (bet. 6th & 7th Sts.), L to 1st Ave., 212-254-2353
222 Seventh Ave. (4th St.), Brooklyn, F to 7th Ave., 718-369-4541
www.miraclegrillny.com

"Kick-ass drinks" – "excellent margaritas", "unbelievable mojitos" – keep these Southwestern "workhorses" chugging along; though some find them "better restaurants than bars", the East Village satellite's "fantastic garden" is "great for a first date"; P.S. the Park Slope branch is new and unrated.

Mission
16 17 15 $9

217 Bowery (bet. Prince & Rivington Sts.), J/M/Z to Bowery, 212-473-3113;
www.missionnewyork.com

"Sink yourself in" for a sortie amid "diverse" loungers at this plush-enough duplex in a lower Bowery locale that may be "a little odd" but at least there's "no need to wait in line"; while heavy spenders will get their mission accomplished, holdouts allow it's "great in theory" but "too loud, too big" and edging "past its prime."

MJ Grill
17 17 18 $9

110 John St. (bet. Cliff & Pearl Sts.), A/C to B'way/Nassau, 212-346-9848

Part "pubby", part "sophisticated", MarkJoseph Steakhouse's Financial District sidekick is an "oasis" for "nice-looking businesspeople" thirsty for "after-work" action; though "quite expensive", it's a "reliable" "mingle" in a nabe where the other "options aren't as upscale."

MO BAR
26 25 21 $14

Mandarin Oriental Hotel, 80 Columbus Circle, 35th fl. (60th St.), 1/A/B/C/D to
59th St./Columbus Circle, 212-805-8800; www.mandarinoriental.com

Elites meet "far away from the riffraff" at the Mandarin Oriental Hotel's "very upscale" bar in the Time Warner Center, a "comfortable", "dimly lit" enclave where the MO includes "unusual drink concepts" and the usual "snooty" stylings; the "stunning" package comes with "mo' of a bill", but it's "worth it" to "impress a date" "at least one time."

Mocca
∇ 20 21 19 $10

78 Reade St. (Church St.), 1/2/3 to Chambers St., 212-233-7570;
www.moccalounge.com

Whether "a coffee bar or a bar bar" suits the mood, this "relaxing" TriBeCa newcomer obliges with java-based cocktails and other enticements to round out cafe fare like espresso and muffins; a metro-retro "European look" and "large windows" make it an "inviting" if "rarely buzzing" hang that's "much needed in the area."

Mod
17 19 15 $9

505 Columbus Ave. (bet. 84th & 85th Sts.), 1 to 86th St., 212-989-3600;
www.modnyc.com

"Enjoy the camp" urge the "twentysomething yuppies" who frequent this "lively" Upper West Side swingerama that channels DJ mojo and "Austin Powers' decorator" into a "'60s-like" sight for kaleidoscope eyes; ok, it's much "too crowded" and maybe even much "too much", but "trendy" types still "love the place", bay-bee.

Moda Outdoors
– – – E

Flatotel, 135 W. 52nd St. (bet. 6th & 7th Aves.), B/D/F/V to 47-50th Sts./
Rockefeller Ctr., 212-887-9880; www.flatotel.com

Set in a breezy covered atrium, this seasonal outdoor adjunct to a Midtown hotel is a "great pit stop" for local worker bees, attracting large, festive crowds; but be aware that the "scene dies off quickly" as the night wears on, so for many it's a "strictly after-work" place.

MODERN, THE   – | – | – | VE

MoMA, 9 W. 53rd St. (bet. 5th & 6th Aves.), E/V to 5th Ave./53rd St., 212-333-1220; www.themodernnyc.com

Danny Meyer's new two-pronged MoMA restaurant offers both casual and formal dining rooms, and falling somewhere between the two is the long marble-topped bar at the entrance; backed by a glass wall housing thousands of wine bottles and bracketed by a floor-to-ceiling photograph of a leafy forest, the minimally chic space is soothing and civilized enough to help ease the sticker shock.

Moe's ⊄   20 | 18 | 20 | $8

80 Lafayette Ave. (S. Portland Ave.), Brooklyn, C to Lafayette Ave., 718-797-9536

A "laid-back and liberal" "local" favorite "with funk", this "*Simpsons*"-inspired saloon is the "longstanding" default haunt for "all of Fort Greene", from "working stiffs" to "the young and hip"; "friendly" regulars and "great DJs" keep it "just crazy enough" for "good times on the low."

Molly's   23 | 20 | 21 | $7

287 Third Ave. (bet. 22nd & 23rd Sts.), 6 to 23rd St., 212-889-3361

"More Irish than Ireland", this "soulful" patch o' sod "always hits the spot" with sticklers for "old-school" essentials like a "layer of sawdust" underfoot, "hard-as-nails booths" and "downright charming" service ("complete with brogues"); loyal lads and lasses count a "wonderful fireplace" for a "winter nightcap" among the "cottage comforts."

Molly Wee Pub   ▽ 15 | 15 | 16 | $6

402 Eighth Ave. (30th St.), A/C/E to 34th St./Penn Station, 212-967-2627; www.mollyweepub.com

As a place to "meet your buddies before a game" or quaff "a quick pint" pre-train, this "consistent" fixture a wee way from Penn Station/MSG offers "genuine throwback" pleasures like TV sports and barmens' blarney; though somewhat "respectablized" these days, it still gets the basics done.

M1-5 Bar   ▽ 21 | 13 | 18 | $8

52 Walker St. (bet. B'way & Church St.), 1 to Canal St., 212-965-1701; www.m1-5.com

This "ginormous", red-lit TriBeCa barroom is "never crowded", despite "very reasonable prices" and plenty to keep one occupied: a pool table, digital jukebox, video games and huge projection TVs; still, critics carp it's "devoid of character" and cite a "10-minute wait to even get noticed" by the bartenders.

Monkey Bar   22 | 22 | 20 | $12

Elysée Hotel, 60 E. 54th St. (bet. Madison & Park Aves.), E/V to Lexington Ave./53rd St., 212-838-2600; www.theglaziergroup.com

The Elysée Hotel's "longtime favorite" for smart-set monkeyshines evokes a "bygone era" with its simian murals and "live piano", and still "gets packed" with "older" denizens of the urban jungle; some say the "stuffy" scene's "getting tired", but after a few "top-notch drinks", the "whimsical" nostalgia works just vine.

Monster, The ⊄   16 | 11 | 17 | $7

80 Grove St. (bet. Waverly Pl. & W. 4th St.), 1 to Christopher St., 212-924-3557; www.manhattan-monster.com

"If you like disco" or classic "Broadway numbers", this "all-inclusive" Village "staple of the gay club" circuit satisfies with a "faaabulous" piano-bar songfest upstairs and a "pulsing" '70s-style dance floor below; those with "traditional" tastes who don't mind "outer-borough" and "tourist" types shrug "what's not to like?"

Moonshine ⌿   – | – | – | M
317 Columbia St. (bet. Hamilton Ave. & Woodhull St.), Brooklyn, F/G to Smith/9th Sts., 718-422-0563
Locals in the Red Hook backwoods take a shine to this new "faux white-trash" joint boasting the requisite "great bourbon selection" (chased with "cheap canned brews"), "country classics" on the juke and a summer "beer garden"; if the whereabouts is a "transportation black hole", that's to be expected for a "diamond in the rough."

Moran's Chelsea   ∇ 20 | 18 | 23 | $9
146 10th Ave. (19th St.), C/E to 23rd St., 212-627-3030;
www.moranschelsea.com
From the "beautiful" fireplaces to the genial service, it's all "warm and friendly" at this Chelsea Gaelic steakhouse lodged in a circa-1834 space that "seems to wrap its arms around you"; tipplers count on a "fair pour" with "little pretense", though to best appreciate the milieu, regulars suggest "be over 40."

Morgans Bar   21 | 21 | 18 | $11
Morgans Hotel, 237 Madison Ave. (bet. 37th & 38th Sts.), 6 to 33rd St., 212-726-7600; www.morganshotelgroup.com
Extra-"dark" and "romantic", this "sexy" downstairs "hideaway" in a Murray Hill hotel is likened to a "genie's bottle" where PYTs perched on velvety seats nurse "designer martinis" by "candlelight"; it's always a "super-cool date spot" – "if you can afford it" – but scenesters acknowledge they're "there to impress, not to linger."

Morrisey Park   – | – | – | M
(fka Openair)
121 St. Marks Pl. (bet. Ave. A & 1st Ave.), L to 1st Ave., 212-979-1459;
www.morriseypark.com
While former occupant Openair was known as a hard-core DJ bar, this new incarnation is more of a middle-of-the-road affair with decent prices, vaguely lodgelike looks and a totally random crowd; a back-room art gallery lends some East Village cred to the scene.

MORTON'S OF CHICAGO   23 | 23 | 24 | $13
551 Fifth Ave. (45th St.), 4/5/6/7/S to 42nd St./Grand Central, 212-972-3315;
www.mortons.com
The "hustle and bustle" at this Midtown outpost of the chophouse chain extends to the bar, which corrals "business" barons out to "close the deal" over martinis and malts poured by "one of the best staffs in the city"; maybe it's "predictable" down to the top-shelf tabs, but "you get what you pay for" and there's "nothing wrong with that."

Mo's Caribbean   16 | 13 | 17 | $7
1454 Second Ave. (76th St.), 6 to 77th St., 212-650-0561;
www.nycbestbars.com
"Woo-hoo!", this "wild" Upper East Side sports bar is "packed and way rockin'" with "fruity frozen" elixirs setting the "happy-go-lucky" "pickup scene" in motion; those "island colors", "surfer trinkets" and "deadly drink deals" make for a mo' "festive" outing, but it may seem "incredibly cheesy" "if you're over 24."

Moto ⌿   – | – | – | M
394 Broadway (Hooper St.), Brooklyn, J/M/Z to Hewes St., 718-599-6895
Authentically "rustic" in Gallic farmhouse mode, this "cool little" tricorner restaurant/bar on the fringe of Williamsburg features quaint

pews, rough-hewn walls and a horseshoe counter dispensing beer and wine; admirers are moto-vated by the "wonderful service", "funky live music" and monthly screenings of films from area auteurs.

Motor City Bar ⌐
21 | 19 | 20 | $6

127 Ludlow St. (bet. Delancey & Rivington Sts.), F/J/M/Z to Delancey/Essex Sts., 212-358-1595

"Rock 'n' roll all night" with "motorcycle types" at this "dark", "grungy" Lower Eastsider, saluting Dee-troit city with "cheap" brews, "biker" colors and a metalhead DJ who "adds some spark" to the proceedings; beneath the "tough" exterior lurks an "overall good vibe" that works especially well for "late-night barhopping."

MOVIDA
– | – | – | VE

28 Seventh Ave. S. (bet. Bedford & Leroy Sts.), 1 to Houston St., 212-206-9600; www.movidanyc.com

Seventh Avenue South gets a chic jolt via this swanky new triplex lounge, a self-described 'psychedelic luxury yacht' with fake portholes framing faux sunsets above a sea of aqua ultrasuede furniture; it feels like something out of *Dynasty*, and with a roster of hot DJs and different theme nights, this one seems primed and ready to set sail.

Mr. Dennehy's
– | – | – | M

63 Carmine St. (bet. Bedford St. & 7th Ave. S.), A/B/C/D/E/F/V to W. 4th St., 212-414-1223

"Your quintessential Irish pub", this West Village "local" is a "down-to-earth" joint equipped with "flat screens" and a "warm staff"; though a "little corporate" for bohemian types, it's "homey enough", especially after a "fantastic Guinness" or two.

Muddy Cup ⌐
▽ 25 | 20 | 22 | $6

388 Van Duzer St. (Beach St.), Staten Island, 718-818-8100; www.muddycup.com

A "breath of fresh air" for Staten Islanders craving a "mellow" place to "unwind", this "funky" coffeehouse offers all the comforts of Berkeley, from the "barn-sale decor" to a "hotbed-of-liberalism" clientele; live music, poetry or theater in the rear performance space bolster its "up-and-coming" rep.

Mug's Ale House
20 | 12 | 20 | $5

125 Bedford Ave. (N. 10th St.), Brooklyn, L to Bedford Ave., 718-384-8494; www.mugsalehouse.com

The "high-quality brews" set this "typical tavern-type" Williamsburg hang apart in the eyes of suds lovers seduced by an impressively "long tap list" featuring "many oddities", all at prices that "put Manhattan bars to shame"; for packs of "sports-loving" pals, it's a "refreshing respite from the hipsters" and the "perfect beginning or end" to a pub crawl.

Mundial
– | – | – | M

(fka Totem)

505 E. 12th St. (Ave. A), L to 1st Ave., 212-982-1282; www.mundialnyc.com

Favored by Euro expats out for a "casual drink" among mates, this East Village bar sports a "very cool design" of the stripped-down school, keeping things spare except for a giant video screen that's apt to be showing soccer; with a DJ and patio seating, it has worldly sorts calling a "local place worth traveling to."

Musical Box
24 | 18 | 20 | $8

219 Ave. B (bet. 13th & 14th Sts.), L to 1st Ave., 212-254-1731

There's "little pretension" at this "Alphabet City stalwart" known for "adept" bartenders, a "great" jukebox and "photos of rock legends" on the walls; in addition, a pool table, "comfy couches" and a "basement feel" make it a real "standby" where the random lament of "too crowded" is the only off note.

Mustang Grill

16 | 15 | 15 | $9

1633 Second Ave. (85th St.), 4/5/6 to 86th St., 212-744-9194
"*Ay caramba!*", "so many tequilas" have the Upper East Side's "fun crowd" stampeding for this "party-type" Southwestern "staple", a favorite site to toss back "stiff margaritas" and "watch the games" (televised or otherwise); but some can't bear to pony up for "pricey drinks" and "vapid" service, even in the loungey downstairs refuge from the "hordes."

Mustang Harry's

16 | 14 | 18 | $7

352 Seventh Ave. (bet. 29th & 30th Sts.), 1/2/3 to 34th St./Penn Station, 212-268-8930; www.mustangharrys.com
A "default" option for any "Garden event", this "old fave" of an Irish joint "succeeds by proximity" to Penn, keeping pre- and "post-game revelers" "well-oiled" with an added dash of tapster "rapport"; otherwise, it's got the horsepower for "a drink after work."

Mustang Sally's

15 | 13 | 19 | $8

324 Seventh Ave. (bet. 28th & 29th Sts.), 1/2/3 to 34th St./Penn Station, 212-695-3806
This "casual" Irish "commuter bar" and "FIT watering hole" near MSG is a standard spot to "meet up" before a "concert or game", to "watch sports" or have a snort with "your boss' secretary on the way home to Long Island"; a few bridle at the "typical" "mullet crowd", but others say it's usually kicking.

ñ ⌀

25 | 19 | 19 | $9

33 Crosby St. (bet. Broome & Grand Sts.), 6 to Spring St., 212-219-8856
SoHo's "hidden" "Spanish treasure", this "narrow hallway" of a tapas bar flaunts its "authentic vibe" with "tantalizing" tipples served amid "velvet curtains" and candlelight that suit everything from "intimate conversation" to the "crazy" Wednesday flamencofests; though it's way *pequeño* and "frequently packed", most "don't mind squeezing" in – "that's part of the appeal."

NA

20 | 16 | 15 | $12

(fka Nell's)
246 W. 14th St. (bet. 7th & 8th Aves.), A/C/E/L to 14th St./8th Ave., 212-675-1567; www.nanightclub.com
"Past a tight velvet rope" lies this new Village club "trying to fill Nell's shoes", offering a ground floor rife with "pretty" neo-Victorian flourishes while on the lower level "consistently choice" DJs pump up the volume; it's kind of "hot right now", so would-be scenemakers "better know somebody" and be prepared to "pay big time."

Naked Lunch

19 | 15 | 15 | $9

17 Thompson St. (bet. Canal & Grand Sts.), A/C/E to Canal St., 212-343-0828
Never mind the "slightly edgy" name, this "jumping" SoHo bar is where "preppy" "recent grads" get their "groove things" in motion to a "greatest-hits" "classic '80s" soundtrack; "if you can stand" "body-to-body" throngs and a "wait in line" overseen by "unfriendly bouncers", the "sloppy partying" can be "sooo fun."

Nancy Whiskey Pub

▽ 18 | 7 | 18 | $5

1 Lispenard St. (W. B'way), 1 to Canal St., 212-226-9943; www.nancywhiskeypub.com
An "eclectic mix" of "hipsters", "union guys" and "social misfits" frequents this TriBeCa relic, a "total dump" made somehow more

"appealing" by simple pleasures like "cheap pitchers" and an "authentic shuffleboard table"; the "lifer" barkeep's "shtick" alone is excuse enough to tumble "off the wagon."

Nation
∇ | 16 | 18 | 18 | $8

12 W. 45th St. (bet. 5th & 6th Aves.), 1/2/3/7/N/Q/R/S/W to 42nd St./ Times Sq., 212-391-8053

Midtown's desk setters "arrive early for happy hour" at this "decent" bar/restaurant, a destination for "casual after-work" libations with "popular music choices" on the sound system and plenty of lounging room upstairs; maybe the nabe's a yawn, but don't tell that to the buttoned-down types with "ties around their heads."

Neogaea
– | – | – | VE

4 E. 28th St. (bet. 5th & Madison Aves.), R/W to 28th St., 212-889-4840

An owner of former hot spot Pangaea hopes to duplicate its bottle-service/velvet-rope success at this new Gramercy lounge, a brick-walled, couches-everywhere affair centered beneath a dome painted with an old-world map; two smallish VIP areas (one a balcony, the other a back room) complete the picture.

Nerveana
– | – | – | M

179 Varick St., 2nd fl. (bet. Charlton & King Sts.), 1 to Houston St., 212-243-1999; www.nerveana.com

Sending up the '90s the same way its downstairs sibling, Culture Club, lambastes the '80s, this new SoHo danceteria features Spice Girl murals, a Monica Lewinsky mannequin and VIP seating in a white Ford Bronco; as for the crowd, it's mostly young, mostly female and mostly bachelorettes.

Nevada Smith's
13 | 10 | 18 | $6

74 Third Ave. (bet. 11th & 12th Sts.), L to 3rd Ave., 212-982-2591; www.nevadasmiths.net

There's "no better place" to "revel in unabashed soccer fervor" than this Village "haven for European football", an "expat" lair for Premier League enthusiasts that's also the Manchester United's local base; beyond "big-screen footy" "in the AM", it's a "plain" "NYU college bar" offering little to cheer for except bi-weekly karaoke.

Newgate Bar & Grill
– | – | – | M

535 La Guardia Pl. (bet. Bleecker & W. 3rd Sts.), A/B/C/D/E/F/V to W. 4th St., 212-358-7995; www.newgatebarandgrill.com

As unpretentious and laid-back as its collegiate following, this new Village bar in the heart of NYU territory is roomy enough to bring the whole dorm and priced for student budgets; a wrong-side-of-the-street address and somewhat generic look are downsides.

New York Comedy Club
∇ | 16 | 10 | 14 | $12

241 E. 24th St. (bet. 2nd & 3rd Aves.), 6 to 23rd St., 212-696-5233; www.newyorkcomedyclub.com

A "night of laughs" awaits at this Gramercy jestfest, hosting "usually very funny" standup with the occasional "stop-in" by big-name yukmeisters; one joker quips if it "were any smaller we'd be sitting outside", but "you come here for the show" so the "great lineup" may blot out digs and service that are "nothing to write home about."

Niagara & Lei Bar
17 | 13 | 17 | $7

112 Ave. A (7th St.), L to 1st Ave., 212-420-9517

"Punks and professionals collide" at this "jammin'" East Village bar and "downstairs tiki room", a "prime location" for "schmoozing" with rafts of followers, from falling-over "frat boys" to the "occasional celeb rocker"; if the surroundings seem "not that special", "with the right crowd" it's a "sweet place to be" and there's always hope "you'll get leied yet."

Nice Guy Eddie's
|16|11|21|$6|

5 Ave. A (Houston St.), F/V to Lower East Side/2nd Ave., 212-253-1666; www.niceguyeddies.com

Nice enough but "not much to look at", this "spacious", "conveniently situated" East Village pitcher 'n' wings purveyor is "dependable" in a "generic", "blue-collar sort of way" when you want to "catch a game", shoot some stick or just "hear yourself talk"; "kick-ass" twofer deals offer some incentive for a stop en route to "where you really want to go."

No Idea
|18|10|19|$6|

30 E. 20th St. (bet. B'way & Park Ave. S.), 4/5/6/L/N/Q/R/W to 14th St./ Union Sq., 212-777-0100; www.noideabar.com

"Get away from the chichi crowd" at this Flatiron "regular bar", an "ideal" choice for a "night you won't remember" noted for its "low-priced pints of mixed drinks" and freebies for "lucky" sots whose "name is the name of the day"; otherwise "expect nothing" but to "kick back" and "watch sports" in a "frat" setting.

No Malice Palace
|21|16|18|$8|

197 E. Third St. (bet. Aves. A & B), F/V to Lower East Side/2nd Ave., 212-254-9184

Acquaintance with this "comfy, sexy" East Villager may "up your cred" with the "too-cool" "neighborhood" types who make it their "other living room", thanks to "plush couches", a DJ "spinning hip-hop" and "sweet bartenders"; "hookups" abound, but even with a "back garden" for overflow, it seems "too many" are "in the know."

No Moore
|17|13|19|$7|

234 W. Broadway (N. Moore St.), 1 to Franklin St., 212-925-2595

Still an "untapped resource", this "unpretentious TriBeCa mainstay" offers "plenty of space" for local "yuppies, artsies and meatheads" to "spread out" and now doubles as a "venue for bands"; a few fret it's "lacking any interesting scene" with "cooler places" beckoning, but most see a "solid" hoodie "hang", no more and no less.

No. 1 Chinese
|–|–|–|E|

50 Ave. B (4th St.), F to 2nd Ave., 212-375-0665

This East Village Chinese restaurant takes the Spice Market approach to nightlife with an extravagantly decorated ground-floor eatery parked above a sprawling subterranean lounge; rife with kitschy fish tanks, hanging lanterns and opium beds imported from China, it's a sexy destination for folks with a sense of humor.

Northsix ⊘
|19|13|17|$6|

66 N. Sixth St. (bet. Kent & Wythe Aves.), Brooklyn, L to Bedford Ave., 718-599-5103; www.northsix.com

A rite of passage for "up-and-coming new bands", this Williamsburg live venue typifies "what indie rock is supposed to be about" with its "value"-priced bevs, "really loud" sound and "lofty" garagelike space; the DIY vibe lets "you know you're in Brooklyn", so all that authenticity is "worth the extra stop on the L."

North West
|18|21|20|$10|

392 Columbus Ave. (79th St.), 1 to 79th St., 212-799-4530

Take the bearings on someone special in the "romantic corners" of the "swanky upstairs lounge" at this "Euro-styled" Upper West Side eatery, where the possibilities also encompass "lively conversation" at the "outside tables" or at the ground-level bar; it's hardly bustling, but at least the "staff gets an A for effort."

Novecento
21 17 19 $11

343 W. Broadway (bet. Broome & Grand Sts.), C/E to Spring St., 212-925-4706; www.novecentogroup.com

Go "loco with the Latin crowd" at this SoHo "Argentinean haven", a Buenos Aires–style steakhouse with an upstairs "Euro lounge" that "routinely entertains" anyone looking to catch a Sunday soccer match or "get loose" after dark (the "later the better"); too bad with so "many hotties on site", there's "never enough room."

Nowhere ⌐
▽ 16 13 23 $6

322 E. 14th St. (bet. 1st & 2nd Aves.), L to 1st Ave., 212-477-4744

"They're not kidding" about the remote locale, so it's up to the "casual" crew at this East Village "neighborhood gay/lesbian bar" to "keep themselves entertained" with a jukebox, pool table and "friendly" banter; ok, it's "not overly exciting", but a "changing crowd from night to night" means there's always a chance of getting somewhere.

Nublu ⌐
▽ 23 19 19 $8

62 Ave. C (bet. 4th & 5th Sts.), F/V to Lower East Side/2nd Ave., 212-979-9925; www.nublu.net

True-blue backers call this East Village lounge an "excellent hideaway" that combines a casually with-it look and a "funky vibe" to draw in an "arty crowd" keen to check out the DJ's "eclectic international beats" or to "listen to live" modern jazz; for fresh-air fiends, the "surprisingly gorgeous" back patio is a bona fide patch of "nature amid the concrete."

Nuyorican Poets Cafe ⌐
23 15 15 $7

236 E. Third St. (bet. Aves. B & C), F/V to Lower East Side/2nd Ave., 212-780-9386; www.nuyorican.org

Rookie rhymesters "discover slam" at Alphabet City's "famous holdover" from the dawn of "poetry jam sessions", a "unique" forum where "tortured souls" versifying onstage "energize the whole place" (as do music and drama acts); if some scoff it's "no longer what it once was" and "needs to get over itself", it's ever popular, so "get there early" for a seat or else "wear a sensible pair of shoes."

NV
14 16 11 $12

289 Spring St. (Hudson St.), C/E to Spring St., 212-929-6868; www.nv289.com

A "clubby crowd" "looking for a good time" frequents this SoHo stalwart for its "perfect mix" of sounds, with hip-hop and R&B to make the lower-level "dancing scene go wild" and a "KTU"-"techno" blend for the "velvety lounge" upstairs; it's exclusive enough to "check out for sure", though vets are "not impressed" by the latest "somewhat cheesy" arrivistes.

NY Perks
– – – M

193 Smith St. (bet. Baltic & Warren Sts.), Brooklyn, F/G to Bergen St., 718-237-2901; www.nyperks.com

Adding some spice to Brooklyn's Smith Street scene is this former coffee bar (as yet not renamed) that's morphed into a self-described 'wine and champagne lounge'; the sprawling, two-story setup features everything from WiFi to a waterfall, and there's a bonus backyard deck for nicotine fiends.

Oak Room
24 23 22 $13

Algonquin Hotel, 59 W. 44th St. (bet. 5th & 6th Aves.), 7/B/D/F/V to 42nd St./6th Ave., 212-840-6800; www.algonquinhotel.com

"So old, so fabulous", the Algonquin Hotel's "elegant", "wood-paneled" retreat oozes "total class" both as a "nostalgic" preserve of "round-table history" and as a showcase for "excellent cabaret"; admittedly "pricey" and "a little snooty", it promises a "romantic evening made to order" for those "of a certain age", so "bring the Amex" and "enjoy the show."

O'Connell's
− | − | − | M

(fka Cannon's Pub)
2794 Broadway (108th St.), 1 to Cathedral Pkwy./110th St., 212-678-9738
Not much has changed beside the name at this Columbia-area Irish bar formerly known as Cannon's Pub; brick walls, cheap pitchers and sports TV sum up a scene that evolves from local drinkers during the day to grad students after dark.

O'Connor's ⊄
19 | 7 | 20 | $4

39 Fifth Ave. (bet. Bergen & Dean Sts.), Brooklyn, 2/3 to Bergen St., 718-783-9721
An "authentic" Depression-era artifact, this "prototypical" Park Slope "old-man dive" wins some "hipster" esteem with amiably "crusty" service, "Elliott Smith on the jukebox" and "serious drinking" that "your wallet won't feel"; it's "scary", "decrepit" and unsuitable "if you want company", but of course "that's the appeal."

ODEA
▽ 25 | 24 | 22 | $11

389 Broome St. (Mulberry St.), 6 to Spring St., 212-941-9222; www.odeany.com
With a "dark and seductive" design courtesy of "the Public folks", this "sleek", "chic" bar/lounge "tucked away" in Little Italy exudes "mystique" from its "bottom-lit onyx bar" to the curtained, "candlelit cabanas" that double as "foolproof" party pods; nightcrawlers looking for "substance" declare it's "definitely a winner" in an "otherwise painful area."

Odeon
19 | 17 | 17 | $11

145 W. Broadway (bet. Duane & Thomas Sts.), 1/2/3 to Chambers St., 212-233-0507; www.theodeonrestaurant.com
"Still one of the hippest" haunts in town, TriBeCa's "original" "upscale" bistro with a "Downtown feel" is a "landmark" to "late-night" living where the "well-weathered" pros behind the bar unfailingly "pour a great cocktail"; if this "suave meat market" for "good-looking people" pales compared to its '80s heyday, it's still "dependable year after year."

Odessa
▽ 19 | 15 | 15 | $12

1113 Brighton Beach Ave. (Seacoast Terrace), Brooklyn, B/Q to Brighton Beach, 718-332-3223; www.restaurantodessa.com
This "old and familiar" Brighton Beach supper club is a model "Russian cabaret" complete with a va-va-voomski floor show, free-flowing vodka and eye-popping eats from the Baltic "equivalent of Balducci's"; *nyet*-sayers deem it "overpriced" and "outdated" measured against "more impressive" rivals, but most confessa it's ever a "fun place."

Off the Wagon
15 | 11 | 16 | $6

109 MacDougal St. (bet. Bleecker & W. 3rd Sts.), A/B/C/D/E/F/V to W. 4th St., 212-533-4487; www.nycbestbars.com
"Throw on your crew shirt" and relive those "wild and crazy college days" at this Village "party central", "always busy" with "sweaty frat boys galore" vying at foosball and pool, "watching sports" and pounding down "tons" of suds; it's "pretty bland" unless you want to get "hammered on a budget", but don't wait till you're "too old."

O'Flaherty's Ale House
19 | 15 | 21 | $6

334-336 W. 46th St. (bet. 8th & 9th Aves.), A/C/E to 42nd St./Port Authority, 212-581-9366; www.oflahertysnyc.com
"Even though it's on Restaurant Row", "neighborhood" vibes hold sway at this durable Irish pub, offering "couldn't be better" service

and "old couches" made for a "group of friends"; with a "backyard garden", "comfy fireplace" and "live music", it's a "cushy" "standby."

O'Flanagan's   17 | 13 | 18 | $6
1215 First Ave. (bet. 65th & 66th Sts.), 6 to 68th St., 212-439-0660
Join "noisy cover bands" belting out classic rock at this Upper East Side Irish saloon, which always works well for a "beer and a game"; the be-brogued barkeeps "know how to take care" of business, too, but even following a "recent makeover", it remains a "typical locals' joint."

O'Flanagan's Ale House   17 | 14 | 19 | $6
1591 Second Ave. (bet. 82nd & 83rd Sts.), 4/5/6 to 86th St., 212-472-2800
Affable Upper East Side regulars and "down-home" Celtic service make this "fairly legit" Irish pub a "solid" place to "start a night" or "spend some time with the boys" cheering on the home team; even the "extremely average" atmo rates a couple of "notches higher" than most others of the breed.

Old Town Bar   22 | 15 | 17 | $7
45 E. 18th St. (bet. B'way & Park Ave. S.), 4/5/6/L/N/Q/R/W to 14th St./Union Sq., 212-529-6732; www.oldtownbar.com
"Touchstones" of "classic bar culture" don't get more "atmospheric" than this "crusty" Flatiron "institution", a 19th-century "blue-collar" boozer that now attracts "all stripes", from the "original patrons still slumped" at the "old wood" counter to "after-work suits" seeking "low-cost" burgers and brews; ever the "ultimate backup plan", it's so staunchly "down to earth" that cell phones are "banned, thankfully."

O'Lunney's   23 | – | 24 | $7
145 W. 45th St. (bet. B'way & 6th Ave.), 1/2/3/7/N/Q/R/S/W to 42nd St./Times Sq., 212-840-6688; www.olunneys.com
On the "upscale" end of Midtown's Irish pub panoply, this longtime Times Square venue offers "warm" service and "closeness to the theaters" as incentives for a "pint of Guinness" and some "sports viewing" before a show; P.S. a recent move one block south into the old Hamburger Harry's space puts its decor score in question.

ONE   21 | 22 | 19 | $11
1 Little W. 12th St. (9th Ave.), A/C/E/L to 14th St./8th Ave., 212-255-9717; www.onelw12.com
The "fun continues" at this "trendy" Meatpacking District lounge/restaurant, where the "look-at-me crowd" unwinds in "swanky", multichambered environs; but "packs of B&Ts" and "poseurs" make the mood "hard to predict", and latecomers should be prepared for "door hassles" and a "mob scene" – this One's just "too popular for its own good."

O'Neals'   18 | 19 | 21 | $10
49 W. 64th St. (bet. B'way & CPW), 1 to 66th St., 212-787-4663; www.oneals.us
A "grown-up-friendly" haven for "option-deprived Lincoln Center" audiences, this long-running Irish pub is always "reliable" for a belt or a bite and sure to be "lively before or after" performances; the "roomy" setup now extends to a "less hectic" cafe, and if the charm is "simple", those "dedicated to the place" simply state "it's all good here."

One & One   ▽ 18 | 14 | 17 | $6
76 E. First St. (1st Ave.), F/V to Lower East Side/2nd Ave., 212-598-9126; www.oneandonenyc.com
Dublin as both an Irish pub and a fish 'n' chips shop, this East Villager supplies pints, plasma TVs and "decent grub" at "reasonable" tabs; folks are of two minds on the atmosphere ("raffish" vs. "boring"), but

all agree it's a "prime location" to "sit outside in the summer" and see "everybody you know" stroll by, if not in.

151 | 19 | 17 | 19 | $8 |
151 Rivington St. (bet. Clinton & Suffolk Sts., downstairs), F/J/M/Z to Delancey/Essex Sts., 212-228-4139
"Down 'n' dirty, just like you like it", this "very rock 'n' roll" Lower Eastsider is a "strictly neighborhood, no-tourist" joint with "cheap" pops and a "really friendly owner"; a "classic '70s" soundtrack and decor channeling "your dad's 1971 wetbar" supply the retro notes.

ONE IF BY LAND, TWO IF BY SEA | 25 | 26 | 25 | $12 |
17 Barrow St. (bet. 7th Ave. S. & W. 4th St.), A/B/C/D/E/F/V to W. 4th St., 212-228-0822; www.oneifbyland.com
"If you want romance", this "venerable" Villager set in Aaron Burr's former abode is "another world" of "aristocratic calm and class" that "impeccably sets the mood" to sip brandy "fireside" while the pianist works the "baby grand"; it's "*the* place to propose", and though undeniably a "big-bucks" expenditure, it'll likely secure a "return on your investment."

119 Bar ⌀ | 17 | 8 | 19 | $7 |
119 E. 15th St. (bet. Irving Pl. & Park Ave. S.), 4/5/6/L/N/Q/R/W to 14th St./Union Sq., 212-777-6158; www.119bar.com
It's a "dive bar for sure", but this "low-key" Union Square "cheapie" is a "nice break from the typical" given its "pleasantly strong" pours, pool action and "close proximity to Irving Plaza"; most don't mind the murky interior since it "definitely looks best with the lights off", as do the "spillover" concertgoers.

One91 | – | – | – | E |
(fka Cafe Lika)
191 Orchard St. (bet. Houston & Stanton Sts.), F/V to Lower East Side/2nd Ave., 212-982-4770; www.one91.com
This spacious Lower Eastsider has undergone several name changes over the years (Mooza, Cafe Lika) and is reborn yet again with more subdued decor and a rejiggered Mediterranean menu; what remains constant, however, is its knockout rear garden, the closest thing to a European piazza in town.

169 Bar | ▽ 15 | 11 | 17 | $7 |
169 E. Broadway (Rutgers St.), F to E. B'way, 212-473-8866; www.169bar.com
Get over the downscale digs and "random location": this Lower East Side "hole-in-the-wall" is a "cool little" asset on "underserved" turf that's "worth the walk" for "cheap" carousing; rising "hip" quotient aside, it's still a "multicultural experience" and regulars who "hope all the tourists stay away" can rest easy.

Onieal's Grand Street | 21 | 19 | 22 | $10 |
174 Grand St. (bet. Centre & Mulberry Sts.), B/D to Grand St., 212-941-9119; www.onieals.com
"Surprisingly preppy and Uptown"-tinged for the "heart of Little Italy", this "warm respite" with a shady past as a '30s speakeasy features "elegant flourishes" like long banquettes and carved woodwork; the "cute bartenders" and "unpretentious" air "hit just the right note", and the setting also factors in "*Sex and the City* lore" "if that's your scene."

ONO | 23 | 25 | 19 | $15 |
Gansevoort Hotel, 18 Ninth Ave. (Gansevoort St.), A/C/E/L to 14th St./8th Ave., 212-660-6766; www.chinagrillmanagement.com
This "posh" restaurant/bar in the Meatpacking District's Gansevoort Hotel draws the "trendiest" of the trendy with its "shimmering"

teahouse design and "outdoor seating" in "cabana hideaways"; ok, the drinks may be "ridiculously overpriced" and service "slow at times", but the "good-looking" crowds alone are enough for many to say "count me in."

Onyx Lounge

▽ 18 | 18 | 21 | $11

168 Sullivan St. (Houston St.), A/B/C/D/E/F/V to W. 4th St., 212-533-9595
Rev up with the "martini list" or "end a night of craziness" at this "cozy" Village boîte with a tin-ceilinged front bar for "not-so-crowded" myxing; down a few steps, a lounge equipped with "wall-to-wall" banquettes, sapphire "mood lights" and a "trance/techno" soundtrack has low-maintenance sorts cheering "talk about a great place to chill."

Opal

17 | 15 | 16 | $8

251 E. 52nd St. (2nd Ave.), 6 to 51st St./Lexington Ave., 212-593-4321; www.opalbar.com
"Young" ones come "alive" at five at this "energetic" Midtowner featuring a "not-bad" "yuppie bar" up front and a "crammed" back-room "party" space with DJs on deck to help "get your schwerve on"; some dub it a "booty call" for the "post-college", "pseudo–Wall Street" set, but overall it's "easy on the eyes", so everyone "keeps going there."

Opaline

17 | 14 | 15 | $8

85 Ave. A (bet. 5th & 6th Sts.), L to 1st Ave., 212-995-8684
Split into loungey "places to chat" and an ample club zone, this "entertaining" East Villager "brings 'em in" for theme soirees (like the "rowdy gay Friday night" and the all-persuasions Saturday "panty party"); if otherwise "not too memorable", "fun folk" out to "make some moves" find "a lot" that moves them here.

Opia

21 | 21 | 18 | $11

Habitat Hotel, 130 E. 57th St., 2nd fl. (bet. Lexington & Park Aves.), 4/5/6/N/R/W to 59th St./Lexington Ave., 212-688-3939; www.opiarestaurant.com
As "trendy" as Midtown gets, the Habitat Hotel's "inviting" bar/restaurant allows the "after-work crowd" and their "Euro friends" some scene space with its "comfortable" luxe-lobby setup, complete with "terraces off the main room"; it also books "excellent" cabaret acts, so if the style's slightly "impersonal", there "aren't any better" bets in the vicinity.

Orchard Bar

18 | 18 | 19 | $8

200 Orchard St. (bet. Houston & Stanton Sts.), F/V to Lower East Side/2nd Ave., 212-673-5350
"If you can find it" behind the "nondescript front door", this durable Lower East Side bar is a "dark" den lined with fish tanks and kewl knickknacks; foes picking up not much of a "discernible vibe" and a "bit of a college" clientele wonder if there's "anyone here from NY."

Orchid

– | – | – | M

765 Sixth Ave. (bet. 25th & 26th Sts.), M/R to 25th St., 212-206-9928; www.orchidny.com
A former florist shop in the heart of Chelsea's Flower District has been remodeled into this airy new bar/lounge that alludes to its leafy past with a clutch of palm trees; now swanked up with banquettes, light bites and weekend jazz, it's part of a burgeoning scene along a stretch of Sixth Avenue where a forest of singles-friendly high rises have recently sprung up.

Orchid Lounge

– | – | – | M

500 E. 11th St. (bet. Aves. A & B), L to 1st Ave., 212-254-4090
The mood's the thing at this sultry new East Village bar/lounge where the funky crimson room is done up Asian-style, an inviting combination

of Japanese lanterns, birdcages and cherry blossoms; regulars lie in wait for the nightly striking of the gong, signaling free shots for all.

Otheroom ⇗   25 | 21 | 24 | $8

143 Perry St. (bet. Greenwich & Washington Sts.), 1 to Christopher St., 212-645-9758; www.theroomsbeerandwine.com

Those bent on "loosening things up" head for this "small", "tucked-away" West Village beer-and-wine bar that's "classy without pretension" for "cuddling" by candlelight; "intimate" "velvet" recesses and "wonderful barkeeps" win it "standing-room-only" devotion to the point that it could use another room.

Otto   25 | 23 | 20 | $10

1 Fifth Ave. (8th St.), A/B/C/D/E/F/V to W. 4th St., 212-995-9559; www.ottopizzeria.com

"Even the most wine-savvy" deem the "zillion bottles" available at Mario Batali's Village pizzeria/enoteca "dizzying", ditto the crowds who pack the "European-style" "stand-up" tables in the "noisy" bar; "modeled after a train station's waiting area", it's "sophisticated" yet "convivial", and the "antipasti-type" grazing's "not bad either."

Otto's Shrunken Head ⇗   17 | 18 | 17 | $7

538 E. 14th St. (bet. Aves. A & B), L to 1st Ave., 212-228-2240

"Easter Island" goes "biker" at this "supremely divey" East Village tiki temple, supplying "strong" grogs to a "punked-out crowd" digging rock DJs in front and live acts in back ("beware if you have no tattoos"); doubters shrink from the "super-kitschy", "semi-embarrassing" style, but "good times" seem to roll all the same.

O2   – | – | – | VE

(fka La Gazelle)

Time Hotel, 224 W. 49th St., 2nd fl. (bet. B'way & 8th Ave.), 1 to 50th St., 212-262-6236; www.oceo.com

The air's chilly at La Gazelle's replacement in the Time Hotel, where a quick glass-elevator ride leads to a suave lounge with low-down leather seating, dim lighting and an even darker back room; in short, there's plenty of breathing room.

OUEST   24 | 24 | 24 | $12

2315 Broadway (bet. 83rd & 84th Sts.), 1 to 86th St., 212-580-8700; www.ouestny.com

Upper Westsiders in quest of a "grown-up cocktail" endorse the "small", "dark" and handsome bar of this tony eatery for its "fabulous" drinks, "super staff" and "airbrushed" ambiance; it's "not cheap" and "walk-ins waiting to get seated" may congregate like "a keg party", but "this kind of quality" is "unusual" for the area and odds are you'll "leave with a few new friends."

Overlook Lounge   – | – | – | M

225 E. 44th St. (bet. 2nd & 3rd Aves.), 4/5/6/7/S to 42nd St./Grand Central, 212-682-7266; www.overlooklounge.com

"Off the beaten track" but not to be overlooked, this Grand Central–area newcomer is a brick-lined barroom animated by a wall-length mural of vintage cartoon characters; otherwise, it sports a pool table, dartboard and flat screens tuned to the games, and territorial "locals want to keep it a secret" from the pub-crawling hordes.

O.W.   ▽ 18 | 19 | 18 | $8

221 E. 58th St. (bet. 2nd & 3rd Aves.), 4/5/6/N/R/W to 59th St./Lexington Ave., 212-355-3395; www.owbar.com

Weeknights aren't too Wilde, but this Upper East Side gay bar "hops on weekends" as the "younger" set gets "boisterous" with go-go boys, a digital jukebox, a deck out back and events for the gents showing on the big screen; for those "comfortable" with a "cruisy" milieu, it's "one of the better choices" north of Chelsea.

Oyster Bar
19 | 17 | 18 | $10

Grand Central Terminal, lower level, 89 E. 42nd St. (Vanderbilt Ave.), 4/5/6/7/S to 42nd St./Grand Central, 212-490-6650; www.oysterbarny.com

"Still peddling tradition" and "worth revisiting" as a "prep for a train ride", Grand Central's circa-1913 "NY original" is a shuckin' "institution" for an "oyster fix" washed down with "draft beer" or "champagne"; the "grandeur" of the "white tile and bright lights" can "make even the most jaded smile", even if it's teeming with "commuters" and "tourists."

Paddy Reilly's Music Bar
22 | 17 | 21 | $7

519 Second Ave. (bet. 28th & 29th Sts.), 6 to 28th St., 212-686-1210; www.paddyreillys.com

This Gramercy pub is primarily known as the "Stone Pony" for Irish bands like Black 47 (who've since departed), but it's also a sure bet for a "draft Guinness" since that's the one brand offered on tap; ignore the "amp feedback" and it's a chance to "spend the night" with "warm, friendly" types having "fun, fun, fun till Paddy takes the music away."

P & G Cafe ♥
▽ 18 | 8 | 17 | $6

279 Amsterdam Ave. (73rd St.), 1/2/3 to 72nd St., 212-874-8568

There's "never a problem getting a table" at this "timeless" Upper Westsider, which boasts "all the elements" of a "perfect 3 AM dive": "dumpy authenticity", "old men and neighborhood dropouts" nursing their jars and "rock 'n' roll on the juke"; though strictly "no-nonsense", "it doesn't try too hard" and that's "oddly appealing."

Paramount Bar
19 | 21 | 16 | $13

Paramount Hotel, 235 W. 46th St. (bet. B'way & 8th Ave.), A/C/E to 42nd St./ Port Authority, 212-413-1010

It's even "worth going to Times Square" to do some "people-watching" in "great style" at this glossy ground-floor bar in the Paramount, where you can sip "overpriced cocktails" and "rub shoulders" with the hipoisie; but the Hard Rock Hotel's planned takeover of the building puts its future in question, so call first.

Paramount Library Bar
▽ 24 | 26 | 21 | $11

Paramount Hotel, 235 W. 46th St. (bet. B'way & 8th Ave.), A/C/E to 42nd St./ Port Authority, 212-764-5500; www.solmelia.com

"Swanky but not stuffy", this mezzanine bar in the Theater District's Paramount Hotel offers enough "beautiful people-watching" to compensate for the "way too high" prices; just make sure to call first, as the hotel has changed hands and its future availability is unknown.

Paris, The
▽ 18 | 17 | 23 | $8

119 South St. (Peck Slip), 2/3/4/5/A/C/J/M/Z to Fulton St./B'way/ Nassau, 212-240-9797; www.theparistavern.com

Hook a few down "right by the fish market" at the South Street Seaport's "historic" 1873 tavern, where Francophiles are scarce among the "mellow crowd" of "serious drinkers" lining the age-old bar; it's "out of the way", but there's time to make the trek since it's "open super-late, which is rare in those parts."

PARK, THE
22 | 24 | 16 | $11

118 10th Ave. (bet. 17th & 18th Sts.), A/C/E/L to 14th St./8th Ave., 212-352-3313

An "adult amusement park" "for all seasons", this "multilevel, multibar" Chelsea scene is a "stunning" preserve for "Prada-loving" chicsters, "metrosexuals" and "loads of hot" playmates; the expansive patio, "atriums with trees" and rooftop "Jacuzzi" ("for those brave enough") distract from the "dearth of service", and if some sense "it's died down", ultimately it still "delivers."

Park Avalon 22 | 23 | 19 | $11

225 Park Ave. S. (bet. 18th & 19th Sts.), 4/5/6/L/N/Q/R/W to 14th St./ Union Sq., 212-533-2500; www.brguestrestaurants.com
"Meet your next sugar daddy (or ex–sugar daddy)" in the "oh-so-yuppie bar" of this "buzzing" restaurant near Union Square, a "sleek" space lit by an "overflow of candles"; it's a "lovely" backdrop "for that first kiss" according to "type-A" types on "expense accounts", who wink it "deserves its longstanding popularity."

Park Avenue Country Club 17 | 16 | 16 | $8

381 Park Ave. S. (27th St.), 6 to 28th St., 212-685-3636
That key "sporting event" will be running on the "tons of TVs" at this "stark" Gramercy clubhouse for "frat boys" turned "businessmen" touching base to "catch all the college" action; ladies better know their "NCAA" before anyone will "even look up from their wings and beer", while "big game" attendees "better make a reservation."

Park Bar 22 | 17 | 19 | $9

15 E. 15th St. (bet. 5th Ave. & Union Sq. W.), 4/5/6/L/N/Q/R/W to 14th St./ Union Sq., 212-367-9085
Snugly parked "right off Union Square", this "relaxed" minibar's "nice lighting" and "tin ceiling" are just upscale enough to work well "after work" or for an "intimate drink before a dinner date"; sticklers remark it's "way too small" and caters to an "even smaller, cliquish crowd", but for a "neighborhoody" haunt, that's par for the course.

Parkside Lounge ∇ 17 | 11 | 17 | $6

317 E. Houston St. (bet. Aves. B & C), F/V to Lower East Side/2nd Ave., 212-673-6270; www.parksidelounge.com
A "wonderful dive", this "unpretentious" Lower Eastsider draws a "diverse crowd" with "cheap" hooch and live "back-room" attractions like the "Friday salsa nights" ("no makeup or expensive attire required"); alright, the proceedings are "typical", but local loyalists sure "keep coming back."

Park Slope Ale House 18 | 16 | 19 | $7

356 Sixth Ave. (5th St.), Brooklyn, F to 7th Ave., 718-788-1756
Slopers ailing "for an old-fashioned bar" declare "this is the place", mainly on the strength of a "thorough draft beer" lineup with some "seasonal specials" thrown in to encourage "conversation with drunken friends"; add a pool table, pub grub and patio seats, and it's a "laid-back hangout" with all the comforts of home.

Parlay Lounge – | – | – | M

206 Ave. A (13th St.), L to 1st Ave., 212-228-6231
Discerning "DJs spin great" beats at this East Village "hip-hop lounge" where "diverse" urbanites parade past the rope to parley and party in a sizable space with a smooth back room; arrivistes "trying too hard" can seem "slightly unhip", but overall, it's got "so much potential" that "everyone's having a good time."

Parlour, The 17 | 15 | 18 | $7

250 W. 86th St. (bet. B'way & West End Ave.), 1 to 86th St., 212-580-8923; www.theparlour.com
For a "casual night out", this Upper West Side "Irish haven" furnishes a "traditional" taproom where regulars gab and "watch soccer", attended to by "warm" staffers who "can pour a pint"; if "just hanging" isn't enough, weekenders can get jiggy with the "fun", "cheezy cover bands" rockin' the "downstairs dance floor."

Passerby
23 | 20 | 20 | $9

436 W. 15th St. (bet. 9th & 10th Aves.), A/C/E/L to 14th St./8th Ave., 212-206-7321

Since there's "no sign", it's easy to pass right by this "low-key" Way West Chelsea barroom and miss out on its "soul and character", not to mention the "groovy" "disco floor" right out of *Saturday Night Fever*; "cozy" enough to be a squeeze "if you have shoulders", it earns "solid" support from "truly arty" patrons peeved that "everyone and their mother found out."

PASTIS
23 | 22 | 18 | $11

9 Ninth Ave. (Little W. 12th St.), A/C/E/L to 14th St./8th Ave., 212-929-4844; www.pastisny.com

"Paris on the Hudson" aka "action city", Keith McNally's "bright", "buzzing" Meatpacking District "brasserie with a bouncer" remains the "scene-iest" for bevies of "well-maintained" boulevardiers set to "strut their stuff" and luck into "a star sighting" ("was that Mary-Kate or Ashley?"); forget the "snail-like service" and "hassle with the crowds": it's "worth fighting" your way in since "this place has it all."

Patio ∅
▽ 20 | 13 | 15 | $9

31 Second Ave. (bet. 1st & 2nd Sts.), F/V to Lower East Side/2nd Ave., 212-460-0992

Once this "laid-back" East Village bar's garagelike front goes up, naturalists insist the "outdoor party" spilling onto the sidewalk is a "warm-weather must"; maybe the "fraternity house–esqe" setup with a "sticky cement floor" is "kinda cheesy", but for "summer" games (with occasional live tunes), it's a lot less trouble than a trip to the 'burbs.

Patio Lounge
22 | 21 | 22 | $6

179 Fifth Ave. (bet. Berkeley & Lincoln Pls.), Brooklyn, M/R to Union St., 718-857-3477; www.patiolounge.com

"Like no other" in Park Slope, this bar/lounge is "so inviting" with its "magical" back garden, "funky" interior featuring a blown-up manga mural and "awesome DJs" to cue the "chilling"; there's "no liquor license", but it "makes good with wine and sake" creations plus such a "crazy beer selection" that they "could easily charge more."

Patrick Conway's Pub
15 | 14 | 21 | $8

40 E. 43rd St. (Madison Ave.), 4/5/6/7/S to 42nd St./Grand Central, 212-286-1873

A "convenient" "after-work gig" given its Grand Central proximity, this veteran Irish "commuter bar" is a "homey" stop where the "friendly barmen" "will get to know your name" even if your boss doesn't; both the space and the clientele "can be a little tight" come rush hour, but otherwise, expect the slow lane.

Patrick Kavanagh's
17 | 13 | 24 | $7

497 Third Ave. (bet. 33rd & 34th Sts.), 6 to 33rd St., 212-889-4304

"Don't even bother to ask for a Cosmo" at this "true Irish pub" in Murray Hill, a "locals-only joint" with gobs of Erin "feeling", "low prices" and sports on the big screen to help "pass away the night"; though no powerhouse, it works for a leisurely "start-out" or "quieter" break from the 'hood's "frat-boy bars."

Patriot Saloon ∅
– | – | – | M

110 Chambers St. (Church St.), 1/2/3 to Chambers St., 212-748-1162

The "beer flows like wine" at this "low-rent" TriBeCa "dump" brought to you by the Village Idiot folks; it "could be heaven" if "dollar burgers", "friendly" barmaids and a "country jukebox" turn you on.

Patroon

22 | 21 | 20 | $11

160 E. 46th St. (bet. Lexington & 3rd Aves.), 4/5/6/7/S to 42nd St./ Grand Central, 212-883-7373; www.patroonrestaurant.com

Mostly a "clubby" affiliate of the "old boys' network", this upmarket Midtown steakhouse offers a "sunny surprise" via a "really cool roof-deck" bar that "caters to young professionals"; sure, it's "pricey", but the patroonage that calls it a "hidden gem" expects no less.

Peasant

22 | 24 | 19 | $11

194 Elizabeth St. (bet. Prince & Spring Sts.), 6 to Spring St., 212-965-9511; www.peasantnyc.com

Emanating enough "true Nolita chic" to keep the commoners at bay, this "rustic Tuscan" is a "warm", "romantic" bower favored for "fabulous" albeit "expensive" vinos; up top it's "more of a restaurant", but grape nuts claim the compact "downstairs wine bar" is "the place to be" "when you don't want to be seen" sampling the wares.

Peculier Pub ∅

18 | 12 | 16 | $6

145 Bleecker St. (bet. La Guardia Pl. & Thompson St.), 1 to Houston St., 212-353-1327

The "mother of all beer lists" awaits at this Village "king of brews", a "grungy frat party" where NYUers "belly up" in ancient wooden booths to chug down a "voluminous" (600-plus) "international" selection of suds; but those wary of the "*Animal House* decor" and "*Fear Factor*" bathrooms posit the "only peculier thing" is its popularity.

Peep

21 | 23 | 20 | $11

177 Prince St. (Sullivan St.), C/E to Spring St., 212-254-7337; www.peepsoho.net

Modest types are leery of the "voyeuristic" "one-way bathroom mirrors" (facing out, thankfully) at this Siamese SoHo-ite, a "funky" spot to Thai one on with "yummy signature cocktails" and "cheap eats"; possessive types deem it a "dinner date" must since you can keep your peepers on your beau as you "powder your nose."

Peggy O'Neill's

15 | 15 | 19 | $7

8123 Fifth Ave. (81st St.), Brooklyn, R to 77th St., 718-748-1400
KeySpan Park, 1904 Surf Ave. (19th St.), Brooklyn, D to Coney Island/ Stillwell Ave., 718-449-3200
www.peggyoneills.com

"Sports on the TV and regulars on their stools" tell the tale of this Brooklyn Irish duo, pegged as "neighborhood staples" that measure up so long as you bring "limited" expectations; karaoke nights provide some kicks, and the KeySpan Park outpost is the "place to hang" on "Cyclones game" days, since there's basically "no other" option.

Penang

18 | 19 | 18 | $10

240 Columbus Ave. (71st St.), 1/2/3 to 72nd St., 212-769-3988
1596 Second Ave. (83rd St.), 4/5/6 to 86th St., 212-585-3838
109 Spring St. (bet. Greene & Mercer Sts.), R/W to Prince St., 212-274-8883
www.penangusa.com

Go Malaysian with a "fancy" potation at this "busy" South Seas restaurant chain, an "authentic" archipelago of "cute decor", "decent" bar scenery and "waiters in sarongs"; the Upper West Side adds an Indo-"industrial" "underground lounge", and though they all could stand to "hip it up a bit", the "lively" style "has its own charm."

Pencil Factory

– | – | – | M

142 Franklin St. (Greenpoint Ave.), Brooklyn, G to Greenpoint Ave., 718-609-5858

As "cool and unpretentious" as "Greenpoint itself", this "neighborhood fave" offers oldfangled saloon surroundings and a "strong feeling of community" to draw area slackers "back again and again"; granted, the "location's not beautiful" or convenient, but sharpened by an "excellent" pop or two, sketchy can seem kinda "cute."

PENTHOUSE EXECUTIVE CLUB | 27 | 24 | 23 | $14 |

603 W. 45th St. (11th Ave.), A/C/E to 42nd St./Port Authority, 212-245-0002; www.penthouseexecutiveclub.com

"Forget Scores", fellas, 'cause this "upscale" Hell's Kitchen strip club is a bi-level juggernaut where "hot girls" onstage wearing "windblown hair" and little else "work it like they're in an '80s rock video"; it's indecently "expensive", but those abreast of the biz claim it does the trick for "a little lift-me-up."

Pen-Top Bar | 24 | 22 | 18 | $14 |

Peninsula Hotel, 700 Fifth Ave., 23rd fl. (55th St.), E/V to 5th Ave./53rd St., 212-903-3097; www.peninsula.com

The panorama alone is "intoxicating" at this open-air bar "overlooking the city" from the summit of Midtown's Peninsula Hotel, and for a "power crowd" uncowed by "sky-high prices" it's the "place to be on a summer evening"; even after a "remodel", the views outdo the "so-so" setup and "pokey" service, but from a vantage point like this, "who cares?"

People | 18 | 18 | 18 | $9 |

163 Allen St. (bet. Rivington & Stanton Sts.), F/V to Lower East Side/ 2nd Ave., 212-254-2668; www.peoplelounge.com

Maybe it's the "great cocktail menu", but folks are "friendlier than most" at this Lower East Side bar/lounge, a lofty space with a "sleek", "minimalist" look and a "comfy", waterfall-equipped "party room" overhead; it attracts a "diverse" following of people persons, but the "buzz hasn't hit yet" so it's still "easy to get in and easy to handle."

Perdition | – | – | – | M |

692 10th Ave. (bet. 48th & 49th Sts.), C/E to 50th St., 212-582-5660; www.perditionnyc.com

The far stretches of 10th Avenue continue to pick up steam with the arrival of this roomy new Hell's Kitchen barroom, a racy-sounding, average-looking Irish pub with a neighborhood vibe; 16 draft beers, big-screen TVs and a variety of board games help pass the time.

Pershing Square/Buzz Bar | 17 | 17 | 18 | $9 |

90 E. 42nd St. (Park Ave.), 4/5/6/7/S to 42nd St./Grand Central, 212-286-9600; www.pershingsquare.com

"Conveniently" tucked "under the overpass" linking Park Avenue to Grand Central, this "commuter haven" hums with "transient" suburbanites out to "kill time" catching a "pricey" buzz; when the street's blocked off for summer, the "outdoor drinking/dining area" offers excellent "people-watching" opportunities.

Peter Dillon's Pub | ▽ 20 | 16 | 21 | $6 |

130 E. 40th St. (bet. Lexington & 3rd Aves.), 4/5/6/7/S to 42nd St./Grand Central, 212-213-3998

A "respite from the strike-a-pose" set is guaranteed at this Grand Central–area Irish bar where the "authentic pub feel" grows more and more "cozy" with each empty jar o' Guinness; the abundance of "dark wood" and "flat-screens for sports" is less than thrillin', but hey, "you come for the company, not the decor."

Peter McManus Cafe ⊖ | 19 | 12 | 19 | $6 |

152 Seventh Ave. (19th St.), 1 to 18th St., 212-929-9691

A '30s-era survivor with the "original decor" and "personality" intact, this Chelsea "local" caters to "cops", "FIT students" and "typical dive" denizens with low-cost sauce poured by "grumpy" characters who "actually know how to tend bar"; genteel types bemoan the "VFW hall" ambiance, but this is a "joint for drinking", so "don't expect anything else."

Peter's
18 | 14 | 18 | $9

182 Columbus Ave. (bet. 68th & 69th Sts.), 1 to 66th St., 212-877-4747
This Upper Westsider is a known "pickup joint" for "thirtysomething", "loosened-tie" "desperados", but it "doesn't claim to be anything else" and singletons "won't be disappointed"; the "narrow" bar space can get "way too crowded" so minglers are typically "seen but not heard", but it "gets the job done" in a nabe that's "starving for more of the same."

Pete's Candy Store
24 | 22 | 22 | $6

709 Lorimer St. (bet. Frost & Richardson Sts.), Brooklyn, G/L to Metropolitan Ave./Lorimer St., 718-302-3770; www.petescandystore.com
"All the hipsters flock" to this "sweet" Williamsburg "hang" to indulge in "scrumptious cocktails" and "tons of events", from the "tricky trivia" and "bingo nights" to eclectic "live music" in the back room "acoustic stage"; fellow revelers are "brainy", "cute and friendly", and in the summer there's an extra bonbon with the "how-cool-am-I" backyard.

PETE'S TAVERN
21 | 16 | 18 | $8

129 E. 18th St. (Irving Pl.), 4/5/6/L/N/Q/R/W to 14th St./Union Sq., 212-473-7676; www.petestavern.com
Dating to 1864, this "venerable" Gramercy "bar's bar" offers a "grubby" "chalkboard-menu" interior and sunnier "sidewalk option", but earns major "mileage" from its "Olde NY image" and rep as a "historical site" ("O. Henry! oh my!"); beyond the "folklore", it's a "functional" watering hole for "swarms" of "underdressed" devotees.

Phebe's
▽ 14 | 12 | 15 | $7

(fka Fuel)
359 Bowery (4th St.), B/D/F/V to B'way/Lafayette St., 212-358-1902; www.phebesnyc.com
Rechristened with its given name after a stint as the alternative Fuel, this all-purpose Bowery bar/eatery is maintaining a "low-key" presence with "lots of space" for flat-screen "sports", a "lounge area" and a deck; though no phenom, it's "popular" with collegiates who hardly miss the original's run-down "charm."

Phoenix ⊅
20 | 10 | 22 | $6

447 E. 13th St. (bet. Ave. A & 1st Ave.), L to 1st Ave., 212-477-9979
"Boys who like boys" but not "Chelsea attitude" migrate to this "no b.s." East Villager as a "relaxed" haven for "reading witty T-shirts as opposed to flashy labels"; the "kick-ass jukebox", pool table and "arcade games" suggest a "college gay bar" ("deodorant optional"), and the heat only "rises" on weekends.

Pianos
18 | 16 | 16 | $8

158 Ludlow St. (bet. Rivington & Stanton Sts.), F/V to Lower East Side/ 2nd Ave., 212-505-3733; www.pianosnyc.com
The keys to "hipster paradise" await at this Lower East Side "music hot spot", a "totally rad" chance to catch "awesome" "unsigned indie bands" on the ground floor, "sip martinis" at the front bar or "shake your groove thang" to "innovative" DJ sets in the "loungey" room upstairs; here's where the "trendy" "slum it", though "meatheaded interlopers" make it predictably jammed.

Pieces ⊘
16 | 10 | 18 | $7

8 Christopher St. (bet. Gay St. & Greenwich Ave.), 1 to Christopher St., 212-929-9291; www.piecesbar.com
"Regularish" guys fit right in at this "welcoming" West Village gay "dive" that "always seems to be crowded" with fans of "campy" theme showcases like the Tuesday "karaoke night" for *American Idol* wannabes"; maybe it "could use a good scrubbing", but "friendliness" and "cheap drinks" make up for the "tacky" display.

Pigalle
20 | 21 | 18 | $10

790 Eighth Ave. (48th St.), C/E to 50th St., 212-489-2233; www.pigallenyc.com
Round-the-clock availability means this "relaxing" Gallic bar/restaurant in the Theater District is as accommodating for "late-night" ramblers as it is for the "pre-show" folks; supporters cite the "thought" put into the wine list, and if there's "not much to speak of" scenewise, few quibble in the wee hours when "there's no other choice" around.

Pig N Whistle
18 | 14 | 19 | $8

922 Third Ave. (bet. 55th & 56th Sts.), 4/5/6/N/R/W to 59th St./Lexington Ave., 212-688-4646; www.pignwhistleon3.com
165 W. 47th St. (bet. 6th & 7th Aves.), R/W to 49th St., 212-302-0112
"Stay as long as you need to" at these "cozy" Irish "staple bars" where it's "easy to strike up a conversation" with "real people" and the "attentive" tapsters are ready to "pat you on your shoulder while you cry into your pint"; though "not fancy", their "comfortable" quarters and ample "leaning space" make for a swine "fallback plan."

Pine Tree Lodge
15 | 19 | 19 | $6
(aka Cabin Club)

326 E. 35th St. (bet. 1st & 2nd Aves.), 6 to 33rd St., 212-481-5490
"*Twin Peaks*" lands in Murray Hill via this "creative", "cabin-themed" bar where the "neat little rooms" look so "sleeping-bag" ready it's "like you died and went to Vermont", with "lots of TVs" and a "courtyard" for consolation; the effect's "hokey but totally fun", and the "long walk from anywhere" helps "you forget you're in NY."

PINK ELEPHANT
22 | 16 | 17 | $11

73 Eighth Ave. (bet. 13th & 14th Sts.), A/C/E/L to 14th St./8th Ave., 212-463-0000; www.pinkelephantclub.com
Throwing its weight around as the Village's latest "tough door", this "intimate", "exclusive" lounge has "30ish" bottle buyers feeling "extremely sexy" amid the chandeliers, curvy banquettes and "fog machine"; despite some "pretension" and those "Euro guys dancing by themselves", it's what every "hot spot aspires to be."

Pink Pony ⊘
19 | 17 | 17 | $8

176 Ludlow St. (bet. Houston & Stanton Sts.), F/V to Lower East Side/2nd Ave., 212-253-1922
Positively "not a cowboy bar", this Lower East Side beer-and-wine cafe is a "laid-back" "literary" lair with book-lined walls and "tag-sale" trappings; aesthetes tickled pink by the "hip 'n' grungy" format can "check out the readings" and art-house flick screenings, but those opposed nag it's too "tired" to trot.

Pioneer Bar
19 | 14 | 18 | $8

218 Bowery (bet. Prince & Spring Sts.), J/M/Z to Bowery, 212-334-0484; www.pioneerbar.com
Intrepid sorts are rewarded with "so much open space" at this massive "party" outpost on a "desolate stretch of the Bowery", a "big draw" that's "not meat market or chichi" but is still rife with "post-college"

"professional" action; even though it's been "discovered", word is it "still delivers."

Pipa
23 | 25 | 19 | $11

ABC Carpet & Home, 38 E. 19th St. (bet. B'way & Park Ave. S.), 4/5/6/N/R/W to 14th St./Union Sq., 212-677-2233; www.abchome.com

Decked out like "Miss Havisham's dream" come true, ABC Carpet's Flatiron tapas bar is an "alluring" enclave of "chandeliers and velvet" where "yummy" nibbles chased with "delicious" sangria will liven up a "significant other" or a "group of friends"; it's "on the expensive side", but the "eclectic" charm is "worth it" despite the "tight" setup.

P.J. Carney's
18 | 14 | 20 | $8

133 E. 56th St. (bet. Lexington & Park Aves.), 4/5/6/N/R/W to 59th St./ Lexington Ave., 212-759-8446
906 Seventh Ave. (bet. 57th & 58th Sts.), N/Q/R/W to 57th St./7th Ave., 212-664-0056
www.pjcarneys.com

You don't need to "change your clothes just to go out" thanks to this Irish twosome where the countermen "remember your name" and the going's "very casual" "without the dive bar" dinge; the wee Westsider can get "cramped", but they'll both accommodate a "thirst-quenching" session amongst "older" habitués who more than likely "live around the corner."

P.J. CLARKE'S
22 | 17 | 19 | $9

915 Third Ave. (55th St.), E/V to Lexington Ave./53rd St., 212-317-1616; www.pjclarkes.com

"Ready for another century", this 1884-vintage Midtowner is a "mainstay" for "elbow-to-elbow" "suits and regular people" "vying for beers" in the "nostalgic" downstairs taproom; though "more pricey" since being "polished up" and fitted out with second-floor dining, it's a "true oldie but goodie", from the "chummy" bustle to the must-see "historic bathrooms."

Plan B
17 | 15 | 16 | $8

339 E. 10th St. (bet. Aves. A & B), L to 1st Ave., 212-353-2303; www.planbny.com

The "lively successor to Drinkland" is this East Village DJ domain with zebra-print banquettes and "intimate back-room" nooks that "get super-crowded" with "younger adults" who attest the "name's appropriate" for a "decent" standby; but the "too-small" "hodgepodge" layout has some foes hoping "plan A will work out."

Planet Rose
∇ 21 | 16 | 19 | $8

219 Ave. A (bet. 13th & 14th Sts.), L to 1st Ave., 212-353-9500; www.planetrose.com

"After a couple of drinks", everyone's "singing up a storm" at this "real karaoke bar" in the East Village, where "sweet sounds" arise as the "talented" and "novices" alike rock the mike; the bloom's off the kitschy safari decor, however, but "who can resist" serenading a "bunch of strangers" instead of "just embarrassing yourself in front of your friends"?

Planet Thailand ⇗
21 | 21 | 16 | $9

133 N. Seventh St. (bet. Bedford Ave. & Berry St.), Brooklyn, L to Bedford Ave., 718-599-5758

"Go for the food and end up hanging" for cocktails and "cryptic DJ" sets at this hiply streamlined Williamsburg Thai restaurant/bar, where "lots of pretty people" gravitate to its "warehouse allure" and "very reasonable prices"; it's "worth the trek to Brooklyn", but plan "to make a day of it" now that the whole world knows.

Play
∇ 23 | 25 | 19 | $11

77-17 Queens Blvd. (Northern Blvd.), Queens, G/R/V to Grand Ave., 718-476-2828; www.play-ny.com
Move up from "your best friend's basement" to this industrial-size Long Island City "activities" center where the focus is on "billiards", "bowling and booze" ("what a great combo!"); featuring four lanes for tenpins, "tons of pool tables" and a lounge area for "any game you could want", it's a "very nice" way to play indeed.

Playwright Tavern
18 | 15 | 20 | $7

732 Eighth Ave. (bet. 45th & 46th Sts.), A/C/E to 42nd St./Port Authority, 212-354-8404
202 W. 49th St. (bet. B'way & 7th Ave.), R/W to 49th St., 212-262-9229
27 W. 35th St. (bet. 5th & 6th Aves.), B/D/F/N/Q/R/V/W to 34th St./ Herald Sq., 212-268-8868
www.playwrighttavern.com
Not the "show biz" hubs that some "incorrectly imagine", these "typical Irish pubs" do set a "friendly" stage for "working stiffs" to "mingle with tourists" under the direction of "witty" barkeeps; though "hardly hot" tickets, they're "well-located" and stick to the script for "economical" brews.

Plaza Athénée Bar Seine
– | – | – | VE

Plaza Athénée Hotel, 37 E. 64th St. (bet. Madison & Park Aves.), 6 to 68th St., 212-606-4647; www.plaza-athenee.com
Simply "beautiful" is the verdict on this *très* chic bar/lounge nestled in the Plaza Athénée with a Moroccan feel and sumptuous details like lacquered walls and leather floors; it's just the spot to rendezvous with your "true love", but bear in mind that the "prices match" the swellegant surroundings.

Plug Uglies
∇ 15 | 12 | 17 | $7

257 Third Ave. (21st St.), 6 to 23rd St., 212-780-1944
Those who proclaim "sawdust shuffleboard" "the greatest bar game there is" slide by this Gramercy Irish "dive" to compete on a free table you just "gotta love"; otherwise, it's a "nondescript" spot to "swill beers and play pool", and some plug the "easygoing" atmosphere so long as you "don't mind all the cops" in the crowd.

PLUNGE
23 | 21 | 15 | $13

(aka Gansevoort Rooftop)
Gansevoort Hotel, 18 Ninth Ave., rooftop (Gansevoort St.), A/C/E/L to 14th St./8th Ave., 212-206-6700; www.chinagrillmanagement.com
"Look down on it all" from this Gansevoort Hotel rooftop perch, packed with "trust-fund babies" admiring the "panoramic Hudson" and "Soho House pool" views while throwing back "ridiculously expensive" elixirs; the "airy" wraparound patio is just the thing come summertime when you're "missing the Hamptons", even though approval ratings plunge for the "annoying door", "snooty" staff and "close, crowded quarters."

PM
22 | 21 | 18 | $13

50 Gansevoort St. (bet. Greenwich & Washington Sts.), A/C/E/L to 14th St./ 8th Ave., 212-255-6676; www.pmloungenyc.com
"Call in your connections" or "get some implants" to access this "exclusive", "high-end" Meatpacking District lounge, a "celeb-spotting" spectacle for the "gorgeous" that many call "*the* place to be right now"; "palm trees" and tropical hues evoke a "chichi island" where "pretension is king", and the "lucky hotties" picked from the "huge lines" can only advise outsiders to "try going earlier."

Pop
19 | 18 | 15 | $9

127 Fourth Ave. (bet. 12th & 13th Sts.), 4/5/6/L/N/Q/R/W to 14th St./ Union Sq., 212-674-8713

An oasis of "modern cuteness" on an "odd street", this East Villager has "good-looking twenties" types populating its "open" bar area and "way-too-comfortable" rear lounge where videos are "projected on the back wall"; though less than poppin' fresh, it's handy for "catching up before moving on."

POP BURGER
22 | 20 | 17 | $10

58-60 Ninth Ave. (bet. 14th & 15th Sts.), A/C/E/L to 14th St./8th Ave., 212-414-8686

"Not your typical fast-food joint", this Meatpacking District whopper of a scene features an "upscale White Castle" vending "munchies" in front and a "totally hip" rear lounge for shooting "pool alongside the model of your choice", with "blaring music" and "soft porn" on the side; a few beef about the prices ("pop goes the wallet") and "holier-than-thou" staff, but it's still a "shame the secret's out."

Porch, The
24 | 18 | 20 | $7

115 Ave. C (bet. 7th & 8th Sts.), L to 1st Ave., 212-982-4034; www.porchbar.com

True to its name, this "inviting" East Village bar is all about its sheltered "back patio" that serves as a "super yard" for some "hang" time whether the "weather is nice" or not, thanks to "outside heat lamps"; the "mellow vibe" extends indoors, though when it's "packed", the rather "intimate" room is "not so tranquil."

Posh
21 | 18 | 23 | $8

405 W. 51st St. (bet. 9th & 10th Aves.), C/E to 50th St., 212-957-2222

A "real-life Cheers for the gay crowd", this "attitude-free" Hell's Kitchen "neighborhood bar" is "perfectly serviceable" (if "not quite posh") for "friendly mingling" supported by "generous" pours; "relaxed" and "homey" sum up both decor and clientele, and there's also a "semi-happening" "comfy back" lounge.

Pravda
23 | 23 | 18 | $11

281 Lafayette St. (bet. Houston & Prince Sts.), 6 to Bleecker St., 212-226-4944; www.pravdany.com

Loungeniks "dig the KGB vibe" at this "secret" SoHo "underground lair", two floors of "plush" perestroika where the various "Kremlin" paraphernalia and "endless selection of vodkas" will red-ily make you "believe you're a Muscovite"; maybe its "heyday" is as "done" as the "Cold War", but loyalists insist it's "so 'out' it's 'in'", albeit with "less edge."

Pressure
18 | 21 | 16 | $10

110 University Pl., 5th fl. (bet. 12th & 13th Sts.), 4/5/6/L/N/Q/R/W to 14th St./ Union Sq., 212-352-1161; www.pressurenyc.com

It's a "trendy pool hall" that more than matches Bowlmor's upmarket alleys downstairs, but this vast Village "megaplex" presses further to "suit your taste", combining trippy "big-screen" video, a "futuristic" look and the semi-private lounge Lucid under a "cool-looking bubble" ceiling; there's "no way to get bored", but some folks say it "needs to be discovered."

Prey
_ | _ | _ | E

4 W. 22nd St. (bet. 5th & 6th Aves.), R/W to 23rd St., 646-230-1444

The short-lived Star Bar has been replaced by this new, pared-down bar/lounge that retains its predecessor's bi-level bones without the fancy design flourishes; similarly, it's drawing local non-scenesters more interested in drinking than posing.

Prohibition
21 | 17 | 19 | $8

503 Columbus Ave. (bet. 84th & 85th Sts.), 1 to 86th St., 212-579-3100; www.prohibition.net

"Celebrate the 21st Amendment" with "those in their thirties" at this Upper Westsider, where everyone's "going strong" thanks to a "sinful cocktail list", "knockout" nightly live bands and a "cool back bar" for shooting stick; a "good time" is virtually "guaranteed", though as the "only decent" "grown-up" option around, it's "way too crowded."

Proof
16 | 15 | 19 | $8

239 Third Ave. (bet. 19th & 20th Sts.), 6 to 23rd St., 212-228-4200; www.proofnyc.com

A "sports hangout" that scores points "even if you're not into" athletics, this Gramercy double-decker boasts a "projection TV" beaming games upstairs and hosts DJs and karaoke in the "candlelit" lower lounge; the "hip"/unhip "combination" proves to be a "good mixed" draw, but antis allege "unremarkable" decor "lets the air out of the ball."

Providence/Triumph Room
_ | _ | _ | E

(fka Le Bar Bat)

311 W. 57th St. (bet. 8th & 9th Aves.), 1/A/B/C/D to 59th St./Columbus Circle, 212-307-0062; www.providencenyc.com

This meandering, multichambered venue near Columbus Circle is focused around a chandeliered, cathedral-ceilinged dining area above which lies a clubby mezzanine with lots of nooks and crannies; if that's not enough, the basement is home to the Triumph Room, a party space complete with an oval hardwood dance floor.

PS 450
_ | _ | _ | M

450 Park Ave. S. (bet. 30th & 31st Sts.), 6 to 33rd St., 212-532-7474; www.ps450.com

From the minds behind the disparate venues Vig Bar and Punch & Judy comes this vast new bar/lounge that's bringing some uplift to the stalled Park Avenue South scene; the traditional, mahogany-lined space features back-room VIP seating and a new twist on bottle service, offering carafes of cocktails instead of fifths of booze.

PUBLIC
25 | 26 | 20 | $12

210 Elizabeth St. (bet. Prince & Spring Sts.), 6 to Spring St., 212-343-7011; www.public-nyc.com

Holding up the "high end" in NoLita, this sleekly spare bar/restaurant is an "airy beauty" inspired by a public library, where the "swank" atmo and "well-concocted" tonics "blend well" with the wooden fixtures, "perfect lighting" and handsome studylike lounge; consensus calls it "glamorous to look at" if "slightly pretentious."

Puck Fair
19 | 17 | 19 | $8

298 Lafayette St. (bet. Houston & Prince Sts.), 6 to Bleecker St., 212-431-1200; www.puckfairbarnyc.com

SoHo's "new formula for the Irish pub", this "large"-scale barroom packs in "attractive" folk like "sardines" for "chummy" imbibing with "tunes blasting"; built around "big wooden booths", a "loft" and a "less hectic" cellar, its plucky "character never gets old", even if that means the "frat party never has to die."

Punch & Judy
23 | 19 | 20 | $9

26 Clinton St. (bet. Houston & Stanton Sts.), F/J/M/Z to Delancey/Essex Sts., 212-982-1116; www.punchandjudynyc.com

That "rare trendy place" where all "feel welcome", this "charming" Lower East Side wine bar uncorks "numerous fabulous" labels in a "sociable" setting overseen by a "knowledgeable" staff that neophytes can "actually learn something" from; with "super" sampler flights and yummy "small dishes", your "casual date" should be pleased as Punch.

Punch Lounge
18 | 18 | 16 | $10

913 Broadway, 2nd fl. (bet. 20th & 21st Sts.), R/W to 23rd St., 212-358-8647; www.punchrestaurant.com
It's "not a huge" attraction, but there's "not a huge line" either at this "warm", red-on-gold Flatiron "standby" above the like-named eatery, where nightcrawlers punch in to chill out with "potent" potations and "funky DJ mixes"; though it's "one of the better finds" in a hard-pressed 'hood, there's usually "no crowding" so everyone can "really relax."

Pussycat Lounge
16 | 12 | 16 | $8

96 Greenwich St. (Rector St.), 1/R/W to Rector St., 212-349-4800; www.pussycatlounge.com
Purring along as a "last bastion" of the "old-fashioned strip clubs", this "grungy" Financial District number is where "brokers rest their weary eyes" on one of the "best non-Broadway shows around" while hepcats check out the "wild bands" and upstairs DJ lounge; it's "skanky" and "kitschy" to a T – and "they'd take that as a compliment."

Pyramid Club
24 | 11 | 15 | $7

101 Ave. A (bet. 6th & 7th Sts.), L to 1st Ave., 212-228-4888
The week-ending "'80s flashback" at this East Village "staple" makes footloose types "wish every night was Friday", but as a "legendary dance gig" it's "still going" on the other days too; the digs are "nothing to look at" and the prevailing "Goth show" is "not everyone's taste", but hey, "where else do they play Yaz?"

Q Lounge
20 | 18 | 15 | $9

220 W. 19th St. (bet. 7th & 8th Aves.), 1 to 18th St., 212-206-7665
"Don't I look pretty shooting pool?" ask the cue-ties at this stylin' Chelsea billiards arcade, a "warehouse"-size layout furnished with 16 tables and "cool" stretches of low-lit, "laid-back" seating; a "mixed" clique says "than-Q" for the DJ soundtrack and "sports-bar" supply of "big screens", even if old-timers opine it "tries too hard."

QT Hotel Bar
– | – | – | E

QT Hotel, 125 W. 45th St. (bet. 6th & 7th Aves.), 1/2/3/7/N/Q/R/S/W to 42nd St./Times Sq., 212-354-2323; www.hotelqt.com
Hotelier André Balazs' new Times Square property is a hip, no-frills affair with a youth hostel feel (i.e. bunk beds) and a quirky, ground-floor bar that abuts the lobby swimming pool; though it's difficult to catch a glimpse of any bathing beauties from your barstool, the scent of chlorine in the air lets you know they're nearby.

Quench ⊄
18 | 21 | 20 | $7

282 Smith St. (Sackett St.), Brooklyn, F/G to Carroll St., 718-875-1500
The "local lounge" of choice for Carroll Gardens swells who "want to feel upscale on Smith Street", this "small" space is "stylish" from the low-key lighting to the "fancy-schmancy" banquettes; the mixology is "nice and professional" too, but skeptics can't quench doubts that it's another "Brooklyn bar" that's not "as cool as it's trying to be."

QUO
21 | 21 | 19 | $11

511 W. 28th St. (bet. 10th & 11th Aves.), C/E to 23rd St., 212-268-5105; www.quonyc.com
Landing in the "crowded market" of West Chelsea dance clubs, this new arrival channels "South Beach" via Cape Canaveral with tropical lighting, "space-age" seating and a grotto-ish "hip-hop room"; the "eclectic" crowd "pays dearly" for access, yet "more selective" folk

rate the "typical" scene strictly status quo: "fun on occasion" but "sort of second tier."

Raccoon Lodge   13 | 10 | 17 | $7
480 Amsterdam Ave. (83rd St.), B/C to 81st St., 212-874-9984
59 Warren St. (bet. Church St. & W. B'way), 1/2/3 to Chambers St., 212-227-9894
"Be a rebel" at these "big-time dives", "cheap but cheerful" "places to kick back" among "rough-and-tumble" regulars with "no teeth" decked out in "biker jackets"; a "jukebox and pool table" amuse "fun-lovers", but these are "authentic dumps" so check all "pretensions at the door."

Rain   20 | 22 | 19 | $10
100 W. 82nd St. (bet. Amsterdam & Columbus Aves.), 1 to 79th St., 212-501-0776; www.rainrestaurant.com
This Pan-Asian Westsider makes a splash with "attractive" urbanites who drop in for "classy" swizzling in a "tranquil bamboo" milieu that enhances the "fabulous fruity cocktails" and "exotic" eats; if the "so-so bar scene" "needs some heating up", at least it's "quiet enough to have a conversation."

RAINBOW GRILL   28 | 27 | 23 | $15
30 Rockefeller Plaza, 65th fl. (49th St.), B/D/F/V to 47-50th Sts./Rockefeller Ctr., 212-632-5145; www.cipriani.com
Flaunting a "showstopper" view from the "top of the town", this "high-rise" Rockefeller Center "treat" is a "gorgeous" deco landmark where "elegant" touches like a piano man scream "special occasion"; this "tourist must" "comes with a price", but paramours promise if you "pop the question, you'll get a 'yes'" here.

Rain Lounge   ▽ 14 | 13 | 19 | $7
216 Bedford Ave. (N. 5th St.), Brooklyn, L to Bedford Ave., 718-384-0100; www.rainlounge.net
Partialists pour "love" on the "super-cool" staff and "excellent DJ" at this Williamsburg bar/lounge, a funky pad sprinkled with deep seating, colored lights and fly "full-bottomed figure" paintings; it's "easy on the wallet" and there's a year-round "garden in the back", though the quirky style is "polarizing" in this dry-humored 'hood.

Raoul's   25 | 20 | 21 | $10
180 Prince St. (bet. Sullivan & Thompson Sts.), C/E to Spring St., 212-966-3518; www.raoulsrestaurant.com
"Everyone's favorite since forever" (well, 1975), this "all-around SoHo charmer" is "alive and kicking" as a "quintessential Frenchie" bistro that "defines classic but hip"; its "ever-fashionable", "black-turtleneck" set savors "well-poured" aperitifs "without being rushed" and reports that the "tiny bar" makes "mingling" mandatory.

Rare   – | – | – | M
416 W. 14th St. (bet. 9th Ave. & Washington St.), A/C/E/L to 14th St./8th Ave., 212-675-2220
"Old-school rock lives on" even in the "gentrified" Meatpacking District courtesy of this live band/DJ venue, a former butcher's locker outfitted with video monitors simulcasting the on-stage action; the subterranean setup's "pretty cool" and alt types declare it well done even if snobs sniff it's "rare to find anyone interesting" here.

Rare View   24 | 20 | 18 | $10
Shelburne Murray Hill Hotel, 303 Lexington Ave. (37th St.), 4/5/6/7/S to 42nd St./Grand Central, 212-689-5200; www.mesuite.com
"Escape the typical" Murray Hill mosh scene on the Shelburne Hotel's "huge" seasonal rooftop deck where even the "good-looking yuppies"

can't compete with the "sweeping" cityscape views; the "incredible" backdrop compensates for the "expensive drinks in plastic cups", but the word's out so "get there early."

Rasputin
23 | 21 | 22 | $14

2670 Coney Island Ave. (Ave. X), Brooklyn, B/Q to Sheepshead Bay, 718-332-8111; www.rasputincabaret.com
"Russian cabaret" connoisseurs are salutin' the "jaw-dropping" hoofers of "both sexes" at this "pumping" Brighton Beach supper club, "infamous" for its over-the-topski floor show, "never-ending amount of food" and "great vodka" ("inexperienced drinkers need not apply"); da, it's "tacky" and "very expensive", but those who steppe in will "definitely be impressed."

Rathbones Pub
18 | 14 | 19 | $7

1702 Second Ave. (88th St.), 4/5/6 to 86th St., 212-369-7361
A "no-prestige", "no-nonsense bar" for "just drinkin'", this Upper East Side "throwback" with "sawdust on the floor" attracts "lots of locals" accustomed to frequent refills and "long stays"; though "rough around the edges", it's "cheap" and "friendly", and "you know what you're getting."

Raven Cafe
– | – | – | M

194 Ave. A (12th St.), L to 1st Ave., 212-529-4712; www.raven-nyc.com
Black lipstick is still welcome, but this East Villager is hardly "just a Goth bar" since such "rec room" staples as "pinball and comfy couches" offer "chill" nesting for all kinds; the DJ sets gratify a "more punk crowd", though critics quoth the decor "leaves something to be desired" – "especially if you like color."

Rawhide ⊅
11 | 7 | 16 | $6

212 Eighth Ave. (21st St.), C/E to 23rd St., 212-242-9332
Still rollin' in Chelsea, this "cruisy" '70s "doozie" sure "sounds like a gay bar" and rounds up mature chaps "from leathermen to preppies" who don't mind the ultra-"seedy" digs; "old school at its oldest" can be a "raw ride", but at least it makes everywhere else in town "look better."

Red and Black ⊅
– | – | – | M

135 N. Fifth St. (bet. Bedford Ave. & Berry St.), Brooklyn, L to Bedford Ave., 718-302-4530
This Billyburg bar/lounge is a roomy, barrel-roofed beaut where the "lighting warrants the name Black" and "dueling DJs" pursue "a good groove"; it's also furnished with an "intimate" front fireplace and a patio, but a few red-flag the "rumpus" as "hit-or-miss, depending on the crowd."

Red Bench
21 | 15 | 17 | $10

107 Sullivan St. (bet. Prince & Spring Sts.), C/E to Spring St., 212-274-9120
"You might need a flashlight" at this "tiny", extra "dark" SoHo bar/lounge, a "quaint" cubbyhole with "lots of charm" that's a "date" rendezvous since the "lighting and booze work to your advantage"; just remember it's also a "living room" for "locals" and "suicidal poets", and they'd "like to keep it that way."

Red Cat
23 | 20 | 22 | $11

227 10th Ave. (bet. 23rd & 24th Sts.), C/E to 23rd St., 212-242-1122; www.theredcat.com
An "accommodating" but "too-small" bar makes all "feel right at home" at this West Chelsea restaurant featuring "creative drinks", "excellent service" and "delectable" "nibbles" ("don't leave without eating"); it's catnip for admirers who claim it "never has an off night", but "three-deep" throngs have them yowling "keep it quiet!"

Redemption
— — — **M**

1003 Second Ave. (53rd St.), E/V to Lexington Ave./53rd St., 212-319-4545;
www.redemptionbar.com

The Second Avenue strip has a new watering hole in this whitewashed
bar/lounge that's much like the rest of the pack save for a massive bar
that's not made of the usual wood, but what looks like poured concrete;
expect the typical trendy post-collegiate types testing the waters.

Redeye Grill
20 **20** **20** **$11**

890 Seventh Ave. (56th St.), N/Q/R/W to 57th St./7th Ave., 212-541-9000;
www.redeyegrill.com

Conveniently sited as an upscale "meeting place", this "big", "busy"
Midtown brasserie brings in "younger professionals after work"
along with Carnegie Hall–bound culturati; a "jazz ensemble" snazzes
up the "lively atmosphere" and the "food's good too", but be redeye
for a scene that's "noisy" and "a tad" spendy.

Red Lion
17 **11** **17** **$7**

151 Bleecker St. (Thompson St.), 1 to Houston St., 212-260-9797;
www.redlion-nyc.com

"Classic rock rocks again" at this Village music bar on the mane
"NYU-area" drag, where "solid live" bands including "some great up-
and-comers" entertain "swarms" of "drunken college kids"; though
"rowdy" and "seedy", it's a low-budget "fallback" "if you're in the mood
for a little headbanging."

Red Rock West
17 **10** **17** **$7**

457 W. 17th St. (10th Ave.), A/C/E/L to 14th St./8th Ave., 212-366-5359;
www.redrockwestsaloon.com

Like an "even trashier Hogs and Heifers", West Chelsea's "good old
all-American bar" is a "hoedown" for "loud bikers", "out-of-towners"
and "bachelorettes" looking to "feel naughty"; the "drooly boys"
watching the "hillbilly" barmaids "shake a tail" on the counter call it
"fun in a vile way", though "you might regret it" the next morning.

RED SKY
20 **20** **18** **$8**

47 E. 29th St. (bet. Madison & Park Aves.), 6 to 28th St., 212-447-1820;
www.redskynyc.com

"Three floors of partying" have postgrad types heading for this
Gramercy "railroad" space, featuring a ground-floor mahogany bar,
red-walled upstairs lounge and "enjoyable" rooftop deck; the formula's
"typical", and much like other "reasonably priced" "twentysomething
pickup joints", but whether it's "blah" or a blast is up to you.

Regency Library Bar
26 **24** **23** **$15**

Regency Hotel, 540 Park Ave. (61st St.), 4/5/6/N/R/W to 59th St./
Lexington Ave., 212-339-4050; www.loewshotels.com

"Plush" is putting it mildly at this "marvelous" Midtown hotel bar,
a "relaxed", book-lined locus for "older" types used to "old-time New
York service"; needless to say, it's "way too expensive", but more
than worth it for "romantic cocktails with someone who may or may
not be your spouse."

Relish
▽ **24** **25** **22** **$8**

225 Wythe Ave. (N. 3rd St.), Brooklyn, L to Bedford Ave., 718-963-4546;
www.relish.com

Relish "film noir" stylishness peppered with Williamsburg "starving-
artist" chic at this "retro chrome diner" tricked out with a "dark back
room" where "local hipsters" have a "burger with a fancy drink"; "old-
school" it ain't, but with a "lovely patio" and "groovy music always
pumpin'", only the hard-boiled can "resist the charm."

Remedy Bar
16 | 14 | 17 | $7

974 Second Ave. (bet. 51st & 52nd Sts.), 6 to 51st St./Lexington Ave., 212-754-0277; www.remedybar.com

"Young businessmen" stuck in "cookie-cutter" Midtown head for this "friendly" refuge where the "real-deal happy hour" delivers a genuine "bang for your buck"; a long bar and "comfy" booths make for easy operating, but "space can be tight" during prime time.

Remote Lounge
17 | 17 | 14 | $8

327 Bowery (2nd St.), F/V to Lower East Side/2nd Ave., 212-228-0228; www.remotelounge.com

"Scoping" assumes "new meaning" at this "futuristic" East Villager where a "TV and camera at every table" allow "Peeping Toms" to zoom in on their quarry and then phone over their "pickup lines"; the blend of "video game" and "dating trend" for the "socially inept" is "cool" enough, but trendsters say the "novelty gets old" fast.

Remy Lounge
▽ 15 | 14 | 14 | $10

104 Greenwich St. (bet. Carlisle & Rector Sts.), 1/R/W to Rector St., 212-267-4646; www.remyloungenyc.com

Livin' large in TriBeCa, this king-sized Latin lounge/dance club is a double-decker fandango featuring "great DJs" who specialize in "sizzling salsa" flava'd up with hip-hop and R&B; it's "a good time" even if the once-plush premises look a little threadbare, and despite the far-flung address it "gets really packed on the weekends."

Reservoir Bar
15 | 10 | 17 | $6

70 University Pl. (bet. 10th & 11th Sts.), R/W to 8th St., 212-475-0770

An "all-around watering hole" frequented by "law students" analyzing brew process, this "cheap", casual Village "staple" is an "efficient" supplier of multiple "sports screens", "Golden Tee", pool matches and "pub grub"; in sum, it's pretty dam ordinary but still "packs them in nightly."

Revival
19 | 16 | 21 | $7

129 E. 15th St. (bet. Irving Pl. & 3rd Ave.), 4/5/6/L/N/Q/R/W to 14th St./ Union Sq., 212-253-8061

Offering a "laid-back pub atmosphere" downstairs "when you want a bar" and "cozy couches" upstairs "when you want a lounge", this Gramercy "find" keeps it "hip without pretense" for "reasonably priced", end-of-day revivifying; a location "off the NYU beaten trail" means there's "plenty of seating", and a "backyard" provides a hint of the "great outdoors."

Rhône
20 | 20 | 16 | $11

63 Gansevoort St. (bet. Greenwich & Washington Sts.), A/C/E/L to 14th St./ 8th Ave., 212-367-8440; www.rhonenyc.com

"Lively but not overwhelming", this "loungey" eatery maintains Meatpacking District "chic without all the fuss" in a "stark", "dark" setting where "cute" customers "wind down" with an "awesome wine list" and rev up when the "eye candy" arrives; despite predictably high prices and an "unpredictable crowd", it "aims to please" and is on a rhôll.

Rififi ⌂
21 | 17 | 21 | $6

332 E. 11th St. (bet. 1st & 2nd Aves.), L to 1st Ave., 212-677-1027; www.cinemaclassics.com

"If indie and '80s is your thing", the DJs at this East Village performance venue oblige with "very cool" set lists while a "friendly bar staff" concocts "volatile drinks"; burlesque nights are also on the lineup, but skeptics see an iffy affair in danger of "hipster overload."

Rink Bar
24 | 20 | 15 | $10

Rockefeller Plaza, 20 W. 50th St. (bet. 5th & 6th Aves.), B/D/F/V to 47-50th Sts./ Rockefeller Ctr., 212-332-7620; www.therinkbar.com

This seasonal alfresco patio set in Rock Center's sunken ice arena is "very popular" for a few 'rinks "on a summer night" when Midtown's "after-work" and tourist multitudes descend; unfortunately it's "over-packed" and "pricey", but skate past "all the hassle" and it's sure to impress, "especially if your date is from out of town."

Rise
25 | 24 | 20 | $15

Ritz-Carlton Battery Park, 2 West St., 14th fl. (Battery Pl.), 4/5 to Bowling Green, 212-344-0800

Drink in "spectacular views of Lady Liberty" from this "mellow" lounge in Battery Park, where "low-key elegance" is the "name of the game"; if the company's "touristy" and the pops "overpriced", the "professional service" and "romantic" outdoor terrace rise to the occasion.

Riviera Cafe
19 | 13 | 20 | $9

225 W. Fourth St. (7th Ave. S.), 1 to Christopher St., 212-929-3250

Situated at a West Village "crossroads", this "decent sports bar" provides "friendly service", sunny "streetside tables" and a "large" indoor layout loaded with TVs; if "not terribly exciting", it's also "not overcrowded" and (not coincidentally) serves as a "Red Sox haven."

Rock Center Cafe
22 | 21 | 20 | $12

Rockefeller Plaza, 20 W. 50th St. (bet. 5th & 6th Aves.), B/D/F/V to 47-50th Sts./ Rockefeller Ctr., 212-332-7620; www.restaurantassociates.com

In wintertime the "lovely" sightlines over the rink at Rockefeller Center make this bar/restaurant "an ice place to take a break" and "watch skaters", and even in balmier seasons it's a "not-to-be-missed NY experience" (translation: a "major tourist destination"); consensus says "you're here for the view", which comes "expensive."

Rocking Horse
19 | 18 | 20 | $10

182 Eighth Ave. (bet. 19th & 20th Sts.), C/E to 23rd St., 212-463-9511

Sí, it's a "rocking scene" at this "offbeat" Chelsea Mexican, thanks to "powerful margaritas" that "wow the taste buds" but may "lighten your wallet" as well as your head; "occasionally ditzy" service hardly hampers the "festive" mood, but the "frenetic bar" is known for "coziness", so "get there early to jockey for position."

Rockwood Music Hall
– | – | – | M

196 Allen St. (bet. Houston & Stanton Sts.), F/V to Lower East Side/2nd Ave., 212-477-4155; www.rockwoodmusichall.com

'Hall' is an overstatement at this shoebox-size Lower East Side music venue where you'll get an up-close-and-personal view of its varied acts unlike anywhere else in town; since the number of seats is extremely limited, arrive early or wear comfortable shoes.

Rocky Sullivan's
∇ 21 | 10 | 20 | $7

129 Lexington Ave. (bet. 28th & 29th Sts.), 6 to 28th St., 212-725-3871; www.rockysullivans.com

Burrow "right back into the old" sod at this Murray Hill "piece of Ireland" where Hibernians "hoist a pint" to the "authentic slumming" and "stellar" diversions including "visiting authors", "pub quiz" Thursdays and live music from "traditional" to "punk"; of course, the "best-tasting Guinness" adds to the "feel-good" mood.

Rodeo Bar
20 | 17 | 18 | $7

375 Third Ave. (27th St.), 6 to 28th St., 212-683-6500; www.rodeobar.com

"Yee-haw!": there's "a little bit of country" in Gramercy at this "no-cover" "Texas-style" jamboree, an "easygoing" place to "enjoy a cold one" with "down-home" bands a-pickin'; the "sawdust" and "peanut shell"–covered floor and "full-size trailer" for a bar round out this "redneck dream come true."

Rogue
▽ 19 | 20 | 21 | $8

757 Sixth Ave. (25th St.), F/V to 23rd St., 212-242-6434; www.roguenyc.com
A "nice neighborhood sports bar", this Chelsea contender comes through with "plenty of flat-panel TVs" lining a high-ceilinged space made for elbow bending or chowing down on "above-average" grub; some request "better music", but most see a "bright spot" in an "otherwise not-so-great neck of the woods."

Romi
▽ 21 | 23 | 21 | $8

19 Rector St. (bet. Greenwich & Washington Sts.), 1 to Rector St., 212-809-1500; www.rominyc.com
The "coolest" the Financial District gets, this "classy" setup spans an airy main-floor bar and a "sexy" upstairs lounge to provide "lots of room" for an "eclectic crowd" of "B&T" commuters and "moderately trendy" locals; but although most "enjoyable" on school nights, some say it can be "dead on weekends."

ROOM, THE ⊭
27 | 22 | 22 | $8

144 Sullivan St. (bet. Houston & Prince Sts.), C/E to Spring St., 212-477-2102
Sip a "quiet glass" "away from the scene" in SoHo at this "mellow" bar/lounge, a "tiny" but "comfortable" upmarket "haunt" specializing in wine and an "extensive selection" of Belgian beers; "lots of candlelight" means the "mood is always right" to "get woozy with your honey", though there's less room on the weekends.

Rosa Mexicano
22 | 21 | 21 | $11

61 Columbus Ave. (62nd St.), 1 to 66th St., 212-977-7700
1063 First Ave. (58th St.), 4/5/6/N/R/W to 59th St./Lexington Ave., 212-753-7407
www.rosamexicano.com
"Delicious", "must-try" pomegranate margaritas and "awesome" guac "fresh-made in front of you" are "all you need to know" about these "modern" Mexicans where the bars are "always jammed"; it's a "big-bucks" buzz, but with an "attentive" staff, vibrantly "attractive" digs and "great energy", it's no problemo to "love them both."

Roseland
20 | 12 | 14 | $8

239 W. 52nd St. (bet. B'way & 8th Ave.), C/E to 50th St., 212-247-0200; www.roselandballroom.com
Land a "great view" of the "best bands in town" at this "industrial-strength" Theater District concert hall, an "SRO" venue bringing "diverse" talent to a "hardwood" ballroom that's "spacious" enough for a couple thousand "closest friends"; the sound's "usually fair at best", but overall it's "still a fave."

Rosemary's Greenpoint Tavern ⊭▽
21 | 14 | 19 | $5

188 Bedford Ave. (bet. N. 6th & 7th Sts.), Brooklyn, L to Bedford Ave., 718-384-9539
"Drink huge" at this "kitschy" Williamsburg dive that pours "beers the size of your head" in "large Styrofoam cups" for "under four bucks"; formerly an "old-folks" headquarters, it now attracts "young hipsters" who dig the year-round "Christmas decorations" and Rosemary, its "good-time owner."

Rose's Turn
22 | 9 | 19 | $8

55 Grove St. (Bleecker St.), 1 to Christopher St., 212-366-5438; www.rosesturn.com
"Belt it, baby", at this gay – or "whatever" – Village piano bar/cabaret where a "talented" crew leads a "silly" songfest and "die-hard show

tune" buffs warble the "Barry Manilow and *Cats*" songbooks; so long as you bring a "sense of humor", the "character and camaraderie" will compensate for a setting that's a bit of a "pit."

ROTHKO
▽ | 19 | 17 | 20 | $7

116 Suffolk St. (bet. Delancey & Rivington Sts.), F/J/M/Z to Delancey/Essex Sts., 212-475-7088; www.rothkonyc.com

Arty "live music lovers" out to catch "cutting-edge" indie acts are making this crimson-tinted venue the Lower East Side's "hottest" new attraction; boasting a "long", lofty stage space plus a downstairs lounge, it throws rotating DJs into the mix and is attracting so many strivers that the "overcrowded" floor's almost "too hip for its own good."

Roxy
19 | 15 | 14 | $11

515 W. 18th St. (bet. 10th & 11th Aves.), A/C/E/L to 14th St./8th Ave., 212-645-5157; www.roxynyc.com

An "old favorite" among "hard-core partiers", this Chelsea "classic" features a "sea of cuties" "shaking their stuff" as "celebrity DJs" drop their "strongest beats"; from "roller-skating on Wednesday" to the "ultimate" Saturday night gay grind, it "never loses its thing" – just "have less than 3% body fat" and "forget about going on a budget."

Royale
▽ | 22 | 22 | 21 | $6

506 Fifth Ave. (bet. 12th & 13th Sts.), Brooklyn, F/M/R to 4th Ave./9th St., 718-840-0089

With a "funky" red-lit bar and a Casablanca-style rear lounge, this "hidden jewel" on an "up-and-coming" Park Slope corner has its grip on the "hip"; "specialty DJs" spin "amazing music", "sexy bartenders" supply the royale treatment and the overall "earthy sophistication" rivals Manhattan – except there's "zero pretension" here.

Royal Oak ⊟
▽ | 22 | 25 | 18 | $5

594 Union Ave. (N. 11th St.), Brooklyn, L to Bedford Ave., 718-388-3884

Williamsburg's "funkiest crowd" says oaky-doke to this "big" and "beautiful" barroom where old-fashioned is in fashion and the "open" layout means there's no trouble landing a throne; the dark tones and "velvet wallpaper" provide the retro "charm", but on "off-nights" the "isolated" locale has some wondering "where is everyone?"

ROYALTON LOUNGE
24 | 26 | 18 | $14

Royalton Hotel, 44 W. 44th St. (bet. 5th & 6th Aves.), 7/B/D/F/V to 42nd St./6th Ave., 212-944-8844; www.morganshotelgroup.com

ROYALTON ROUND BAR

Royalton Hotel, 44 W. 44th St. (bet. 5th & 6th Aves.), 7/B/D/F/V to 42nd St./6th Ave., 212-869-4400; www.morganshotelgroup.com

"Prepare to be checked out" at this "swank-contempo" Theater District hotel lounge where "black is the color" to don and those testing the "trendy" waters find it "still reasonably cool" for a "chic rendezvous"; "platinum"-strength tabs to the contrary, this is a joint where even the "men's room is a site to be seen"; P.S. don't miss the "minuscule" padded-leather Round Bar, tucked in a corner just off the entrance.

RUBY FALLS
23 | 23 | 18 | $12

609 W. 29th St. (bet. 11th & 12th Aves.), C/E to 23rd St., 212-643-6464

"Hype is half the battle" at this red "hot", "high-energy" West Chelsea clubzilla set in a "towering warehouse" lined with canvases (it's an "art gallery" by day); after dark, the "glam" split-level space still feels "spacious even when packed" with "sexy" sorts "flirting with everyone", so just "bring money" and you'll have fun – this one's definitely running "on the right track."

Ruby Foo's
21 | 23 | 19 | $11

2182 Broadway (77th St.), 1 to 79th St., 212-724-6700
1626 Broadway (49th St.), R/W to 49th St., 212-489-5600
www.brguestrestaurants.com
"Swanky" but "not haute", this "jumping" Pan-Asian pair serves "imaginative" specialty drinks that make a "potent" match for the "kitschy" "movie-set" decor; though apt to be "standing room only" and "touristy" at the Times Square branch, they're a "convenient backup" so long as you ignore the "decibel level" and "bring a fat wallet."

Rubyfruit
17 | 17 | 17 | $7

531 Hudson St. (bet. Charles & W. 10th Sts.), 1 to Christopher St.,
212-929-3343; www.rubyfruitnyc.com
One of the "longest-lasting" hangouts for "ladies who like ladies", this "refined, relaxing" West Villager attracts "30+" types with mellow "live music", "candlelit" downstairs dining and plenty of "sofas and comfy chairs" for fireside chats; a Sapphic circuit staple, it's also "welcoming" enough to "cater to all."

Ruby's Tap House
13 | 11 | 16 | $7

1754 Second Ave. (bet. 91st & 92nd Sts.), 6 to 96th St., 212-987-8179
There's always "plenty of beer on tap" at this "standard" Upper East Side keg kicker where "cheap" prices attract hordes of "unruly" types; despite "greasy" wings and a pool table, many label it a "lame" scene.

Rudy's Bar ⌖
18 | 9 | 20 | $5

627 Ninth Ave. (bet. 44th & 45th Sts.), A/C/E to 42nd St./Port Authority,
212-974-9169
This Hell's Kitchen "all-time fave" "sets the standard for dive bars" as "local boozehounds rub elbows" with "broke college kids" in "deteriorating" digs made more hospitable by "free hot dogs" and an "eccentric jukebox"; it's "tried and true" for "dirt-cheap" drinking and guaranteed to be "at least interesting."

Rue B
26 | 22 | 22 | $9

188 Ave. B (bet. 11th & 12th Sts.), L to 1st Ave., 212-358-1700
"Sweet", "small" and "exquisitely retro", this East Village French "hideaway" leaves admirers breathless with "astonishingly good" cocktails; the "lively yet relaxed" tempo is set by live jazz nightly and a "warm feel" that's a "nice" surprise in an "inelegant part of town."

Rue 57
20 | 20 | 20 | $11

60 W. 57th St. (6th Ave.), F to 57th St., 212-307-5656; www.rue57.com
"Stop by after work" to make the most of the "cool-enough" bar at this "solid" Midtown brasserie, the Uptown take on "Pastis" with "open-air" streetside seating and "low wait times" if you decide to stay for *dîner*; a few rue the "boring" scene, but given the area's limited pickings, it "could be worse."

Rufus
– | – | – | M

640 10th Ave. (bet. 45th & 46th Sts.), A/C/E to 42nd St./Port Authority,
212-333-2227
Flea-market furniture and framed album covers comprise the decor at this funky Hell's Kitchen watering hole with a bar up front that leads to a comfortable rear lounge; a local following and amiable staff add to its neighborhoody feel.

Rum House
– | – | – | M

Edison Hotel, 228 W. 47th St. (bet. B'way & 8th Aves.), 1 to 50th St.,
212-869-3005
Ok, it's not exactly the chicest Theater District spot, but this down-to-earth watering hole in the funky Hotel Edison is a low-key locus with

a split personality, half piano bar and half sports-TV pub; the two personalities coexist peacefully enough with the pianist winning out post-theater.

Rumor
21 | 20 | 20 | $9

130 W. Third St. (bet. MacDougal St. & 6th Ave.), A/B/C/D/E/F/V to W. 4th St., 212-777-7745; www.rumornyc.com
Hearsay has it this Village basement lounge is a "groovy" source of "thumpin' hip-hop" with a "nice big dance floor" and a "diverse young crowd to hang out with"; "open mike nights" create some extra buzz, but holdouts consider the ropeline posturing and "expensive drinks" a scandal since "you won't find Jay-Z or P. Diddy" in the house.

Rumours
18 | 18 | 19 | 6

933 Eighth Ave. (55th St.), 1/A/B/C/D to 59th St./Columbus Circle, 212-757-2373
"Strong drinks" and "big TVs" sum up the scene at this Hell's Kitchen Irish pub, a "quintessential neighborhood" joint to "watch the game and enjoy a pint" courtesy of the "quick" boyos behind the bar; even the tunes issuing from the "churchlike" DJ booth are ecumenical enough to "satisfy everyone."

Russian Samovar
20 | 16 | 19 | $10

256 W. 52nd St. (bet. B'way & 8th Ave.), C/E to 50th St., 212-757-0168; www.russiansamovar.com
"Infused vodkas galore" keep the mood lively at this "real Russian" bar/restaurant in the Theater District, where "helpful" barkeeper comrades siphon "stiff shots" to the strains of a Slavic piano-strings combo; the "tacky" "old-style" trappings may be due for a "rethink", but it's a godsend for a bracer to "get you through the second act."

Russian Vodka Room
21 | 17 | 18 | $10

265 W. 52nd St. (bet. B'way & 8th Ave.), C/E to 50th St., 212-307-5835
"No one remembers leaving" this Theater District Russian redoubt owing to its "limitless selection" of "delicious" but "lethal" infused vodkas ("they make their own"); the "dark" premises are "mobbed" with expatchiks who "really know how to drink", but there always seems to be room to "toss back" a few more.

Ryan's Daughter
19 | 15 | 22 | $6

350 E. 85th St. (bet. 1st & 2nd Aves.), 4/5/6 to 86th St., 212-628-2613
Keeping it "totally laid-back" for the "twentysomething" lads, this Upper East Side "Irish local" is a "quite popular" but "manageable" hang where the countermen "always have a joke" and pool, darts and video games await; though "typical" of the breed, it's been home to the "same regulars" for years.

Ryan's Irish Pub
∇ 15 | 13 | 18 | $6

151 Second Ave. (bet. 9th & 10th Sts.), 6 to Astor Pl., 212-979-9511; www.ryansnyc.com
This "down-to-earth" East Village pub is a "friendly joint" whose "Irishness" boils down to dark-wood booths and "eclectic characters" aiming to guzzle Guinness and "watch a game" for "cheap"; indeed, it's such a "standard" "hole-in-the-wall" that some suspect a "dive bar" in disguise.

SAKAGURA
27 | 26 | 27 | $11

211 E. 43rd St. (bet. 2nd & 3rd Aves.), 4/5/6/7/S to 42nd St./Grand Central, 212-953-7253; www.sakagura.com
"Like walking into Tokyo", this "real" Japanese bar "hidden" in Midtown below a "corporate lobby" is a chance to "expand your sake palate" with an "unbeatable" lineup ("over 200 types"); aficionados who go

"wild" with the sipping and "upscale" nibbles warn you'll "quickly run a large bill."

Sake Hana
23 | 23 | 20 | $10

466 Amsterdam Ave. (bet. 82nd & 83rd Sts.), B/C to 81st St., 212-874-0369
265 E. 78th St. (bet. 2nd & 3rd Aves.), 6 to 77th St., 212-327-0582
www.sushihana.com
So "small" and "stylish" it "feels like the Village", this Upper East Side Japanese lounge (steps away from its sire, Sushi Hana) will "satisfy your taste" for sake with an "excellent selection" served in "quiet", "intimate" environs "perfect for a first date"; the West Side edition is a bar within the restaurant, but it maintains the same "serene" vibe.

Sala
23 | 21 | 19 | $9

344 Bowery (Great Jones St.), 6 to Bleecker St., 212-979-6606
35 W. 19th St. (bet. 5th & 6th Aves.), R/W to 23rd St., 212-229-2300
www.salanyc.com
You "can't beat the authentic" feel at this *muy rústico* NoHo Spaniard, a "great date place" where dim lighting sets the scene for "delicious sangria and tapas", abetted by a "hip yet comfy" lounge; P.S. the Flatiron outpost is new and unrated.

SALON
– | – | – | E

505 West St. (Jane St.), A/C/E/L to 14th St./8th Ave., 212-929-4303;
www.salonnyc.net
'Swanky' barely does justice to this new West Village ultra-lounge set in a former ballroom that's been revamped in high deco style from the checkerboard floor and velvety banquettes to the art moderne screen mounted above the bar; its second-floor perch overlooking the Hudson makes it a natural for sunset cocktails, but the interior is so smashing that it will impress at any hour.

Saloon
▽ 15 | 11 | 16 | $6

1584 York Ave. (bet. 83rd & 84th Sts.), 4/5/6 to 86th St., 212-570-5454;
www.saloonnyc.com
Upper Eastsiders "fresh out of college" and hankering to hit the dance floor flock to this large, "lively" bar-cum-boogiethon; it's "great for a big group" since there's "no long wait to get in", though some say the scent of "cologne and hair gel" signals a "super-cheese pickup" scene.

Salt Bar
▽ 23 | 17 | 22 | $8

29A Clinton St. (bet. Houston & Stanton Sts.), F/J/M/Z to Delancey/Essex Sts., 212-979-8471
Plain-looking but a "real draw" for "quality drinks and conversation", this Lower Eastsider's dangerously tempting "specialty cocktails" and "warm atmosphere" lay the groundwork for "seductive dates"; it's also worth its you-know-what eatswise, serving a "well-chosen" small-bites menu "too tasty to be called bar food."

San Marcos
▽ 18 | 18 | 20 | $7

12 St. Marks Pl. (bet. 2nd & 3rd Aves.), 6 to Astor Pl., 212-995-8400
Nacho typical scruffy East Villager, this Mexican themer offers a chance to "chill out" over tequila-laced "frozen drinks" in a cantina-style setting that's "cheerful" if not entirely convincing; it's a "welcome hangout" for "bargain"-seeking students and a "popular" sidewalk option, though cred-conscious locals are still "not sure why."

Sapphire Lounge
19 | 12 | 14 | $9

249 Eldridge St. (Houston St.), F/V to Lower East Side/2nd Ave., 212-777-5153;
www.sapphirenyc.com
It's all about dancing at this "jumpin' small club" on the Lower East Side, a "dark" temple to hip-hop and house where the volume's

turned "way, way, way" high and the footloose get freaky; whether your groove's "hands down or hands up", this "standby" "rocks all night."

Sardi's
20 | 20 | 17 | $11

234 W. 44th St. (bet. B'way & 8th Ave.), A/C/E to 42nd St./Port Authority, 212-221-8440; www.sardis.com
"Celebrity gawkers" see "their favorites staring back" via the "legendary drawings" on display at this Theater District "original"; it "hasn't changed much" in its 80-plus years (though its "'in'-place" days are "long gone") and, "yeah, it's tourist bait", but "when all else fails" it's a fallback "guilty pleasure."

Satalla
▽ 18 | 13 | 17 | $8

37 W. 26th St. (bet. B'way & 6th Ave.), R/W to 28th St., 212-576-1155; www.satalla.com
World music wonks meet their match at this Chelsea performance venue, host to "excellent live" groups spanning African to zydeco to every obscure niche in between; the rainbow-hued, black-lighted space and multiculti crowd make a "nice" impression overall, though there's not much competition to measure by.

Satelite
– | – | – | I

505 E. Sixth St. (bet. Aves. A & B), 6 to Astor Pl., 212-777-2555
'Basic' is putting it mildly at this ultra no-frills East Village dive with cheap pops, zero decor and a rock 'n' roll soul; pool and foosball tables, open mike night and a makeshift stage showcasing local bands supply the diversions here.

Savalas
– | – | – | M

285 Bedford Ave. (bet. Grand & S. 1st Sts.), Brooklyn, L to Bedford Ave., 718-599-5565; www.savalasnyc.com
Part of Williamsburg's booming south side is this DJ-focused newcomer that's just as cool as its more northerly brethren, but somewhat cozier due to warm colors and a publike vibe; swell happy-hour deals help attract neighborhood swillers.

Savannah Steak
▽ 18 | 21 | 20 | $10

7 E. 48th St. (bet. 5th & Madison Aves.), B/D/F/V to 47-50th Sts./ Rockefeller Ctr., 212-935-2500; www.savannahsteak.com
Take care of "business after work" at this Midtown steakhouse where the "robust" bar corrals a "high ratio of bankers" with "big cigars" and the "women who chase them"; the energy often "dies off" by dinnertime, but the "excellent (if pricey) wines" and "friendly" service hold their own even when it's a meatery that's only "trying to be" a meet market.

SCHILLER'S
24 | 22 | 19 | $10

131 Rivington St. (Norfolk St.), F/J/M/Z to Delancey/Essex Sts., 212-260-4555; www.schillersny.com
"Balthazar/Pastis mastermind" Keith McNally "strikes again" with "Lower East Side swagger" at this "impeccable", perpetually packed "white-tile facsimile" of a "'20s French cafe" that gives "chic" sorts the chillers; "edgier" and "slightly cheaper" than its brethren, it's just as "hectic" and "self-impressed", so even if the backdrop "feels like a restaurant", it's still "worth fighting your way in."

Scopa
20 | 20 | 19 | $11

79 Madison Ave. (bet. 28th & 29th Sts.), 6 to 28th St., 212-686-8787; www.scoparestaurant.com
A "classy" standby in a lacking neighborhood is the scoopa on this Gramercy restaurant/bar that turns "busy" when the "nearby corporate" hives empty out; proponents praise the handsome room

with its endless stretch of burnished bar, but contras cite a "random" clientele that skews on the "older" side.

SCORES
23 | 17 | 20 | $14

333 E. 60th St. (bet. 1st & 2nd Aves.), 4/5/6/N/R/W to 59th St./Lexington Ave., 212-421-3600

536 W. 28th St. (bet. 10th & 11th Aves.), C/E to 23rd St., 212-868-4900
www.scoresnewyork.com

"Silicone never looked so good" as at these "high-end" stripperamas, jiggling "off the hook" with scores of "gorgeous" g-stringers proffering "G-rated lap dances"; "obscene" prices mean the other "plastic" on display will be "corporate cards", and some boobs titter this is where "lemmings follow their leader – Howard Stern."

Scratcher
∇ 23 | 16 | 22 | $6

209 E. Fifth St., downstairs (bet. 2nd & 3rd Aves.), 6 to Astor Pl., 212-477-0030

East Villagers itching for a "perfect pint" of "creamy" Guinness duck "underground" into this "small Irish bar" where the bevvy's "super-affordable" and the crowd comprised of a "wider age range"; the "warm and fuzzy hospitality" makes for a "low-key" "break from all the attitude in the area", so regulars would prefer to "keep it a semi-secret."

Scruffy Duffy's
15 | 11 | 16 | $7

743 Eighth Ave. (bet. 46th & 47th Sts.), A/C/E to 42nd St./Port Authority, 212-245-9126; www.scruffyduffys.com

"Get all the sports you want" at this Hell's Kitchen "bar-hop" fixture, a "cheap dive" that nonetheless "draws a crowd" with "tons of flat-screen" viewing augmented by "pool, darts" and "greasy" grub; "teeming" with "scruffy young fellas", it's "rowdy", dingy and "reeks of beer" – in other words, the "ideal place to watch any game."

SEA
25 | 27 | 21 | $8

114 N. Sixth St. (Berry St.), Brooklyn, L to Bedford Ave., 718-384-8850; www.searestaurant.com

See Williamsburg go "over the top" at this Thai restaurant, an "eye-catching" extravaganza where the "Buddha"-equipped "reflection pool", "swinging chairs" and "way cool" circular bar add up to a heady "experience"; fans report "wall-to-wall hipster watching" in this "over-trendy" "zoo" that's worth cruising by for its "crazy restrooms" alone.

Second Nature
17 | 17 | 18 | $8

221 Second Ave. (bet. 13th & 14th Sts.), L to 3rd Ave., 212-254-2222; www.secondnaturenyc.com

Gemini Lounge's "surprisingly decent second coming", this East Village bar draws a "cute", "social" mix of "yuppies" and "NYU coeds" into its "swanky" but "not overdone" confines; its "friendly" door and "groovy" DJ soundtrack lead to a "packed house", so crowding naturally arises.

SELECT
– | – | – | E

49 W. 24th St. (bet. 5th & 6th Aves.), F/V to 23rd St., 212-255-9200; www.selectny.com

Choosy night-owls select this new Flatiron lounge for its Technicolor Gothic glamour, with carved-wood arches, stained glass and heavy chandeliers setting the darkly stylish mood, echoed by a staff that's "friendly if a bit distracted" (and "distracting, too"); although it does get "crowded", some say it's still trying to "find its footing."

Senor Swanky's
13 | 11 | 14 | $8

142 Bleecker St. (La Guardia Pl.), A/B/C/D/E/F/V to W. 4th St., 212-979-9800

513 Columbus Ave. (bet. 84th & 85th Sts.), 1 to 86th St., 212-579-2900

Join "college kids" for "flavored margaritas" on the "summertime" patios at these "generic" Mexican joints where the "loud decor" simulates a "bar in Cabo"; those who find them "annoying even if you're just walking by" see "nothing swanky" in sight here.

Sequoia
18 | 18 | 17 | $9

Pier 17, 89 Fulton St. (South St.), 2/3 to Fulton St., 212-732-9090;
www.arkrestaurants.com

The "pretty view of the Brooklyn Bridge" makes this South Street Seaport bar/restaurant "just classy enough" to draw crowds "after work"; though planted on "touristy" turf, it's a "popular" stop, "especially in the summer" when it goes disco on Fridays for those who just "wanna drink and dance" at week's end.

SERAFINA
21 | 19 | 18 | $11

Dream Hotel, 210 W. 55th St. (B'way), N/Q/R/W to 57th St./7th Ave.,
212-315-1700
38 E. 58th St. (bet. Madison & Park Aves.), 4/5/6/N/R/W to 59th St./
Lexington Ave., 212-832-8888
29 E. 61st St. (bet. Madison & Park Aves.), 4/5/6/N/R/W to 59th St./
Lexington Ave., 212-702-9898
393 Lafayette St. (4th St.), 6 to Astor Pl., 212-995-9595
1022 Madison Ave., 2nd fl. (79th St.), 6 to 77th St., 212-734-2676
www.serafinarestaurant.com

Practice "English as a second language" at these "cute", "easy" Italians where "pretty Euros" "chill out after a day of shopping"; the Midtown outlets are distinctly "not as chic" as the "model"-friendly Village original, though its "sex appeal" lingers despite "heavy" tabs and "lots of attitude."

Serena
21 | 19 | 16 | $11

Chelsea Hotel, 222 W. 23rd St. (bet. 7th & 8th Aves.), C/E to 23rd St.,
212-255-4646; www.serenanyc.com

Still a "trusted go-to" for "intimate" lounging, this "underground" enclave beneath the Chelsea Hotel is styled as a "dark, sexy boudoir" with "velvet couches"; "everyone looks stunning" as they plan their next "tryst", but antis allege it's "seen its better days" – someone should tell the "difficult doormen" the "snob appeal" is fading.

Session 73
19 | 17 | 16 | $8

1359 First Ave. (73rd St.), 6 to 77th St., 212-517-4445; www.session73.com

It's a "rockin' good time" at this "busy", "roomy" Upper Eastsider as "bands with talent" hold jazzy jam sessions for a "party"-minded clientele too "upscale" for the "monotonous row of sports bars" that rules the nabe; even if the hobnobbing can be "hit-or-miss", it's "always there if you're feeling lonely."

7B
19 | 11 | 15 | $6

(aka Horseshoe Bar)
108 Ave. B (7th St.), L to 1st Ave., 212-473-8840

"One of the originals" for "old-school" East Village grunge, this "dingy dump" features "blasting metal on the jukebox", "awesome" prices and "surly service" from "tattooed, pierced" gents behind the "horseshoe-shaped bar"; it's frequented by both "alternative" types and Uptowners who sneak in and "brag about it the next day."

17
∇ 19 | 18 | 19 | $11

37 W. 17th St. (bet. 5th & 6th Aves.), 1 to 18th St., 212-924-8676

There's not much floor space, so "dress to impress" to "make it past the velvet rope" at this "hot" new Chelsea lounge from the team "who brought you Suite 16", offering bottle service, "awesome" hard-rock DJing and Friday night "karaoke, baby"; despite few frills, "its 10 minutes" are ticking so it's worth a detour to "see who's coming in and out."

17 Home
18 | 17 | 18 | $9

17 Stanton St. (bet. Bowery & Chrystie St.), F/V to Lower East Side/2nd Ave., 212-598-2145; www.17home.net

Slightly "off the beaten path", this Lower Eastsider matches "simple" beige-on-white decor with an "interesting" layout featuring a "big back room" and a basement labyrinth that's like being "lost in Hipster World"; "twenties" loungers grouse it's "empty sometimes", but weekends "get busy" as prodigals come home to "party."

17 Murray
– | – | – | I

17 Murray St. (bet. B'way & Church St.), R/W to City Hall, 212-608-3900; www.17murray.com

Hard by City Hall, this Financial District fixture is "great fun" "once you get to know the friendly staff" and courthouse regulars who make it a hub of after-hours scuttlebutt; even outsiders find it "surprisingly good" for a belt and a bite, though it would be impolitic to expect much more.

Shade
▽ 19 | 16 | 20 | $8

241 Sullivan St. (bet. Bleecker & W. 3rd Sts.), A/B/C/D/E/F/V to W. 4th St., 212-982-6275

An unexpected find "in the raucous NYU area", this "romantic, shadowy" Village wine bar forgoes the kid stuff for a "touch of Europe" complete with "wonderful" vinos and "yummy crêpes"; the "small" setup doesn't throw much shade, but it's a rare "gem" on turf more accustomed to roaming frat parties.

Shag
▽ 21 | 21 | 21 | $9

4 Eighth Ave. (bet. Bleecker & W. 12th Sts.), A/C/E/L to 14th St./8th Ave., 212-242-0220; www.shagbar.com

Fans of the "kitschy" '60s dig the "trademark shag-lined" walls at this "casual-trendy" West Villager, a "totally adorable" tribute to mod where the "innovative cocktail list" is as "sweet" as the Marc Jacobs–clad staff; with tapas-style "comfort food" as an added attraction, it's no surprise that "cute" young things "end up here a lot."

SHALEL LOUNGE
26 | 26 | 20 | $9

65½ W. 70th St., downstairs (bet. Columbus Ave. & CPW), B/C to 72nd St., 212-873-2300

Take an "unexpected" trip to some "far-away" Mediterranean land at this "intriguing underground grotto" tucked below an Upper West Side Greek eatery; its "mysterious" honeycomb setup with "walls of rough-cut stone" and plenty of "nooks and crannies to snuggle in" is made for "romance", though so many are in on the "secret" that it can "get a little too cozy" these days.

Shark Bar
20 | 19 | 20 | $12

307 Amsterdam Ave. (bet. 74th & 75th Sts.), 1/2/3 to 72nd St., 212-874-8500; www.sharkbar.com

Everything's fin and dandy at this Upper West Side "buppie hangout" where "beautiful people" from the realms of "sports and music" are "always in the house"; the "narrow" bar area is usually "packed", though a snarky few feel the "overrated" scene's just treading water.

Shebeen
– | – | – | E

202 Mott St. (bet. Kenmare & Spring Sts.), 6/J/M/N/Q/R/W/Z to Canal St., 212-625-1105

It's "hidden out of the way", so expect a "quiet drink rather than a raucous night out" at this NoLita bar/lounge where the "understated cool" and "interesting" mixology (i.e. those "fantastic lychee martinis") lend a "sophisticated" air; fans say it's "better than the trendy" stops in the nabe for "cozy conversation."

Shelly's New York
18 | 19 | 19 | $11

104 W. 57th St. (6th Ave.), F to 57th St., 212-245-2422;
www.shellysnewyork.com

When day is done and "great martinis" are in order, desk jockeys
adjourn to the upstairs lounge at this splashy Midtown restaurant,
whose amenities include "good-looking seafood" apps and live jazz;
it's a prime "place for businesspeople to bring clients" on expense
accounts since the tabs can be a serious shellacking.

Shelter ⊘
– | – | – | E

20 W. 39th St. (bet. 5th & 6th Aves.), 7/B/D/F/V to 42nd St./6th Ave.,
212-719-4479; www.clubshelter.com

If you need sanctuary "to get your dance on", this gargantuan Garment
District club is an "urban melting pot" where "big-name DJs" keep
the floor in a swelter; some sense "sketchy" company and "B&T"
infringement, but there's no question "this is a party that will
make you move."

Sherwood Cafe ⊘
▽ 23 | 25 | 16 | $7

195 Smith St. (bet. Baltic & Warren Sts.), Brooklyn, F/G to Bergen St.,
718-596-1609; www.sherwoodcafe.com

Get your "hip kitsch" to go from this Boerum Hill Gallic eatery, a patch
of "Paris in Brooklyn" chock-full of "eccentric" curios that are mostly
for sale; the *petit* bar and "lovely" garden are just the ticket for some
"wine by the glass", and it's "priced well – what more do you need?"

Ship of Fools
17 | 13 | 17 | $6

1590 Second Ave. (bet. 82nd & 83rd Sts.), 4/5/6 to 86th St.,
212-570-2651

Catch up "with the boys" at this "prototypical" Upper East Side sports
bar, a "massive" vessel with "flat screens in any direction you tilt your
head"; bar food and brewskis by the bucketful fuel the unruly, "no-frills
fun", and "hard-core" jocks "don't think it gets much better."

Show
18 | 20 | 13 | $10

135 W. 41st St. (bet. B'way & 6th Ave.), 1/2/3/7/N/Q/R/S/W to 42nd St./
Times Sq., 212-278-0988; www.shownightclub.com

"You don't know where to look first" at this Times Square showstopper,
an old burlesque house revamped into a "club maven's dream" with
miles of red velvet, "Moulin Rouge–type" stage spectacles and a
"whole lot of freaks" on the "big dance floor"; the "gorgeous" crowds
are "out of control" and staffers "think they're God", but "forgive the
attitude" and it's surefire "entertainment."

Siberia ⊘
18 | 11 | 15 | $6

356 W. 40th St. (bet. 8th & 9th Aves.), A/C/E to 42nd St./Port Authority,
212-333-4141; www.siberiany.com

Even if this Port Authority–area "dump" is "not quite the original"
(formerly housed in an "IRT station"), it's still as "weird" and "grungy"
as before with "tag-sale furniture" and a basement stage for "indie
bands"; it's a favorite of hipsters and journalists, so if you can't locate
the "mystery" entrance, you "aren't meant to be here."

Sidetracks
17 | 17 | 20 | $8

45-08 Queens Blvd. (bet. 45th & 46th Sts.), Queens, 7 to 46th St.,
718-786-3570; www.sidetracksny.com

Known for railroad decor including a built-in caboose, this Sunnyside
bar/eatery is a "favorite local" where it's obvious the singles are
"from the neighborhood"; normally a whistlestop for a "quick" nip, on
weekend nights it switches tracks to become a club with DJs and lots
of loco motion.

Sidewalk
21 | 14 | 18 | $6

94 Ave. A (6th St.), L to 1st Ave., 212-473-7373
This "super laid-back" East Villager hosts an "always original" roster of "free live" music in its back room, running the gamut from the "talented" to the "bizarre"; if the "bar patrons leave something to be desired", there's also "outside seating" and an adjacent "24-hour restaurant."

Silverleaf Tavern
– | – | – | E

70 Park Ave. Hotel, 43 E. 38th St. (Park Ave.), 4/5/6/7/S to 42nd St./ Grand Central, 212-973-2550; www.silverleaftavern.com
Away from it all in a Murray Hill hotel lies this intimate new bar that's separated from the adjoining restaurant by a long communal table; the posh feel is more 1940s cocktail lounge than tavern, and the drinks list, created by master mixologist Dale DeGroff, offers new spins on old favorites; a late-night bar menu seals the deal.

Sin-é ⌐
20 | 13 | 18 | $6

150 Attorney St. (bet. Houston & Stanton Sts.), F/J/M/Z to Delancey/ Essex Sts., 212-388-0077; www.sin-e.com

Sin-é Bar ⌐
146 Attorney St. (Stanton St.), F/J/M/Z to Delancey/Essex Sts., 212-388-0077; www.sin-e.com
Take a break from the "terminally trendy Lower East Side" at this high-cred "classic", a music club that "books solid bands" and offers "great sound" and an "open" layout so fans "can see everything"; since it's "wine and beer only", hepcats head for its new, fully stocked sibling set nearby in a former bodega.

Single Room Occupancy ⌐
(aka SRO)
25 | 21 | 23 | $8

360 W. 53rd St. (bet. 8th & 9th Aves.), C/E to 50th St., 212-765-6299
The "easily missed" entrance and "door buzzer" are aptly "speakeasy-esque" at this "tiny" Hell's Kitchen "hideaway", a bastion of "back-alley chic" serving "beer and wine only" in "sweet", "intimate" digs; its "secret society" of admirers runs from "artist types" to "suits and ties", and knowing your way in will surely "impress a date."

Sing Sing Karaoke
∇ 23 | 9 | 17 | $7

81 Ave. A (bet. 5th & 6th Sts.), L to 1st Ave., 212-674-0700
9 St. Marks Pl., 2nd fl. (bet. 2nd & 3rd Aves.), 6 to Astor Pl., 212-387-7800
"Bring a party", "grab a Kirin and cut loose" at this "divey" East Village karaoke joint where would-be warblers are always the "main attraction"; maybe the "actual bar is slightly sketchy", but once you're penned up with friends in a private room "singing Elvis", you'll be having "too much fun" to notice; P.S. the St. Marks Place branch is new and unrated.

Sin Sin/Leopard Lounge
18 | 16 | 16 | $8

248 E. Fifth St. (2nd Ave.), 6 to Astor Pl., 212-253-2222; www.leopardloungenyc.com
"Two levels of fun" prove that "dual personality works" at this "reasonably priced" East Village spot split into a "toned-down" ground-floor bar and a packed (verging on claustrophobic) upstairs lounge; maybe the "crowd isn't the trendiest", but it's still an "attractive enough" mix.

6's & 8's
18 | 16 | 17 | $8

205 Chrystie St. (Stanton St.), F/V to Lower East Side/2nd Ave., 212-477-6688
Though outwardly "a little tough", this Lower Eastsider is just a plain old "rock bar" with "nonstop loud" tunes in the booth-lined upstairs and a "spacious downstairs" rec room; odds-makers see a "diamond

in the rough", though a potential snake-eyes scenewise "if you don't bring a posse."

66 22 | 23 | 20 | $13

241 Church St. (Leonard St.), 1/2/3 to Chambers St., 212-925-0202; www.jean-georges.com
"Excellent signature drinks" are dispensed in the "über-minimalist" lounge of this "sexy", "subdued" TriBeCa restaurant via Jean-Georges Vongerichten; even if most of the loungers are merely "biding time until their table opens up" and the "off-the-beaten-path" locale means there's "not enough foot traffic", it's certainly a "cool environment" for "relaxing", "exquisitely expensive" imbibing.

Skinny, The – | – | – | M
(fka Angel)

174 Orchard St. (Stanton St.), F/J/M/Z to Delancey/Essex Sts., 212-228-3668
"Well, it's narrow" is the early take on this new Lower Eastsider where long, high walls lined with canvases from area artists allow slim space for the bar and DJ booth; so far, the skinny is it "looks good" but has yet to "figure out its personality."

Slainte – | – | – | M

304 Bowery (bet. Bleecker & Houston Sts.), B/D/F/V to B'way/Lafayette St., 212-253-7030; www.slaintenyc.com
Get that "Irish bar feeling" in "spacious", clean-cut quarters at this new NoHo pub done in traditional mahogany and brick with a boothy back area; "friendly barkeeps" and "TVs to catch games on" make it "welcoming in every way", maybe even poised to "take off."

Slane – | – | – | M
(fka Nikita)

102 MacDougal St. (Bleecker St.), A/B/C/D/E/F/V to W. 4th St., 212-505-0079; www.slanenyc.com
This standard-issue Village Irish pub is "not very trendy", but it's "not crowded either" given the "adult" feel in a "mostly student neighborhood"; some say its "only appeal is the open doors" facing the street, rendering it "not so appealing when it's cold outside."

Slate 20 | 19 | 19 | $10

54 W. 21st St. (bet. 5th & 6th Aves.), F/V to 23rd St., 212-989-0096; www.slate-ny.com
Way "nicer than regular pool rooms", this "upscale" Flatiron billiards parlor is an "airy", split-level affair boasting "plenty of tables" plus a "happening" bar that's "appealing to both sexes"; it's a "neat concept" for shooting stick or just sticking to "people-watching", though a spell on the felt will rack up a "pricey" bill.

Slaughtered Lamb Pub 18 | 18 | 16 | $8

182 W. Fourth St. (Jones St.), A/B/C/D/E/F/V to W. 4th St., 212-727-3350; www.slaughteredlambpub.com
Channeling *An American Werewolf in London*, this "olde" West Village pub pours "beers from around the world" in a multiroom "dungeon" decked with campy horror decor; it's a "consistent if uninventive" lair for "packs of NYU students" and "out-of-towners", though foes fear it's just bloody "weird."

SLIDE, THE ∇ 21 | 15 | 22 | $7

356 Bowery, downstairs (bet. 4th & Great Jones Sts.), 6 to Astor Pl., 212-420-8885
Slide into something "decadent but cozy" at this East Village gay bar, a (barely) refurbished 19th-century cellar updated for "modern-day shenanigans" with low lights, low lifes and "scandalous go-go boys";

brought to you by the Marion's Continental folks, it's a "joyfully sleazy" opportunity to get "a little naughty", though sober types shrug "trashy."

Slipper Room   ▽ 23 | 16 | 19 | $7

167 Orchard St. (Stanton St.), F/V to Lower East Side/2nd Ave., 212-253-7246; www.slipperroom.com

Inhibitions slip away as this "unique" Lower Eastsider stages "hilarious burlesque" à la ironic comics, "drag kings" and "sexy striptease" chicks; it's "too damn funny when you're drunk" and also works when "straight people want to have a near-gay experience."

SMALLS ∅   – | – | – | M

183 W. 10th St. (7th Ave.), 1 to Christopher St., 212-675-7369; www.fatcatjazz.com

After a year-and-a-half hiatus, this much loved Village jazz joint is jumping again in its former digs, all spruced up with a shiny new liquor license to boot; as in the past, the cover charge is $10, and even though there's now a two-drink minimum, diehards declare it's a modest price to pay for the avant-garde acts gracing its intimate stage.

Smoke   22 | 17 | 19 | $11

2751 Broadway (bet. 105th & 106th Sts.), 1 to 103rd St., 212-864-6662; www.smokejazz.com

"If you love jazz", break out the "black beret and scarf" and head for this "intimate" Upper West Side "godsend" where "young phenoms" mix it up onstage with the "old guard"; the "cramped quarters" ensure an "exclusive" feel and there's "good sound everywhere", generating all-around "awesome vibes."

Snapper Creek   14 | 12 | 16 | $6

1589 First Ave. (bet. 82nd & 83rd Sts.), 4/5/6 to 86th St., 212-327-1319

Upper Eastsiders up the creek for options turn to this "roomy" "local yokel" bar where "junior investment bankers" can "watch a game" and groove to "'80s hits" while pool sharks "may actually get on the table"; sure, its staunchest supporters are "too young to know any better", but at least it's "there when you need it."

SNITCH   ▽ 25 | 18 | 17 | $8

59 W. 21st St. (bet. 5th & 6th Aves.), F/V to 23rd St., 212-727-7775

Velvet Revolver goes "velvet ropey" at this Flatiron upstairs bar (part-owned by members of the band) where flat-screen TVs air sports, "amazing DJs" keep it "authentic" and "impromptu jam sessions" happen on the small stage; fans run the gamut from "hipsters" to "reformed metalheads" with "lots of tattoos", and informants squeal "this place rocks."

S.O.B.'s ∅   21 | 18 | 16 | $10

204 Varick St. (Houston St.), 1 to Houston St., 212-243-4940; www.sobs.com

"*The* place to samba", this SoHo Latin club features some of the "best in world entertainment" with a "rotating selection" of "slamming DJs" and "amazing live shows"; all that "Carnaval flavor" combined with "killer caipirinhas" fires up a "diverse" crowd that doesn't mind dropping some *dinero* for the chance to "get wild."

Social   19 | 18 | 19 | $8

795 Eighth Ave. (bet. 48th & 49th Sts.), C/E to 50th St., 212-459-0643; www.socialbarnyc.com

"Lots of partying singles" turn up at this Hell's Kitchen triplex, offering "multilevel fun" from the ground-floor Irish sports bar to the "sleek" upper-level lounge and "refreshing" outdoor deck; it's a chance to "be social with strangers", though some snub the "tacky pickup" scene.

Soda Bar
∇ 23 | 20 | 24 | $6

629 Vanderbilt Ave. (bet. Prospect & St. Mark's Pls.), Brooklyn, 2/3/4 to Grand Army Plaza, 718-230-8393
An "old soda fountain" that's traded egg creams for the hard stuff, this "friendly" Prospect Heights joint lures "multicultural locals" with "cheap" potables and "bar eats"; favored for its rear garden, "free" pool table and "comprehensive jukebox", it's "laid-back" but "funky" – "just like the neighborhood."

Soho Billiards ⊅
– | – | – | M

56 E. Houston St. (Mott St.), B/D/F/V to B'way/Lafayette St., 212-925-3753
There are "plenty of pool tables available" at this sprawling billiard hall on the NoHo/SoHo border, since it's "usually empty"; maybe that's because it "needs a complete rehaul", but at least you won't have to wait around to get your game on.

Soho House
22 | 23 | 17 | $12

29-35 Ninth Ave. (W. 14th St.), A/C/E/L to 14th St./8th Ave., 212-627-9800; www.sohohouseny.com
Think urban "country club" (with "dark wood and leather everywhere") to get the gist of this six-floor private club in the Meatpacking District offering a bar, restaurant, library and hotel rooms as well as a cool pool on the roof; it also supplies "sanctuary from the hordes" outside, though some say for best results a "British accent is better than a membership card."

SOHO: 323
∇ 19 | 21 | 18 | $11

323 W. Broadway (bet. Canal & Grand Sts.), C/E to Spring St., 212-334-2232; www.soho323.com
"High Miami style" brings fashionable types to this "swanky" SoHo newcomer, a loftlike duplex with a "mellow bar" that contrasts with the "hot upstairs lounge"; "fantastic" martinis and select DJs ensure "long lines", but it's "worth it" so long as you can handle the "attitude at the door."

Solas
19 | 18 | 20 | $7

232 E. Ninth St. (bet. 2nd & 3rd Aves.), 6 to Astor Pl., 212-375-0297; www.solasbar.com
"Young partiers" choose from "different vibes" at this plus-size East Villager, boasting a "low-key bar" downstairs and DJs spinning up top, as well as "chill" private niches; believers thank the "gods of going out" for the "cheap drinks", "convivial" staffers and "meat market" prospects ("you won't be solas for long").

SON CUBANO
23 | 22 | 19 | $11

405 W. 14th St. (Washington St.), A/C/E/L to 14th St./8th Ave., 212-366-1640; www.soncubanonyc.com
Guaranteed to "get the party started", this "caliente" Meatpacking District Cuban is a "tropical mini-vacation" that brings out the "Latin lover" in its "international crowd" via "killer mojitos" and "really loud" live salsa rhythms; it's "packed" at "prime times" since everyone needs a "respite from its pretentious neighbors."

Sonny's Bar & Grill
∇ 19 | 17 | 21 | $7

305 Smith St. (Union St.), Brooklyn, F/G to Carroll St., 718-643-3293
The "big windows" and sunny "outdoor tables" offer primo "people-watching" at this Carroll Gardens newbie, a "conventional" bar/restaurant that invites patrons to "hang out as long as you want"; the "family-oriented" ambiance "misses the mark" for drinking-oriented sorts, but it still "passes if you're in a jam."

Sophie's ⌀
∇ | 20 | 11 | 20 | $5

507 E. Fifth St. (bet. Aves. A & B), F/V to Lower East Side/2nd Ave., 212-228-5680
A slice of "quintessential East Village" low life, this '40s vet is "the diviest of dive bars" where "wannabe artists" mix with "bums off the street"; note to neophytes: don't look for the name outside (there's none) and "pray you don't need to use the bathroom."

Southpaw ⌀
24 | 20 | 22 | $8

125 Fifth Ave. (bet. Sterling & St. Johns Pls.), Brooklyn, B/Q to 7th Ave., 718-230-0236; www.spsounds.com
Park Slopers into "cutting-edge" bands "don't have to take the F train home" thanks to this "top-notch rock club", a user-friendly venue with top "indie" talent, sufficient seating and "real bartenders" pouring drinks "without hipster attitude"; the "awesome sound" and "reasonable prices" are pitch-perfect for a "youthful night out."

SouthWest NY
18 | 20 | 16 | $10

2 World Financial Ctr. (bet. Liberty St. & South End Ave.), 1/2/3 to Chambers Sts., 212-945-0528; www.southwestny.com
"When the weather's right", the "Wall Street crowd" invests in the "after-work meat market" at this "water's-edge" WFC outpost with "amazing", "can't-be-beat" Hudson River views; a few find the scenery indoors "subpar", but at least it's "convenient" in an area with limited options.

SPICE MARKET
25 | 27 | 18 | $13

403 W. 13th St. (9th Ave.), A/C/E/L to 14th St./8th Ave., 212-675-2322; www.jean-georges.com
Expect lots of "über-fabulous" types (and some wannabes) at this "sceney" Meatpacking District entry, an outrajahs Asian eatery via Jean-Georges Vongerichten that comes complete with a "sexy, mysterious" downstairs lounge featuring "hidden cabanas" made for having a "Bali"; it's high "drama to get in", so expect "maddening waits" to "see what all the fuss is about."

Spider Club
∇ | 18 | 18 | 15 | $10

47 W. 20th St. (6th Ave.), F/V to 23rd St., 212-807-7780; www.avalonnewyorkcity.com
Avalon's VIP room, "with its own name and entrance", this Flatiron District club within a club is still "trying to establish some sort of exclusivity" with varying degrees of success; it's not as packed as the mother ship, maybe because of the "overpriced drinks" and "Studio 54–wannabe" crowd.

Spike Hill
– | – | – | M

184 Bedford Ave. (N. 7th St.), Brooklyn, L to Bedford Ave., 718-218-9737
Thirst comes first at this youngish yet old-school Irish saloon in Williamsburg, where traditional values ensure a "large selection of beers" and "professional" tapmeisters who pride themselves on their way with "high-end classics"; topers attest the dark-wood "Manhattan feel" makes it a "great place to gather."

Spirit
17 | 16 | 14 | $11

530 W. 27th St. (bet. 10th & 11th Aves.), C/E to 23rd St., 212-268-9477; www.spiritnewyork.com
"Twilo is back – well, sort of" – at this "huge" West Chelsea club, a "hedonistic" excuse to "go nuts dancing" to "house/trance" music that's "six months ahead" of its time (with live shows also in the mix); but foes who call it "played out" cite a "dank" atmo, "attitude problems" and "long lines."

Spirit Cruises
25 | 21 | 22 | $14

Chelsea Piers, Pier 62 (W. 23rd St.), C/E to 23rd St., 212-727-2789; www.spiritcruises.com

"Hop on board" at Chelsea Piers for this "scenic" dinner cruise on a "pleasure yacht circling Manhattan", offering the "most fantastic" sights to distract voyagers "from the daily grind"; those not in the spirit dismiss it as "overpriced" bait for "out-of-towners", but "even the most jaded" secretly concede it's "a good time", at least "once or twice."

Splash ⏀
(aka SBNY)
20 | 19 | 16 | $8

50 W. 17th St. (bet. 5th & 6th Aves.), F/L/V to 14th St./6th Ave., 212-691-0073; www.splashbar.com

"Looks will definitely get you far" at this pumped-up Flatiron gay bar, a "cattle call" for "very hot beefcake" from "go-go" boys to "buff" barkeeps to maybe even the "man of your dreams"; if that's not enough, there's a new "lounge space downstairs" and the kind of DJ playlist "you want to hear", even if cynics call it a "stuck-up cliché" studded with "suburban folk."

SPOTTED PIG
24 | 20 | 21 | $10

314 W. 11th St. (Greenwich St.), 1 to Christopher St., 212-620-0393; www.thespottedpig.com

Despite the name, this "so-hyped" West Village corner of "jolly old London" is never a boar for "gastro-pub lovers" who dig the house-brewed ale, brick-lined charm and "pig" eating; since it's "way too cramped" for the "unbelievable" mobs hogging the "cozy" space, a "crazy wait" is "inevitable."

Spring Lounge
18 | 10 | 17 | $7

48 Spring St. (Mulberry St.), 6 to Spring St., 212-965-1774

"Everyone's a regular" at this "true NoLita staple" with a "loyal following" of "totally low-key" locals partial to "cheap brews", "well-worn" surroundings and "giant fish decor"; it gets particularly "sloppy on the weekends" as "frat brothers" keep it "crowded" to the max.

Sputnik
– | – | – | M

262 Taaffe Pl. (bet. DeKalb & Willoughby Aves.), Brooklyn, G to Classon Ave., 718-398-6666; www.barsputnik.com

Bohos have liftoff in Clinton Hill at this "spacious refuge" split into a main-floor lounge/cafe and a "retro space-age" downstairs where "unknown greats" stage "amazing" jam sessions; an art gallery, rotating DJs and "killer drinks" round out this "cool, cultured" cosmos prized for its "lack of hipsters."

Spuyten Duyvil
▽ 24 | 21 | 20 | $8

359 Metropolitan Ave. (Havemeyer St.), Brooklyn, L to Bedford Ave., 718-963-4140; www.spuytenduyvilnyc.com

The Dutch name invokes the devil, but the "endless selection of beer" comes from "on high" at this Williamsburg brew bar, featuring "far-out obscurities" and "a lot of Belgian" labels; since the "thrift-shop" furnishings and other knickknacks can be purchased, it's the spuyten image of a very "social garage sale."

Stain ⏀
– | – | – | M

766 Grand St. (bet. Graham Ave. & Humboldt St.), Brooklyn, L to Grand St., 718-387-7840; www.stainbar.com

"Imaginative" is the word for this off-the-beaten-path Williamsburg bar/lounge known for a selection of wine and beer that's "entirely NY-centric", along with enough "local artwork and performances" to make for a "cozy" boho feel.

St. Andrews
21 | 19 | 21 | $7

120 W. 44th St. (bet. B'way & 6th Ave.), 1/2/3/7/N/Q/R/S/W to 42nd St./
Times Sq., 212-840-8413
"Service with a smile" from barmen "in kilts" marks the "true Scottish"
manners at this Theater District pub where Tartans are heartened by
"fair prices", a "vast beer menu" and one of the "best selections of
single-malts" this side of Glasgow; it may seem "predictable", but
that doesn't mean it won't be "mobbed after work with suits."

Stand-Up NY Comedy Club
21 | 13 | 16 | $8

236 W. 78th St. (bet. Amsterdam Ave. & B'way), 1 to 79th St., 212-595-0850;
www.standupny.com
Seriously "funny" comics bring on "belly-aching" mirth at this Upper
West Side gigglefest where the lineup's liable to include "quite
famous" faces, though off nights may be a bit "subpar"; knockers
mock the "squashed" seating, but loyalists claim this "good time"
"won't break the bank."

Stan's
19 | 9 | 17 | $8

836 River Ave. (opp. Yankee Stadium), Bronx, 4/B/D to Yankee Stadium,
718-993-5548
"Prep for a Yanks game" at this Bronx sports bar where "bleacher
creatures" cram in to "get the blood up" and bums without tickets can
bench it and still "hear the roar of the stadium"; P.S. since it's "only
open during baseball season", you shouldn't "go out of your way."

Stanton Social
– | – | – | E

99 Stanton St. (Ludlow St.), F/J/M/Z to Delancey/Essex Sts.,
212-995-0099
On the ground level, this new Lower Eastsider is a small-plate dining
room, so nightcrawlers head upstairs to its mellow bar/lounge with a
retro air courtesy of the red-hot designers of Odea and Public; classy
leather banquettes, votive candles galore and screens adorned with
cherry blossoms make for cozy cocktailing and canoodling.

Starlight ⌀
21 | 20 | 18 | $8

167 Ave. A (bet. 10th & 11th Sts.), L to 1st Ave., 212-475-2172;
www.starlightbarlounge.com
A "key stop on the gay circuit", this "trendy" but "nonthreatening"
East Villager is populated by "attractive" "junior publicists on the
make", and thus the "tight quarters" are "often packed"; DJs add a
"happening" soundtrack, and Sunday's lesbian Starlette affair shines
as just about the "best girl's party" going.

Star 64
▽ 16 | 13 | 15 | $7

(fka Starfoods)
64 E. First St. (bet. 1st & 2nd Aves.), F/V to Lower East Side/2nd Ave.,
212-260-3116
It's "no chichi" scene, but cred-hungry "hipsters and Eurotrash alike"
flock to this two-sided East Villager for its flawlessly "retro vibe" and
"outta this world" weekend DJs; no matter which you choose, both
the front bar and "comfort food" rear restaurant are user "friendly."

Stay
– | – | – | E

(fka Abaya)
244 E. Houston St. (bet. Aves. A & B), F/V to Lower East Side/2nd Ave.,
212-982-3532; www.stay-nyc.com
The former Abaya has been lightly renovated into this new bar/lounge
on the East Village/Lower East Side border that still retains much
of its original mod decor; on the other hand, the crowd seems less
pretentious now, maybe because there's no velvet rope in sight.

St. Dymphna's   ▽ 22 | 15 | 19 | $6

*118 St. Marks Pl. (bet. Ave. A & 1st Ave.), L to 1st Ave., 212-254-6636;
www.stdymphnas.com*
It's named for the "patron saint of insanity", but this "unpretentious"
East Villager is a perfectly sensible choice for an "honest", "affordable"
pint of Guinness matched with a "real Irish pub feel"; the "boisterous
but well-behaved" "neighborhood" regulars swear by the "warm"
service and snug back patio, insisting "even the food is good."

Still   – | – | – | M
(fka Tavaru)
*192 Third Ave. (bet. 17th & 18th Sts.), 4/5/6/L/N/Q/R/W to 14th St./Union Sq.,
212-471-9807; www.stillnyc.com*
Gramercy's Tavaru is now reborn as "just a regular bar" with the
standard brick, hardwood and row of stools, but when the workday's
done it's "very crowded" with "post-college" types; the mix of meet
market and "strong drinks" is anything but mellow, so "bring earplugs."

Stir   23 | 21 | 21 | $11
*1363 First Ave. (bet. 73rd & 74th Sts.), 6 to 77th St., 212-744-7190;
www.stirnyc.com*
Finally, "a bit of a scene" is stirring on the Upper East Side at this
"trendy" new lounge where "upbeat" DJs and "fabulous martinis"
wow a "younger" clientele; with "comfy" banquettes and "soft
candlelight" to cushion the "steep" prices, it's a "decidedly cool" port
in a "sea of frat-boy bars."

Stitch   – | – | – | M
*247 W. 37th St. (bet. 7th & 8th Aves.), 1/2/3 to 34th St./Penn Station,
212-852-4826; www.stitchnyc.com*
The snoozy Garment District gets a wake-up call via this new bar/
lounge, a vast, high-ceilinged space that still retains its original 19th-
century bones, jazzed up with a long oak bartop, plasma screens and
a mezzanine level overlooking the action; it's a mega–after work
scene owing to its proximity to Penn Station and Port Authority, but is
much more subdued (and intimate) on weekends.

St. Marks Ale House   15 | 10 | 18 | $6
2 St. Marks Pl. (3rd Ave.), 6 to Astor Pl., 212-260-9762
"Drink cheaply" with the "Cooper Unioners" at this divey East Village
"college hangout", a "typical wings-and-beer" specialist with "many
TVs for the sports fan" and a "seat if you want one"; it's a "decent"
enough base for a "guy's football night", even if some ask "why a frat
bar on St. Marks?"

Stoned Crow   19 | 15 | 20 | $6
*85 Washington Pl. (bet. 6th Ave. & Washington Sq. W.), F/L/V to 14th St./
6th Ave., 212-677-4022; www.thestonedcrowny.com*
Just wing it at this "nontrendy" West Village basement bar, known for
"cheap" sauce, "abundant popcorn", walls papered with "old movie
stills" and some competitive pool in the back; it's the "perfect hideaway"
for "getting sloshed", at least until all of "NYU" flutters in.

Stonehome Wine Bar   ▽ 27 | 24 | 23 | $9
*87 Lafayette Ave. (bet. S. Elliott Pl. & S. Portland Ave.), Brooklyn, G to
Fulton St., 718-624-9443; www.stonehomewinebar.com*
With its pleasing bouquet of "homey" and "stylish", this "adorable
wine bar" is a "nice change" for Fort Greene's yupscale set parlaying
an "impressive" roster of labels poured by "helpful", "super-friendly"
staffers; the "warm" setting's curvy bartop and back garden both work
well for "laid-back" sipping.

STONE ROSE
23 | 25 | 19 | $13

Time Warner Ctr., 10 Columbus Circle, 4th fl. (60th St.), 1/A/B/C/D to 59th St./Columbus Circle, 212-823-9769; www.mocbars.com

"Get a rise" from the "expansive views" of Columbus Circle and Central Park at Rande Gerber's Time Warner Center "swankatorium", a handsome, "high-ceilinged" spot for "professionals" sipping "well-made" cocktails and apps conveyed by scantily clad "Kate Moss wannabes"; some suspect it's "overhyped", but there's "great mingling" to be had so long as "money is no object."

Stonewall
17 | 10 | 16 | $8

53 Christopher St. (bet. 7th Ave. S. & Waverly Pl.), 1 to Christopher St., 212-463-0950

"If you're gay, you gotta go" to this historic West Village bar that earns "homage" for its role in the '69 civil disobedience when the "movement started"; still, many say it's "kind of tired" and "needs patching up", proving there's a downside to "living in the past."

Suba
23 | 26 | 18 | $10

109 Ludlow St. (bet. Delancey & Rivington Sts.), F/V to Lower East Side/2nd Ave., 212-982-5714; www.subanyc.com

"Trendy" types give three cheers ("sexy, sexy, sexy!") to this Lower Eastsider featuring an "ultracool bar" at ground level and two "darkly elegant" dining rooms below (especially that "grottoesque" enclave bordered by an "amazing" moat); flamenco dancing and "strong cocktails fuel the fire", keeping the mood "lively" here.

Subway Inn ⊄
13 | 6 | 14 | $6

143 E. 60th St. (Lexington Ave.), 4/5/6/N/R/W to 59th St./Lexington Ave., 212-223-8929

A "real dive bar" from "before the term became ironic", this "poor man's paradise" near Bloomie's delivers the "down 'n' dirty" goods in all their "seedy glory" with "morning customers falling off" their stools and a treacherous "tilted floor" in the bathroom; the "amazingly cheap drinks" "make you feel welcome", but afterwards "go straight to AA."

SUEDE
20 | 20 | 16 | $11

161 W. 23rd St. (bet. 6th & 7th Aves.), 1 to 23rd St., 212-633-6113; www.suedelounge.com

"Still holding its own", this "celeb"-friendly Chelsea hot spot remains a "well-decorated den" that's "chock-full o' models" and other "pretty people" striking poses on "super-soft" banquettes until inspired to "get up and shake it"; it's "not impossible to get in" and thus "filled to maximum capacity", even if trendoids sniff "so two years ago."

Sugar
19 | 20 | 17 | $10

311 Church St. (bet. Lispenard & Walker Sts.), 1 to Canal St., 212-431-8642; www.sugarnyc.com

A sweet spot in TriBeCa, this "mod", bi-level bar/lounge flaunts a "cheeky" Danish Modern/African design, plus a downstairs that looks like "someone's basement" turned into a "sweaty" danceathon; a few say it's "a bit played", but most say this honey has "staying power."

Sugar Bar
∇ 19 | 21 | 18 | $11

254 W. 72nd St. (bet. B'way & West End Ave.), 1/2/3 to 72nd St., 212-579-0222; www.sugarbarnyc.com

"Owned by Ashford and Simpson" of Motown renown, this Upper West Side bar/eatery comes in "as smooth as can be" with a "beautiful" African-accented look and "great live entertainment"; a clientele that "feels local and friendly" says the chances of sugar-coated satisfaction are solid as a rock.

SUGARCANE
– | – | – | E

243 Park Ave. S. (bet. 19th & 20th Sts.), 4/5/6/L/N/Q/R/W to 14th St./ Union Sq., 212-475-9377; www.sushisamba.com

Connected to the Flatiron SushiSamba, this jazzy new offshoot looks more samba than sushi, with a sexy Amazon jungle vibe via abstract leaves on the ceiling and a red-lit, tunnel-like space; trendy is the vibe, beautiful is the crowd and sake is the thing to drink here.

Sullivan Room
∇ | 18 | 15 | 16 | $8

218 Sullivan St. (bet. Bleecker & W. 3rd Sts.), A/B/C/D/E/F/V to W. 4th St., 212-252-2151; www.sullivanroom.com

"Underground" both literally and in spirit, this West Village DJ lair offers prime audiophile downtime as "top-notch international" deckmeisters drop "quality house" mixes; the sub–street level space is "too sketchy to be chichi", "too glam to be a dive" but just clubby enough for "a little naughtiness."

Sunita
– | – | – | M

106 Norfolk St. (bet. Delancey & Rivington Sts.), F/J/M/Z to Delancey/ Essex Sts., 917-250-8118

Nestled in a tiny storefront on a (relatively) tame Lower East Side block, this quiet boîte is a charming, no-frills neighborhood hangout for those looking for a hassle-free drink; the eponymous owner/ barkeep hosts every night, with a sweet experimental jazz program in play on Tuesdays.

Sunny's ⌐
– | – | – | M

253 Conover St. (bet. Beard & Reed Sts.), Brooklyn, 2/3/4/5/M/R to Borough Hall, 718-625-8211

You can "smell the waterfront" at this "middle of nowhere" Red Hook "neighborhood bar" that's been dispensing spirits since the 1890s under different names and today is run by the great-grandson of the original owner; sure, it's a kitschy, "paraphernalia"-laden joint, but its hippie-artist-beatnik following finds it "nostalgic" and "beyond charming."

Superfine
26 | 23 | 23 | $8

126 Front St. (bet. Jay & Pearl Sts.), Brooklyn, F to York St., 718-243-9005; www.eatatsuperfine.com

"Supercool" and "superfriendly", this spacious Dumbo bar/restaurant offers an "open" industrial space outfitted with "funky" furnishings, "comfortable" couches and a "free pool table"; arty natives call it the "right bar in the right place", and with intermittent live entertainment it's "interesting" enough to merit a "trip over the bridge."

SUPREME TRADING
– | – | – | M

213 N. Eighth St. (bet. Driggs Ave. & Roebling St.), Brooklyn, L to Bedford Ave., 718-218-6538

Doing drinkers, "artists and spectators" a "genuine service", this super-size Williamsburg newcomer trades on its "incredible" floor space to accommodate not only a barroom but "installations" and fashion shows as well; with a garden, two galleries and a generous lounge area, this "big but not too trendy" venue aspires "to be supreme."

Sushi Generation
12 | 11 | 14 | $9

1571 Second Ave. (bet. 81st & 82nd Sts.), 4/5/6 to 86th St., 212-249-2222

This Upper Eastsider generates interest by merging a "sushi and sports" bar into a one-stop "combo" with jocks "on the TVs" and rolls on the menu; some trying to referee the "identity issue" rule it's more an "average" Japanese restaurant, yet on "certain game nights, expect a wait."

SUSHISAMBA   23 | 23 | 18 | $12

*245 Park Ave. S. (bet. 19th & 20th Sts.), 4/5/6/L/N/Q/R/W to 14th St./
Union Sq., 212-475-9377*
87 Seventh Ave. S. (Barrow St.), 1 to Christopher St., 212-691-7885
www.sushisamba.com
"Rio meets Tokyo" at these "chic multicultural" nightspots that
are "faves among scenesters" and "fashionistas" thanks to "sexy",
"lively" vibes as well as "faboo drinks" and fusion fare; the Village
outpost's "open-air rooftop" is "cool" when you're "feeling hot, hot,
hot", but all that "hyped-up" spice makes for a "price to match."

Sutra   _ | _ | _ | M
(fka The Flat)
*16 First Ave. (bet. 1st & 2nd Sts.), F/V to Lower East Side/2nd Ave.,
212-677-9477; www.sutranyc.com*
Channeling "swanky" karma as The Flat's reincarnation, this East
Villager suits youthful acolytes with its gold Buddhist icons and
"sexy", scarlet-lined back room; the ample downstairs lounge is
suffused with "inviting" candlelight, and if there's nothing "really that
different" in the mix, it's still an "altogether good time."

SUTTON PLACE   17 | 15 | 15 | $8
*1015 Second Ave. (bet. 53rd & 54th Sts.), E/V to Lexington Ave./53rd St.,
212-207-3777; www.suttonplacenyc.com*
"Just-out-of-college preppies" feeling "frisky" throw on "Abercrombie
button-downs" and pack into this tri-level Upper East Side "mating
ground" till they're "squished" like the "6 train during rush hour"; it's
a "go-to in the summer" when the "rooftop bar rocks", but it still puts
you right "back at the frat house" for more of "the same old."

Sway   21 | 18 | 16 | $10
*305 Spring St. (bet. Greenwich & Hudson Sts.), 1 to Houston St.,
212-620-5220; www.swaylounge.com*
Exuding Casablanca "chic" in West SoHo, this "high-energy" souk
("hidden" behind the 'McGovern's Bar' sign) sways "beautiful but
easygoing" revelers into dubbing it "*the* place" for "late-night
dancing" to "fab flashback music"; expect "no pretension inside",
though the "difficult" door could "lose the 'tude."

Sweet & Vicious   17 | 14 | 15 | $8
*5 Spring St. (bet. Bowery & Elizabeth St.), 6 to Spring St., 212-334-7915;
www.sweetandvicious.com*
As the name suggests, this NoLita Turkish bar merges the "divey"
with the "divine", drawing "tons of twentysomethings" to its "dark,
roomy" digs; the "casual" setup sports hoop "chandeliers", "plank
floors" and an "amazing" back garden, but the overall scene's "too
popular" and ergo "not as hip as it used to be."

Sweet Rhythm   _ | _ | _ | M
*88 Seventh Ave. S. (bet. Bleecker & Grove Sts.), A/B/C/D/E/F/V to W. 4th St.,
212-255-3626; www.sweetrhythmny.com*
Set in the former Sweet Basil space on Seventh Avenue South, this
Village music club offers a diverse roster of acts, from jazz to blues to
merengue and beyond; somewhat underpopulated, it's just the ticket for
low-key listening with reasonably priced covers and drink minimums.

Sweetwater ⊄   ∇ 17 | 15 | 18 | $6
*105 N. Sixth St. (bet. Berry St. & Wythe Ave.), Brooklyn, L to Bedford Ave.,
718-963-0608*
Thanks to "new ownership" determined to "expunge" its "punk bar
past", this "cleaned up" Williamsburger is now in a "bistro groove"

with snug booths, "lace curtains" and even "fancy food"; it's still a handy watering hole, though headbangers sigh it's "just not the same" since they "kept the name but took away the soul."

Swift
| 21 | 20 | 20 | $6 |

34 E. Fourth St. (bet. Bowery & Lafayette St.), 6 to Astor Pl., 212-227-9438; www.swiftbarnyc.com

"Anyone can feel comfortable" at this "low-key" but comparatively "upscale" NoHo Irish pub where an "admirable beer selection" is poured with "flair" by "bartenders right off the boat"; "decent prices" and swift-talking "characters" "add to the charm", particularly if you like company "a little on the middle-aged side."

Swing 46 Jazz Club
| 18 | 14 | 17 | $12 |

349 W. 46th St. (bet. 8th & 9th Aves.), 1/2/3/7/N/Q/R/S/W to 42nd St./ Times Sq., 212-262-9554; www.swing46.com

"If you like to swing", shuffle over to this Restaurant Row supper club where "live bands" bring on the classics and the dance floor gets "jam-packed" with "serious" hoofers jumpin' and jivin'; even "non-swingers" can get in the mood with free lessons that make learning "much fun."

Tabla
| 24 | 24 | 23 | $12 |

11 Madison Ave. (25th St.), 6 to 23rd St., 212-889-0667; www.tablany.com

"Still a classic and for good reason", this "oasis of cool" via Danny Meyer offers "great specialty drinks" in deco Indian environs enhanced by a seasonal patio with mighty swell "vistas of Madison Square Park"; desk jockeys "celebrating their release from the daily grind" couldn't care less that it's on the "expensive" side.

TABLE 50
| 23 | 21 | 19 | $10 |

643 Broadway, downstairs (Bleecker St.), 6 to Bleecker St., 212-253-2560; www.table50.com

Named for Walter Winchell's Stork Club roost, this NoHo basement "ultralounge" recalls a shadowy, "hip" speakeasy with exposed brick, "cool vibes" and "great DJs" turning tables for a "beautiful" clientele; "bottle buyers" lining the banquettes inhabit "pricey" terrain, but with "celeb sightings" and a "surprisingly attitude-free staff", it's gaining steam as another reason "not to go to the Meatpacking District."

Tainted Lady Lounge
| – | – | – | M |

318 Grand St. (bet. Havemeyer St. & Marcy Ave.), Brooklyn, L to Bedford Ave., 718-302-5514; www.taintedladylounge.com

"Sex appeal" is busting out all over at this "cute" Billyburg bar where photos of "alluring beauties" flashing "T&A" adorn the walls and strippers unpeel on vintage videos; with a "female artist"–only jukebox and "delicious concoctions" named for famous femmes, it's a "friendly" hang that grows "more attractive" as the night wears on.

Taj
| 20 | 25 | 18 | $11 |

48 W. 21st St. (bet. 5th & 6th Aves.), R/W to 23rd St., 212-620-3033; www.tajlounge.com

"Hip without being off-putting", this "sultry" Flatiron bar/lounge offers "gorgeous" Ganges decor and "inventive cocktails" supplying the "edge"; DJs "get the room moving" since "dancing is key" to the "consistently solid" scene, though some are downcaste that it "doesn't seem to get a top crowd."

TAO
| 24 | 26 | 19 | $12 |

42 E. 58th St. (bet. Madison & Park Aves.), 4/5/6/N/R/W to 59th St./ Lexington Ave., 212-888-2288; www.taonyc.com

"Big Buddha is watching" the "sugar daddies", "glamour kitties" and "Hamptons types" at this "vibrant" Midtown "must-see", a "quintessentially trendy" spot to "hobnob" assuming you can "find some wiggle room"; "scintillating cocktails" and "tons of energy" justify the "stiff prices", and if doubters deem it "overdone", it's still "overrun by 5:01."

Tap a Keg

∇ 12 | 8 | 16 | $5

2731 Broadway (bet. 104th & 105th Sts.), 1 to 105th St., 212-749-1734
The boozing's "good and cheap" at this Upper West Side gin mill, a "nothing-special" spot where diehards drink up and feed the juke till they're all tapped out; meanwhile, those not "already completely intoxicated" cite a "weird crowd" that's either "just out of school" or "over 75."

Tapas Lounge

21 | 20 | 19 | $10

1078 First Ave. (59th St.), 4/5/6/N/R/W to 59th St./Lexington Ave., 212-421-8282
There's "authentic Spanish" spirit on a "desolate stretch" of East Midtown at this "mission-style" outpost where the sangria's "delightful" and the finger food's a "pretty good" match; all the "hardwood and wrought iron" may seem "a little Goth" and it's "pricey" to boot, but it still works well for an "informal" outing.

Tavern on Jane

21 | 15 | 23 | $7

31 Eighth Ave. (Jane St.), A/C/E/L to 14th St./8th Ave., 212-675-2526;
www.tavernonjane.com
A "quaint bar on a cute street", this "hidden" West Villager is a "homey" refuge from the hustle and bustle where the "bartender remembers your drink" and the regulars lend a "Cheers feel" to the proceedings; throw in "reasonable" prices, and it's just what "every nabe needs."

Tavern on the Green

23 | 23 | 20 | $13

Central Park W. (bet. 66th & 67th Sts.), B/C to 72nd St., 212-873-3200;
www.tavernonthegreen.com
Done up in "Fabergé egg" decor suited to "your grandmother's era", this "glitzy" Central Park "landmark" is "still going strong" as a "big-name" "default destination"; though some locals are bummed by "out-of-towners snapping pics", "a night in the garden" can be "terribly romantic" and even cynics say "get there at least once."

Tea Lounge ⊅

22 | 22 | 21 | $6

350 Seventh Ave. (10th St.), Brooklyn, F to 7th Ave., 718-768-4966
837 Union St. (bet. 6th & 7th Aves.), Brooklyn, M/R to Union St., 718-789-2762
"Alternative living rooms" for "mommies with tots" and "bohemians with iMacs", these "much-needed" Park Slopers provide "funky couches" where you can "stay for hours" sampling coffees, teas, treats and organic wines; but even in "mellow" mode, it may take "a drink just to handle" the mobs ("oh, for a little solitude!").

Teddy's Bar & Grill

23 | 17 | 18 | $6

96 Berry St. (N. 8th St.), Brooklyn, L to Bedford Ave., 718-384-9787
A de facto "bar museum" dating to 1894, this Williamsburg "drinker's staple" maintains its "old tile floor and tin ceiling" as well as old-fashioned "cheap" pricing; maybe it's a bit "run-of-the-mill", but regulars insist it's still "worth checking out."

Telephone Bar

16 | 16 | 17 | $7

149 Second Ave. (bet. 9th & 10th Sts.), 6 to Astor Pl., 212-529-5000;
www.telebar.com
London's calling at this East Village–meets–"Piccadilly Circus" theme bar where a row of "English phone booths" marks a "publike" sanctum for Anglophiles craving a "pint of imported ale"; even if the "kitschy" feel "doesn't thrill" everyone, it's ever a "dependable stop" to chat up "Bridget Jones" clones and other "attractive strangers."

Tempest Bar
_ | _ | _ | M

407 Eighth Ave. (bet. 30th & 31st Sts.), A/C/E to 34th St./Penn Station, 212-643-1502

This budget Garment District bar is a popular port in a storm for FIT students and MSG attendees who flood in to "grab a drink" and get "loud"; the front room can be a "squeeze", but there's "plenty of room in back" for fans of darts and Buck Hunter.

TEMPLE
_ | _ | _ | E

(fka Float)

240 W. 52nd St. (bet. B'way & 8th Ave.), C/E to 50th St., 212-489-7656; www.templenewyork.com

Theater District movers and shakers get jiggy at this new tri-level danceteria, a revamp of Float that centers the dance floor under a dome ringed by balcony seating and lots of nooks and crannies; private parties, promoter nights and a booming sound system keep things lively, while bottle service and a velvet rope come with the territory.

Temple Bar
24 | 24 | 23 | $11

332 Lafayette St. (bet. Bleecker & Houston Sts.), 6 to Bleecker St., 212-925-4242

"Bring a date" to this "slick" NoHo lounge, a "martini lover's Xanadu" that "oozes class" with expert mixologists and "intimate", "smooth surroundings" so "dark" you might "need a seeing-eye dog"; the going can be "expensive", but its "romantic" cachet virtually guarantees you'll "seal the deal."

Tenement
19 | 20 | 18 | $9

157 Ludlow St. (bet. Rivington & Stanton Sts.), F/V to Lower East Side/ 2nd Ave., 212-766-1270; www.tenementlounge.com

Don't expect to slum it at this Lower East Side bar/eatery, a fairly "stylish place" offering Victorian flourishes mixed with contemporary "cool"; the DJs run the gamut from "good to awesome", but overall it's "quiet" enough to "actually talk" since the room's "usually not too busy."

Ten's
_ | _ | _ | VE

35 E. 21st St. (bet. B'way & Park Ave. S.), R/W to 23rd St., 212-254-2444; www.tensnyc.com

See double as the dancers undrape at this Flatiron "skin city", one of the "classier" strip club options even if tabs "more expensive than Tokyo" threaten to bust the bank; knockers contend the talent's "not the best looking" in town, but after a few nips, one "plastic surgery" job is as good as another.

Xth Ave Lounge
∇ 19 | 19 | 22 | $9

642 10th Ave. (bet. 45th & 46th Sts.), A/C/E to 42nd St./Port Authority, 212-245-9088

Both "gays and straights mingle" at this Hell's Kitchen bar/lounge that's one of the "best places" in these parts to "drink and talk with friends" yet "out of the way enough to avoid the tourists"; the "friendly" staff keeps standards high, but "you'll tip them well" anyway just "'cause they're so damn cute."

Tequilaville
11 | 12 | 15 | $9

12-14 Vanderbilt Ave. (bet. 42nd & 43rd Sts.), 4/5/6/7/S to 42nd St./ Grand Central, 212-681-8441; www.rieserestaurants.com

"Commuters with margaritas" make for a "loud" combination at this "quick stop" near Grand Central, specializing in "strong" drinks to facilitate siesta time on the LIRR; "convenient" and "reasonably priced" it may be, but foes still dismiss the "mediocre" milieu as a ticket to dullsville.

Terra Blues

▽ 19 | 17 | 18 | $8

149 Bleecker St., 2nd fl. (bet. La Guardia Pl. & Thompson St.), A/B/C/D/E/F/V to W. 4th St., 212-777-7776; www.terrablues.com

A "friendly", down-to-terra "place to hear the blues", this Village fixture pours a decent "selection of scotch" to drown your sorrows while jamsters take the stage; it may have a "dive" vibe, but backers say the "selling point is the live music", period.

T.G. Whitney's

12 | 9 | 16 | $6

244 E. 53rd St. (bet. 2nd & 3rd Aves.), E/V to Lexington Ave./53rd St., 212-888-5772; www.tgwhitneys.com

Ok, it's a "typical Midtown" barroom, but the staff at this bi-level Irish joint will "make sure your glass is full" during "happy hour and beyond"; it's a "cheap" choice if you don't mind socializing with "heavy-drinking" folk in a "narrow" space, but "not something you'd make a night of."

Thady Con's

21 | 18 | 19 | $7

915 Second Ave. (bet. 48th & 49th Sts.), 6 to 51st St./Lexington Ave., 212-688-9700

"Like coming home" to "true old Ireland", this Turtle Bay hideaway blends "fast, friendly" tapsters, "traditional music" and a "winter fireplace" to make for a "very cozy" mood; indeed, for a "tame night of conversation", it's way "above average" for the genre.

THERAPY

24 | 26 | 20 | $9

348 W. 52nd St. (bet. 8th & 9th Aves.), C/E to 50th St., 212-397-1700; www.therapy-nyc.com

"Chelsea comes to Hell's Kitchen" at this "sleek" "gay bar of the moment", a "real beauty" with a "high-style" bi-level layout "chock-full of future ex-boyfriends"; although "pricey", "fashionable" frills like a reflecting pool and a "central staircase for making grand exits" make this one a no-brainer when you need "professional help."

Third & Long

13 | 8 | 16 | $6

523 Third Ave. (35th St.), 6 to 33rd St., 212-447-5711

With a playbook based on "lots of testosterone and no dress code", this Murray Hill "hole-in-the-wall" is "popular" among "rowdy" "early twenties" fratsters out for a "cheap" buzz; expect to "watch games" with the guys ("and that's about it") since female turnout is a long shot.

Thirsty Scholar

17 | 14 | 17 | $6

155 Second Ave. (bet. 9th & 10th Sts.), 6 to Astor Pl., 212-777-6514; www.ryansnyc.com

More "unpretentious" than highbrow, this East Village Irish bar holds a "certain appeal for locals" since it's "never too crowded" to chat, throw darts or nurse a pint; deep thinkers find "nothing interesting" here, but fans swear "you'll leave happier than when you arrived."

13

15 | 12 | 15 | $8

35 E. 13th St. (University Pl.), 4/5/6/L/N/Q/R/W to 14th St./Union Sq., 212-979-6677; www.bar13.com

"Loud crowds" of "NYU college kids" let loose at this bi-level Village bar/lounge that evokes "memories of frat parties" what with the "sticky floors", "cheesy music" and all that "grinding"; some shrug "so-so", but it's certainly "doable" for the "great rooftop" alone.

13 Little Devils ⊘

14 | 11 | 17 | $9

120 Orchard St. (bet. Delancey & Rivington Sts.), F/J/M/Z to Delancey/Essex Sts., 212-420-1355

This "little" Lower Eastsider is a "dark, funky" walk "on the trashy side" with bartop poles for devil-may-care displays of "cardio striptease" moves and a "see-through floor" that gives "Peeping Toms" downstairs a "peek up"; but critics who call it "hit-or-miss" find the "somewhat empty" nights rather "hellish."

Thom Bar
| 22 | 23 | 18 | $12 |

60 Thompson Hotel, 60 Thompson St., 2nd fl. (bet. Broome & Spring Sts.), C/E to Spring St., 212-219-3200; www.thompsonhotels.com
Expect the "once-over" to make sure "you've got the look" at this "swank" SoHo prototype of "boutique hotel cool", a "loungey" enclave peopled by "I'm-beautiful" types sipping "classy drinks" priced for the "well-to-do"; though "sophisticated" enough to confirm "you've arrived", it's less "intimate" now that it's "no longer a secret."

THOR Lobby Bar
| – | – | – | E |

The Hotel on Rivington, 107 Rivington St. (bet. Essex & Ludlow Sts.), F/J/M/Z to Delancey/Essex Sts., 212-475-2600; www.hotelonrivington.com
Swell in a very Lower East Side way, this second-floor bar in The Hotel on Rivington juxtaposes the usual plush banquettes and tricky lighting with something completely different: floor-to-ceiling windows offering a splendid view of a streetlight and the Economy Candy sign across the street; the makeshift, nothing-special bar setup is trumped by the international hipster crowd.

Three of Cups
| 20 | 17 | 19 | $7 |

83 First Ave. (5th St.), 6 to Astor Pl., 212-388-0059; www.threeofcupsnyc.com
For folks "into metal", the "dank downstairs bar" at this East Village spot is an "entertaining hole" with a "working-class" vibe and a fist-pumping soundtrack; disorderly fans are "sometimes annoying", but it's always "good for hiding out", "kicking off the night" or letting a "nostalgic rocker" lift a glass to "the way it was."

Time Out
| 14 | 10 | 15 | $6 |

349 Amsterdam Ave. (bet. 76th & 77th Sts.), 1 to 79th St., 212-362-5400
It's "not the epitome of class", but this "cheap and grungy" Upper West Side clubhouse for "dudes watching sports" does have "lots and lots of TVs"; bench-warmers admit there's "not much more" on the program except a "beer pong table", "in case you didn't play enough in college."

Tin Lizzie
| 13 | 10 | 13 | $6 |

1647 Second Ave. (bet. 85th & 86th Sts.), 4/5/6 to 86th St., 212-288-7983
Join a "frat reunion" at this Upper East Side "party" bar populated by "huge crowds" of "meatheads in sports jerseys" and "Long Island" girls in "tiny tops"; with "no decor" to speak of and "tone-deaf" acoustics, it's "not a great place to be sober."

Tír na Nóg
| 18 | 17 | 18 | $7 |

5 Penn Plaza (8th Ave., bet. 33rd & 34th Sts.), A/C/E to 34th St./Penn Station, 212-630-0249; www.tirnanognyc.com
As "Irish as it gets", this Penn Plaza pub is a "respectable" island "in a sea of nothingness" near MSG for those wanting to "unwind" over an "after-work Guinness" or get wound up "before the game"; it can get "a bit crowded", but that warm Gaelic feel makes it easy to justify "a few more before catching your train."

Tom & Jerry's ⌿
(aka 288)
| 21 | 14 | 22 | $6 |

288 Elizabeth St. (bet. Bleecker & Houston Sts.), 6 to Bleecker St., 212-260-5045
Soak up some "mixology history" via the "Tom & Jerry mugs display" at this "serviceable" NoHo "hangout", a "standby" for "simple" pleasures like "friendly barkeeps" and "ever-changing exhibits of local art"; indeed, the "laid-back" mood here is made for a "casual beer."

Tonic ⌐̸   20 | 15 | 19 | $7 |

*107 Norfolk St. (bet. Delancey & Rivington Sts.), F/J/M/Z to Delancey/
Essex Sts., 212-358-7501; www.tonicnyc.com*
A shot in the arm for "avant-garde music" aficionados, this "alternative"
Lower Eastsider presents "not-yet-famous acts" getting jazzy and
experimental; in addition, its "basement DJ sets" and "old wooden
wine barrels" converted into seating round out a "funky" time that
fans insist should "not be missed."

TONIC/MET LOUNGE   20 | 19 | 18 | $9 |

*727 Seventh Ave. (bet. 48th & 49th Sts.), 1 to 50th St., 212-382-1059;
www.thetonicbar.com*
Looming "bigger than life" even for Times Square, this three-floor
drink-and-dine colossus offers everyone from "tourists" to the
"Morgan Stanley" crowd plenty of space to roam around in along
with enough "big-screen TVs" to be "heaven for sports fans"; but
despite all the flash, a few think it's still "missing something" ("where
are the swanky people?").

Tool Box ⌐̸   ∇ 11 | 8 | 13 | $8 |

1742 Second Ave. (bet. 90th & 91st Sts.), 4/5/6 to 86th St., 212-348-1288
The Upper East Side's "only gay bar", this "seedy" "hole-in-the-wall"
is strictly "run-of-the-mill" with "hard-core porn" on the tube and
"hot go-go boyz on Tuesday nights"; foes say it's "so small you tend
to walk past it . . . and you should."

Top of the Tower   25 | 23 | 21 | $12 |

*Beekman Tower Hotel, 3 Mitchell Pl. (1st Ave. & 49th St.), 6 to 51st St./
Lexington Ave., 212-980-4796; www.affinia.com*
The view provides the "wow" factor at this "high in the sky" Midtown
aerie, an upholder of "old-fashioned charm" that "pairs well with the
wine" and "live piano"; the "quiet atmosphere" is tops for that "'I
really like you' talk", though down-to-earth sorts warn that romance
here comes "at a price."

Tortilla Flats   20 | 16 | 17 | $7 |

*767 Washington St. (W. 12th St.), A/C/E/L to 14th St./8th Ave., 212-243-1053;
www.tortillaflatsnyc.com*
"Get ready to party" at this "out of control" Village Mexican vet
where the "sensory overload" is fueled by "dangerously cheap"
margaritas, "crazy" hula-hoop and bingo competitions and plenty of
"Cinco de Mayo kitsch"; the "rowdy" "birthday and bachelorette"
fiestas can be "obnoxious", ditto the inevitable "severe hangovers."

Total Wine Bar   – | – | – | M |

*74 Fifth Ave. (bet. St. Marks Pl. & Warren St.), Brooklyn, 2/3 to Bergen St.,
718-783-5166*
Park Slope's yupwardly mobile are totally grateful for this new wine
bar and its "creative" seasonal list, including some more "eclectic"
labels accompanied by "poetic" menu descriptions; the "comfy"
room with a rounded wooden bar is on the small side, but when the
vino's flowing that "makes meeting new people easy."

TOWN   24 | 26 | 22 | $13 |

*Chambers Hotel, 15 W. 56th St. (bet. 5th & 6th Aves.), F to 57th St.,
212-582-4445; www.townnyc.com*
When you're on the town and "feeling luxe", this Midtown hotel's
"chic" mezzanine bar is a "striking" backdrop for "who's who" types
coddled by the "creative cocktail list" and "outstanding service"; this
"classy" act will certainly "impress a date", while "expense-account"
pricing "keeps the right clientele" around.

Town Crier
11 | 10 | 17 | $6

303-305 E. 53rd St. (bet. 1st & 2nd Aves.), E/V to Lexington Ave./53rd St., 212-223-3157
Maybe it's just another "cheap", "unassuming" local bar, but "early thirties" folks needing a "place to meet up" rally to this "narrow, train car"–like Midtowner; regulars go to view sports and "get trashed with buddies", while the ladies flirt with the "cute guest bartenders."

Townhouse ⌀
16 | 16 | 18 | $10

236 E. 58th St. (bet. 2nd & 3rd Aves.), 4/5/6/N/R/W to 59th St./Lexington Ave., 212-754-4649; www.townhouseny.com
"Men over 50" and the "younger men who cater to them" call this East Side gay bar a "tolerable alternative" to the typical scene; "quaint" decor suits the "suited" set, who praise the "lively" pianist and say "thank God there's no more smoke with your show tunes."

Town Tavern
▽ 14 | 13 | 19 | $7

134 W. Third St. (bet. MacDougal St. & 6th Ave.), A/B/C/D/E/F/V to W. 4th St., 212-253-6955; www.towntavernnyc.com
This "casual" new Villager offers two floors of "frat house fun" enhanced by an "attractive crowd" and "great burgers"; the fireplace-equipped upstairs lends "a hint of lounge" to the proceedings, but overall it's best if you've "graduated but still think you're in college."

Tracy J's Watering Hole
17 | 12 | 19 | $7

106 E. 19th St. (bet. Irving Pl. & Park Ave. S.), 4/5/6/L/N/Q/R/W to 14th St./Union Sq., 212-674-5783
"Way to go, Art!" cheer team players at "basketball legend" Art Heyman's Gramercy "hangout", a local "after-work magnet" for a few brews and some "friendly" facing off; even though it's a bit of a "dump", regulars "go for the karaoke" and "stay for the humiliation."

Trailer Park
18 | 21 | 19 | $7

271 W. 23rd St. (bet. 7th & 8th Aves.), C/E to 23rd St., 212-463-8000; www.trailerparklounge.com
"It doesn't get any tackier" than this Chelsea "guilty pleasure", a city slicker's "Middle American nightmare" done up as a "wacky museum of trash" (i.e. "velvet paintings", "pink flamingos", "Elvis impersonators"); maybe it's only "serving up irony to jaded Downtowners", but it still works when you feel like a "PBR" and a "good laugh."

Trash ⌀
– | – | – | M

256 Grand St. (bet. Driggs Ave. & Roebling St.), Brooklyn, L to Bedford Ave., 718-599-1000; www.thetrashbar.com
This Williamsburg space changes its tune to become a "wild rock 'n' roll" showcase with a no-cover "main bar in front" and "ongoing bands" thrashing away in the back; the general feel of a biker clubhouse littered with metalheads is pitch "perfect if that's what you're looking for."

Tribe
▽ 20 | 17 | 19 | $7

132 First Ave. (St. Marks Pl.), L to 1st Ave., 212-979-8965
DJ devotees are "glad to join the tribe" at this "chill" East Village lounge where adept deckmeisters "spin infusions of pop and hip-hop" that "appeal to post-collegians"; insiders are relieved it's still "under the radar", since conditions are already "hot" and "cramped" enough.

Tribeca Grill
22 | 21 | 22 | $13

375 Greenwich St. (Franklin St.), 1 to Franklin St., 212-941-3900; www.myriadrestaurantgroup.com
"Considering how long it's been around", this "hip" TriBeCan from Robert De Niro and Drew Nieporent deserves an "Oscar" for its ongoing

role as a "cosmopolitan" favorite for Downtown denizens; granted, its "overhyped" rep draws "touristy" types, but overall it's a "pleasurable backup" as well as a "Nobu" holding pen.

Tribeca Rock Club
— — — M

16 Warren St. (bet. B'way & Church St.), 1/2/3 to Chambers St., 212-766-1070; www.tribecarockclub.com

Catch garage bands in what "looks like a basement" at this frill-free TriBeCa music club that draws "dedicated" rockers psyched to "see their favorite little-known" groups gigging on a "small" stage; flea-market couches encourage lingering "for hours" and you'll "never feel the need to rush" off since it's "not near anything."

Tribeca Tavern
17 13 17 $7

247 W. Broadway (bet. Walker & White Sts.), A/C/E to Canal St., 212-941-7671

A rare "nontrendy bar in TriBeCa", this "old-school tavern" is a "low-key hideout" where the only demands are "guzzling beer" and choosing between "pool or Pac-Man"; "you almost think you're in Ohio", but at least it's there when "nothing else comes to mind."

Trinity Public House
20 16 21 $6

229 E. 84th St. (bet. 2nd & 3rd Aves.), 4/5/6 to 86th St., 212-327-4450; www.trinitypubnyc.com

Aye, they "pull a mean pint" at this "hopping" Upper East Side Irish pub, a "tiny" joint that's like "home away from home" for those won over by "catchy tunes" on the jukebox and "always smiling" service "with a brogue"; since it's "as good as you're gonna get" hereabouts, it's "usually packed to the gills."

TRIPLE CROWN
— — — M

108 Bedford Ave. (N. 11th St.), Brooklyn, L to Bedford Ave., 718-388-8883; www.triplecrownpage.com

"Upping the ante" for Williamsburg's DJ scene, this "very smooth" newcomer is off to the races hosting nightly derbies on the decks in a minimalist, whitewashed space with lots of blonde wood; those finding it "a touch sterile" call for "more graffiti" like the spray-can glyphs adorning one wall.

Trousdale
— — — E

Amsterdam Court Hotel, 226 W. 50th St. (bet. B'way & 8th Ave.), C/E to 50th St., 212-262-4070; www.trousdalebar.com

Radiating swank à la Sinatra-era Tinseltown, this Midtown boutique hotel's chandeliered bar is done in shades of blue and beige to provide a "pretty" backdrop as you "relax with a martini"; it's first class for a tony tête-à-tête, "but not to meet new people" since the room's typically "underpopulated."

Turkey's Nest ⌂
∇ 14 8 17 $4

94 Bedford Ave. (N. 12th St.), Brooklyn, L to Bedford Ave., 718-384-9774

A longtime "guy's bar", this Williamsburg dive is where "disgruntled blue-collar" types "get trashed" on "cheap beer in Styrofoam cups" while "watching the game"; it nonetheless "welcomes all", so the "hipsters" gobble it up ("just don't step on anybody's toes").

TURKS & FROGS
∇ 24 23 24 $8

323 W. 11th St. (bet. Greenwich & Washington Sts.), A/C/E/L to 14th St./8th Ave., 212-691-8875

An antiques store with a license to pour, this "cozy" new West Village wine bar is stocked with cash-and-carry tchotchkes that double as decor; with vinos "from all over the world", "Turkish appetizers" and a "warm" staff, it's an "undiscovered" pad in the neighborhood pond and partisans plead "don't let the secret out!"

Turtle Bay
15 | 14 | 16 | $8 |
987 Second Ave. (bet. 52nd & 53rd Sts.), E/V to Lexington Ave./53rd St., 212-223-4224; www.turtle-bay.com
Meet a "twentysomething in a suit" at this Midtown "after-work hot spot", a "perennial favorite" for "frat pack" types who come to "guzzle" hooch, "watch big TVs" and par-tay in the upstairs lounge; predictably, this "loud mob scene" attracts "more men" than femmes.

Twelve
– | – | – | M |
206 E. 34th St. (3rd Ave.), 6 to 33rd St., 212-545-9912; www.twelvenewyork.com
An Irish pub on steroids, this new Murray Hill barroom boasts all the state-of-the-art bells and whistles, starting with the mini-TVs mounted on the beer taps; big and brash and proud of it, it's already pulling in a crowd off the Third Avenue corridor.

12" Bar
– | – | – | M |
179 Essex St. (bet. Houston & Stanton Sts.), F/V to Lower East Side/ 2nd Ave., 212-505-6027
"Cool" album covers line the walls of this Lower East Side beer-and-wine bar, an altar to the vinyl LP where 'open table' nights let would-be DJs spin their own sets; it may measure just above a "dive", but at least the lo-fi mood and "out-of-the-way" locale help "insure privacy."

24/7
▽ 23 | 23 | 24 | $10 |
247 Eldridge St. (bet. Houston & Stanton Sts.), F/V to Lower East Side/ 2nd Ave., 212-505-7600
Though not the endless party the name suggests, this Lower Eastsider keeps its "low-key cool" with hippity-hop DJs doing the honors in brick-walled quarters with low lounge seating and copper-top tables; space can be tight, but "nice bartenders" help loosen things up.

21 Club
24 | 24 | 23 | $14 |
21 W. 52nd St. (bet. 5th & 6th Aves.), B/D/F/V to 47-50th Sts./ Rockefeller Ctr., 212-582-7200; www.21club.com
"They don't make them like this anymore" say the "old boys" networking at this "legendary" Midtowner, a "former speakeasy" where the "classy" cocktails and "impeccable" service come at "premium" prices best expensed "on the firm", and if the "clubby" confines are "sort of stuffy", that's "just as it should be"; P.S. "don't forget your jacket and tie" at the dinner hour.

2A
18 | 14 | 17 | $7 |
25 Ave. A (2nd St.), F/V to Lower East Side/2nd Ave., 212-505-2466
Definitely "not for suits", this East Village "staple" is where "locals chill out" with "decently priced drinks and cool music" either in the "rocking bar" or upstairs on "grungy couches" fronting "full-length windows"; whether as a "pit stop" or to "park yourself" for a while, it's got "decades" of "totally dependable" cred.

2 by 4 ⊘
8 | 6 | 14 | $7 |
68 Second Ave. (4th St.), F/V to Lower East Side/2nd Ave., 212-254-5766
The "mostly male patrons" of this "supreme dive" in the East Village perk up when the "half-naked" barmaids "dance on top of the bar"; but critics say this "Coyote Ugly wannabe" is an option "only when you have nowhere else to go", given the "weird crowd" and "sloppy" digs.

200 Fifth
16 | 13 | 18 | $8 |
200 Fifth Ave. (bet. Sackett & Union Sts.), Brooklyn, M/R to Union St., 718-638-2925; www.200fifth.net
If you're up for "watching the game" with a "native Brooklyn crowd", this long-standing Park Slope sports bar offers 40 "beers on tap" and

enough TVs to "put Best Buy to shame"; it goes the distance for "basic" mixing and drinking, even if some shudder it "feels like the suburbs."

2i's
▽ | 12 | 7 | 12 | $9

248 W. 14th St. (bet. 7th & 8th Aves.), A/C/E/L to 14th St./8th Ave., 212-807-1775

For "late-night dancing" to "straight-up hip-hop", this bi-level West Village club/lounge is a "crowded but not impossible" playpen; come Friday and Saturday, it hosts the strip show HunkMania, serving up beefcake for the bachelorettes.

203 Spring
18 | 17 | 16 | $10

203 Spring St. (Sullivan St.), C/E to Spring St., 212-334-3855;
www.203lounge.com

"Let your hair down" and still "be cool" at this "dark", "clique-y" bar on a SoHo corner where the "all-too-fabulous" crowd claims patches of "velvet upholstery"; though prone to "spacier-than-thou service", it's "reliable" for a "pricey" martini or three to "either start or end a night."

212
18 | 18 | 17 | $11

133 E. 65th St. (bet. Lexington & Park Aves.), 6 to 68th St., 212-249-6565;
www.212restaurant.com

Pack your cell phone and put on an "accent" for best results at this "fashionable" Upper East Side bar/eatery where "beautiful Euros" and "Match.com" preps get cozy over "infused vodkas"; outsiders say it "tries too hard", but locals feel "lucky" to have some "eye candy" in this "lacking" neighborhood.

Ty's ∅
▽ | 15 | 12 | 17 | $6

114 Christopher St. (bet. Bleecker & Hudson Sts.), 1 to Christopher St., 212-741-9641

Both the bar and clientele go back a "hound's age" and "show it" at this longtime Village gay bar, an "unpretentious" place for old ty-mers to enjoy cheap sauce; if "a bit clannish", it's still "decent" enough for strangers out "to make a friend for the night."

ULYSSES
21 | 18 | 16 | $8

95 Pearl St. (off Hanover Sq.), 4/5 to Bowling Green, 212-482-0400;
www.ulyssesbarnyc.com

"After a tough day", Wall Street dudes "slip off their wedding rings" and hit this "atmospheric" Irish pub to trade on their "equity"; it draws "huge" crowds in an area where action is "otherwise nonexistent", and come summer everyone pours out onto a rear "cobblestoned" lane that's "like a movie set of old NY."

Uncle Jack's Steakhouse
21 | 20 | 21 | $11

440 Ninth Ave. (34th St.), A/C/E to 34th St./Penn Station, 212-244-0005
39-40 Bell Blvd. (40th Ave.), Queens, LIRR to Bayside, 718-229-1100
www.unclejacks.com

"Class acts" in underserved areas, this chophouse duo maintains a "comfortable" gentleman's club ambiance with "generous drinks" and "bartenders who remember a face"; they're a relatively "good bet" for tossing back martinis and "hearing the person next to you", but "prepare to spend money", Jack.

Uncle Ming's
21 | 20 | 19 | $8

225 Ave. B, 2nd fl. (bet. 13th & 14th Sts.), L to 1st Ave., 212-979-8506;
www.unclemings.com

Those "in-the-know" go for this East Village lounge up an "unmarked stairwell" that's home to a "clubby" DJ soundtrack and flamboyantly "funky" furnishings fit for your "dirty uncle's bachelor pad"; it's an "awesome hideaway" for "chill" thrills, though scenewise it all "depends when you catch it."

Underbar

20 | 21 | 16 | $11

W Union Square Hotel, 201 Park Ave. S. (bet. 17th & 18th Sts.), 4/5/6/L/N/Q/R/W to 14th St/Union Sq., 212-358-1560; www.midnightoilbars.com

"Wealthy trendoids" dub the W Union Square Hotel's "sensual", "dimly lit" underground lounge the "ultimate make-out bar", with servers in "skimpy" attire, a strategically placed bed and "curtains on the booths to keep you guessing"; the "sleek" style "never loses its cool", though the underwhelmed say "passé."

Underground Lounge

∇ 19 | 14 | 17 | $6

955 West End Ave. (107th St.), 1 to Cathedral Pkwy./110th St., 212-531-4759; www.theundergroundnyc.com

Have a "hip night (for the Upper West Side)" at this "accommodating" basement lounge/performance space hosting comedy, jazz and "open mike" acts; it's "flaky" but affordable for Columbia scholars who find it "refreshing" in an area that's "kind of a desert."

Under the Volcano

19 | 17 | 19 | $8

12 E. 36th St. (bet. 5th & Madison Aves.), 6 to 33rd St., 212-213-0093

Named for the Malcolm Lowry novel, this Murray Hill bar boasts an "expansive tequila list" as well as an appropriate "south-of-the-border" vibe; it's a "decent option for the neighborhood" and an easy "alternative" to the "overcrowded" Ginger Man across the street, but "don't expect a hotbed of activity."

Union Pool

21 | 20 | 20 | $5

484 Union Ave. (Meeker Ave.), Brooklyn, G/L to Metropolitan Ave./ Lorimer St., 718-609-0484

A "swimming" example of Williamsburg cool, this "relaxed" but "upbeat" hangout occupies an "understated" space in a former pool supply store, where "rock 'n' roll DJs" and random "concert nights" have even "Manhattanites" plunging in; an "outside terrace" invites "summertime chilling", though the "too-hip" milieu drives a few off "the deep end."

Union Square Cafe

24 | 22 | 23 | $12

21 E. 16th St. (bet. 5th Ave. & Union Sq. W.), 4/5/6/L/N/Q/R/W to 14th St/ Union Sq., 212-243-4020

"Not your everyday" joint, Danny Meyer's Union Square exercise in "urban chic" puts a "warm", "civilized" face on "upper-class" elegance, making it a "favorite" for "wonderful" wines and "dinner at the bar"; big spenders confirm it's "worth every penny" to "check out everyone" squeezing in, but "get there early" for a "strategic seat."

Uptown Lounge

20 | 20 | 20 | $8

1576 Third Ave. (bet. 88th & 89th Sts.), 4/5/6 to 86th St., 212-828-1388; www.uptownloungenyc.com

Despite the name there's a distinct "Downtown feel" to this Upper East Side bar/lounge where a youthful crew keeps "rocking most of the night" and looking their "hottest" thanks to "nice lighting" and "yummy" specialty martinis; all acknowledge it's "sorely needed" to "fill the void" in the otherwise "frat-heavy" local lineup.

Urge, The ⌐

17 | 12 | 18 | $7

33 Second Ave. (bet. 1st & 2nd Sts.), F/V to Lower East Side/2nd Ave., 212-533-5757; www.urgenyc.com

Live it up at this East Village "anti-Chelsea" gay bar, a "former funeral home" turned "comfortable" haunt (with "just a hint of sleaze") where "cuties" and "plasma screens" vie for your attention; some say it's gotten "sanitized" and "a bit boring", but "mellow" fellows confess an "urge" to "keep coming back."

Vapor
_ | _ | _ | E

(fka Room 143)

*143 Madison Ave. (bet. 31st & 32nd Sts.), 6 to 33rd St., 212-686-6999;
www.vapornyc.com*

Perhaps the most impressive remake of a constantly changing space
(fka China White, fka Room 143), this fuchsia-lit Murray Hill duplex
boasts one of the sleekest back rooms in town and follows up with a
cool, candlelit underground lounge; so far, it also appears to have
much less attitude than its earlier incarnations, and is even open for
after-work drinks.

Varjak
_ | _ | _ | M

(fka Hannah's Lava Lounge)

923 Eighth Ave. (bet. 54th & 55th Sts.), C/E to 50th St., 212-245-3212

Taking its name from Holly Golightly's beau in *Breakfast at Tiffany's*,
this Hell's Kitchen entry is a smooth spot "for locals to gather" and dig
occasional "evening jazz" from boppin' combos working the "cozy"
room; otherwise, it's a "typical" place to kick back and sip a Guinness
(the only brew on tap).

Vasmay Lounge ⌀
_ | _ | _ | M

(fka Meow Mix)

269 E. Houston St. (Suffolk St.), F/V to Lower East Side/2nd Ave., 212-228-0820

A refuge for those dismayed by Lower East Side gentrification, this
downscale newcomer keeps the focus on swilling suds and shooting
stick; the basement's being primed for live bands, but for now black-
leather types can bang their heads to the punk standards on the juke.

V Bar
∇ 23 | 20 | 21 | $9

*225 Sullivan St. (bet. Bleecker & W. 3rd Sts.), A/B/C/D/E/F/V to W. 4th St.,
212-253-5740; www.vbar.net*

It's "easy to be casual" at this "cozy" Greenwich Village wine bar where
"overeducated NYU grad students" linger in the "living room"–like
setting; "entertaining" staffers make sure a "great time is had by all",
though regulars report "sardine-can" conditions "when strangers
invade" on weekends.

Vegas
∇ 14 | 16 | 19 | $6

*135 Smith St. (bet. Bergen & Dean Sts.), Brooklyn, F/G to Bergen St.,
718-875-8308*

Smith Street's low rollers do their lounging and "pool playing" at
this roomy bar known for "Gothic" tinged decor and the "nicest"
tapmeisters who keep the sauce coming "without attitude"; but when
the chips are down, some find it "not too exciting."

VELA
22 | 22 | 18 | $12

*55 W. 21st St. (bet. 5th & 6th Aves.), R/W to 23rd St., 212-675-8007;
www.velarestaurant.com*

Once the "lights go down" at this Flatiron fusion eatery, "fashionistas"
teetering on "pointy-toed shoes" toddle in for some "late-night"
lounging; decorwise, the waterfall, Japanese lanterns and other
"beautiful" touches are "definitely worth a look", but the vela-vet
rope scene at the door is "all attitude."

Velvet
∇ 15 | 19 | 15 | $10

*223 Mulberry St. (bet. Prince & Spring Sts.), 6 to Spring St., 212-965-0439;
www.velvetnyc.com*

The velvety antique couches are both "interesting" to look at and
easy to settle back on at this louche NoLita lounge; if some of the
"luster has dulled", hipsters with a soft spot for Victoriana still head
over for a "quiet drink."

Velvet Cigar Lounge ⊄

`- | - | - | E`

80 E. Seventh St. (bet. 1st & 2nd Aves.), 4/5/6/L/N/Q/R/W to 14th St./ Union Sq., 212-533-5582

The name hints at the relaxed, clubby mood at this intimate, 12-seat East Village cigar lounge that draws an only-in-NY mix of stogie aficionados; supplemented by a well-curated selection of beer and wine (with an emphasis on port), this is an old-school salute to the joy of smoking, even if cigarette puffing is not permitted.

VERITAS

`25 | 21 | 26 | $14`

43 E. 20th St. (bet. B'way & Park Ave. S.), 4/5/6/L/N/Q/R/W to 14th St./ Union Sq., 212-353-3700; www.veritas-nyc.com

An oenophile's veritable "dream list" awaits at this "classy" Flatiron restaurant's compact wine bar where the "superb" selection is decanted by "knowledgeable sommeliers" always ready for a "good chat"; the "snooty" scene's veri "expensive" but "worth it" – sipping "doesn't get much better" than this.

Verlaine

`24 | 21 | 19 | $9`

110 Rivington St. (bet. Essex & Ludlow Sts.), F/J/M/Z to Delancey/ Essex Sts., 212-614-2494

Named for decadent poet Paul Verlaine, this Lower East Side lounge pours "delish" "eclectic" cocktails in a "plush" setting with "great background music"; it's a go-to if you "want to be cool", and even starving bards can "keep on ordering" since the twofer deal lasts "till 10 PM."

Vero

`22 | 18 | 19 | $10`

1483 Second Ave. (bet. 77th & 78th Sts.), 6 to 77th St., 212-452-3354; www.veronyc.com

The "Village meets the Upper East Side" at this "friendly little" wine and panini purveyor where adults meet and greet over primo vino by the glass; the "cozy" space and "key outdoor seating" fill up quickly since it's "one of a kind" in this nabe and the "locals love it."

Viceroy

`18 | 18 | 18 | $11`

160 Eighth Ave. (18th St.), A/C/E/L to 14th St./8th Ave., 212-633-8484

Still "bumpin'", this Chelsea bar/restaurant hosts "hordes of muscle boys" in "film noir–ish" digs staffed by buff "model servers"; it's a "basic" but "fun" fixture where "all orientations" sit by the window and "watch the night come to life", though a few party-poopers sigh it's "lost its zing."

View Bar ⊄

`14 | 15 | 17 | $7`

232 Eighth Ave. (bet. 21st & 22nd Sts.), C/E to 23rd St., 212-929-2243; www.viewbarnyc.com

With its "facade open to the street", this "airy" Chelsea gay bar "right on the Eighth Avenue strip" affords choice views of the "eye candy" outside since the company inside is usually "not much to look at"; although "quiet" verging on "tired", it works for downing a "quick" one "before hitting the clubs."

View Lounge

`23 | 18 | 16 | $12`

Marriott Marquis Hotel, 1535 Broadway, 48th fl. (bet. 45th & 46th Sts.), 1/2/3/7/N/Q/R/S/W to 42nd St./Times Sq., 212-704-8900; www.nymarriottmarquis.com

Putting a "dizzy spin" on sightseeing, this revolving hotel bar high above Times Square commands "breathtaking views" but remains an "otherwise basic" venue with all the allure of a "pricey" "airport lounge"; still, it's "irresistible" for "out-of-town folks", even if city slickers sigh "strictly amateur hour."

Vig Bar
20 | 15 | 18 | $9

12 Spring St. (Elizabeth St.), 6 to Spring St., 212-625-0011

"Neighborhood" boosters boast this "chill" NoLita bar has "everything you could ask for": a "good-looking" crowd, "edgy" tunes, "awesome" DJs and some of the "friendliest bartending" around; when the "intimate" front room gets "overly packed", vigilant types head to the back for more "private relaxing."

Village Karaoke
∇ 14 | 7 | 15 | $7

27 Cooper Sq. (bet. 5th & 6th Sts.), 6 to Astor Pl., 212-254-0066

Indulge your inner pop star with "no public embarrassment" at this BYO East Village "karaoke den" where parties "pay by the hour" for "brothel-esque" private rooms equipped with everything from "international music" to the "Backstreet Boys"; just be prepared for a "sketchy" setup and a "wait."

Village Lantern
16 | 11 | 17 | $9

167 Bleecker St. (bet. Sullivan & Thompson Sts.), A/B/C/D/E/F/V to W. 4th St., 212-260-7993; www.villagelantern.com

With live music and DJs plus "comedy downstairs", this "convenient" Village bar/restaurant is a bright spot on turf otherwise ruled by NYU tykes; the unenlightened call it "mediocre", but for most it's "reliable" enough, "without the hassle" of hipper joints.

Village 247
∇ 19 | 19 | 19 | $8

247 Smith St. (bet. Degraw & Douglass Sts.), Brooklyn, F/G to Bergen St., 718-855-2848; www.village247.com

This Carroll Gardens eatery's interior is a "fun little" mockup of an olden village, with a "cozy" pub in the basement that's like a "grown-up version of a frat bar" for "reasonable" quaffing; but despite the cool "garden in the back" skeptics sense a "strangely suburban" vibe.

Village Vanguard ⊘
23 | 15 | 16 | $10

178 Seventh Ave. S. (11th St.), 1/2/3 to 14th St., 212-255-4037; www.villagevanguard.com

"Hallowed" ground for jazz lovers, this "down-low" Village "institution" attracts "reverent" fans primed for an earful of "top" bebop; it may be a "worn"-looking "time warp", but there's "still magic in the air" since hepcats know "it's all about the music", daddy-o.

VILLARD
23 | 26 | 23 | $14

Palace Hotel, 455 E. 51st St. (bet. Madison & Park Aves.), 6 to 51st St./Lexington Ave., 212-303-7757; www.newyorkpalace.com

Midtown meets Versailles at this "high-end" hideaway in the Palace Hotel, a luxe "step back in time" with "velvet sofas" and "rich colors" fit for a "French bordello"; the "expense-account" prices don't faze its "business" crowd seeking a little peace and "quiet", though commoners contend it takes itself "way too seriously."

Vine
19 | 20 | 19 | $12

25 Broad St. (Exchange Pl.), 2/3/4/5 to Wall St., 212-344-8463; www.vinefood.com

Traders tout this "small" Wall Street wine bar as an "after-work gathering" option, though it's more for quiet tête-à-têtes and not "if you're looking for a scene"; hedgers hint it's "a little too snooty" and "expensive", yet it's "close" to the Exchange so most "can't complain."

Vintage
21 | 18 | 21 | $10

753 Ninth Ave. (bet. 50th & 51st Sts.), C/E to 50th St., 212-581-4655

The "book"-length list of "fabulous" martinis and "extensive" wine selection keep the thirsty coming back to this Hell's Kitchen "find", a "classy" but "comfortable" setup with "vintage furniture" and "sweet", "skilled" service; if the tabs are "fairly high", the "mellow" milieu favored by "actors" and their "hangers-on" is "sooo worth it."

VIP Club

▽ 18 | 16 | 18 | $12

20 W. 20th St. (bet. 5th & 6th Aves.), R/W to 23rd St., 212-633-1199; www.vipny.com

If you're "looking for naked chicks", this Flatiron stripteaser showcases "actually attractive" dancers entertaining gents who "get exactly what they expect" so long as they flash a "stack of bills"; jugheads gripe "talent is scarce" and suggest you "go to Vegas" for the real deal.

Viscaya

18 | 19 | 16 | $11

191 Seventh Ave. (bet. 21st & 22nd Sts.), 1 to 23rd St., 212-675-5980; www.viscayalounge.com

Making a "big scene" in Chelsea, this "popular" but "not mega" lounge has "hot young thangs" marching to a "hip-hop" beat, from the platinum-hued front rooms to a rear "VIP section" that's every bottle buyers' "place to be"; it's a "def return" destination in clubland, even if foes bemoan "just another expensive" club.

Vol de Nuit

▽ 27 | 22 | 22 | $8

148 W. Fourth St. (bet. MacDougal St. & 6th Ave.), A/B/C/D/E/F/V to W. 4th St., 212-979-2616

"Show off your knowledge of the Village" by heading to this secluded "Belgian beer bar", a "laid-back" retreat whose "unpretentious" Euro-rustic looks enhance an "awesome" list of imported brews; there's a "courtyard" for "fresh air" and they serve "great mussels and fries too", though the liquid diet alone is good enough to "survive on."

Von

▽ 23 | 21 | 21 | $9

3 Bleecker St. (bet. Bowery & Elizabeth St.), 6 to Bleecker St., 212-473-3039; www.vonnyc.com

Sophistos "bored with the pubs and dives" slip away to this candlelit NoHo "gem", a simple yet "appealing" wood-and-brick barroom that's kept "nice and dark"; it's an "easy place to meet" strangers since they'll be "rubbing up against you" in the "narrow" space.

Vong

22 | 22 | 20 | $13

200 E. 54th St. (3rd Ave.), E/V to Lexington Ave./53rd St., 212-486-9592; www.jean-georges.com

"East meets West" in the "exotic" bar of Jean-Georges Vongerichten's Midtown flagship, a "sexy" sanctuary of "Zen mystique" where "beautiful" types toy with "expensive" cocktails and nibbles; to some it "seems so '80s", but adherents say it's "exquisite" enough to "revisit", provided you "go late or early" to avoid the "waiting dining crowd."

V Steakhouse

22 | 24 | 23 | $14

Time Warner Ctr., 10 Columbus Circle, 4th fl. (60th St.), 1/A/B/C/D to 59th St./Columbus Circle, 212-823-9500; www.jean-georges.com

Make it "first class all the way" at Jean-Georges Vongerichten's Time Warner Center cash cow where the "gorgeous baroque" environs include a "small yet sufficient bar" for "intimate" conversation lubricated by an "unbelievable" wine list; it's "not a scene", but "be prepared to melt some plastic" for just being there.

Vudu

15 | 17 | 13 | $10

1487 First Ave. (bet. 77th & 78th Sts.), 6 to 77th St., 212-249-9540; www.vudulounge.com

"Pickup" lines and "hair gel" work their magic at this Upper East Side dance club where the "decent DJs" cast a spell over "college" castaways; though it's "convenient" when "you can't think of anywhere else", liabilities include a "stuffy" staff and "cheeseball" atmosphere.

Vue
17 | 19 | 16 | $11

151 E. 50th St. (bet. Lexington & 3rd Aves.), 6 to 51st St./Lexington Ave., 212-753-1144; www.vuenyc.com
Some are "hypnotized" by the video display on the soaring dome at this Midtown club, a bi-level behemoth that offers "plenty of space to dance"; it's where "white collars" get loosened up, though a few rue there's "usually a cover" for scenery that's "not up to the hype."

Waikiki Wally's
16 | 19 | 15 | $9

101 E. Second St. (bet. Ave. A & 1st Ave.), F/V to Lower East Side/2nd Ave., 212-673-8908; www.waikikiwallys.com
Escape to a "tropical" isle at this "grass-thatched" East Villager, a "Hawaiian-themed" bar "complete with waterfall" and "fiery" tiki drinks that draws "raucous" "bachelorettes" and "NYU kids"; yes, it's "really tacky", but most have "fuzzy memories" of a "totally fun" time.

Walker's
20 | 14 | 20 | $8

16 N. Moore St. (Varick St.), 1 to Franklin St., 212-941-0142
A "solid" NY tavern, this TriBeCa "staple" walks the "old-school" walk with "vintage" digs and the "coolest" service, allowing locals to "watch the game in peace"; if it "doesn't look like much", that's because it's the kind of "real people bar" that "every neighborhood needs."

Warsaw ⊘
▽ 20 | 15 | 19 | $9

261 Driggs Ave. (Eckford St.), Brooklyn, G/L to Metropolitan Ave./ Lorimer St., 718-387-0505; www.warsawconcerts.com
"Like traveling to Poland" with some "darn good bands" in tow, this Greenpoint cultural center serves up budget suds and kielbasa while alt/punk acts rock the old-world ballroom; the premises may be lacking in polish, but hipper "fans of live music" should "hightail it over."

Waterfront Ale House
20 | 14 | 20 | $7

540 Second Ave. (30th St.), 6 to 33rd St., 212-696-4104
155 Atlantic Ave. (bet. Clinton & Henry Sts.), Brooklyn, 2/3/4/5/M/R to Borough Hall, 718-522-3794
www.waterfrontalehouse.com
"Beer lovers" stoutly tout the "tons" of "esoteric" options at these "low-key" brewrooms, homes to "prompt service", "TV sports" and "free popcorn"; they're "solid" stops even if snobs sneer "standard issue", adding there's "no waterfront in sight."

Waterloo Tavern
14 | 13 | 16 | $6

1629 Second Ave. (bet. 84th & 85th Sts.), 4/5/6 to 86th St., 212-535-4472
"Pick up a prepster" at this Upper East Side hang, a meat market/ sports bar "composite" where "ex–frat boys" "try to hook up" while watching the game at the same time; "as unoriginal as they come", it's still a draw for "Loyola alumni" on a "weekend bar crawl."

Water Street Bar
▽ 13 | 15 | 14 | $7

66 Water St. (bet. Dock & Main Sts.), Brooklyn, A/C to High St., 718-625-9352; www.waterstreetbar.com
This whale of a venue on the Dumbo waterfront is a "brass rail" Irish pub with a bar "as long as a football field" perched above an industrial performance area hosting DJs and live music; but the generous "physical space" is "rarely full" owing to a location so remote "no one seems to know it's there."

WCOU Radio ⊘
– | – | – | M

115 First Ave. (7th St.), L to 1st Ave., 212-254-4317
Though "nothing fancy", this long-running East Village "dive" (aka "Tile Bar") gets a good reception from "subdued" sorts who like their

imbibing "plain and simple"; it may be on the "unspectacular" side, but it's still a "quintessential neighborhood bar."

Webster Hall   17 | 15 | 13 | $10

125 E. 11th St. (bet. 3rd & 4th Aves.), 4/5/6/L/N/Q/R/W to 14th St./Union Sq., 212-353-1600; www.websterhall.com

Expect "quite a show" at this "loud", multifloored East Village megaclub where "theme rooms" pulsating with "hot" tunes keep dancers "sweaty"; while there's much "crazy stuff" to explore, contras call it a "cheesy" choice frequented by "tourists", "first-time clubgoers" and "random weirdos."

Welcome to the Johnsons ⌦   18 | 17 | 19 | $5

123 Rivington St. (bet. Essex & Norfolk Sts.), F/J/M/Z to Delancey/ Essex Sts., 212-420-9911

"Kitschy" is the word on this "easygoing" Lower Eastsider, a "priceless" re-creation of a "'70s basement rec room" complete with tacky "paneling" and "plastic-covered couches"; it's a "no-frills" place to crash and crack open "cheap cans of PBR", but "bring a date here and it's goodbye."

West   19 | 19 | 19 | $8

425 West St. (11th St.), A/C/E/L to 14th St./8th Ave., 212-242-4375; www.west-nyc.com

"Make the trek at sunset" for the "scenic" Hudson vistas at this "very far west" Villager, a "spacious" "modern" lounge that lures "too-cool-for-school" settlers with DJs and "indie films"; despite a "stark" design, most say it's worth going "out of the way" especially on "quiet" weekday nights.

West End   14 | 11 | 13 | $7

2911 Broadway (bet. 113th & 114th Sts.), 1 to 116th St., 212-662-8830; www.thewestendnyc.com

A "former Kerouac haunt" and trove of "old Columbia memories", this Morningside Heights "undergrad institution" is just the spot to "throw back a few" on a "student budget"; fans doff their "baseball caps" to the "karaoke nights" and "beer pong", though some alums grumble "it ain't what it used to be."

Westside Brewing Co.   18 | 16 | 18 | $7

340 Amsterdam Ave. (76th St.), 1/2/3 to 72nd St., 212-721-2161; www.westsidebrewingco.com

Your "standard neighborhood tavern", this Upper Westsider caters to the "preppy" set in "casual" mode with a "solid beer selection" fortified by "many" microbrews (even if it doesn't make its own); whether to "watch sports" or relax at the "outside tables", count on plenty of "home-town" company.

Wet Bar   22 | 22 | 18 | $11

W Court Hotel, 130 E. 39th St. (Lexington Ave.), 4/5/6/7/S to 42nd St./ Grand Central, 212-592-8844; www.mocbars.com

Have a "chance encounter" with a "metrosexual" at this "dark", "swanky" Murray Hill hotel bar where "yuppified" loungers and "out-of-towners" sip "overpriced cocktails" fetched by servers in "tight black dresses"; if too many "pretenders" dampen the scene, at least "cheating spouses" will appreciate the "rooms upstairs."

Whiskey, The   22 | 21 | 19 | $11

W Times Square Hotel, 1567 Broadway, downstairs (47th St.), R/W to 49th St., 212-930-7444; www.midnighttoilbars.com

"Beautiful people" are "wild" about this "spendy" Times Square club, a "lively" place to dance or just take in the kaleidoscopic "gel square" floor and "unisex" loos; but foes of "tourists" and "outer borough" types contend it "should be more glam" after the "hyped" buildup.

Whiskey Blue
20 | 21 | 16 | $12

W New York Hotel, 541 Lexington Ave. (bet. 49th & 50th Sts.), 6 to 51st St./ Lexington Ave., 212-486-1591; www.mocbars.com
The blue-chip "suits-and-stilettos" scene "keeps on ticking" at this "sleek, dark" Midtown hotel bar where the "foo-foo" digs and "miniskirt-and-boots" service are "perennially chic"; still, critics deem it "too pricey" and "too impressed with itself."

Whiskey Park
21 | 21 | 18 | $12

Trump Parc, 100 Central Park S. (6th Ave.), N/R/W to 5th Ave./59th St., 212-307-9222; www.midnightoilbars.com
Throw on "all black" to fit in at this "über-cool" Central Park South bar/lounge, an "expensive abode" where "model-like waitresses" prowl a "sexy, candlelit" room; the "no longer crowded" premises provide some "quiet space" for that "after-work martini", though scenesters shrug "was hot, now not."

Whiskey River
_ | _ | _ | M

(fka Nectar)
575 Second Ave. (bet. 31st & 32nd Sts.), 6 to 33rd St., 212-679-6799
Picking up where former tenant Nectar left off, this new, off-the-beaten-path Murray Hill barroom remains a spread-out affair with plenty of room to move around in; its secret weapon, a cool backyard patio, is still intact, welcoming both smokers and fresh-air fiends.

WHISKEY WARD
25 | 22 | 25 | $6

121 Essex St. (bet. Delancey & Rivington Sts.), F/J/M/Z to Delancey/ Essex Sts., 212-477-2998
Common ground for everyone from "preps" to "tattoo artists", this Lower East Side watering hole is a "surprisingly fun" way to ward off the blues as the "friendliest" barkeeps dispense top-shelf whiskey at "reasonable prices"; with DJs and a "lively pool table" to keep things "interesting", stalwarts "accept no substitutes."

White Horse Tavern ∅
21 | 14 | 17 | $7

567 Hudson St. (11th St.), A/C/E/L to 14th St./8th Ave., 212-989-3956
An "enduring" fave on any "Village tour", this circa-1880 "landmark" "where Dylan Thomas drank his last drink" corrals "throngs" drawn to its "bohemian history" and "streetside picnic tables"; maybe the patrons "wish they were back in college", but all that "dirty charm" ensures "it's never empty."

White Rabbit
▽ 18 | 16 | 17 | $9

(fka Idlewild)
145 E. Houston St. (bet. Eldridge & Forsyth Sts.), F/V to Lower East Side/ 2nd Ave., 212-477-5005; www.whiterabbitnyc.com
Swapping Idlewild's plane looks for glossy "minimalist surroundings", this new Lower Eastsider is all bright white surfaces and "comfy" contempo seating made for feeding your head with "pricey drinks"; "chill-out tunes" and videos "projected on the back wall" kindle the scene, but a few fuss the concept's "cooler than the vibe."

Wicked Monk
18 | 19 | 20 | $8

8415 Fifth Ave. (84th St.), Brooklyn, R to 86th St., 718-921-0601; www.wickedmonk.com
Tricked out "like an Irish monastery", this Bay Ridge "favorite" is an otherwise "standard bar" where the "local" congregation "sips a Guinness", "plays darts and just hangs"; but there's no vow of silence when "cover bands" play at "a deafening pitch."

Wild Spirits ♥

– | – | – | M

1843 First Ave. (bet. 95th & 96th Sts.), 6 to 96th St., 212-427-7127;
www.wildspiritsnyc.com

Leave the Upper East Side mindset waaay behind at this new rock 'n'
roll bar channeling CBGB's and featuring nightly live bands that are
uniformly loud; dress down and be ready to flash your tats to fit in with
the punks, bikers and headbangers in the crowd.

Windfall

∇ 22 | 17 | 24 | $7

23 W. 39th St. (bet. 5th & 6th Aves.), 4/5/6/7/S to 42nd St./Grand Central,
212-869-4606

Bring a "group to make your own fun" at this "large" Garment District
bar that's a "happy-hour" magnet on weekdays (but closed weekends);
the staff is "friendly" enough to "take a couple of shots with you."

Winnie's ♥

∇ 21 | 12 | 18 | $7

104 Bayard St. (bet. Baxter & Mulberry Sts.), A/C/E to Canal St., 212-732-2384

Prep your pipes for "energetic revelry" at this Chinatown karaoke
palace–cum–"dive bar" hosted under the "fair but stern" supervision of
mama-sans who may "start singing with you"; discount drinks make
the crowd "a little rowdy", but the "hilarious" show is a sure winner.

Wogie's ♥

∇ 18 | 16 | 20 | $6

39 Greenwich Ave. (Charles St.), F/L/V to 14th St./6th Ave., 212-229-2171

Best known for its "tremendous" Philly cheese steaks, this "relaxed"
Village newcomer also vends typical "pub grub" along with "cheap"
drinks; parked on a high-traffic Greenwich Avenue corner, it offers
plenty of "people-watching" opportunities, starting with the "ever-
changing crowd" at the bar.

Wollensky's Grill

20 | 18 | 21 | $11

201 E. 49th St. (3rd Ave.), 6 to 51st St./Lexington Ave., 212-753-0444;
www.smithandwollensky.com

An "upscale crowd" with "cash to burn" jams into the "small" bar
area of this Midtown steakhouse; regulars are relieved that the staff
"isn't composed of aspiring models" and add "you can always stay to
eat" – the kitchen's open till 2 AM.

Wonderland

– | – | – | E

(fka Social Club)

14 E. 27th St. (bet. 5th & Madison Aves.), R/W to 28th St., 212-686-1400;
www.wonderlandnewyork.com

What was once Gramercy's Social Club has been scaled down
and refashioned into this blue-lit subterranean lounge featuring a
horseshoe-shaped bar and curtained 'cabanas' equipped with fully
stocked mini-fridges; it's more intimate than before now that the ground-
floor level is exclusively reserved for private parties.

World Bar

21 | 21 | 22 | $16

845 UN Plaza (1st Ave. at 47th St.), 6 to 51st St./Lexington Ave.,
212-935-9361; www.hospitalityholdings.com

"Get away from it all" at this "elegant" lounge near the UN that's just
the ticket for a "sexy, quiet and very expensive" drink delivered by a
staff that "treats you like gold"; however, there's "no buzz" in the air
given the way-off-the-beaten-path address, so it's "often empty."

World Yacht

24 | 21 | 21 | $13

Pier 81, W. 41st St. & Hudson River, A/C/E to 42nd St./Port Authority,
212-630-8100; www.worldyacht.com

"Something different", this cruise ship offers dining, dancing and
"fantastic" Manhattan skyline views in one "unique" package; sure,

it's pricey and "touristy" (and the food just "ok"), but most call it an "exceptional" experience that's perfect for "anniversary" celebrations.

W Times Square Living Room   23 | 24 | 18 | $12
W Times Square Hotel, 1567 Broadway, 7th fl. (47th St.), R/W to 49th St., 212-930-7447; www.midnightoilbars.com

"Put your trendiest foot forward" at this "intimidatingly cool" Times Square hotel bar upholstered in "white leather" and serviced by "gorgeous" gals in "short black dresses" and "high black boots"; be prepared for "overpriced" drinks and lots of "tourists doing their one-night-out-in-NY thing" – but at least they're "hip tourists."

W Union Square Living Room   22 | 24 | 18 | $12
W Union Square Hotel, 201 Park Ave. S. (17th St.), 4/5/6/L/N/Q/R/W to 14th St./Union Sq., 212-253-9119; www.starwood.com

"Oh-so-cool" and "metropolitan", this "plush" Union Square hotel bar is favored by the "fashion-savvy set" toting "Gucci or Kiehl's shopping bags" and toying with "appletinis or Cosmos"; the "coveted window seats" offer premium "people-watching" perches, but the overall "living room setup" is "best for groups, not for mingling."

WXOU Radio ⊅   19 | 12 | 20 | $7
558 Hudson St. (bet. Perry & W. 11th Sts.), A/C/E/L to 14th St./8th Ave., 212-206-0381

There's "lots of character (and characters") to be found at this Village watering hole, a "no-nonsense" "little bar that always delivers" the goods, starting with the "helpful" staff and "great jukebox"; regulars report the "front booths" overlooking Hudson Street are "prime real estate" and advise you "get there early to snag one."

xes lounge   20 | 20 | 21 | $8
157 W. 24th St. (bet. 6th & 7th Aves.), 1 to 23rd St., 212-604-0212; www.xesnyc.com

"Pronounced 'excess'", this "great new addition to the Chelsea gay scene" may be "not quite there yet" but seems to be "gaining momentum" thanks to "stylish" decor and a "nice-looking" following; its best feature is seasonal: a "fabulous backyard patio" that's a favorite for "smoking" and "low-key" cruising.

Xicala   _ | _ | _ | M
151 Elizabeth St. (bet. Broome & Kenmare Sts.), 6 to Spring St., 212-219-0599; www.xicala.com

"Delicious" tapas and a "nice selection" of Spanish wines are the draws at this Little Italy wine bar, a place that's as "dark" as it is "fabulous"; the really "tiny" setup works well for intimate tête-à-têtes, but definitely "not for groups."

XL ⊅   22 | 24 | 18 | $9
357 W. 16th St. (bet. 8th & 9th Aves.), A/C/E/L to 14th St./8th Ave., 646-336-5574; www.xlnewyork.com

"Even off-nights are on" at this "snazzy" Chelsea gay bar, an "ultra-modern", "LA meets Miami" thing bathed in blue "halogen lighting" and boasting a "justifiably legendary" bathroom with a "fish tank urinal"; maybe the pops are "pretty pricey" and the beyond-"buff" bartenders "sexier than you'll ever be", but for "state-of-the-art" cruising – with a side of "top-tier attitude" – look no further.

XR Bar   ∇ 19 | 16 | 19 | $9
128 W. Houston St. (Sullivan St.), 1 to Houston St., 212-674-4080; www.xrbar.com

"Not bad for a quick drink", this "low-key" bar on the Village/SoHo border brings in a "mixed crowd" with its "welcoming feel" and "delish cocktails"; maybe the music can get too "loud for conversation", but at least the "tunes are good so you don't mind having to yell."

Xunta
22 | 15 | 17 | $8

*174 First Ave. (bet. 10th & 11th Sts.), L to 1st Ave., 212-614-0620;
www.xuntatapas.com*
"Potent sangria and delicious tapas steal the show" at this East Villager that's "been around for a while now" but remains as "loud and crowded" as ever; no one minds the "less than attractive setting" (an eclectic mix of "fishnet", "Christmas tree lights" and "barrel-shaped tables") since you can "get a buzz on here for not much dough."

Yaffa Cafe
19 | 20 | 16 | $7

97 St. Marks Pl. (bet. Ave. A & 1st Ave.), 6 to Astor Pl., 212-674-9302
"After a night of heavy drinking", "wind down" at this 24/7 East Village cafe serving "healthy", "veggie-friendly" grub that's "not badly priced"; sure, the "zoned-out service" and "busy" decor can be annoying, but the overall "relaxed" vibe and "great backyard" compensate.

Yankee Tavern
20 | 16 | 16 | $9

*72 E. 161st St. (Gerard Ave.), Bronx, 4/B/D to Yankee Stadium, 718-292-6130;
www.yankeetavern.com*
"Only true Yankee fans need apply" to this vintage sports bar a block from the stadium that's good "before or after any game" or when you "couldn't score tickets"; diehards say this "Bronx treasure" is "better than the overcrowded Stan's", with the "coldest beer" in these parts.

Yello Bar
17 | 15 | 20 | $8

*32 Mulberry St. (Mosco St.), 4/5/6/J/M/Z to Chambers/Centre Sts.,
212-964-3410; www.yellobarnyc.com*
Something "different" in Chinatown, this "fun" spot is a neighborhood "favorite" for "nice drinks" in the upstairs bar and "free karaoke" in the downstairs lounge; maybe the location is "not super appealing", but most say it's got "lots of potential, but has yet to find its groove."

Ye Olde Tripple Inn
14 | 9 | 17 | $6

*263 W. 54th St. (bet. B'way & 8th Ave.), 1/A/B/C/D to 59th St./Columbus Circle,
212-245-9849*
"Year-round Christmas lights" brighten this "hole-in-the-wall" dive, an "olde style" Theater District "camp classic" that recalls what drinking was like "back in the day"; it's a favorite stop for "cops, firemen" and "slummers", though picky tipplers show up "only as a last resort."

Yogi's ⌿
▽ 16 | 8 | 18 | $5

2156 Broadway (bet. 75th & 76th Sts.), 1 to 79th St., 212-873-9852
What might be the "cheapest drinks on the Upper West Side" is the claim to fame of this "classic dance-on-the-bar dive" where the word "'trashy' is a compliment"; you sure "don't go for the scene (there isn't one")", but rather for the "hot barmaids", "free peanuts" and "corny country music" on the jukebox.

Yuca Bar
– | – | – | M

111 Ave. A (7th St.), L to 1st Ave., 212-982-9533; www.yucabarnyc.com
"Great mojitos" enhance the Latin mood at this East Villager, a cozy, candlelit refuge from the Avenue A madness; there's also a "summer alfresco" scene going on featuring some "excellent people-watching."

Zablozki's
– | – | – | M

*107 N. Sixth St. (bet. Berry St. & Wythe Ave.), Brooklyn, L to Bedford Ave.,
718-384-1903*
Williamsburg's hopping North Sixth Street strip continues to pop with the arrival of this "welcoming" new watering hole where "everyone

knows the owner's name"; it's a "real", irony-free bar with a "young, eccentric" following that likes the "unpretentious" vibe and "cheap beers like the old days."

Zanzibar
| 18 | 19 | 15 | $9 |

645 Ninth Ave. (45th St.), A/C/E to 42nd St./Port Authority, 212-957-9197; www.zanzibarnyc.com

A "nice contribution to the Hell's Kitchen scene", this "never-too-packed" bar/lounge/eatery is "quite sophisticated" for the area, featuring a cool circular fireplace and French doors made for "Ninth Avenue people-watching"; foes find service "seriously lacking" and suggest "turning down the attitude."

Zarela
| 20 | 17 | 18 | $10 |

953 Second Ave. (bet. 50th & 51st Sts.), 6 to 51st St./Lexington Ave., 212-644-6740; www.zarela.com

Just make sure to "pace yourself" at this "lively" Midtown cantina famed for its "atomic", "fall-down-the-stairs" margaritas ("buyer beware: more than two and you're in trouble"); small wonder that it "always feels like a party" overseen by "Zarela herself", parked on a "prime barstool."

Zebulon
| – | – | – | M |

258 Wythe Ave. (bet. Metropolitan Ave. & N. 3rd St.), Brooklyn, L to Bedford Ave., 718-218-6934; www.zebuloncafeconcert.com

There's serious listening to be had at this "suave" new music venue in Williamsburg; the "warm" French–North African sensibility (à la the Village's Casimir, by the same owner) works well with the jazz and world music showcased here.

Zinc Bar
| 22 | 20 | 18 | $10 |

90 W. Houston St. (bet. La Guardia Pl. & Thompson St.), 1 to Houston St., 212-477-8337; www.zincbar.com

Village people line up at this "underground" live music spot and pay "low covers" for the nightly "alternative" jazz and Latin rhythms; the "moody" Moroccan digs consist of a "small front room" and "more loungey" back area that complements the "smooth, sultry sounds."

Zoë
| 22 | 21 | 21 | $12 |

90 Prince St. (bet. B'way & Mercer St.), R/W to Prince St., 212-966-6722

As "subdued" as any SoHo restaurant/bar can be, this "sleek" mainstay offers a "superbly crafted" "old-time cocktail" menu (via mixologist Dale DeGroff) and a "large selection of American wines"; while tabs are on the "expensive" side, the "romantic" mood makes it a "great launch pad for a night out."

Zombie Hut
| 23 | 24 | 21 | $7 |

263 Smith St. (Degraw St.), Brooklyn, F/G to Carroll St., 718-875-3433

The "frozen zombies will steal your soul" at this "tiki-licious" Smith Street themer (think "Trader Vic's in Brooklyn") where "sweet", "island-inspired concoctions" and cheap PBRs make for "rip-roaring fun" – and some "legendary hangovers"; it "tends to get very crowded", but that only adds to the "spring break in Daytona" vibe.

Zum Schneider ⊘
| 24 | 17 | 19 | $8 |

107-109 Ave. C (7th St.), L to 1st Ave., 212-598-1098; www.zumschneider.com

"*Ein mass, bitte!*" bellow beer nuts at this "brew lovers' Bavarian hall", a "year-round Oktoberfest" on Avenue C fueled by "giant steins" of "tasty" suds; though the "dark" "faux Black Forest" digs are "not especially appealing", the alfresco imbibing is nothing short of "*wunderbar*."

Indexes

LOCATIONS
SPECIAL APPEALS

LOCATIONS

(Venue name followed by its street location.
A = Avenue, s = Street, e.g. 1A/116s= First Ave. at 116th
St.; 3A/82-3s = Third Ave. between 82nd & 83rd Sts.)

MANHATTAN

Chelsea
(24th to 30th Sts., west of 5th;
14th to 24th Sts., west of 6th)
Amuse *18s/6-7A*
Avalon *6A/20s*
Barracuda *22s/7-8A*
Bar Veloce *7A/20-1s*
Bateaux NY *23s/Hudson River*
BED New York *27s/10-1A*
Biltmore Room *8A/24-5s*
Black Door *26s/6-7A*
Blarney Stone *9A/29-30s*
Bongo *10A/27-8s*
Brite Bar *10A/27s*
Bungalow 8 *27s/10-1A*
Cabanas *9A/16-7s*
Cafeteria *7A/17s*
Cain *27s/10-1A*
Cajun *8A/16-17s*
Chelsea Brewing *18s/Hudson River*
Chelsea Piers Bowling *18s/Hudson River*
Coral Room *29s/10-1A*
Cotton *27s/6-7A*
Crobar *28s/10-1s*
Dewey's Flatiron *5A/25-6s*
Diner 24 *8A/15s*
Dusk *24s/6-7A*
Eagle, The *28s/10-1s*
Earth *10A/17-8s*
East of Eighth *23s/7-8A*
El Flamingo *21s/10-1A*
elmo *7A/18-9s*
El Quijote *23s/7-8A*
Flannery's *14s/7-8A*
Flight 151 *8A/17-8s*
40/40 *25s/Bway-6A*
Frying Pan *23s/W. Side Hwy.*
g *19s/7-8A*

Glass *10A/26-7s*
Glo *16s/9-10A*
Gstaad *26s/Bway-6A*
GYM Sportsbar *8A/18-9s*
Half King *23s/10-1A*
Heaven *6A/16-7s*
Helen's *8A/18-9s*
Hiro *17s/9A*
Jake's Saloon *23s/7-8A*
Kanvas *9A/23-4s*
Kavehaz *26s/Bway-6A*
La Bottega Caffé *9A/16s*
Le Singe Vert *7A/19-20s*
Lot 61 *21s/10-1A*
Marquee *10A/26-7s*
Matsuri *16s/9A*
Merchants, NY *7A/16-7s*
Moran's Chelsea *10A/19s*
Mustang Harry's *7A/29-30s*
Mustang Sally's *7A/28-9s*
Orchid *6A/25-6s*
Park *10A/17-8s*
Passerby *15s/9-10A*
Peter McManus *7A/19s*
Q Lounge *19s/7-8A*
Quo *28s/10-11A*
Rawhide *8A/21s*
Red Cat *10A/23-4s*
Red Rock West *17s/10A*
Rocking Horse *8A/19-20s*
Rogue *6A/25s*
Roxy *18s/10-1A*
Ruby Falls *29s/11-2A*
Satalla *26s/5-6A*
Scores *28s/10-1A*
Serena *23s/7-8A*
Spirit *27s/10-1A*
Spirit Cruises *23s/Hudson River*
Suede *23s/6-7A*
Taj *21s/5-6A*

Trailer Park *23s/7-8A*
Viceroy *8A/18s*
View Bar *8A/21-2s*
Viscaya *7A/21-2s*
xes lounge *24s/6-7A*
XL *16s/8-9A*

Chinatown
(Bet. Hester & Pearl Sts., bet. Bowery & Bway)
Winnie's *Bayard/Baxter-Mulberry*
Yello Bar *Mulberry/Mosco*

East Village
(14th to Houston Sts., east of Bway)
Ace Bar *5s/Aves. A-B*
Alphabet Lounge *Ave. C/7s*
alt.coffee *Ave. A/8-9s*
Anatomy Bar *6s/Aves. A & B*
Angel's Share *Stuyvesant/9s-3A*
Anyway Cafe *2s/Bowery-2A*
Apocalypse Lounge *3s/Aves. A-B*
Babel Lounge *Ave. C/8s*
Baraza *Ave. C/8-9s*
Bar None *3A/12-3s*
Bar on A *Ave. A/10-1s*
Bar Veloce *2A/11-12s*
Beauty Bar *14s/2-3A*
Big Bar *7s/1-2A*
Black & White *10s/3-4A*
Bleecker St. Bar *Blkr./Bway-Lafayette*
Blue and Gold *7s/1-2A*
Boiler Room *4s/1-2A*
Bouche Bar *5s/Aves. A-B*
Bowery Poetry *Bowery/Blkr.-Houston*
Boxcar Lounge *Ave. B/10-1s*
Boys Room *Ave. A/Houston-2A*
Brewsky's *7s/2-3A*
B-Side *Ave. B/12-3s*
B3 *Ave. B/3s*
Bua *St. Marks/Ave. A-1A*
Buddha Lounge *3s/2A*
Bull McCabe's *St. Marks/2-3A*
Burp Castle *7s/2-3A*
Butter *Lafayette/Astor-4s*
Cafe Deville/Bar Bleu *3A/13s*

Casimir *Ave. B/6-7s*
CBGB's *Bowery/Blkr.*
CB's 313 *Bowery/Blkr.*
Cellar, The *14s/1-2A*
Central Bar *9s/3-4A*
Cheap Shots *1A/9s-St. Marks*
Cherry Tavern *6s/Ave. A-1A*
Cloister Cafe *9s/2-3A*
Clubhouse *9s/Ave. C*
C-Note *Ave. C/9-10s*
Cock *Ave. A/12s*
Company *10s/1-2A*
Continental *3A/9s-St. Marks*
Corner Billiards *4A/10-1s*
Coyote Ugly *1A/9s*
Crif Dogs *St. Marks/Ave. A-1A*
Croxley Ales *Ave. B/2-3s*
d.b.a. *1A/2-3s*
Decibel *9s/2-3A*
Detour *13s/1-2A*
Dick's *2A/12s*
Doc Holliday's *Ave. A/8-9s*
Duke's *Ave C/8-9s*
East 4th St. Bar *4s/Bowery-2A*
Edge, The *3s/1-2A*
Eleventh St. Bar *11s/Aves. A-B*
Forbidden City *Ave A./13-4s*
Grassroots *St. Marks/2-3A*
Hanger *3s/Aves. B-C*
Hi-Fi *Ave. A/ 10-1s*
Holiday Cocktail *St. Marks/1-2A*
Hop Devil Grill *St. Marks/Ave. A*
Il Posto Accanto *2s/Aves. A-B*
International Bar *1A/7s-St. Marks*
In Vino *4s/Aves. A-B*
Joe's Bar *6s/Aves. A-B*
Joe's Pub *Lafayette/Astor-4s*
Joey's *Ave. B/11-12s*
Jules *St. Marks/1-2A*
Kabin *2A/5-6s*
Karma *1A/3-4s*
Keybar *13s/Ave. A-1A*
KGB *4s/2-3A*
King's Head *14s/2-3A*
Korova *Ave. A/12-3s*
Lakeside Lounge *Ave. B/10-1s*
La Linea *1A/1-2s*
Lava Gina *Ave. C/7-8s*

Le Souk *Ave. B/3-4s*
Library *Ave. A/Houston-2s*
Life Cafe *10s/Ave. B*
Lit *2A/5-6s*
Louis *9s/Aves. B-C*
Luca Bar/Lounge *multi. loc.*
Lucy's *Ave. A/9s-St. Marks*
Lunasa *1A/St. Marks-7s*
Mama's Bar *3s/Ave. B*
Manitoba's *Ave. B/6-7s*
Mars Bar *1s/2A*
McSorley's *7s/2-3A*
Micky's Blue Room *Ave. C/10-1s*
Miracle Grill *1A/6-7s*
Morrisey Park *St. Marks/Ave. A*
Mundial *12s/Ave. A*
Musical Box *Ave. B/13-4s*
Nevada Smith's *3A/11-2s*
Niagara/Lei Bar *Ave. A/7s*
Nice Guy Eddie's *Ave. A/Houston*
No Malice Palace *3s/Aves. A-B*
No. 1 Chinese *Ave. B/4s*
Nowhere *14s/1-2A*
Nublu *Ave. C/4-5s*
Nuyorican Poets *3s/Aves. B-C*
One & One *1s/1A*
Opaline *Ave. A/5-6s*
Orchid Lounge *11s/Aves. A-B*
Otto's Shrunken *14s/Aves. A-B*
Parkside *Houston/Aves. B-C*
Parlay *Ave. A/13s*
Patio *2A/1-2s*
Phoenix *13s/Ave. A-1A*
Plan B *10s/Aves. A-B*
Planet Rose *Ave. A/13-4s*
Pop *4A/12-3s*
Porch *Ave. C/7-8s*
Pyramid *Ave. A/6-7s*
Raven *Ave. A/12s*
Remote Lounge *Bowery/2s*
Rififi *11s/1-2A*
Rue B *Ave. B/11-2s*
Ryan's Irish Pub *2A/9-10s*
San Marcos *St. Marks/2-3A*
Satelite *6s/Aves. A-B*
Scratcher *5s/2-3A*
Second Nature *2A/13-4s*
Serafina *Lafayette/4s*

7B *Ave. B/7s*
Sidewalk *Ave. A/6s*
Sing Sing *multi. loc.*
Sin Sin/Leopard *2A/5s*
Solas *9s/2-3A*
Sophie's *5s/Aves. A-B*
Starlight *Ave. A/10-1s*
Star 64 *1s/1-2A*
Stay *Houston/Aves. A-B*
St. Dymphna's *St. Marks/Ave. A*
St. Marks Ale *St. Marks/3A*
Sutra *1A/1-2s*
Telephone *2A/9-10s*
Thirsty Scholar *2A/9-10s*
Three of Cups *1A/5s*
Tribe *1A/St. Marks*
2A *Ave. A/2s*
2 by 4 *2A/4s*
Uncle Ming's *Ave. B/13-4s*
Urge, The *2A/1-2s*
Velvet Cigar *7s/1-2A*
Village Karaoke *Cooper/5-6s*
Waikiki Wally's *2s/Ave. A-1A*
WCOU *1A/7s*
Webster Hall *11s/3-4A*
Xunta *1A/10-1s*
Yaffa *St. Marks/Ave. A-1A*
Yuca Bar *Ave. A/7s*
Zum Schneider *Ave. C/7s*

East 40s

Alamo *48s/2A*
Annie Moores *43s/Mad-Vanderbilt*
Beer Bar/Cafe Centro *45s/Vanderbilt*
Blarney Stone *3A/44-45s*
Bliss *49s/2-3A*
B1 Drink Club *45s/Lex-3A*
Bull & Bear *Lex/49s*
Calico Jack's *2A/42-3s*
Campbell Apt. *Vanderbilt/42-3s*
Capital Grille *42s/Lex-3A*
Connolly's *multi. loc.*
Django *Lex/46s*
Docks Oyster *3A/40s*
English Is Italian *3A/40s*
Lea *Park/45-6s*
LQ *Lex/47-8s*

Maggie's *47s/5A-Mad*
Mambi Lounge *2A/49-50s*
McFadden's *2A/42s*
Métrazur *42s/Park*
Michael Jordan's *42s/Vanderbilt*
Morton's *5A/45s*
Overlook Lounge *44s/2-3A*
Oyster Bar *42s/Vanderbilt*
Patrick Conway's *43s/Mad*
Patroon *46s/Lex-3A*
Pershing Sq. *42s/Park*
Peter Dillon's *40s/Lex-3A*
Sakagura *43s/2-3A*
Savannah Steak *48s/5A-Madison*
Tequilaville *Vanderbilt/42-3s*
Thady Con's *2A/48-9s*
Top of the Tower *Mitchell/1A-49s*
Whiskey Blue *Lex/49-50s*
Wollensky's *49s/3A*
World Bar *1A/47s*

East 50s
Azaza *1A/50s*
Bar Room *2A/52-3s*
Bice *54/5A-Mad*
Bill's Gay 90's *54s/Mad-Park*
BlackFinn *53s/2-3A*
Bottega del Vino *59s/5A*
Branch *54s/2-3A*
Brasserie *53s/Lex-Park*
Casa La Femme *1A/58-9s*
Divine Bar *51s/2-3A*
58 *58s/Mad-Park*
Fifty Seven 57 *57s/Park*
Fizz *55s/Lex-3A*
Four Seasons Bar *52s/Lex-Park*
Fubar *50s/1-2A*
Guastavino's *59s/1A-York*
Harry Cipriani *5A/59-60s*
Houston's *54s/3A*
Jameson's *2A/51-2s*
Jimmy Walker's *55s/2-3A*
King Cole Bar *55s/5A*
Le Bateau Ivre *51s/2-3A*
Le Colonial *57s/Lex-3A*
Le Jazz Au Bar *58s/Mad-Park*
Light *54s/Lex-Park*
Local *2A/53s*

Metro 53/Loft *53s/1-2A*
Mica Bar *51s/2-3A*
Monkey Bar *54s/Mad-Park*
Opal *52s/2A*
Opia *57s/Lex-Park*
O.W. *58s/2-3A*
Pig N Whistle *3A/55-6s*
P.J. Carney's *56s/Lex-Park*
P.J. Clarke's *3A/55s*
Redemption *2A/53s*
Remedy *2A/51-2s*
Rosa Mexicano *1A/58s*
Serafina *58s/Mad-Park*
Sutton Place *2A/53-4s*
Tao *58s/Mad-Park*
Tapas Lounge *1A/59s*
T.G. Whitney's *53s/2-3A*
Town Crier *53s/1-2A*
Townhouse *58s/2-3A*
Turtle Bay *2A/52-3s*
Villard *51s/Mad-Park*
Vong *54s/3A*
Vue *50s/Lex-3A*
Zarela *2A/50-1s*

East 60s
Baker St. Pub *1A/63s*
Barbalùc *65s/Lex-Park*
Becky's *1A/63-4s*
Blue Room *2A/60s*
Café Pierre *61s/5A*
Club Macanudo *63s/Mad-Park*
Dangerfield's *1A/61s*
Daniel *65s/Mad-Park*
Feinstein's/Regency *Park/61s*
Geisha *61s/Mad-Park*
Merchants, NY *1A/62s*
O'Flanagan's *1A/65-6s*
Plaza Athénée Bar Seine *64s/*
    Mad-Park
Regency Library Bar *Park/61s*
Scores *60s/1-2A*
Serafina *61s/Mad-Park*
Subway Inn *60s/Lex*
212 *65s/Lex-Park*

East 70s
American Trash *1A/76-7s*
Bandol *78s/Lex-3A*

Baraonda *2A/75s*
Bar Coastal *1A/78s*
Bemelmans *76s/Mad*
Boat House *72s/Park Dr. N.*
Bounce *2A/73s*
Brother Jimmy's *2A/77-78s*
Cabin Fever *York/76-7s*
Cafe Carlyle *76s/Mad*
Canyon Road *1A/76-7s*
Cocktail Room *73s/1-2A*
David Copperfield *York/74s*
Doc Watson's *2A/77-8s*
Finnegans Wake *1A/73s*
Hi-Life *1A/72s*
Iggy's *2A/75-76*
J.G. Melon *3A/74s*
Lenox Room *3A/73-4s*
Lexington Bar/Books *Lex/73s*
Luke's B&G *3A/79-80s*
Mark's Bar *77s/Mad*
Mo's Caribbean *2A/76s*
Sake Hana *78s/2-3A*
Serafina *Mad/79s*
Session 73 *1A/73s*
Stir *1A/73-4s*
Vero *2A/77-8s*
Vudu *1A/77-8s*

East 80s

Auction House *89s/1-2A*
Back Page *3A/83-4s*
Bar @ Etats-Unis *81s/2-3A*
Brandy's Piano *84s/2-3A*
Comic Strip *2A/81-2s*
Dorrian's *2A/84s*
Dt.Ut *2A/84-5s*
Fiona's *1A/86-7s*
Fondue *80s/1-2A*
Gaf Bar *1A/89s*
Mad River *3A/81-2s*
Manhattan Lounge *2A/88-9s*
Martell's *83s/3A*
Met. Museum Roof *5A/81s*
Mustang Grill *2A/85s*
O'Flanagan's Ale *2A/82-3s*
Penang *2A/83s*
Rathbones *2A/88s*
Ryan's Daughter *85s/1-2A*

Saloon *York/83-4s*
Ship of Fools *2A/82-3s*
Snapper Creek *1A/82-3s*
Sushi Generation *2A/81-2s*
Tin Lizzie *2A/85-6s*
Trinity Public Hse. *84s/2-3A*
Uptown Lounge *3A/88-9s*
Waterloo *2A/84-5s*

East 90s & 100s

(Bet. 90th & 110th Sts.)
American Spirits *2A/90-1s*
Bar East *1A/90s*
Biddy's *91s/1-2A*
Big City *3A/90s*
Big Easy *2A/92-3s*
Blondies *2A/92-3s*
Brother Jimmy's *3A/92s*
Coogan's Parrot Bay *3A/93-4s*
Kinsale *3A/93-4s*
Ruby's Tap House *2A/91-2s*
Tool Box *2A/90-1s*
Wild Spirits *1A/95-6s*

Financial District

(South of Murray St.)
A&M Roadhouse *Murray/ Church-W Bway*
Bayard's *Hanover Sq./Pearl-Stone*
Blarney Stone *Trinity/Morris*
Bridge Cafe *Water/Dover*
Dakota Roadhse. *Park/Church-W. Bway*
Full Shilling *Pearl/Pine-Wall*
Jeremy's Ale *Front/Beekman- Peck Slip*
John Street B&G *John/Bway- Nassau*
Mercantile Grill *Pearl/Hanover- Wall*
MJ Grill *John/Cliff-Pearl*
Paris, The *South/Peck Slip*
Pussycat Lounge *Greenwich/ Rector*
Raccoon Lodge *Warren/Church*
Rise *West s/Battery Pl*
Romi *Rector/Greenwich- Washington*

17 Murray *Murray/Bway-Church*
SouthWest NY *World Fin./Liberty-South End*
Ulysses *Pearl/Hanover Sq.*
Vine *Broad/Exchange*

Flatiron District
(Bet. 14th & 24th Sts., 6th Ave. & Park Ave. S., excluding Union Sq.)
Angelo & Maxie's *Park S./19s*
Chango *Park S./19-20s*
Chetty Red *23s/Mad-Park S.*
Cutting Room *24s/Bway-6A*
Deep *22s/5-6A*
Discothèque *19s/5-6A*
Duvet *21s/5-6A*
Eugene *24s/5-6A*
Flatiron Lounge *19s/5-6A*
Flûte *20s/Bway-Park S.*
Gotham Comedy *22s/5-6A*
Gramercy Tavern *20s/Bway-Park*
Gypsy Tea *24s/5-6A*
Justin's *21s/5-6A*
Lemon, The *Park S./18-9s*
L'Express *Park S./20s*
Live Bait *23s/5A-Mad*
Mesa Grill *5A/15-6s*
No Idea *20s/Bway-Park S.*
Old Town Bar *18s/Bway-Park S.*
Park Avalon *Park S./18-9s*
Park Bar *15s/5A-Union Sq. W*
Pipa *19s/Bway-Park S.*
Prey *22s/5-6A*
Punch Lounge *Bway/20-1s*
Sala *19s/5-6A*
Select *24s/5-6A*
17 *17s/5-6A*
Slate *21s/5-6A*
Snitch *21s/5-6A*
Spider Club *20s/6A*
Splash *17s/5-6A*
Sugarcane *Park S./19-20s*
SushiSamba *Park S./19-20s*
Ten's *21s/Bway-Park S.*
Underbar *Park S./17-8s*
Vela *21s/5-6A*
Veritas *20s/Bway-Park S.*
VIP Club *20s/5-6A*

Garment District
(30th to 40th Sts., west of 5th)
Bellevue *9A/39-40s*
Blarney Stone *multi. loc.*
Copacabana *34s/11A*
Door *9A/38-9s*
Escuelita *39s/8-9A*
Hammerstein Ballrm *34s/8-9A*
Heartland Brewery *5A/34s*
Katwalk *35s/5-6A*
Keens Steak *36s/5-6A*
Lobby *38s/8-9A*
Local *33s/7-8A*
Metro Grill Roof *35s/5-6A*
Molly Wee *8A/30s*
Playwright *35s/5-6A*
Shelter *39s/5-6A*
Stitch *37s/7-8A*
Tempest Bar *8A/30-1s*
Tír na Nóg *Penn Pl.: 8A/33-4s*
Uncle Jack's *9A/34s*
Windfall *39s/5-6A*

Gramercy Park
(24th to 30th Sts., east of 5th; 14th to 24th Sts., east of Park)
Aubette *27s/Lex-Park S.*
Barfly *3A/20s*
Bar Jamón *Irving/17s*
Belmont *15s/Irving-Park S.*
Black Bear *3A/21-2s*
Blue Smoke *27s/Lex-Park S.*
Bull's Head *3A/22-3s*
Cibar *Irving/17-18s*
Desmond's *5A/29-30s*
Dos Caminos *Park S./26-7s*
Duke's *19s/Park S.*
Eleven Madison Pk. *Mad/24s*
Enoteca I Trulli *27s/Lex-Park S.*
Failte *2A/29-30s*
Fitzgerald's *3A/25s*
Galaxy Global *Irving/15s*
Gallery *27s/5A-Mad*
Houston's *Park S./27s*
Irving Plaza *Irving/15s*
Jazz Standard *27s/Lex-Park S.*
Le 26 *Madison/26s*
Link *15s/Irving*

McCormack's *3A/26s*
McSwiggan's *2A/22-3s*
Molly's *3A/22-3s*
Neogaea *28s/5A*
New York Comedy *24s/2-3A*
119 Bar *15s/Irving-Park S.*
Paddy Reilly's *2A/28-9s*
Park Ave. Country *Park S./27s*
Pete's Tavern *18s/Irving*
Plug Uglies *3A/21s*
Proof *3A/19-20s*
Red Sky *29s/Mad-Park*
Revival *15s/Irving-3A*
Rocky Sullivan's *Lex/28-9s*
Rodeo *3A/27s*
Scopa *Mad/28-9s*
Still *3A/17-8s*
Tabla *Mad/25s*
Tracy J's *19s/Irving-Park S.*
Wonderland *27s/5A-Mad*

Greenwich Village
(Houston to 14th Sts., west of Bway, excluding NoHo and Meatpacking District)
Absolutely 4th *4s/7A S.-10s*
Alibi *MacDougal/Bleecker-3s*
Art Bar *8A/Horatio-Jane*
Arthur's Tavern *Grove/Bleecker-7A S.*
Automatic Slim's *Washington/Bank*
Back Fence *Bleecker/Thompson*
Baggot Inn *3s/Sullivan-Thompson*
Barrow St. Ale *Barrow/7A S.-4s*
Bar 6 *6A/12-3s*
Bitter End *Blkr./La Guardia-Thompson*
Blind Tiger Ale *Hudson/10s*
Blue Mill *Commerce/Barrow*
Blue Note *3s/6A*
Boston Comedy *3s/Sullivan-Thompson*
Bowlmor Lanes *University/12-3s*
Boxers *4s/Barrow*
Cafe de Bruxelles *Greenwich/13s*
Cafe Wha? *MacDougal/Blkr.-3s*
Caffe Dante *MacDougal/Blkr.-Houston*

Caffe Rafaella *7A S./Charles-10s*
Caffe Reggio *MacDougal/Blkr.-3s*
Caliente Cab *multi. loc.*
Cedar Tavern *University/11-2s*
Chow Bar *4s/10s*
Chumley's *Bedford/Barrow-Grove*
Comedy Cellar *MacDougal/Blkr.-3s*
Cornelia St. Cafe *Cornelia/Blkr.*
Corner Bistro *4s/Horatio*
Cowgirl *Hudson/10s*
Cubby Hole *12s/4s*
Daddy-O *Bedford/Leroy*
Dove *Thompson/Bleecker-3s*
Down the Hatch *4s/6-7A*
Dublin 6 *Hudson/Bank-11s*
Dugout *Christopher/Wash.-West*
Duplex *Christopher/7A S.*
1849 *Bleecker/MacDougal-Sullivan*
Employees Only *Hudson/Christopher-10s*
EN Japanese Brasserie *Hudson/Leroy*
Falucka *Bleecker/Sullivan-Thompson*
Fat Black Pussy Cat *3s/MacDougal-6A*
Fat Cat *Christopher/Blkr.-7A S.*
Fiddlesticks *Greenwich/6A-7A S.*
55 Bar *Christopher/6A-7A S.*
49 Grove *Grove/Bleecker*
Four-Faced Liar *4s/6A-7A S.*
French Roast *6A/11s*
Fuelray *3s/LaGuardia-Thompson*
Garage *7A S./Barrow-Grove*
Gotham B&G *12s/5A-University*
Greenwich Brewing *6A/9s*
Grey Dog's *Carmine/Bedford-Blkr.*
Groove *MacDougal/3s*
Hangar *Christopher/Blkr.-Hudson*
Henrietta Hudson *Hudson/Morton*
Hudson Bar/Books *Hudson/Horatio-Jane*
Hue *Charles/Bleecker*
Hunk Mania *14s/7-8A*
I.C.U. *Washington/12s*
Indochine *Lafayette/Astor-4s*

Locations

I Tre Merli *10s/4s*
Jekyll & Hyde *7A S./Barrow-4s*
Johnny's Bar *Greenwich A/12-3s*
Josie Wood's *Waverly/Greene-Mercer*
Julius *10s/Waverly*
Kenny's Castaways *Bleecker/Sullivan-Thompson*
Kettle of Fish *Christopher/7A S.-Waverly*
Knickerbocker B&G *University/9s*
La Lanterna *MacDougal/3-4s*
Le Figaro *Bleecker/MacDougal*
Lion's Den *Sullivan/Bleecker-3s*
Lips *Bank/Greenwich*
Luke & Leroy *7A S./Leroy*
MacDougal St. Ale *MacDougal/Bleecker-3s*
Madame X *Houston/La Guardia-Thompson*
Marie's Crisis *Grove/7A S.*
Miracle Grill *Bleecker/Bank-11s*
Monster *Grove/Waverly Pl.-4s*
Movida *7A S./Bedford-Leroy*
Mr. Dennehy's *Carmine/7A S.*
NA *14s/7-8A*
Newgate Bar & Grill *La Guardia/Bleecker-3s*
Off the Wagon *MacDougal/Bleecker-3s*
One if by Land *Barrow/7A S.-4s*
Onyx *Sullivan/Houston*
Otheroom *Perry/Greenwich A-Washington*
Otto *5A/8s*
Peculier Pub *Bleecker/La Guardia-Thompson*
Pieces *Christopher/Gay-Greenwich A*
Pink Elephant *8A/13-4s*
Pressure *University/12-3s*
Red Lion *Bleecker/Thompson*
Reservoir *University/10-1s*
Riviera *4s/7A S.*
Rose's Turn *Grove/Bleecker*
Rubyfruit *Hudson/Charles-10s*
Rumor *3s/MacDougal-6A*
Salon *West/Jane*
Senor Swanky's *Bleecker/La Guardia*
Shade *Sullivan/3s*
Shag *8A/Bleecker-12s*
Slane *MacDougal/Bleecker*
Slaughtered Lamb *4s/Jones*
Smalls *10s/7A S.*
Spotted Pig *11s/Greenwich s*
Stoned Crow *Wash. Pl./6A*
Stonewall *Christopher/7A S.-Waverly*
Sullivan Room *Sullivan/Blkr.-3s*
SushiSamba *7A S./Barrow*
Sweet Rhythm *7A S./Bleecker-Grove*
Tavern on Jane *8A/Jane*
Terra Blues *Bleecker/La Guardia-Thompson*
13 *13s/University*
Tortilla Flats *Washington/12s*
Town Tavern *3s/MacDougal-6A*
Turks & Frogs *11s/Greenwich-Washington*
2i's *14s/7-8A*
Ty's *Christopher/Bleecker-Hudson*
V Bar *Sullivan/Bleecker-3s*
Village Lantern *Bleecker/Sullivan-Thompson*
Village Vanguard *7A S./11s*
Vol de Nuit *4s/MacDougal-6A*
West *West s/11s*
White Horse *Hudson/11s*
Wogie's *Greenwich A/Charles*
WXOU *Hudson/Perry-11s*
XR Bar *Houston/Sullivan*
Zinc Bar *Houston/La Guardia-Thompson*

Harlem/East Harlem
(West of Morningside Ave., bet. 125th & 157th Sts.; bet. 5th & Morningside Aves., bet. 110th & 157th Sts.; east of 5th Ave., north of 100th St.)
Lenox Lounge *Lenox/125s*

Little Italy

(Bet. Canal & Delancey Sts., &
Bowery & Lafayette St.)

Double Happiness *Mott/Broome-
Grand*

M Bar *Broome/Bowery-Elizabeth*

Odea *Broome/Mulberry*

Onieal's Grand St. *Grand/Centre-
Mulberry*

Xicala *Elizabeth/Broome-Kenmare*

Lower East Side

(Houston to Canal Sts., east of
Bowery)

Arlene Grocery *Stanton/Ludlow-
Orchard*

Barramundi *Clinton/Rivington-
Stanton*

Barrio Chino *Broome/Ludlow-
Orchard*

Belly *Rivington/Clinton-Suffolk*

Bereket *Houston/Orchard*

Bob *Eldridge/Houston-Stanton*

Boss Tweed's *Essex/Delancey-
Rivington*

Bowery Ballroom *Delancey/
Bowery-Chrystie*

Café Charbon *Orchard/Stanton*

Chibi's Sake/Chibitini *Clinton/
Rivington-Stanton*

Crash Mansion/BLVD *Bowery/
Spring*

Dark Room *Ludlow/Houston-
Stanton*

Delancey *Delancey/Attorney-
Clinton*

East Side Co. *Essex/Grand*

Eleven *Orchard/Stanton-Rivington*

Epstein's Bar *Stanton/Allen*

Essex *Essex/Rivington*

Freemans *Rivington/Bowery-
Chrystie*

Girls Room *Rivington/Pitt*

Good World B&G *Orchard/Canal-
Division*

Happy Ending *Broome/Eldridge-
Forsythe*

Iggy's *Ludlow/Rivington-Stanton*

'inoteca *Rivington/Ludlow*

Kos *Bowery/Houston-Prince*

Kush *Chrystie/Rivington-Stanton*

La Caverna *Rivington/Essex-
Norfolk*

Laugh Lounge *Essex/Rivington-
Stanton*

Les Enfants Terribles *Canal/
Ludlow*

Libation *Ludlow/Rivington-Stanton*

Living Room *Ludlow/Rivington-
Stanton*

Local 138 *Ludlow/Rivington-
Stanton*

Lolita *Broome/Allen*

Loreley *Rivington/Bowery-Chrystie*

Lotus Lounge *Clinton/Stanton*

Lucky Jack's *Orchard/Delancey-
Rivington*

Magician *Rivington/Essex*

Martignetti Liquors *Houston/
Allen-Eldridge*

Max Fish *Ludlow/Houston-Stanton*

Mercury Lounge *Houston/Essex-
Ludlow*

Milk and Honey *Eldridge/Broome-
Delancey*

Mission *Bowery/Prince-Rivington*

Motor City Bar *Ludlow/Delancey-
Rivington*

151 *Rivington/Clinton-Suffolk*

One91 *Orchard/Houston-Stanton*

169 Bar *E. B'way/Rutgers*

Orchard Bar *Orchard/Houston-
Stanton*

People *Allen/Rivington-Stanton*

Pianos *Ludlow/Rivington-Stanton*

Pink Pony *Ludlow/Houston-
Stanton*

Punch & Judy *Clinton/Houston-
Stanton*

Rockwood Music *Allen/Houston-
Stanton*

Rothko *Suffolk/Delancey-Rivington*

Salt Bar *Clinton/Stanton*

Sapphire *Eldridge/Houston*

Schiller's *Rivington/Norfolk*

17 Home *Stanton/Bowery-Chrystie*
Sin-é *Attorney/Stanton*
6's & 8's *Chrystie/Stanton*
Skinny *Orchard/Stanton*
Slipper Room *Orchard/Stanton*
Stanton Social *Stanton/Ludlow*
Suba *Ludlow/Delancey-Rivington*
Sunita *Norfolk/Delancey-Rivington*
Tenement *Ludlow/Rivington-Stanton*
13 Little Devils *Orchard/Delancey-Rivington*
THOR Lobby Bar *Rivington/Essex-Ludlow*
Tonic *Norfolk/Delancey-Rivington*
12" Bar *Essex/Houston-Stanton*
24/7 *Eldridge/Houston-Stanton*
Vasmay Lounge *Houston/Suffolk*
Verlaine *Rivington/Essex-Ludlow*
Welcome/Johnsons *Rivington/Essex-Norfolk*
Whiskey Ward *Essex/Delancey-Rivington*
White Rabbit *Houston/Eldridge-Forsyth*

Meatpacking District
(Gansevoort to 15th Sts., west of 9th Ave.)
Aer *13s/9A-Washington*
APT *13s/9A-Washington*
Ara Wine Bar *9A/13-4s*
Brass Monkey *Little W. 12s/10A-Washington*
Cielo *Little W. 12s/9A-Washington*
5 Ninth *9A/Little W. 12s*
Florent *Gansevoort/Greenwich-Wash.*
Gaslight/G2 *multi. loc.*
Highline *Washington/Little W. 12s*
Hog Pit *9A/13s*
Hogs & Heifers *Wash./13s*
Level V *Hudson/14s*
Lotus *14s/9A-Washington*
Markt *14s/9A*
Meet *Gansevoort/Washington*
One *Little W. 12s/9A*
Ono *9A/Gansevoort*
Pastis *9A/Little W. 12s*

Plunge *9A/Gansevoort*
PM *Gansevoort/Greenwich-Wash.*
Pop Burger *9A/14-5s*
Rare *14s/9A-Washington*
Rhône *Gansevoort/Greenwich-Wash.*
Soho House *9A/14s*
Son Cubano *14s/Washington*
Spice Market *13s/9A*

Murray Hill
(30th to 40th Sts., east of 5th)
Asia de Cuba *Mad/37-8s*
Banc Cafe *3A/30s*
Bar 515 *3A/34-5s*
Black Sheep *3A/38-9s*
Bogart's *Park/39s*
Cherry *39s/Lexington-Park*
Coda *34s/5A-Mad*
Dip *3A/29-30s*
El Rio Grande *38s/3A*
Ginger Man *36s/5A-Mad*
Hairy Monk *3A/25s*
Hook and Ladder *2A/33-4s*
Joshua Tree *3A/34-5s*
Margarita & Murphy *3A/38-9s*
Mercury Bar *3A/33-4s*
Mica Bar *3A/38-9s*
Morgans Bar *Mad/37-8s*
Patrick Kavanagh's *3A/33-4s*
Pine Tree Lodge *35s/1-2A*
PS 450 *Park/30-1s*
Rare View *Lex/37s*
Silverleaf *38s/Park*
Third & Long *3A/35s*
Twelve *34s/3A*
Under the Volcano *36s/5A-Mad*
Vapor *Mad/31-2s*
Waterfront Ale Hse. *2A/30s*
Wet Bar *39s/Lex*
Whiskey River *2A/31-2s*

NoHo
(Bet. Houston & 4th Sts., Bowery & Bway)
Ace of Clubs *Great Jones/Lafayette*
Agozar! *Bowery/Bleecker*

B Bar *4s/Bowery-Lafayette*
Bond Street *Bond/Bway-Lafayette*
Crime Scene *Bowery/Bleecker-Houston*
Five Points *Gr. Jones/Bowery*
Gonzalez/Gonzalez *Bway/Blkr.-Houston*
Great Jones Cafe *Gr. Jones/Bowery*
Mannahatta *Bowery/Bleecker*
Marion's Continental *Bowery/4s-Gr. Jones*
Phebe's *Bowery/4s*
Sala *Bowery/Great Jones*
Slainte *Bowery/Bleecker-Houston*
Slide *Bowery/4s-Gr. Jones*
Soho Billiards *Houston/Mott*
Swift *4s/Bowery-Lafayette*
Table 50 *Bway/Bleecker*
Temple Bar *Lafayette/Blkr.-Houston*
Tom & Jerry's *Elizabeth/Bleecker-Houston*
Von *Bleecker/Bowery-Elizabeth*

NoLita

(Bet. Delancey & Houston Sts., Bowery & Lafayette St.)
Botanica *Houston/Mott-Mulberry*
Cafe Gitane *Mott/Houston-Prince*
Chibi's Sake/Chibitini *Mott/Prince-Spring*
Eight Mile Creek *Mulberry/Prince*
Gatsby's *Spring/Lafayette-Mulberry*
Mexican Radio *Cleveland/Kenmare-Spring*
Peasant *Elizabeth/Prince-Spring*
Pioneer *Bowery/Prince-Spring*
Pravda *Lafayette/Houston-Prince*
Public *Elizabeth/Prince-Spring*
Shebeen *Mott/Kenmare-Spring*
Spring Lounge *Spring/Mulberry*
Sweet & Vicious *Spring/Bowery-Elizabeth*
Velvet *Mulberry/Prince-Spring*
Vig Bar *Spring/Elizabeth*

SoHo

(Bet. Canal & Houston Sts., west of Lafayette St.)
Antarctica *Hudson/Spring*
Balthazar *Spring/Bway-Crosby*
Bar 89 *Mercer/Broome-Spring*
BINY *Thompson/Canal-Grand*
Blue Ribbon *Sullivan/Prince-Spring*
Broome St. Bar *W. Bway/Broome*
Cafe Noir *Grand/Thompson*
Cipriani Downtown *W. Bway/Broome-Spring*
Circa Tabac *Watts/6A-Thompson*
Cub Room *Sullivan/Prince*
Culture Club *Varick/Charlton-King*
Cupping Room *W. Bway/Broome*
Diva *W. Bway/Broome-Grand*
Don Hill's *Greenwich/Spring*
Dos Caminos *W. Bway/Houston*
Ear Inn *Spring/Greenwich-Washington*
Falls, The *Lafayette/Kenmare-Spring*
Fanelli's *Prince/Mercer*
Fiamma Osteria *Spring/6A-Sullivan*
Flow *Varick/Spring-Vandam*
46 Grand *Grand/Thompson-W. Bway*
Grand Bar *Bway/Canal-Grand*
Green Room *Spring/Hudson-Varick*
Ideya *W. Bway/Broome-Grand*
I Tre Merli *W. Bway/Houston-Prince*
Jazz Gallery *Hudson/Spring*
Kaña *Spring/Greenwich-Washington*
L'Orange Bleue *Broome/Crosby*
Lucky Strike *Grand/W. Bway*
Lure Fishbar *Mercer/Prince*
Merc Bar *Mercer/Houston-Prince*
Mercer Bar *Prince/Mercer*
Milady's *Prince/Thompson*
ñ *Crosby/Broome-Grand*
Naked Lunch *Thompson/Grand*

Nerveana *Varick/Charlton-King*
Novecento *W. Bway/Broome-Grand*
NV *Spring/Hudson*
Peep *Prince/Sullivan*
Penang *Spring/Greene-Mercer*
Puck Fair *Lafayette/Houston-Prince*
Raoul's *Prince/Sullivan-Thompson*
Red Bench *Sullivan/Prince-Spring*
Room *Sullivan/Houston-Prince*
S.O.B.'s *Varick/Houston*
Soho: 323 *Bway/Canal-Grand*
Sway *Spring/Greenwich-Hudson*
Thom Bar *Thompson/Broome-Spring*
203 Spring *Spring/Sullivan*
Zoë *Prince/Bway-Mercer*

South Street Seaport
Harbour Lights *South s/Fulton*
Heartland Brewery *South s/Fulton*
Sequoia *Fulton/South s*

TriBeCa
(Bet. Canal & Murray Sts., west of Bway)
Anotheroom *W. Bway/Beach-N. Moore*
Brandy Library *N. Moore/Hudson-Varick*
Bubble Lounge *W. Bway/Franklin-White*
Buster's Garage *W. Bway/Leonard-Worth*
Canal Room *W. Bway/Canal*
Church Lounge *6A/White*
City Hall *Duane/Church-W. Bway*
Dekk *Reade/Greenwich-Hudson*
Dylan Prime *Laight/Greenwich*
Flor de Sol *Greenwich/Franklin-Harrison*
Grace *Franklin/Church-W. Bway*
Harrison, The *Greenwich/Harrison*
Knitting Factory *Leonard/Bway-Church*
Le Zinc *Duane/Church-W. Bway*

Lush *Duane/Bway-Church*
Megu *Thomas/Church-W. Bway*
Mehanata *Bway/Canal*
Mocca *Reade/Church*
M1-5 Bar *Walker/Bway-Church*
Nancy Whiskey *Lispenard/W. Bway*
No Moore *W. Bway/N. Moore*
Odeon *W. Bway/Duane-Thomas*
Patriot Saloon *Chambers/Church*
Remy *Greenwich/Carlisle-Rector*
66 *Church/Leonard*
Sugar *Church/Lispenard-Walker*
Tribeca Grill *Greenwich/Franklin*
Tribeca Rock Club *Warren/Bway-Church*
Tribeca Tavern *W. Bway/Walker-White*
Walker's *N. Moore/Varick*

Union Square
(Bet. 14th & 17th Sts., Union Sq. E. & W.)
Blue Water Grill *Union Sq. W./16s*
Coffee Shop *Union Sq. W./16s*
Heartland Brewery *Union Sq. W./16-7s*
Isis *Park S./17-8s*
Luna Park *17s/Bway-Park S.*
Union Sq. Cafe *16s/Union Sq. W*
W Union Square Living Room *Park S./17s*

Washington Hts. & Up
(North of W. 157th St.)
Bleu Evolution *187s/Ft. Wash.-Pinehurst*

West 40s
Algonquin *44s/5-6A*
Bar 41 *41s/7A*
Barrage *47s/9-10A*
B. B. King Blues *42s/7-8A*
Birdland *44s/8-9A*
Blarney Stone *47/8-9A*
Blue Fin *Bway/47s*
Broadway Lounge *Bway/45-6s*
Bryant Park *40s/5-6A*
Bull Moose *44s/8-9A*

Carolines *Bway/49-50s*
Cellar Bar *40s/5-6A*
Channel 4 *48s/5-6A*
Chez Josephine *42s/9-10A*
China Club *47s/Bway-8A*
Collins Bar *8A/46-7s*
Connolly's *45s/6-7A*
Croton Reservoir *40s/Bway-6A*
Daltons *9A/43-4s*
Danny's *multi. loc.*
Del Frisco's *6A/49s*
Delta Grill *9A/48s*
Don't Tell Mama *46s/8-9a*
ESPN Zone *Bway/42s*
Fashion 40 *40s/7-8A*
Film Center Cafe *9A/44-5s*
Gaf Bar *48s/9-10A*
Heartland Brewery *43s/Bway-6A*
House of Brews *46s/8-9A*
Irish Rogue *44s/8-9A*
Jade Terrace *47s/Bway-8A*
Jimmy's Corner *44s/Bway-6A*
Joe Allen *46s/8-9A*
Joshua Tree *46s/8-9A*
Kemia *44s/9A*
Kevin St. James *8A/46s*
Koi *40s/5-6A*
Latitude *8A/47-8s*
Laugh Factory *8A/42s*
Leisure Time *8A/42s*
Marseille *9A/44s*
M Bar *44s/5-6A*
McHales *8A/46s*
Mercury Bar *9A/46s*
Nation *45s/5-6A*
Oak Room *44s/5-6A*
O'Flaherty's Ale *46s/8-9A*
O'Lunney's *45s/Bway-6A*
O2 *49s/Bway-8A*
Paramount Bar *46s/Bway-8A*
Paramount Library Bar *46s/ Bway-8A*
Penthse Exec. Club *45s/11A*
Pigalle *8A/48s*
Pig N Whistle *47s/6-7A*
Playwright *multi. loc.*
QT Hotel Bar *45s/6-7A*

Rainbow Grill *Rock Plaza/49s*
Royalton *44s/5-6A*
Ruby Foo's *Bway/49s*
Rudy's *9A/44-5s*
Rufus *10A/45-6s*
Rum House *47s/Bway-8A*
Sardi's *44s/Bway-8A*
Scruffy Duffy's *8A/46-7s*
Show *41s/Bway-6A*
Siberia *40s/8-9A*
Social *8A/48-9s*
St. Andrews *44s/Bway-6A*
Swing 46 *46s/8-9A*
Xth Ave Lounge *10A/45-6s*
Tonic/Met Lounge *7A/48-9s*
View Lounge *Bway/45-6s*
Whiskey *Bway/47s*
World Yacht *41s/Hudson River*
W Times Square Living Room *Bway/47s*
Zanzibar *9A/45s*

West 50s
Ava Lounge *55s/Bway*
Bar Nine *9A/53-4s*
Brasserie 8½ *57s/5-6A*
Carnegie Club *56s/6-7A*
Cité Grill *51s/6-7A*
Coliseum Bar *58s/8-9A*
Cosmo *54s/8-9A*
'disiac *54s/9-10A*
Divine Bar *54s/Bway-8A*
Dream Lounge *55s/Bway-7A*
Druids *10A/50-1s*
Exit *56s/12A*
Faces & Names *54s/6-7A*
Flashdancers *Bway/52-3s*
Flûte *54s/Bway-7A*
Frederick's *58s/5-6A*
Fusion *10A/54-5s*
Hard Rock *57s/Bway-7A*
Heartland Brewery *6A/51s*
Hooters *56s/Bway-7A*
Hudson Hotel Bar *58s/8-9A*
Hudson Hotel Library *58s/8-9A*
Hustler Club *51s/12A*
Iguana *54s/Bway-8A*
Improv *53s/8-9A*

Iridium *Bway/50-1s*
Jake's Saloon *10A/57s*
Juniper Suite *56s/5-6A*
Kennedy's *57s/8-9A*
K Lounge *52s/5-6A*
Maison *Bway/53-4s*
Mars 2112 *Bway/51s*
Matt's Grill *8A/55-6s*
McCormick/Schmick *6A/52s*
McGee's *55s/Bway-8A*
Mickey Mantle's *CPS/5-6A*
Moda Outdoors *52s/6-7A*
Modern, The *53s/5-6A*
Pen-Top Bar *5A/55s*
Perdition *10A/48-9s*
P.J. Carney's *7A/57-8s*
Posh *51s/9-10A*
Providence/Triumph Room *57s/8-9A*
Redeye *7A/56s*
Rink Bar *50s/5-6A*
Rock Center Cafe *50s/5-6A*
Roseland *52s/Bway-8A*
Rue 57 *57s/6A*
Rumours *8A/55s*
Russian Samovar *52s/Bway-8A*
Russian Vodka Rm. *52s/Bway-8A*
Serafina *55s/Bway*
Shelly's NY *57s/6A*
Single Rm. Occup. *53s/8-9A*
Temple *52s/Bway-8A*
Therapy *52s/8-9A*
Town *56s/5-6A*
Trousdale *50s/Bway-8A*
21 Club *52s/5-6A*
Varjak *8A/54-5s*
Vintage *9A/50-1s*
Whiskey Park *CPS/6A*
Ye Olde Tripple Inn *54s/Bway-8A*

West 60s

Bar Masa *Columbus Circle/60s*
Café des Artistes *67s/Columbus-CPW*
Café Gray *Columbus Circle/60s*
Dizzy's Club *Columbus Circle/60s*
Jean Georges *CPW/60-1s*
Makor *67s/Columbus-CPW*

MO Bar *60s/Bway-Col.*
O'Neals' *64s/Bway-CPW*
Peter's *Columbus/68-9s*
Rosa Mexicano *Columbus/62s*
Stone Rose *Columbus Circle/60s*
Tavern on Green *CPW/66-7s*
V Steakhouse *Columbus Circle/60s*

West 70s

All State *72s/Bway-W. End*
Amsterdam Billiards *Amst./76-7s*
Beacon *Bway/74s*
Blondies *79s/Amst.-Bway*
Boat Basin *79s/Hudson River*
Bourbon St. *Amst./79-80s*
Burton Pub/Kama Lounge *Col/78s*
Cafe Luxembourg *70s/Amst.-W. End*
Candle Bar *Amsterdam/74-5s*
'Cesca *75s/Amst.*
Citrus B&G *Amst./75s*
Dive 75 *75s/Amst.-Col*
Dublin House *79s/Amst.-Bway*
Eight of Clubs *75s/Bway-West End*
Harrison's Tavern *Amsterdam/77s*
Malachy's *72s/Bway-Columbus*
North West *Columbus/79s*
P & G Cafe *Amst./73s*
Penang *Columbus/71s*
Ruby Foo's *Bway/77s*
Senor Swanky's *Columbus/84-5s*
Shalel *70s/CPW-Columbus*
Shark Bar *Amst./74-75s*
Stand-Up NY *78s/Amst.-Bway*
Sugar Bar *72s/Bway-West End*
Time Out *Amst./76-7s*
Westside Brewing *Amst./76s*
Yogi's *Bway/75-6s*

West 80s

Brother Jimmy's *Amst./80-1s*
Cafe Lalo *83s/Amst.-Bway*
Calle Ocho *Col./81-2s*
Dead Poet *Amst./81-2s*
Docks Oyster *Bway/89-90s*
Edgar's Cafe *84s/Bway-W. End*
Fez *Bway/85s*

Firehouse *Col./85-6s*
4₂0 *Amst./80s*
French Roast *Bway/85s*
Fujiyama Mama *Col./82-3s*
George Keeley's *Amst./83-4s*
Gin Mill *Amst./81-2s*
Hi-Life *Amst./83s*
Jake's Dilemma *Amst./80-1s*
Jean-Luc *Col./84-5s*
McAleer's Pub *Amst./80-1s*
Mod *Columbus/84-5s*
Ouest *Bway/83-4s*
Parlour *86s/Bway-West End*
Prohibition *Columbus/84-5s*
Raccoon Lodge *Amsterdam/83s*
Rain *82s/Amst.-Columbus*
Sake Hana *Amsterdam/82-3s*

West 90s
Cleopatra's Needle *Bway/92-3s*
Dive Bar *Amst./95-6s*

West 100s
(West of Morningside Ave.)
Abbey Pub *105s/Amst.-Bway*
Broadway Dive *Bway/101-02s*
Ding Dong Lounge *Col./105-06s*
Eden *Bway/104-05s*
Heights B&G *Bway/111-12s*
O'Connell's *Bway/108s*
Smoke *Bway/105-06s*
Tap a Keg *Bway/104-05s*
Underground *West End/107s*
West End *Bway/113-14s*

BRONX

An Béal Bocht *238s/Greystone-Waldo*

Stan's *River A/Yankee Stad.*
Yankee Tavern *161s/Gerard*

BROOKLYN

Bay Ridge
Delia's *3A/93s*
Legacy *88s/4-5A*
Peggy O'Neill's *5A/81s*
Wicked Monk *5A/84s*

Boerum Hill
Apartment 138 *Smith/Dean-Bergen*
BarTabac *Smith/Dean*
Boat *Smith/Warren-Wyckoff*
Brazen Head *Atlantic/Boerum-Court*
Brooklyn Inn *Hoyt/Bergen*
Hank's Saloon *3A/Atlantic*
Sherwood *Smith/Baltic*
Vegas *Smith/Bergen-Dean*

Brighton Beach
Odessa *Brighton Beach/Seacoast*
Rasputin *Coney Island/Ave. X*

Brooklyn Heights
Eamonn's *Montague/Clinton-Court*
Floyd *Atlantic/Clinton-Henry*

Magnetic Field *Atlantic/Henry-Hicks*
Waterfront Ale Hse. *Atlantic/Clinton-Henry*

Bushwick
Life Cafe *Flushing/Bogart-Central*

Carroll Gardens
Angry Wade's *Smith/Butler*
Boudoir Bar *Smith/Degraw-Sackett*
Brooklyn Social *Smith/Carroll-President*
B61 *Columbia/Degraw*
Gowanus Yacht *Smith/President*
miniBar *Court/4s-Luquer*
NY Perks *Smith/Baltic-Warren*
Quench *Smith/Sackett*
Sonny's B&G *Smith/Union*
Village 247 *Smith/Degraw-Douglass*
Zombie Hut *Smith/Degraw*

Clinton Hill
Sputnik *Taaffe/DeKalb-Willoughby*

Locations

Cobble Hill
Bar Below *Smith/Baltic-Butler*
Joya *Court/Warren*
Last Exit *Atlantic/Clinton-Henry*

Coney Island
Peggy O'Neill's *Surf/19s*

Downtown
BAMcafé *Lafayette/Ashland*
Kili *Hoyt/Atlantic-State*

Dumbo
Superfine *Front/Jay-Pearl*
Water St. Bar *Water/Dock-Main*

Fort Greene
Butta' Cup *Adelphi/DeKalb*
Five Spot *Myrtle/Washington-Waverly*
Frank's Cocktail *Fulton/Hudson-Rockwell*
Moe's *Lafayette/Portland*
Stonehome *Lafayette/Elliott-Portland*

Greenpoint
Enid's *Manhattan/Driggs*
Matchless *Manhattan/Driggs*
Pencil Factory *Franklin/Greenpoint*
Warsaw *Driggs/Eckford*

Manhattan Beach
Anyway Cafe *Oriental/West End*

Park Slope
Barbès *9s/6A*
Bar 4 *7A/15s*
Bar Reis *5A/5-6s*
Blue Ribbon Bklyn. *5A/1s-Garfield*
Buttermilk *5A/16s*
Commonwealth *5A/12s*
Excelsior *5A/6-7s*
Gate, The *5A/3s*
Ginger's *5A/5-6s*
Great Lakes *5A/1s*
Lighthouse *5A/Carroll-Garfield*
Loki *5A/2s*

Long Tan *5A/Berkeley-Union*
Lucky 13 *13s/5-6A*
Miracle Grill *7A/4s*
O'Connor's *5A/Bergen-Dean*
Park Slope Ale *6A/5s*
Patio Lounge *5A/Berkeley-Lincoln*
Royale *5A/12-3s*
Southpaw *5A/Sterling-St. Johns*
Tea Lounge *multi. loc.*
Total Wine Bar *5A/St. Marks-Warren*
200 Fifth *5A/Sackett-Union*

Prospect Heights
Freddy's *Dean/6A*
Half Wine Bar *Vanderbilt/Prospect-Park*
Soda Bar *Vanderbilt/Prospect-St. Mark's*

Red Hook
Hook *Commerce/Columbia-Richards*
Lillie's *Beard/Dwight*
Moonshine *Columbia/Hamiton-Woodhull*
Sunny's *Conover/Beard-Reed*

Sheepshead Bay
Anyway Cafe *Gravesend Neck/16s*

Sunset Park
Koze Lounge *5A/20-1s*

Williamsburg
Abbey *Driggs/N. 7-8s*
Alligator Lounge *Metropolitan/Lorimer*
Anytime *N. 6s/Berry-Wythe*
Barcade *Union/Ainslie-Powers*
Bembe *S. 6s/Berry*
Black Betty *Metropolitan/Havemeyer*
Blu Lounge *N. 8s/Driggs*
Boogaloo *Marcy/Bway-Wooster*
Brooklyn Ale *Berry/N. 8s*
Brooklyn Brewery *N. 11s/Berry-Wythe*
Capone's *N. 9s/Driggs-Roebling*

Locations

Clem's *Grand/Roebling*
D.O.C. Wine Bar *N. 7s/Kent-Wythe*
Duff's *N. 3s/Kent*
East River *S. 6s/Bedford-Berry*
Fun House *N. 4s/Bedford-Driggs*
Galapagos *N. 6s/Kent-Wythe*
Grand Press *Grand/Havemeyer-Roebling*
Iona *Grand/Bedford-Driggs*
Laila Lounge *N. 7s/Berry-Wythe*
Larry Lawrence *Grand/Havemeyer-Roebling*
Levee, The *Berry/Metropolitan*
Lucky Cat *Grand/Driggs-Roebling*
Metropolitan *Lorimer/Devoe-Metropolitan*
Moto *Bway/Hooper*
Mug's Ale *Bedford/N. 10s*
Northsix *N. 6s/Kent-Wythe*
Pete's Candy Store *Lorimer/Frost-Richardson*
Planet Thailand *N. 7s/Bedford-Berry*
Rain Lounge *Bedford/N. 5s*

Red and Black *N. 5s/Bedford-Berry*
Relish *Wythe/N. 3s*
Rosemary's Greenpoint *Bedford/N. 6-7s*
Royal Oak *Union/N. 11s*
Savalas *Bedford/Grand-S. 1s*
SEA *N. 6s/Berry*
Spike Hill *Bedford/N. 7s*
Spuyten Duyvil *Metropolitan/Havemeyer*
Stain *Grand/Graham-Humboldt*
Supreme Trading *N. 8s/Driggs-Roebling*
Sweetwater *N. 6s/Berry-Wythe*
Tainted Lady *Grand/Havemeyer-Marcy*
Teddy's *Berry/N. 8s*
Trash *Grand/Driggs-Roebling*
Triple Crown *Bedford/N. 11s*
Turkey's Nest *Bedford/N. 12s*
Union Pool *Union/Meeker*
Zablozki's *N. 6s/Berry-Wythe*
Zebulon *Wythe/Metropolitan-N. 3s*

QUEENS

Astoria
Athens Cafe *30A/32-3s*
Bohemian Hall *24A/31s*
Byzantio *31s/Newtown*
Cafe Bar *36s/34A*
Cávo *31A/42-3s*
Central *Steinway/20A-20r*
Life *Newtown/30s*

Bayside
Byzantio *Bell/Northern*
Donovan's *41A/Bell*
First Edition *Bell/41st*

Uncle Jack's *Bell/40A*

Forest Hills
Bartini's *Station Sq./71A*

Long Island City
Play *Queens/Northern*

Sunnyside
Sidetracks *Queens/45-6s*

Woodside
Donovan's *Roosevelt/58s*

STATEN ISLAND

Big Nose Kate's *Arthur Kill/ St. Luke's*
Cargo *Bay/Slosson Terrace*
Jade Island *Richmond/Yukon*

Killmeyer's *Arthur Kill/Sharrotts*
Martini Red *Van Duzer/Beach*
Muddy Cup *Van Duzer/Beach*

SPECIAL APPEALS

(Indexes list the best in each category. Multi-location nightspots' features may vary by branch. For some categories, schedules may vary; call ahead or check Web sites for the most up-to-date information.)

After Work

Amuse
Angelo & Maxie's
Annie Moores
Aubette
Ava Lounge
Bar Below
Bar 515
Bar Nine
Bar Room
Bayard's
Beer Bar/Cafe Centro
Bice
Black Door
Bliss
Blue Room
Blue Water Grill
Blu Lounge
Boat Basin
Bogart's
B1 Drink Club
Branch
Brasserie 8½
Brazen Head
Bryant Park
Bull & Bear
Café Gray
Campbell Apt.
Capital Grille
Cherry
Church Lounge
Cibar
Cité Grill
City Hall
Connolly's
Croton Reservoir
Del Frisco's
Delta Grill
Divine Bar
Django

Docks Oyster
Eamonn's
El Rio Grande
Faces & Names
Fashion 40
Fifty Seven 57
Flûte
Four Seasons Bar
Full Shilling
Gaf Bar
Ginger Man
Grace
Guastavino's
Heartland Brewery
Houston's
Hudson Hotel Bar
Iguana
Isis
Jake's Saloon
Jameson's
Jeremy's Ale
John Street B&G
Juniper Suite
Katwalk
Kevin St. James
King Cole Bar
La Linea
Le Colonial
Lemon, The
Le 26
Light
Local
Luna Park
Mad River
Maggie's
Mambi Lounge
M Bar (West 40s)
McCormick/Schmick
McFadden's
McGee's

Special Appeals

Mercantile Grill
Merchants, NY
Mercury Bar
Metro 53/Loft
Mica Bar
MJ Grill
Moda Outdoors
Mug's Ale
Nation
No Idea
O'Flaherty's Ale
Old Town Bar
O'Lunney's
Opal
Opia
Paramount Bar
Park Bar
Patrick Conway's
Pen-Top Bar
Pershing Sq.
Pig N Whistle
P.J. Carney's
P.J. Clarke's
PS 450
Q Lounge
Redemption
Redeye
Remy
Rink Bar
Romi
Rosa Mexicano
Rosemary's Greenpoint
Royalton
Rue 57
Savannah Steak
Scruffy Duffy's
Sequoia
Shelly's NY
Social
SouthWest NY
Spike Hill
Splash
St. Andrews
Stitch
Sutton Place
Tao
Tír na Nóg

Tracy J's
Turtle Bay
21 Club
Ulysses
Under the Volcano
Vapor
Varjak
Villard
Vine
Walker's
Wet Bar
Whiskey
Whiskey Blue
Whiskey Park
Windfall
Wollensky's
XL
Zablozki's

All-Night Dining
Bereket
Cafeteria
Diner 24
Florent
French Roast
L'Express
Maison
Pigalle
Yaffa

Art Bars
Apocalypse Lounge
Art Bar
Bowery Poetry
CB's 313
Freddy's
Fun House
Galapagos
Half King
Kanvas
KGB
Lucky Cat
Nublu
Nuyorican Poets
Passerby
Rififi
Supreme Trading

Bachelor Parties
Del Frisco's
ESPN Zone
Flashdancers
40/40
Hogs & Heifers
Hustler Club
Park Ave. Country
Penthse Exec. Club
Pussycat Lounge
Red Rock West
Scores
Ten's
VIP Club

Bachelorette Parties
Automatic Slim's
Cafe Wha?
Culture Club
El Flamingo
Hogs & Heifers
Hunk Mania
Lips
Nerveana
Tortilla Flats
Xunta

Bathrooms to Visit
Baraza
Bar 89
Brasserie
Bungalow 8
Casa La Femme
Dusk
Duvet
ESPN Zone
Glass
Jekyll & Hyde
M Bar (Little Italy)
Ono
Peep
P.J. Clarke's
Royalton
Schiller's
SEA
Slide
Splash
Tao

Xth Ave Lounge
Whiskey
XL

Beautiful People
APT
Asia de Cuba
Ava Lounge
Balthazar
Blue Ribbon
Bond Street
Brasserie 8½
Bungalow 8
Cabanas
Cafeteria
Cain
Canal Room
Cellar Bar
Cherry
Cibar
Cielo
Coffee Shop
Discothèque
Eugene
Flow
Frederick's
g
Grand Bar
Guastavino's
Hiro
Hudson Hotel Bar
Hue
Indochine
Koi
La Bottega Caffé
Le Colonial
Light
Lot 61
Lotus
Marquee
Matsuri
Meet
Mercer Bar
Morgans Bar
Movida
Odeon
Paramount Bar
Park

Pastis
Pink Elephant
Pop Burger
Pravda
Raoul's
Royalton
Ruby Falls
Schiller's
Select
Spice Market
SushiSamba
Sway
Table 50
Tao
Thom Bar
203 Spring
Underbar
Villard
Viscaya
Wet Bar
Whiskey
Whiskey Blue
XL

Bed-ridden
APT
Ava Lounge
BED New York
Cotton
Duvet
Highline
Hue
No. 1 Chinese
Underbar
Whiskey Blue

Biker Bars
American Trash
Ear Inn
Hogs & Heifers
Raccoon Lodge
Red Rock West

Bottle Service
(Bottle purchase sometimes
required to secure a table)
Avalon
Bliss
Bungalow 8

Cain
Canal Room
China Club
Cielo
Coral Room
Cotton
Discothèque
Earth
Eugene
58
40/40
49 Grove
Glo
Gypsy Tea
Hiro
Level V
Lot 61
Lotus
LQ
Marquee
Martignetti Liquors
Mission
Movida
NA
Pink Elephant
PM
Providence/Triumph Room
Quo
Rumor
Select
Serena
Show
Spirit
Stay
Suede
Sway
Table 50
Taj
Temple
Underbar
Vudu
Vue
Wonderland

Cabaret
Cafe Carlyle
Danny's
Don't Tell Mama

Duplex
Feinstein's/Regency
Joe's Pub
Lips
Oak Room
Odessa
Rasputin
Rose's Turn

Cheap Drinks
Abbey
American Spirits
Bar East
Big Easy
Blind Tiger Ale
Blue and Gold
Bohemian Hall
Boxcar Lounge
Brazen Head
Brooklyn Brewery
B61
Bull McCabe's
Cheap Shots
Cherry Tavern
Corner Bistro
Desmond's
Doc Holliday's
Down the Hatch
Dublin House
Edge, The
Enid's
Flannery's
Floyd
Freddy's
Gowanus Yacht
Grassroots
Holiday Cocktail
Iona
Jimmy's Corner
Lillie's
Mad River
Magnetic Field
Manitoba's
Mars Bar
McAleer's Pub
McSorley's
Milady's
Motor City Bar

Nancy Whiskey
O'Connor's
Off the Wagon
P & G Cafe
Plug Uglies
Rosemary's Greenpoint
Rudy's
Ryan's Irish Pub
Sophie's
St. Marks Ale
Subway Inn
Sweetwater
Tap a Keg
Town Crier
Warsaw
Welcome/Johnsons
Yogi's

Coffeehouses
alt.coffee
Athens Cafe
Byzantio
Cafe Gitane
Cafe Lalo
Caffe Dante
Caffe Rafaella
Caffe Reggio
Dt.Ut
Edgar's Cafe
French Roast
Grey Dog's
Kavehaz
Le Figaro
Lotus Lounge
Lucky Cat
Muddy Cup
Pink Pony
Tea Lounge

Comedy Clubs
(Call ahead to check nights, times, performers and covers)
Boston Comedy
Carolines
Comedy Cellar
Comic Strip
Dangerfield's
Gotham Comedy

Improv
Laugh Factory
Laugh Lounge
New York Comedy
Stand-Up NY

Commuter Oases
Grand Central
  Annie Moores
  Beer Bar/Cafe Centro
  Blarney Stone
  B1 Drink Club
  Campbell Apt.
  Capital Grille
  Lea
  Métrazur
  Michael Jordan's
  Oyster Bar
  Patrick Conway's
  Pershing Sq.
  Peter Dillon's
  Tequilaville
Penn Station
  Blarney Stone
  Local
  Molly Wee
  Playwright
  Tír na Nóg
  Uncle Jack's
Port Authority
  Bar 41
  Bellevue
  Croton Reservoir
  Daltons
  Door
  Fashion 40
  Siberia

Critic-Proof
(Very popular, despite so-so ratings)
Bar 515
Bar None
Blarney Stone
Brother Jimmy's
Caliente Cab
Dorrian's
Gaslight/G2

Heartland Brewery
Hi-Life
Hogs & Heifers
Joshua Tree
Lemon, The
Mad River
McFadden's
Mercury Bar
Metro 53/Loft
Mo's Caribbean
Off the Wagon
Turtle Bay
West End

Dance Clubs
Avalon
Branch
China Club
Cielo
Copacabana
Coral Room
Crobar
Culture Club
Deep
Discothèque
El Flamingo
Escuelita
Eugene
Exit
58
Glo
Gonzalez/Gonzalez
Heaven
Legacy
LQ
Luke & Leroy
Mannahatta
Monster
NA
Nerveana
NV
Providence/Triumph Room
Quo
Remy
Roxy
Saloon
Sapphire
Shelter

Show
Spirit
Swing 46
Temple
13
2i's
Vudu
Vue
Webster Hall

Dinner Cruises
Bateaux NY
Spirit Cruises
World Yacht

Dives
Ace Bar
Ace of Clubs
All State
American Spirits
American Trash
Automatic Slim's
Back Fence
Baggot Inn
Bar East
Barfly
Bar None
Bellevue
Blarney Stone
Bleecker St. Bar
Blue and Gold
Boiler Room
Botanica
Broadway Dive
B-Side
Bull McCabe's
Candle Bar
Cheap Shots
Cherry Tavern
Cock
Continental
Coyote Ugly
Desmond's
Dick's
Ding Dong Lounge
Dive Bar
Doc Holliday's
Don Hill's
Down the Hatch

Duke's (East Village)
East River
Eight of Clubs
55 Bar
Flannery's
Frank's Cocktail
Freddy's
Fubar
Gin Mill
Girls Room
Grassroots
Hog Pit
Holiday Cocktail
I.C.U.
Iggy's
International Bar
Jake's Dilemma
Jimmy's Corner
Jimmy Walker's
Joe's Bar
Johnny's Bar
John Street B&G
Josie Wood's
Lakeside Lounge
Library
MacDougal St. Ale
Mad River
Mars Bar
McAleer's Pub
McHales
McSwiggan's
Micky's Blue Room
Milady's
Moonshine
Nevada Smith's
O'Connor's
151
119 Bar
169 Bar
P & G Cafe
Parkside
Peculier Pub
Pieces
Plug Uglies
Pussycat Lounge
Pyramid
Rathbones
Red Lion

Red Rock West
Rosemary's Greenpoint
Ruby's Tap House
Rudy's
Satelite
Scruffy Duffy's
7B
Ship of Fools
Siberia
Sidewalk
Sing Sing
Soho Billiards
Sophie's
Stoned Crow
Subway Inn
Sweetwater
Tap a Keg
T.G. Whitney's
Third & Long
Tin Lizzie
Town Crier
Trash
Tribeca Rock Club
2 by 4
Vasmay Lounge
WCOU
Whiskey Ward
Winnie's
Ye Olde Tripple Inn
Yogi's

DJs

APT
Avalon
Black Betty
Bob
Branch
Cain
Canal Room
Capone's
China Club
Cielo
Clubhouse
Copacabana
Coral Room
Crobar
Culture Club
Deep

Discothèque
Double Happiness
El Flamingo
Escuelita
Eugene
Exit
58
Galapagos
Glo
Gonzalez/Gonzalez
Grand Bar
Gypsy Tea
Heaven
Legacy
Lit
Lolita
Lot 61
Lotus
LQ
Luke & Leroy
Mannahatta
Marquee
M Bar (Little Italy)
Moe's
Monster
Movida
NA
Nerveana
Nublu
NV
Opaline
Orchard Bar
Park
Pianos
Plan B
Providence/Triumph Room
Quo
Red and Black
Remy
Roxy
Royale
Saloon
Sapphire
Savalas
Serena
Shelter
Show

Snitch
Spirit
Sullivan Room
Swing 46
Table 50
Temple
13
Tribe
Triple Crown
12" Bar
2i's
Vudu
Vue
Webster Hall

Drag Shows
Barracuda
Boys Room
Escuelita
Lips
O.W.
Slipper Room

Drink Specialists
Beer
(* Microbreweries)
Anotheroom
Baker St. Pub
Barcade
Barrow St. Ale
Beer Bar/Cafe Centro
Blind Tiger Ale
Blue Smoke
Bohemian Hall
Boxcar Lounge
Brass Monkey
Brazen Head
Brewsky's
Brooklyn Ale
Brooklyn Brewery*
Bull Moose
Burp Castle
Cafe de Bruxelles
Chelsea Brewing*
Croxley Ales
David Copperfield
d.b.a.
Dewey's Flatiron
Gate, The

Ginger Man
Greenwich Brewing*
Heartland Brewery*
Hop Devil Grill
House of Brews
Iona
Jake's Dilemma
Jeremy's Ale
Killmeyer's
King's Head
Kinsale
Loreley
MacDougal St. Ale
Markt
Matchless
McSorley's
Moto
Mug's Ale
O'Flaherty's Ale
O'Flanagan's Ale
Otheroom
Park Slope Ale*
Peculier Pub
Pioneer
Puck Fair
Room
Ruby's Tap House
Slaughtered Lamb
Spike Hill
Spuyten Duyvil
St. Andrews
St. Marks Ale
Swift
Tír na Nóg
200 Fifth
Ulysses
Vol de Nuit
Waterfront Ale Hse.
Westside Brewing*
Zum Schneider

Champagne
Bubble Lounge
Flûte
Royalton

Cocktails
Angel's Share
Asia de Cuba

Aubette
Baraza
Bemelmans
Blue Mill
Bond Street
Brandy Library
Brooklyn Social
Bungalow 8
Calle Ocho
Chow Bar
Church Lounge
Cibar
City Hall
Cocktail Room
Cosmo
Dylan Prime
East Side Co.
Employees Only
Fez
Fifty Seven 57
5 Ninth
Five Points
Flatiron Lounge
Forbidden City
Freemans
Galaxy Global
Good World B&G
Grand Bar
Great Jones Cafe
Harry Cipriani
Juniper Suite
Kanvas
Korova
Last Exit
Le Colonial
Long Tan
Lot 61
Madame X
Manhattan Lounge
Marion's Continental
M Bar (Little Italy)
Milk and Honey
Modern, The
Niagara/Lei Bar
Penang
Pravda
Ruby Foo's

Rue B
Silverleaf
Slipper Room
SushiSamba
Tabla
Tao
Town
Verlaine
Vintage
Vong
Waikiki Wally's
Whiskey
World Bar
Zanzibar
Zoë

Martinis
Angelo & Maxie's
Angel's Share
Asia de Cuba
Aubette
Balthazar
Bar Below
Bar 89
Bar 4
Bar Nine
Bartini's
Bayard's
Blue Ribbon Bklyn.
Café Pierre
Carnegie Club
Cellar Bar
Cibar
Circa Tabac
Cocktail Room
Divine Bar
Dylan Prime
Fifty Seven 57
Four Seasons Bar
Grace
Kanvas
Lemon, The
Le Souk
Long Tan
Lot 61
Marion's Continental
Métrazur
MO Bar

Onieal's Grand St.
Onyx
Pravda
Rue B
Shebeen
Stir
Temple Bar
Tribeca Grill
21 Club
203 Spring
Vintage

Sake
Chibi's Sake/Chibitini
Decibel
EN Japanese Brasserie
Forbidden City
Fujiyama Mama
Matsuri
Megu
Ono
Sakagura
Sake Hana
Sugarcane
SushiSamba

Scotch/Single Malts
Angelo & Maxie's
Aubette
Blind Tiger Ale
Brandy Library
Brazen Head
Bridge Cafe
Bull & Bear
Carnegie Club
Club Macanudo
d.b.a.
Hudson Bar/Books
Keens Steak
Lexington Bar/Books
Spike Hill
St. Andrews
Swift
Tír na Nóg
Whiskey Ward

Tequila
Alamo
Barrio Chino
Chango

Citrus B&G
Dos Caminos
Mesa Grill
Mexican Radio
Mustang Grill
Rocking Horse
Under the Volcano

Vodka
Anyway Cafe
Odessa
Opal
Pravda
Rasputin
Royalton
Russian Samovar
Russian Vodka Rm.
Temple Bar
212

Wine Bars
Ara Wine Bar
Bandol
Bar @ Etats-Unis
Barbalùc
Bar Jamón
Bar Veloce
Bottega del Vino
Boudoir Bar
Divine Bar
D.O.C. Wine Bar
Enoteca I Trulli
Flûte
Half Wine Bar
Il Posto Accanto
'inoteca
In Vino
Le Bateau Ivre
Michael Jordan's
NY Perks
Peasant
Punch & Judy
Rhône
Shade
Stonehome
Total Wine Bar
Turks & Frogs
V Bar
Vine

Special Appeals

Von
Xicala
Wine by the Glass
Anotheroom
Bar 6
Eleven Madison Pk.
Gotham B&G
Gramercy Tavern
Iridium
Lexington Bar/Books
Le Zinc
Louis
ñ
Otheroom
Otto
Room
Shelly's NY
Silverleaf
Single Rm. Occup.
Smoke
Tabla
Tavern on Green
Tribeca Grill
21 Club
Union Sq. Cafe
Veritas
Zoë

Euro
Asia de Cuba
Balthazar
Baraonda
Barbalùc
Bar 6
Bar Veloce
Bice
Bungalow 8
Cafe Gitane
Cafe Noir
Cain
Casimir
Cielo
Cipriani Downtown
Circa Tabac
Coffee Shop
Diva
Florent
Flûte

Frederick's
Freemans
French Roast
Geisha
Grand Bar
Harry Cipriani
Indochine
I Tre Merli
Kaña
Le Bateau Ivre
Le Colonial
Les Enfants Terribles
Le Singe Vert
Le Souk
Le 26
L'Orange Bleue
Lotus
Lucky Strike
Mercer Bar
Novecento
NV
Opia
Pastis
Raoul's
Royalton
Schiller's
Serafina
Soho House
Sway
Thom Bar
212
Velvet
Villard

Expense-Accounters
Asia de Cuba
Balthazar
Bar Masa
Bateaux NY
Bayard's
Bemelmans
Bice
Blue Fin
Blue Note
Bond Street
Brandy Library
Brasserie
Brasserie 8½

Bubble Lounge
Bull & Bear
Cafe Carlyle
Café des Artistes
Cafe Luxembourg
Café Pierre
Campbell Apt.
Capital Grille
Carnegie Club
Cellar Bar
Cherry
Church Lounge
Club Macanudo
Daniel
Del Frisco's
Django
Eleven Madison Pk.
Enoteca I Trulli
Fiamma Osteria
Fifty Seven 57
Flow
Flûte
Four Seasons Bar
Gotham B&G
Gramercy Tavern
Grand Bar
Guastavino's
Harry Cipriani
Hudson Hotel Bar
Hudson Hotel Library
Indochine
Jean Georges
Keens Steak
King Cole Bar
Koi
Le Colonial
Lot 61
Mark's Bar
Megu
Michael Jordan's
MO Bar
Modern, The
Monkey Bar
Morton's
Oak Room
One if by Land
Pen-Top Bar

Plaza Athénée Bar Seine
Rainbow Grill
Regency Library Bar
Rink Bar
Rise
Royalton
Sakagura
Savannah Steak
Stone Rose
Tabla
Tao
Tavern on Green
Town
21 Club
212
Uncle Jack's
Underbar
Union Sq. Cafe
Veritas
Villard
Vong
V Steakhouse
Whiskey
Whiskey Blue
Whiskey Park
Wollensky's
World Bar

Fine Dining Too
Amuse
Asia de Cuba
Balthazar
Bar Masa
Bayard's
Biltmore Room
Blue Fin
Blue Ribbon
Blue Ribbon Bklyn.
Blue Water Grill
Café des Artistes
Café Gray
Capital Grille
'Cesca
Daniel
Dos Caminos
Eleven Madison Pk.
English Is Italian
Fiamma Osteria

Fifty Seven 57
5 Ninth
Four Seasons Bar
Gotham B&G
Gramercy Tavern
Jean Georges
Le Colonial
Marseille
Matsuri
Megu
Mercer Bar
Mesa Grill
Michael Jordan's
Modern, The
Ono
Otto
Ouest
Public
66
Spice Market
Spotted Pig
Tabla
Town
21 Club
Union Sq. Cafe
Vong
V Steakhouse

Fireplaces
Amsterdam Billiards
Angry Wade's
Art Bar
Aubette
Big City
Black Bear
Boat
Burton Pub/Kama Lounge
Byzantio
Carnegie Club
Central Bar
Chumley's
Cibar
Delancey
Delia's
Delta Grill
Divine Bar
Donovan's
Dorrian's

Dublin 6
Employees Only
Faces & Names
Failte
5 Ninth
Garage
Gaslight/G2
Gin Mill
Harbour Lights
Highline
Hudson Hotel Library
Iguana
Jekyll & Hyde
Josie Wood's
Keens Steak
Kennedy's
Keybar
Kili
La Lanterna
Latitude
Le Figaro
Lexington Bar/Books
Loki
McGee's
Merchants, NY
Metropolitan
Molly's
Moran's Chelsea
O'Flaherty's Ale
One if by Land
Park
Pig N Whistle
Playwright
Rain Lounge
Raoul's
Red and Black
Redeye
Revival
Riviera
Rubyfruit
Senor Swanky's
Serafina
Shelly's NY
Sherwood
Sutton Place
Tavern on Jane
Teddy's

Telephone
Tenement
T.G. Whitney's
Thady Con's
Therapy
Thom Bar
Time Out
Town Tavern
Turtle Bay
21 Club
Velvet Cigar
Water St. Bar
Westside Brewing
Wet Bar
Whiskey River
Zanzibar
Zombie Hut

First Date
Angel's Share
Anotheroom
Art Bar
Aubette
Bar 4
Bar 6
Bemelmans
Black Door
Blue Smoke
Boat Basin
Boat House
Bongo
Bowlmor Lanes
Bubble Lounge
Cafe Carlyle
Caffe Reggio
Calle Ocho
Casimir
Cibar
Cub Room
Delia's
Dizzy's Club
D.O.C. Wine Bar
Double Happiness
Dylan Prime
Edgar's Cafe
Eight Mile Creek
Eleven Madison Pk.
Enoteca I Trulli

Fez
Flor de Sol
Forbidden City
Frederick's
Hudson Hotel Library
Il Posto Accanto
Jazz Standard
Le Colonial
Le Zinc
Louis
Marseille
MO Bar
Morgans Bar
North West
Onieal's Grand St.
Otheroom
Park Bar
Pen-Top Bar
Pipa
Punch & Judy
Raoul's
Red Bench
Room
Royalton
Sake Hana
Sala
Temple Bar
Town
203 Spring
Von
Zanzibar

Foreign Feeling
French
Balthazar
Bandol
Barbès
Bar 6
BarTabac
Café Charbon
Cafe Gitane
Cafe Luxembourg
Chez Josephine
Daniel
French Roast
Indochine
Jules
La Bottega Caffé

Le Bateau Ivre
Le Figaro
Le Singe Vert
L'Express
Le Zinc
L'Orange Bleue
Lucky Strike
Maison
Marseille
Pastis
Pigalle
Pink Pony
Raoul's
Rue B
Schiller's
Sherwood
Zebulon

German
Bohemian Hall
Killmeyer's
Loreley
Zum Schneider

Indian
Burton Pub/Kama Lounge
Earth
K Lounge
Spice Market
Sutra
Taj

Irish
An Béal Bocht
Annie Moores
Baggot Inn
Baker St. Pub
Bar East
Biddy's
Black Sheep
Blarney Stone
Boss Tweed's
Bua
Bull McCabe's
Bull Moose
Central Bar
Channel 4
Connolly's
Coogan's Parrot Bay
Dead Poet

Desmond's
Doc Watson's
Donovan's
Dorrian's
Druids
Dublin House
Dublin 6
Eamonn's
Eleventh St. Bar
Failte
Fiddlesticks
Finnegans Wake
Fiona's
Fitzgerald's
Flannery's
Four-Faced Liar
Full Shilling
Gaf Bar
Gatsby's
George Keeley's
Hairy Monk
Half King
Iggy's
Iona
Irish Rogue
Jake's Saloon
Jameson's
Jimmy Walker's
Josie Wood's
Kennedy's
Kevin St. James
Kinsale
Local 138
Lucky Jack's
Lunasa
Maggie's
Malachy's
Margarita & Murphy
McAleer's Pub
McCormack's
McFadden's
McGee's
McHales
McSorley's
McSwiggan's
Mercantile Grill
Molly's

Molly Wee
Moran's Chelsea
Mr. Dennehy's
Mustang Harry's
Mustang Sally's
O'Connell's
O'Connor's
O'Flaherty's Ale
O'Flanagan's
O'Flanagan's Ale
O'Lunney's
O'Neals'
One & One
Paddy Reilly's
Parlour
Patrick Conway's
Patrick Kavanagh's
Peggy O'Neill's
Perdition
Peter Dillon's
Peter McManus
Pig N Whistle
P.J. Carney's
Playwright
Plug Uglies
Puck Fair
Rocky Sullivan's
Rumours
Ryan's Daughter
Ryan's Irish Pub
Scratcher
Scruffy Duffy's
Slainte
Slane
Social
Spike Hill
St. Dymphna's
Swift
T.G. Whitney's
Thady Con's
Thirsty Scholar
Tír na Nóg
Trinity Public Hse.
Twelve
Ulysses
Waterloo
Water St. Bar
Wicked Monk

Latin
Agozar!
Baraza
Barrio Chino
Calle Ocho
Coffee Shop
Copacabana
El Flamingo
El Quijote
Escuelita
Flor de Sol
Gonzalez/Gonzalez
Ideya
Kaña
LQ
Mambi Lounge
ñ
Novecento
Nuyorican Poets
Pipa
Remy
Sala
S.O.B.'s
Son Cubano
Tapas Lounge
Xunta
Yuca Bar
Zinc Bar

Middle Eastern/Moroccan
Babel Lounge
Bar 6
Black Betty
Cafe Gitane
Casa La Femme
Casimir
Door
Falucka
Fez
Karma
Kemia
Kush
Le Souk
L'Orange Bleue
Marseille
Plaza Athénée Bar Seine
Royale
Shalel
Sway

Zebulon
Zinc Bar

Russian
Anyway Cafe
KGB
Odessa
Pravda
Rasputin
Russian Samovar
Russian Vodka Rm.

Frat House

American Spirits
American Trash
Bar Coastal
Bar East
Bar 515
Bar None
Barrow St. Ale
Big City
Big Easy
Bleecker St. Bar
Bounce
Bourbon St.
Brother Jimmy's
Bull's Head
Calico Jack's
Crime Scene
Dewey's Flatiron
Dive Bar
Doc Watson's
Down the Hatch
1849
Falls, The
Fiddlesticks
Firehouse
Gin Mill
Iggy's
Jake's Dilemma
Jeremy's Ale
Joshua Tree
Josie Wood's
Kabin
Kenny's Castaways
MacDougal St. Ale
Mad River
Martell's
McFadden's
Mo's Caribbean

No Idea
Off the Wagon
Park Ave. Country
Peculier Pub
Proof
Raccoon Lodge
Rathbones
Ruby's Tap House
Ryan's Daughter
Saloon
Senor Swanky's
Ship of Fools
Slainte
Snapper Creek
Still
Sutton Place
Tap a Keg
Third & Long
Time Out
Tin Lizzie
Tortilla Flats
Town Tavern
Turtle Bay
West End

Games
Bocce Ball
Floyd
Bowling
Bowlmor Lanes
Chelsea Piers Bowling
Leisure Time
Play
Darts
A&M Roadhouse
Ace Bar
American Spirits
American Trash
Angry Wade's
Back Page
Bar Coastal
Bar East
Barfly
Barrow St. Ale
Biddy's
Blarney Stone
Bleecker St. Bar
Blondies
Boss Tweed's

Special Appeals

Brazen Head
Broadway Dive
Bull McCabe's
Bull's Head
Cabin Fever
Cheap Shots
Collins Bar
Coyote Ugly
Dakota Roadhse.
David Copperfield
Desmond's
Dive Bar
Down the Hatch
Duke's (East Village)
Eamonn's
Edge, The
Fat Black Pussy Cat
Fitzgerald's
Flannery's
Gaf Bar
Gate, The
George Keeley's
Ginger's
Grand Press
Grassroots
GYM Sportsbar
Hook and Ladder
Iggy's
Iona
Jake's Dilemma
Jimmy Walker's
John Street B&G
Josie Wood's
Kettle of Fish
Lighthouse
Loki
MacDougal St. Ale
McAleer's Pub
McSwiggan's
Micky's Blue Room
M1-5 Bar
Moonshine
O'Connell's
Off the Wagon
O'Flaherty's Ale
Overlook Lounge
Paddy Reilly's

Patriot Saloon
Peggy O'Neill's
Red Rock West
Ruby's Tap House
Ryan's Daughter
Scruffy Duffy's
Shag
Ship of Fools
Snapper Creek
Tap a Keg
Tempest Bar
T.G. Whitney's
Thirsty Scholar
Time Out
Turkey's Nest
Underground
West End
Wicked Monk
Ye Olde Tripple Inn
Yogi's
Zablozki's

Foosball
Apartment 138
Back Page
Bar 4
BarTabac
Dakota Roadhse.
Down the Hatch
East River
ESPN Zone
Gin Mill
Grand Press
Hog Pit
Jake's Dilemma
Luca Bar/Lounge
Matchless
M1-5 Bar
Off the Wagon
Parkside
Satelite
Soho House

Photo Booths
American Trash
Buttermilk
Enid's
Grand Press
Lakeside Lounge

Lemon, The
Magnetic Field
Niagara/Lei Bar
Opaline
Otto's Shrunken
7B
Trailer Park
Union Pool

Pinball
Ace Bar
Bellevue
Big Easy
Bleecker St. Bar
Boat
Boiler Room
Cellar, The
Dick's
Dugout
Enid's
Fat Cat
Flight 151
Hi-Fi
Kettle of Fish
Leisure Time
Levee, The
Lucy's
Max Fish
Mod
Motor City Bar
Nowhere
Otto's Shrunken
Peculier Pub
Phoenix
Raven
Rawhide
7B
Sherwood
Siberia
Stonewall
Zablozki's

Pool Halls
Amsterdam Billiards
Corner Billiards
Fat Cat
Play
Pressure
Q Lounge

Slate
Soho Billiards

Pool Tables
A&M Roadhouse
Abbey
Ace Bar
American Spirits
American Trash
Anatomy Bar
Angry Wade's
Antarctica
Apartment 138
Back Page
Barcade
Bar Coastal
Bar East
Barfly
Bar Reis
Barrow St. Ale
Big City
Bleecker St. Bar
Blondies
Blue and Gold
Blue Room
Boiler Room
Boss Tweed's
Brooklyn Ale
Brooklyn Inn
Brooklyn Social
B-Side
B61
Bull McCabe's
Bull Moose
Bull's Head
Cabin Fever
Candle Bar
Capone's
Cargo
Chelsea Piers Bowling
Cherry Tavern
Crime Scene
Dakota Roadhse.
Dead Poet
Dewey's Flatiron
Dick's
Dip
Dive Bar

Doc Holliday's	McSwiggan's
Doc Watson's	Metropolitan
Dugout	Micky's Blue Room
Duke's (East Village)	Milady's
Duplex	M1-5 Bar
Dusk	Moonshine
Eagle, The	Mo's Caribbean
East 4th St. Bar	Musical Box
East River	No Idea
Edge, The	Nowhere
1849	Off the Wagon
Failte	O'Flaherty's Ale
Fat Black Pussy Cat	O'Flanagan's
40/40	119 Bar
Freddy's	169 Bar
Fubar	Overlook Lounge
Ginger's	O.W.
Gin Mill	Parkside
Grand Press	Park Slope Ale
GYM Sportsbar	Patio
Hangar	Patriot Saloon
Harrison's Tavern	Peter Dillon's
Henrietta Hudson	Phoenix
Hi-Fi	Pieces
Hog Pit	Pioneer
Hogs & Heifers	Plug Uglies
Hook and Ladder	Pop Burger
Hudson Hotel Library	Prohibition
Iggy's	Raccoon Lodge
Jake's Dilemma	Raven
Jimmy Walker's	Rawhide
Joe's Bar	Red Rock West
John Street B&G	Reservoir
Josie Wood's	Ruby's Tap House
Kabin	Ryan's Daughter
King's Head	San Marcos
Latitude	Satelite
Levee, The	Scruffy Duffy's
Lighthouse	Second Nature
Loki	Ship of Fools
Lucky Jack's	Sin-é
Lucy's	Snapper Creek
MacDougal St. Ale	Soho House
Magnetic Field	Sophie's
Manitoba's	Stoned Crow
Matchless	Superfine
Max Fish	Sutra

Tap a Keg
Time Out
Tool Box
Town Crier
Trash
Tribeca Tavern
Turkey's Nest
2 by 4
Underground
Vasmay Lounge
Vegas
Water St. Bar
Webster Hall
Welcome/Johnsons
Whiskey Ward
Wicked Monk
Zablozki's

Video Games
Abbey
Ace Bar
Alligator Lounge
American Spirits
American Trash
Amsterdam Billiards
Angry Wade's
Apartment 138
Back Page
Barcade
Bar Coastal
Bar East
Barfly
Bar 4
Barrow St. Ale
Bellevue
Big Easy
Big Nose Kate's
BINY
Black Bear
Black Sheep
Blarney Stone
Bleecker St. Bar
Boat
Bohemian Hall
Boiler Room
Boss Tweed's
Broadway Dive
Brooklyn Ale

Brother Jimmy's
B-Side
Bull's Head
Cabin Fever
Candle Bar
Cellar, The
Cheap Shots
Chelsea Brewing
Coogan's Parrot Bay
Coyote Ugly
Crif Dogs
Dakota Roadhse.
David Copperfield
Desmond's
Dick's
Ding Dong Lounge
Dive Bar
Doc Holliday's
Donovan's
Down the Hatch
Dublin House
Duff's
Dugout
Duke's (East Village)
Duplex
Eagle, The
East 4th St. Bar
East River
1849
Eight of Clubs
Enid's
ESPN Zone
Failte
Fat Black Pussy Cat
Firehouse
First Edition
Gaf Bar
George Keeley's
Ginger's
Gin Mill
GYM Sportsbar
Hank's Saloon
Harrison's Tavern
Henrietta Hudson
Hi-Fi
Hog Pit
Hogs & Heifers

Holiday Cocktail
Hook and Ladder
Iona
Jake's Dilemma
Jekyll & Hyde
Jeremy's Ale
Jimmy's Corner
Jimmy Walker's
Joey's
Johnny's Bar
John Street B&G
Josie Wood's
Kabin
Kenny's Castaways
Kettle of Fish
King's Head
Lakeside Lounge
Leisure Time
Lemon, The
Levee, The
Library
Luca Bar/Lounge
Lucy's
Magnetic Field
Mambi Lounge
Manitoba's
Mars 2112
McAleer's Pub
McSwiggan's
Metropolitan
Micky's Blue Room
Milady's
Mod
Moe's
M1-5 Bar
Moonshine
Mo's Caribbean
Motor City Bar
Nevada Smith's
No Moore
Nowhere
Off the Wagon
169 Bar
Otto's Shrunken
Paris, The
Patio
Patriot Saloon

Peculier Pub
Peggy O'Neill's
Peter Dillon's
Peter McManus
Peter's
Phoenix
Pine Tree Lodge
P.J. Carney's
Pussycat Lounge
Raccoon Lodge
Rathbones
Raven
Rawhide
Red Rock West
Remote Lounge
Reservoir
Rosemary's Greenpoint
Ruby's Tap House
Rudy's
Ryan's Daughter
Satelite
Scruffy Duffy's
7B
Ship of Fools
Siberia
6's & 8's
Skinny
Slaughtered Lamb
Snapper Creek
Southpaw
Sputnik
Star 64
Stitch
St. Marks Ale
Stonewall
Subway Inn
Tap a Keg
Tempest Bar
T.G. Whitney's
Tom & Jerry's
Town Crier
Trash
Tribeca Tavern
Turkey's Nest
12" Bar
Ty's
Underground

Varjak
Vasmay Lounge
Vegas
View Bar
Water St. Bar
Welcome/Johnsons
Whiskey River
Yankee Tavern
Yello Bar
Ye Olde Tripple Inn
Yogi's

Gay

(See also Lesbian; * certain nights only)
Barracuda
Barrage
Boiler Room
Boys Room
Candle Bar
Clubhouse
Cock
Dick's
Discothèque*
Dugout
Duplex
Eagle, The
Eight of Clubs
Escuelita
Excelsior
g
GYM Sportsbar
Hangar
Heaven
Julius
Lips
Marie's Crisis
Metropolitan
Monster
Nowhere
Opaline*
O.W.
Phoenix
Pieces
Posh
Rawhide
Rose's Turn
Roxy*

Slide
Splash
Starlight
Stonewall
Therapy
Tool Box
Townhouse
Ty's
Urge, The
View Bar
xes lounge
XL

Group-Friendly

Ace Bar
Amsterdam Billiards
Antarctica
Bar 515
Boat Basin
Bohemian Hall
Bourbon St.
Bowlmor Lanes
Brooklyn Brewery
Brother Jimmy's
Bryant Park
Bull Moose
Cafe Wha?
Chelsea Brewing
Chelsea Piers Bowling
Connolly's
Corner Billiards
Culture Club
d.b.a.
Dewey's Flatiron
El Flamingo
El Quijote
ESPN Zone
Gowanus Yacht
Hogs & Heifers
Iggy's
Kaña
Killmeyer's
Leisure Time
Luna Park
Nerveana
Pioneer
Pressure
Q Lounge

Special Appeals

Remote Lounge
Rodeo
Saloon
Sing Sing
Slate
Soho Billiards
St. Marks Ale
Tom & Jerry's
Tortilla Flats
Village Karaoke
Webster Hall
Winnie's
Zum Schneider

Grown-Ups
Algonquin
Bandol
Bar @ Etats-Unis
Barbalùc
Bar Masa
Bemelmans
Bice
Biltmore Room
Brandy Library
Brasserie 8½
Bull & Bear
Cafe Carlyle
Café des Artistes
Cafe Luxembourg
Café Pierre
Campbell Apt.
Carnegie Club
'Cesca
Club Macanudo
Daniel
Dizzy's Club
Django
Docks Oyster
Dove
Eleven Madison Pk.
Feinstein's/Regency
Fifty Seven 57
Four Seasons Bar
Geisha
Gotham B&G
Guastavino's
Harry Cipriani
Jean Georges

J.G. Melon
King Cole Bar
Le Colonial
Le Jazz Au Bar
Lexington Bar/Books
Mark's Bar
M Bar (West 40s)
Monkey Bar
Oak Room
Ouest
P.J. Clarke's
Plaza Athénée Bar Seine
Rainbow Grill
Sardi's
Tavern on Green
Top of the Tower
Town
Townhouse
21 Club
Uncle Jack's
Union Sq. Cafe
Village Vanguard
Villard
V Steakhouse
World Bar

Happy Hour
Angry Wade's
Back Page
Baggot Inn
Baker St. Pub
Bar Coastal
Bar None
Barrage
Barrow St. Ale
Big Easy
Bleecker St. Bar
Blondies
Blu Lounge
Bob
Boss Tweed's
Botanica
Bounce
Bourbon St.
Boxers
Brazen Head
Brother Jimmy's
B3

Bull McCabe's

Bull's Head

Cafe Deville/Bar Bleu

Cajun

Calico Jack's

Cellar, The

Chango

Cloister Cafe

Collins Bar

Company

Continental

David Copperfield

Dead Poet

Doc Holliday's

Double Happiness

Down the Hatch

Dugout

Eamonn's

El Rio Grande

Enid's

Epstein's Bar

Fat Black Pussy Cat

55 Bar

First Edition

Five Spot

Flight 151

46 Grand

4_2O

Full Shilling

g

Gate, The

Gatsby's

George Keeley's

Gin Mill

Greenwich Brewing

Heights B&G

Iggy's

Iguana

Jameson's

Joey's

Johnny's Bar

John Street B&G

Karma

Kenny's Castaways

Kevin St. James

Laila Lounge

Lakeside Lounge

La Linea

Life Cafe

Lit

Local 138

Lolita

Mad River

Magnetic Field

Manitoba's

McGee's

Métrazur

Metro 53/Loft

Metropolitan

Mica Bar

Nancy Whiskey

Nation

Nevada Smith's

Off the Wagon

O'Flaherty's Ale

O.W.

Paddy Reilly's

Parlour

Pieces

Plug Uglies

Posh

Raven

Rawhide

Remedy

Riviera

Rocky Sullivan's

Russian Vodka Rm.

Sapphire

Scopa

7B

Shade

Ship of Fools

Sidewalk

Slainte

Snitch

Splash

St. Dymphna's

St. Marks Ale

Superfine

Tap a Keg

Thirsty Scholar

Time Out

Tortilla Flats

Town Crier

Town Tavern
Tracy J's
Turtle Bay
Vasmay Lounge
Viceroy
View Bar
Waterloo
WCOU
Welcome/Johnsons
WXOU
xes lounge

Hotel Bars

Algonquin Hotel
  Algonquin
  Oak Room
Amsterdam Court Hotel
  Trousdale
Beekman Tower Hotel
  Top of the Tower
Bryant Park Hotel
  Cellar Bar
  Koi
Carlyle Hotel
  Bemelmans
  Cafe Carlyle
Chambers Hotel
  Town
Chelsea Hotel
  Serena
Dream Hotel
  Ava Lounge
  Dream Lounge
  Serafina
Edison Hotel
  Rum House
Elysée Hotel
  Monkey Bar
Flatotel
  Moda Outdoors
Four Seasons Hotel
  Fifty Seven 57
Gansevoort Hotel
  Ono
  Plunge
Gershwin Hotel
  Gallery

Habitat Hotel
  Opia
Hotel 41 at Times Square
  Bar 41
Hotel on Rivington, The
  THOR Lobby Bar
Hudson Hotel
  Hudson Hotel Bar
  Hudson Hotel Library
Inn at Irving Place
  Cibar
Mandarin Oriental Hotel
  MO Bar
Mansfield Hotel
  M Bar (West 40s)
Maritime Hotel
  Cabanas
  Hiro
  La Bottega Caffé
  Matsuri
Mark Hotel
  Mark's Bar
Marriott Marquis Hotel
  Broadway Lounge
  View Lounge
Mercer Hotel
  Mercer Bar
Metro Hotel
  Metro Grill Roof
Morgans Hotel
  Asia de Cuba
  Morgans Bar
Palace Hotel
  Villard
Paramount Hotel
  Paramount Bar
  Paramount Library Bar
Peninsula Hotel
  Pen-Top Bar
Pickwick Arms Hotel
  Le Bateau Ivre
Pierre Hotel
  Café Pierre
Plaza Athénée Hotel
  Plaza Athénée Bar Seine
QT Hotel
  QT Hotel Bar

Radisson Lexington Hotel
LQ
Regency Hotel
Feinstein's/Regency
Regency Library Bar
Ritz-Carlton Battery Park
Rise
Royalton Hotel
Royalton
70 Park Ave. Hotel
Silverleaf
Shelburne Murray Hill Hotel
Rare View
Sherry Netherland Hotel
Harry Cipriani
60 Thompson Hotel
Thom Bar
SoHo Grand Hotel
Grand Bar
St. Regis Hotel
King Cole Bar
Time Hotel
02
Tribeca Grand Hotel
Church Lounge
Trump Int'l Hotel
Jean Georges
Waldorf-Astoria Hotel
Bull & Bear
W Court Hotel
Wet Bar
W New York Hotel
Whiskey Blue
W Times Square Hotel
Blue Fin
Whiskey
W Times Square Living Room
W Tuscany Hotel
Cherry
W Union Square Hotel
Underbar
W Union Square Living Room

Jacket Required
Cafe Carlyle
Café Pierre
Four Seasons Bar
Harry Cipriani

Lexington Bar/Books
Rainbow Grill
21 Club

Jazz Clubs
Arthur's Tavern
B. B. King Blues
Birdland
Blue Note
Cleopatra's Needle
Detour
Dizzy's Club
Fat Cat
55 Bar
Iridium
Jazz Gallery
Jazz Standard
Kavehaz
Le Jazz Au Bar
Lenox Lounge
Smalls
Smoke
Swing 46
Village Vanguard
Zinc Bar

Jukeboxes
Abbey
Abbey Pub
Alligator Lounge
All State
American Spirits
American Trash
Angry Wade's
Antarctica
Apartment 138
Arlene Grocery
Art Bar
Back Page
Bar Coastal
Bar East
Barfly
Barrow St. Ale
Becky's
Bellevue
Biddy's
Big Nose Kate's
Black Bear

Black Betty
Black Sheep
Blarney Stone
Blondies
Blue and Gold
Blue Smoke
Blu Lounge
Boat
Bohemian Hall
Boiler Room
Boss Tweed's
Boxers
Brazen Head
Broadway Dive
Brooklyn Ale
Brooklyn Inn
Brooklyn Social
Broome St. Bar
B-Side
B61
Bull McCabe's
Bull's Head
Buster's Garage
Buttermilk
Cabin Fever
Candle Bar
Cedar Tavern
Cellar, The
Cheap Shots
Chelsea Brewing
Cherry Tavern
Chumley's
Clem's
Coliseum Bar
Collins Bar
Commonwealth
Connolly's
Corner Bistro
Coyote Ugly
Crime Scene
Cubby Hole
Cutting Room
Dakota Roadhse.
Dark Room
David Copperfield
d.b.a.
Dead Poet

Desmond's
Dick's
Dive Bar
Dive 75
Doc Holliday's
Doc Watson's
Donovan's
Dorrian's
Druids
Dublin House
Duff's
Dugout
Duke's (East Village)
Duplex
Dusk
Eamonn's
East 4th St. Bar
East River
Edge, The
1849
Eight of Clubs
Enid's
Excelsior
Falls, The
Fat Black Pussy Cat
Fat Cat
Film Center Cafe
Fiona's
Firehouse
First Edition
Fitzgerald's
Flannery's
Flight 151
Floyd
Four-Faced Liar
Fubar
Full Shilling
Fun House
Gaf Bar
Gate, The
George Keeley's
Ginger's
Grand Press
Grassroots
Great Jones Cafe
Great Lakes
GYM Sportsbar

Hanger
Hank's Saloon
Hi-Fi
Hog Pit
Hogs & Heifers
Holiday Cocktail
Hook and Ladder
Iggy's
International Bar
Jake's Dilemma
Jake's Saloon
Jameson's
Jeremy's Ale
J.G. Melon
Jimmy's Corner
Jimmy Walker's
Joe's Bar
Johnny's Bar
John Street B&G
Joshua Tree
Josie Wood's
Kennedy's
Kettle of Fish
King's Head
Kinsale
Korova
La Bottega Caffé
Lakeside Lounge
La Linea
Lenox Lounge
Levee, The
Library
Lighthouse
Lillie's
Loki
Lucy's
MacDougal St. Ale
Magician
Magnetic Field
Malachy's
Mama's Bar
Manitoba's
Mars Bar
Matchless
Max Fish
McAleer's Pub
McCormack's

McGee's
McSwiggan's
Mercury Bar
Metropolitan
Micky's Blue Room
Milady's
Molly's
Molly Wee
M1-5 Bar
Musical Box
Newgate Bar & Grill
No Idea
No Moore
Nowhere
O'Connell's
O'Connor's
Off the Wagon
O'Flaherty's Ale
O'Flanagan's Ale
Otto's Shrunken
O.W.
Paddy Reilly's
P & G Cafe
Paris, The
Parkside
Passerby
Patrick Conway's
Patrick Kavanagh's
Patriot Saloon
Peculier Pub
Peter Dillon's
Peter McManus
Peter's
Pete's Tavern
Phoenix
Pig N Whistle
Pink Pony
P.J. Carney's
P.J. Clarke's
Playwright
Plug Uglies
Quench
Raccoon Lodge
Rawhide
Red and Black
Red Rock West
Reservoir

Riviera
Rocky Sullivan's
Rosemary's Greenpoint
Rubyfruit
Rudy's
Rufus
Rum House
Ryan's Daughter
Satalla
Scruffy Duffy's
Senor Swanky's
7B
Sherwood
Ship of Fools
Siberia
Sidetracks
Sin-é
Snapper Creek
Soda Bar
Sophie's
Southpaw
Spring Lounge
Spuyten Duyvil
Stitch
St. Marks Ale
Stoned Crow
Subway Inn
Sweet & Vicious
Tainted Lady
Tap a Keg
Teddy's
Tempest Bar
Thirsty Scholar
13 Little Devils
Time Out
Tom & Jerry's
Tool Box
Town Tavern
Tribeca Tavern
Trinity Public Hse.
Turkey's Nest
12" Bar
Underground
Varjak
Vasmay Lounge
Vegas
WCOU

Welcome/Johnsons
Whiskey River
Whiskey Ward
White Horse
Wicked Monk
WXOU
Yankee Tavern
Ye Olde Tripple Inn
Yogi's

Jury Duty
(Near Manhattan
courthouses)
A&M Roadhouse
City Hall
Dakota Roadhse.
John Street B&G
Raccoon Lodge
17 Murray

Karaoke Bars
(Call to check nights, times
and prices)
BINY
Planet Rose
Sing Sing
Village Karaoke
Winnie's

Lesbian
(* Certain nights only; call
ahead)
Cubby Hole
Ginger's
Girls Room
Henrietta Hudson
Metropolitan
Nowhere
Rubyfruit
Starlight*

Live Entertainment
(See also Cabaret, Comedy
Clubs, Drag Shows, Jazz
Clubs, Karaoke Bars, Music
Clubs, Piano Bars, Spoken
Word, Strip Clubs)
Absolutely 4th (jazz/karaoke)
Agozar! (Latin)

American Spirits (karaoke)
American Trash (bands)
An Béal Bocht (Irish)
Angel's Share (jazz)
Anyway Cafe (bands)
Baker St. Pub (guitar)
Bar Nine (rock)
Bar on A (blues)
Bateaux NY (jazz)
Bemelmans (piano)
Big Easy (bands)
Big Nose Kate's (bands)
Black & White (spoken word)
Blue Fin (jazz)
Blue Water Grill (jazz)
Boat Basin (classical)
Bohemian Hall (bands)
Boogaloo (bands)
Broadway Lounge (piano)
Bubble Lounge (bands)
Bull's Head (bands)
Butta' Cup (bands)
Café Pierre (piano)
Cajun (jazz/swing)
Campbell Apt. (jazz)
Cargo (jazz/swing)
Carnegie Club (swing)
Central Bar (rock)
Chetty Red (bands)
Chez Josephine (jazz)
Club Macanudo (bands)
Connolly's (bands)
Copacabana (Latin dance)
Culture Club (vocals)
Delta Grill (bands)
Desmond's (bands)
Doc Watson's (Irish)
Dos Caminos (jazz)
Eight Mile Creek (bands)
El Flamingo ("The Donkey
   Show")
Fifty Seven 57 (piano)
Flannery's (rock)
Flor de Sol (flamenco/jazz)
Flûte (jazz)
Fujiyama Mama (karaoke)
Garage (jazz)

Gonzalez/Gonzalez (Latin)
Gowanus Yacht (jazz)
Great Lakes (bands)
Hook and Ladder (folk)
Houston's (jazz)
Iggy's (karaoke/bands)
Jules (jazz)
Justin's (R&B/soul)
King's Head (rock)
Knickerbocker B&G (jazz)
Laila Lounge (open mike)
Lava Gina (belly dancer)
Le Bateau Ivre (jazz)
Leisure Time (karaoke)
Lillie's (bands)
Lit (karaoke)
L'Orange Bleue (Mid. Eastern)
Louis (jazz)
Manitoba's (bands)
M Bar (West 40s) (Latin)
McGee's (bands)
Merchants, NY (jazz)
Micky's Blue Room (bands)
Mo's Caribbean (reggae)
Moto (blues/jazz)
Mustang Grill (karaoke)
ñ (flamenco)
Nevada Smith's (karaoke)
O'Flaherty's Ale (rock)
One if by Land (piano)
Paddy Reilly's (Irish)
Park Avalon (jazz)
Parlour (comedy)
Prohibition (R&B/soul)
Proof (karaoke)
Rawhide (male go go dancers)
Redeye (jazz)
Remy (Latin)
Rocky Sullivan's (bands)
Ruby's Tap House (karaoke)
Rue B (jazz)
Russian Vodka Rm. (jazz/piano)
Shelly's NY (jazz)
Sidewalk (open mike)
Splash (drag)
St. Andrews (Celtic)
Starlight (vocals)

Star 64 (rock)
Suba (flamenco)
Superfine (comedy/fashion)
Swift (Irish)
Tavern on Green (piano)
Teddy's (bands)
T.G. Whitney's (karaoke)
Tin Lizzie (rock)
Tír na Nóg (Irish)
Top of the Tower (piano)
Tracy J's (karaoke)
Urge, The (go go boys)
View Bar (drag)
Vue (light show)
Walker's (jazz)
West End (jazz/karaoke)
World Yacht (bands)
XL (cabaret/disco)
XR Bar (jazz)

Meat Markets

Aer
Automatic Slim's
Bar 89
Bar 515
Barrage
Bar 6
B Bar
Belmont
Bice
Big Easy
Bliss
Bogart's
Bounce
Bourbon St.
Boys Room
Branch
Brother Jimmy's
Bryant Park
Butter
Cafeteria
Cain
Cherry
China Club
Church Lounge
Cock
Cocktail Room
Coffee Shop

Cotton
Culture Club
Discothèque
Divine Bar
Dorrian's
Dos Caminos
Duvet
Eagle, The
El Rio Grande
Eugene
Glo
Grand Bar
Gypsy Tea
Houston's
Hudson Hotel Bar
Iguana
Joshua Tree
Lemon, The
Level V
Libation
Light
Luna Park
Mad River
McFadden's
Meet
Mercer Bar
Mica Bar
Monkey Bar
NA
NV
Opal
Park
Park Avalon
Parlour
Plunge
Quo
Red Sky
Remote Lounge
Revival
Roxy
Saloon
Select
17
Shark Bar
Sin Sin/Leopard
Splash
Sugar

Sutton Place
Tao
Therapy
13
Tin Lizzie
Tortilla Flats
Turtle Bay
2A
212
Underbar
Vudu
Vue
Webster Hall
Wet Bar
Whiskey
Whiskey Blue
Whiskey Park
xes lounge
XL

Music Clubs
(see also Jazz Clubs & Piano Bars)
Ace of Clubs
Arlene Grocery
Back Fence
Baggot Inn
Barbès
Beacon
Bitter End
Bowery Ballroom
Cafe Wha?
CBGB's
CB's 313
C-Note
Coda
Continental
Crash Mansion/BLVD
Cutting Room
Delancey
Don Hill's
Freddy's
Galapagos
Groove
Hammerstein Ballrm
Hank's Saloon
Hook
Irving Plaza

Joe's Pub
Knitting Factory
Lakeside Lounge
Lion's Den
Living Room
Mercury Lounge
No Moore
Northsix
Nublu
Otto's Shrunken
Pete's Candy Store
Pianos
Rare
Red Lion
Rockwood Music
Rodeo
Roseland
Rothko
Satalla
Session 73
Sin-é
S.O.B.'s
Southpaw
Sugar Bar
Sweet Rhythm
Terra Blues
Tonic
Trash
Tribeca Rock Club
Warsaw
Wild Spirits
Zebulon

Noteworthy Newcomers (172)
Ace of Clubs
Aer
Alamo
Apartment 138
Babel Lounge
Barcade
Bar Masa
BED New York
Blue Mill
Blue Room
Bogart's
B1 Drink Club
Boss Tweed's

Bottega del Vino
Bounce
Boys Room
Brandy Library
Brass Monkey
Brooklyn Social
Bua
Buddha Lounge
Burton Pub/Kama Lounge
Cabanas
Cabin Fever
Café Gray
Cain
Capital Grille
Capone's
Cellar, The
Channel 4
Cheap Shots
Commonwealth
Coogan's Parrot Bay
Cotton
Crime Scene
Daltons
Dark Room
Dekk
Delancey
Diner 24
Dizzy's Club
Dove
Dream Lounge
Duff's
Duvet
Earth
East River
East Side Co.
Eleven
Employees Only
English Is Italian
EN Japanese Brasserie
Epstein's Bar
Falls, The
58
5 Ninth
Fizz
Floyd
49 Grove
Frederick's

Freemans
Fun House
Girls Room
Glo
Green Room
GYM Sportsbar
Gypsy Tea
Hanger
Helen's
Highline
Hop Devil Grill
House of Brews
Hustler Club
I.C.U.
Irish Rogue
Isis
Juniper Suite
Kabin
Koi
Kos
Koze Lounge
Latitude
Laugh Factory
Le 26
Levee, The
Level V
Libation
Luca Bar/Lounge
Lucky Jack's
Lure Fishbar
Mambi Lounge
Margarita & Murphy
Martignetti Liquors
McCormick/Schmick
miniBar
MJ Grill
Mocca
Modern, The
Moonshine
Morrisey Park
Movida
Mundial
NA
Neogaea
Nerveana
Newgate Bar & Grill
NY Perks

O'Connell's
One91
Ono
Orchid
Orchid Lounge
Overlook Lounge
Perdition
Pink Elephant
Plunge
Prey
Providence/Triumph Room
PS 450
QT Hotel Bar
Quo
Redemption
Red Sky
Rockwood Music
Rogue
Ruby Falls
Salon
Satelite
Savalas
Select
17
Silverleaf
Skinny
Slainte
Slane
Snitch
Soho: 323
Sonny's B&G
Spotted Pig
Stain
Stanton Social
Stay
Still
Stir
Stitch
Sugarcane
Sunita
Supreme Trading
Sutra
Table 50
Tainted Lady
Temple
THOR Lobby Bar
Total Wine Bar

Town Tavern
Triple Crown
Turks & Frogs
Twelve
12" Bar
Vapor
Varjak
Vasmay Lounge
Vela
Velvet Cigar
V Steakhouse
Whiskey River
White Rabbit
Wild Spirits
Wonderland
xes lounge
Zablozki's
Zebulon

Noteworthy Closings (136)

Abaya
Acme Underground
Angel
Anju
Antique Lounge
Arshile
Bar D'O
Bar Harbour
Bauhaus
B-52
Big Sur
Black
B'Lo
Blur
Bottom's Up!
Cafe Lika
Cannon's Pub
Canteen
Carnaval
Carriage House
Carvao Bar & Grill
Centro-Fly
Chazal
Cheetah
Chez Es Saada
City Lighting
Climate Eight
Club Masa

Club New York
Code
Crazy Moose Saloon
Cuba Libre
Decade
Dorothy's
Dorsia
Downtime
Edelweiss
Etoile
Evelyn Lounge
Ferrier
Filter 14
Finally Fred's
First
Flat, The
Float
Freight
Fuel
Funky Nassau
Gaiety Theater
Global 33
Go
Gowanus Lounge
Gramercy Park Bar
Grotto
Hannah's Lava Lounge
Hell
High Bar
Ike
industry (food)
Infrared Lounge
Jimmy's Downtown
Jimmy's Uptown
Johnny Fox's
JUdson Grill
Kafeen
Kava Lounge
Lansky Lounge
Le Cirque 2000
Liquor Store Bar
Lola
Lounge 68
Ludlow Bar
Luna Lounge
Meow Mix
Milieu

Myne
Natural 9
Nectar
9½
Noa
Noca
Noche
Nocturne
Nowbar
Oak Bar
Ola
Open
Openair
Opium Den
Otis
Oyster Bar at the Plaza
Pangaea
Patria
Plaid
Plant
Play (Greenwich Village)
Poolbeg Street Pub
Potion Lounge
Red Light Lounge
Revolution
Rivertown Lounge
Room 143
Sage
Smithfield
Snackbar
Social Club
Soha
Sol
Sound Factory
Sparky's Ale House
Spectrum
Splendid
Sporting Club
Standard
Stanhope Supper Club
Stinger Club
Stingy Lulu's
Suite 16
SX 137
Tammany Hall
Tangerine
Taperia Madrid

Tavaru
Tenth Street Lounge
Tiki Room
Totem Lounge
Tupelo
Tuscan
Village Idiot
Void
Volume
Who's On First
Wonder Bar
Wye Bar
X.O.
Yabby's

NY State of Mind

Algonquin
Arlene Grocery
Arthur's Tavern
Bemelmans
Bill's Gay 90's
Bitter End
Blue and Gold
Blue Note
Boat House
Brasserie
Bridge Cafe
Brooklyn Inn
Brooklyn Social
Café des Artistes
Cafe Luxembourg
Caffe Dante
Caffe Reggio
CBGB's
Cedar Tavern
Chumley's
City Hall
Copacabana
Corner Bistro
Dorrian's
Eagle, The
Ear Inn
El Quijote
Fanelli's
Fifty Seven 57
Film Center Cafe
Florent
Four-Faced Liar

Geisha
Gotham B&G
Jeremy's Ale
J.G. Melon
Keens Steak
King Cole Bar
Lenox Lounge
Luna Park
MacDougal St. Ale
Mannahatta
Marie's Crisis
Matsuri
McAleer's Pub
McHales
McSorley's
Met. Museum Roof
Michael Jordan's
Mickey Mantle's
Moto
Nuyorican Poets
Odeon
Old Town Bar
One if by Land
Ouest
Oyster Bar
Pete's Tavern
P.J. Clarke's
Rainbow Grill
Roseland
Rudy's
Sardi's
Schiller's
Slide
Smalls
Stan's
Stonewall
Tavern on Green
21 Club
Village Vanguard
Webster Hall
White Horse

Old New York
(50+ yrs.; year opened;
* building)
1767 One if by Land
1817 Ear Inn
1847 Fanelli's

1851 Bayard's*
1854 McSorley's
1864 Pete's Tavern
1873 Paris, The
1880 White Horse
1884 P.J. Clarke's
1885 Keens Steak
1890 Sunny's
1892 Old Town Bar
1894 Teddy's
1902 Algonquin
1906 Hammerstein Ballrm
1910 Bohemian Hall
1913 Oyster Bar
1915 Caffe Dante
1917 Café des Artistes*
1919 55 Bar
1920 Milady's
1921 Sardi's
1922 Chumley's
1923 Campbell Apt.*
1924 Bill's Gay 90's
1924 Molly's
1926 El Quijote
1927 Caffe Reggio
1927 Dublin House
1927 P.J. Carney's
1928 Beacon
1928 Yankee Tavern
1929 Marie's Crisis
1929 21 Club
1930 Café Pierre
1930 O'Connor's
1932 Film Center Cafe
1934 Rainbow Grill
1934 Rudy's
1934 Subway Inn
1935 7B
1935 Village Vanguard
1936 Monkey Bar
1936 Peter McManus
1937 Arthur's Tavern
1938 Bowlmor Lanes
1939 Lenox Lounge
1940 Sophie's
1942 P & G Cafe
1945 Back Fence
1945 Holiday Cocktail
1947 Bemelmans

1948 First Edition
1949 King Cole Bar
1950 Kettle of Fish
1950 Marion's Continental
1952 Boat House
1952 Duplex
1952 McHales
1953 McAleer's Pub
1954 Cedar Tavern
1955 Cafe Carlyle
1955 Candle Bar
1955 Parkside
1955 Rosemary's Greenpoint
1956 Roseland

Outdoor Spaces
Garden
Aer
Anyway Cafe
Apartment 138
Bar Reis
B Bar
Black Betty
Bohemian Hall
Boudoir Bar
Boxcar Lounge
Brazen Head
Brooklyn Social
Bryant Park
Bull McCabe's
Casimir
Central
Cibar
Cloister Cafe
Croxley Ales
d.b.a.
Doc Watson's
Druids
East of Eighth
Eight Mile Creek
Eight of Clubs
Excelsior
5 Ninth
Fuelray
Fusion
Glass
Gowanus Yacht
Grand Press
Half King

I.C.U.
International Bar
Iona
Joey's
Joya
Killmeyer's
Laila Lounge
Last Exit
Lighthouse
Lillie's
Loki
Long Tan
Loreley
Luca Bar/Lounge
Lucky Cat
Luna Park
Lunasa
Madame X
Miracle Grill
Moonshine
Mug's Ale
Mustang Grill
No Malice Palace
Nublu
O'Flaherty's Ale
One91
Park
Pencil Factory
Pete's Candy Store
Porch
Relish
Revival
Rudy's
Rue B
Sherwood
Spuyten Duyvil
Stain
St. Dymphna's
Stonehome
Sugar Bar
Sunny's
Sweet & Vicious
Sweetwater
Tavern on Green
Tenement
Triple Crown
Yaffa

Patio/Terrace
Avalon
Barcade
BarTabac
Beer Bar/Cafe Centro
Belmont
Bleu Evolution
Blue Water Grill
Blu Lounge
Boat Basin
Boat House
B1 Drink Club
Boogaloo
Boss Tweed's
Buster's Garage
Butta' Cup
Cafe Deville/Bar Bleu
Capone's
Cargo
Cávo
Cellar, The
Chelsea Brewing
Cielo
City Hall
Clem's
Coogan's Parrot Bay
'disiac
Divine Bar
Django
Dos Caminos
Duff's
Duke's (East Village)
East River
El Rio Grande
Frank's Cocktail
Fun House
Gate, The
Ginger's
Good World B&G
Guastavino's
GYM Sportsbar
Half Wine Bar
Harbour Lights
Heartland Brewery
Hook
Hook and Ladder
Hooters
Hudson Hotel Bar

Jean Georges
Jekyll & Hyde
La Bottega Caffé
Larry Lawrence
Maison
Merchants, NY
Metropolitan
Mica Bar
Michael Jordan's
Miracle Grill
Moda Outdoors
Mundial
Musical Box
Newgate Bar & Grill
No. 1 Chinese
NY Perks
Ono
Opia
O.W.
Patio Lounge
Patroon
Pine Tree Lodge
Pressure
Rain Lounge
Red and Black
Rink Bar
Rock Center Cafe
Rubyfruit
Select
Senor Swanky's
Sequoia
Serafina
Social
Soda Bar
Sonny's B&G
SouthWest NY
Supreme Trading
Swing 46
Tabla
Tapas Lounge
Telephone
T.G. Whitney's
Thom Bar
Time Out
Top of the Tower
Total Wine Bar
Tribeca Grill

Tribeca Tavern
212
Ulysses
Underground
Union Pool
Village 247
Vintage
West End
Whiskey River
xes lounge

Rooftop
Ava Lounge
BED New York
Boogaloo
Cabanas
Delancey
Eagle, The
Heights B&G
Jade Terrace
Latitude
Metro Grill Roof
Met. Museum Roof
Pen-Top Bar
Plunge
Rare View
Red Sky
SushiSamba
Sutton Place
13

Sidewalk
American Spirits
Athens Cafe
Banc Cafe
Barfly
Bar 6
Bice
Big City
Bliss
Blue Smoke
Bottega del Vino
Boxers
B3
Bua
Butta' Cup
Cafe Bar
Cafe Gitane
Cafeteria

Special Appeals

Caffe Dante
Caffe Rafaella
Caffe Reggio
Caliente Cab
Casa La Femme
Chow Bar
Cipriani Downtown
Citrus B&G
Coffee Shop
Cornelia St. Cafe
Cowgirl
Diva
Doc Watson's
Dt.Ut
East 4th St. Bar
EN Japanese Brasserie
Epstein's Bar
Fiddlesticks
Finnegans Wake
Firehouse
Five Points
Flor de Sol
Florent
Four-Faced Liar
French Roast
Garage
Groove
Harrison, The
Heartland Brewery
Henrietta Hudson
Hi-Life
Il Posto Accanto
Jake's Dilemma
Jake's Saloon
Jean-Luc
J.G. Melon
Joe's Pub
Joshua Tree
Jules
Kaña
Le Figaro
Le Singe Vert
Le 26
Life Cafe
Link
Local
L'Orange Bleue

Luke's B&G
Markt
Martell's
McAleer's Pub
McCormick/Schmick
Meet
Mickey Mantle's
Moran's Chelsea
Mo's Caribbean
Mustang Sally's
North West
Odeon
One
One & One
Opal
Paris, The
Park Slope Ale
Pastis
Penang
Pershing Sq.
Pete's Tavern
Pioneer
Pipa
Prohibition
Redemption
Red Lion
Riviera
Rocking Horse
Romi
Rue 57
Ryan's Irish Pub
San Marcos
Savalas
Senor Swanky's
Serafina
Session 73
Sidewalk
Slaughtered Lamb
Sunita
Sushi Generation
SushiSamba
Teddy's
Three of Cups
Tortilla Flats
Uptown Lounge
Vero
Viceroy

Walker's
Waterloo
Westside Brewing
White Horse
Wogie's
Wollensky's
Zanzibar
Zum Schneider

Waterside
Bateaux NY
Boat Basin
Boat House
Chelsea Brewing
Harbour Lights
Heartland Brewery
Sequoia
SouthWest NY
Spirit Cruises
World Yacht

Piano Bars
Brandy's Piano
Danny's
Don't Tell Mama
Duplex
Helen's
Marie's Crisis
Monster
Rose's Turn
Rum House
Townhouse

Pub Grub
A&M Roadhouse
Abbey Pub
Annie Moores
Baker St. Pub
Bar East
Blarney Stone
Broome St. Bar
Bull Moose
Burton Pub/Kama Lounge
Cedar Tavern
Company
Connolly's
Coogan's Parrot Bay
Corner Bistro
Crif Dogs

Croton Reservoir
Croxley Ales
Daltons
David Copperfield
Desmond's
Doc Watson's
Donovan's
Druids
Fanelli's
Fiddlesticks
Finnegans Wake
Fiona's
Firehouse
Fitzgerald's
Flannery's
George Keeley's
Half King
Heartland Brewery
Hop Devil Grill
Iggy's
Jake's Saloon
Jekyll & Hyde
J.G. Melon
Kevin St. James
Kinsale
Latitude
Mad River
Malachy's
McAleer's Pub
McCormack's
McFadden's
McGee's
McHales
Molly's
Molly Wee
Mug's Ale
O'Connell's
Old Town Bar
O'Lunney's
O'Neals'
Patrick Conway's
Patrick Kavanagh's
Patriot Saloon
Peculier Pub
Peter Dillon's
Pig N Whistle
P.J. Clarke's

PS 450
Puck Fair
Rathbones
Rumours
Ryan's Irish Pub
17 Murray
Slainte
Slane
Slaughtered Lamb
Snitch
Social
St. Andrews
St. Dymphna's
Swift
Time Out
Tír na Nóg
Trinity Public Hse.
Waterfront Ale Hse.
Waterloo
Water St. Bar
White Horse
Wogie's

Punk Bars
Bellevue
CBGB's
Continental
Ding Dong Lounge
Duff's
Korova
Lucky 13
Manitoba's
Mars Bar
Siberia
Trash
Wild Spirits

Quiet Conversation
alt.coffee
Angel's Share
Anotheroom
Ara Wine Bar
Bandol
Bar @ Etats-Unis
Bemelmans
Bleu Evolution
Blue Mill
Bongo
Bouche Bar

Boxcar Lounge
Brandy Library
Burp Castle
Cafe de Bruxelles
Café des Artistes
Café Pierre
Caffe Dante
Caffe Rafaella
Caffe Reggio
Cibar
Cloister Cafe
Cupping Room
Decibel
Dt.Ut
Enoteca I Trulli
Flûte
Four Seasons Bar
Hudson Bar/Books
Hudson Hotel Library
Il Posto Accanto
Jean Georges
King Cole Bar
Louis
Lucky Cat
Manhattan Lounge
Mark's Bar
M Bar (West 40s)
Milk and Honey
Onieal's Grand St.
Otheroom
Paramount Library Bar
Plaza Athénée Bar Seine
Rainbow Grill
Regency Library Bar
Scratcher
Silverleaf
Tea Lounge
Temple Bar
Tenement
Top of the Tower
Total Wine Bar
Velvet Cigar
Von
World Bar

Roadhouse
A&M Roadhouse
Bar None

Special Appeals

Bellevue
Big Easy
Coyote Ugly
Dakota Roadhse.
Delta Grill
Doc Holliday's
Duke's (Gramercy)
Great Jones Cafe
Hog Pit
Hogs & Heifers
Live Bait
Red Rock West
Rodeo
Trailer Park
Yogi's

Romantic
Angel's Share
Auction House
Balthazar
Bandol
Bateaux NY
Bemelmans
Blue Water Grill
Boat House
Bubble Lounge
Buddha Lounge
Cafe Noir
Caffe Rafaella
Casa La Femme
Casimir
Cellar Bar
Chez Josephine
Cibar
Cloister Cafe
Cub Room
Daniel
Decibel
Divine Bar
Dylan Prime
Employees Only
Enoteca I Trulli
Fez
Flatiron Lounge
Flor de Sol
Flûte
Hudson Bar/Books
Hudson Hotel Library

Il Posto Accanto
I Tre Merli
Jules
King Cole Bar
K Lounge
Kush
La Lanterna
Le Bateau Ivre
Le Colonial
Le Singe Vert
Lexington Bar/Books
Madame X
M Bar (West 40s)
Met. Museum Roof
Milk and Honey
MO Bar
Monkey Bar
Morgans Bar
North West
Oak Room
Odea
One if by Land
Onieal's Grand St.
Park Avalon
Park Bar
Peasant
Rainbow Grill
Raoul's
Regency Library Bar
Rubyfruit
Rue B
Shalel
Spice Market
Spirit Cruises
Tavern on Green
Temple Bar
Top of the Tower
Townhouse
Velvet
Villard
World Yacht
Zoë

Sleepers
(Good to excellent ratings, but little known)
An Béal Bocht
Barbès

Bar on A
Bateaux NY
Bayard's
Bembe
Blu Lounge
Bouche Bar
Buttermilk
Caffe Rafaella
Daddy-O
Detour
Ding Dong Lounge
D.O.C. Wine Bar
Dublin 6
Duke's (East Village)
Edge, The
Eleventh St. Bar
Excelsior
55 Bar
Fitzgerald's
Freddy's
Galaxy Global
Ginger's
Great Jones Cafe
Iona
Jimmy's Corner
Kaña
Kavehaz
Keybar
La Lanterna
Lava Gina
Lea
Le 26
Local 138
Lucy's
Marion's Continental
McCormack's
Metro Grill Roof
Metropolitan
Moran's Chelsea
Muddy Cup
Nublu
O'Lunney's
Onieal's Grand St.
Peter Dillon's
Planet Rose
Rasputin
Relish

Rocky Sullivan's
Rosemary's Greenpoint
Scratcher
Sherwood
Sing Sing
Slide
Slipper Room
Soda Bar
Sophie's
Stand-Up NY
St. Dymphna's
Tribe
V Bar
Von
Whiskey Ward
Windfall
World Yacht

Smoking Permitted
(* Cigars only)
Carnegie Club
Circa Tabac
Club Macanudo
40/40*
Hudson Bar/Books
Karma
Lexington Bar/Books
Merchants, NY (East 60s)
Velvet Cigar*

Spoken Word
Back Fence
BAMcafé
Barbès
Bowery Poetry
Cornelia St. Cafe
Cutting Room
Dekk
Dt.Ut
Ear Inn
Four-Faced Liar
Freddy's
Half King
Happy Ending
Joe's Pub
KGB
Knitting Factory
Life Cafe

Lucky Cat
Magnetic Field
Nuyorican Poets
Parkside
Pete's Candy Store
Pink Pony
Remote Lounge
Telephone
13
Underground
Zinc Bar

Sports Bars
Back Page
Bar Coastal
Bar 515
Barfly
Bar None
Becky's
Big City
BlackFinn
Black Sheep
Blondies
Bounce
Bourbon St.
Brother Jimmy's
Bull Moose
Buster's Garage
Central Bar
Coogan's Parrot Bay
Croxley Ales
Desmond's
Down the Hatch
ESPN Zone
Firehouse
First Edition
Fitzgerald's
40/40
Gin Mill
GYM Sportsbar
Irish Rogue
Jake's Dilemma
John Street B&G
Joshua Tree
Katwalk
Kevin St. James
Kinsale
MacDougal St. Ale

Malachy's
McAleer's Pub
McCormack's
McFadden's
Mickey Mantle's
Mo's Caribbean
Nevada Smith's
Off the Wagon
O'Flanagan's
Overlook Lounge
Park Ave. Country
Proof
Rathbones
Red Lion
Reservoir
Riviera
Rogue
Ryan's Daughter
Scruffy Duffy's
Ship of Fools
Social
Stan's
Stitch
St. Marks Ale
Sushi Generation
Sutton Place
Time Out
Tonic/Met Lounge
Tracy J's
Turtle Bay
Twelve
200 Fifth
Waterloo
Yankee Tavern

Strip Clubs
Flashdancers
Hunk Mania
Hustler Club
Penthse Exec. Club
Pussycat Lounge
Scores
Ten's
VIP Club

Suits
Angelo & Maxie's
Barbalùc

Bar 41
Bayard's
Beer Bar/Cafe Centro
Biltmore Room
Bliss
Blue Water Grill
Brandy Library
Bryant Park
Bull & Bear
Café Gray
Campbell Apt.
Capital Grille
Carnegie Club
Cellar Bar
'Cesca
Church Lounge
Cité Grill
Club Macanudo
Croton Reservoir
Del Frisco's
Divine Bar
Django
English Is Italian
Fifty Seven 57
Frederick's
Full Shilling
Geisha
Ginger Man
Heartland Brewery
Houston's
Jameson's
John Street B&G
Keens Steak
K Lounge
Lea
Le Colonial
Luna Park
Mambi Lounge
Mark's Bar
McCormick/Schmick
Mercantile Grill
Michael Jordan's
MO Bar
Moda Outdoors
Morton's
Nation
Old Town Bar

O2
P.J. Clarke's
Rink Bar
Rock Center Cafe
Romi
Savannah Steak
Scores
Shelly's NY
Silverleaf
SouthWest NY
St. Andrews
Stone Rose
Sutton Place
Tao
Top of the Tower
Town
Townhouse
21 Club
Ulysses
Villard
V Steakhouse
Whiskey Blue
Wollensky's
World Bar
W Times Square Living Room

Swanky

Aer
Asia de Cuba
Aubette
Ava Lounge
Balthazar
Brandy Library
Brasserie
Brasserie 8½
Bubble Lounge
Bungalow 8
Butter
Cafe Carlyle
Café Gray
Cain
Calle Ocho
Campbell Apt.
Canal Room
Carnegie Club
Cellar Bar
Church Lounge
Cibar

Club Macanudo
Daniel
Del Frisco's
Dos Caminos
Eugene
Feinstein's/Regency
Fiamma Osteria
Fifty Seven 57
Fizz
Flûte
Four Seasons Bar
Frederick's
Geisha
Glo
Grand Bar
Guastavino's
Hudson Hotel Library
Juniper Suite
King Cole Bar
K Lounge
Le Colonial
Light
Mark's Bar
Marquee
MO Bar
Monkey Bar
Movida
One
O2
Paramount Library Bar
Plunge
Rainbow Grill
Royalton
Salon
Silverleaf
66
Spice Market
Stone Rose
Top of the Tower
Trousdale
Villard
V Steakhouse
Wet Bar
World Bar

Theme Bars
Barcade
Beauty Bar

Big Easy
Big Nose Kate's
Black Bear
Boudoir Bar
Bourbon St.
Burp Castle
Coogan's Parrot Bay
Coral Room
Cowgirl
Crime Scene
Culture Club
ESPN Zone
Firehouse
Flight 151
Fun House
Gstaad
Hard Rock
Hook and Ladder
Hooters
Jade Island
Jekyll & Hyde
KGB
K Lounge
Korova
La Caverna
Mars 2112
Nerveana
Otto's Shrunken
Pine Tree Lodge
Remote Lounge
Rodeo
Sidetracks
Slaughtered Lamb
Tainted Lady
Trailer Park
Waikiki Wally's
Wicked Monk
Zombie Hut

Tourist Favorites
Arthur's Tavern
Bateaux NY
B. B. King Blues
Bitter End
Blue Fin
Blue Note
Broadway Lounge
Cafe Wha?

Special Appeals

Caffe Reggio
Carolines
China Club
Coyote Ugly
Culture Club
ESPN Zone
Faces & Names
Garage
Groove
Harbour Lights
Hard Rock
Heartland Brewery
Hogs & Heifers
Hooters
Iridium
Jekyll & Hyde
Joe Allen
Le Figaro
Mars 2112
McSorley's
Met. Museum Roof
Mickey Mantle's
Oyster Bar
Playwright
Rainbow Grill
Rink Bar
Rock Center Cafe
Ruby Foo's
Sardi's
Sequoia
Spirit Cruises
Splash
Stonewall
Tavern on Green
Tonic/Met Lounge
View Lounge
Village Vanguard
White Horse
World Yacht

Trendy
Aer
Balthazar
BED New York
Biltmore Room
Bungalow 8
Cabanas
Cain

Canal Room
Cellar Bar
Cielo
Coral Room
Cotton
Crobar
Dream Lounge
Duvet
Earth
East Side Co.
Employees Only
Eugene
5 Ninth
40/40
Frederick's
Freemans
Glo
Green Room
Gypsy Tea
Highline
Hiro
Hue
'inoteca
Koi
La Bottega Caffé
Level V
Libation
Marquee
Matsuri
NA
Odea
One
Pastis
Pink Elephant
Plunge
PM
Pop Burger
Public
Quo
Ruby Falls
Rumor
Schiller's
Select
66
Soho: 323
Spice Market
Starlight

Stone Rose
Suede
Sugarcane
Sway
Table 50
Tao
Therapy
Triple Crown
Viscaya
XL

Velvet Rope

Aer
APT
Bungalow 8
Cabanas
Cain
China Club
Cielo
Copacabana
Cotton
Crobar
Discothèque
Eugene
Flow
49 Grove
Frederick's
Glo
Green Room
Gypsy Tea

Hiro
Kos
Level V
Libation
Lobby
Lot 61
Lotus
Marquee
NA
NV
One
Pink Elephant
Plunge
PM
Quo
Ruby Falls
Rumor
Select
17
Show
Snitch
Suede
Sway
Table 50
Tao
Temple
Viscaya
Vue

Wine Vintage Chart

This chart is designed to help you select wine to go with your meal. It is based on the same 0 to 30 scale used throughout this *Survey*. The ratings (prepared by our friend **Howard Stravitz,** a law professor at the University of South Carolina) reflect both the quality of the vintage and the wine's readiness for present consumption. Thus, if a wine is not fully mature or is over the hill, its rating has been reduced. We do not include 1987, 1991–1993 vintages because they are not especially recommended for most areas. A dash indicates that a wine is either past its peak or too young to rate.

	'85	'86	'88	'89	'90	'94	'95	'96	'97	'98	'99	'00	'01	'02	'03
WHITES															
French:															
Alsace	24	–	22	28	28	27	26	25	25	26	25	26	27	25	–
Burgundy	26	25	–	24	22	–	28	29	24	23	26	25	23	27	24
Loire Valley	–	–	–	–	24	–	20	23	22	–	24	25	23	27	26
Champagne	28	25	24	26	29	–	26	27	24	24	25	25	26	–	–
Sauternes	21	28	29	25	27	–	21	23	26	24	24	24	28	25	26
Germany	25	–	25	26	27	25	24	27	24	23	25	24	29	27	–
California (Napa, Sonoma, Mendocino):															
Chardonnay	–	–	–	–	–	–	–	24	26	25	25	24	27	29	–
Sauvignon Blanc/Semillon	–	–	–	–	–	–	–	–	–	25	25	23	27	28	26
REDS															
French:															
Bordeaux	24	25	24	26	29	22	26	25	23	25	24	28	26	23	24
Burgundy	23	–	21	24	26	–	26	28	25	22	28	22	24	27	–
Rhône	25	19	27	29	29	24	25	23	24	28	27	27	26	–	25
Beaujolais	–	–	–	–	–	–	–	–	–	–	23	24	–	25	28
California (Napa, Sonoma, Mendocino):															
Cab./Merlot	27	26	–	21	28	29	27	25	28	23	26	23	27	25	–
Pinot Noir	–	–	–	–	–	–	–	–	24	24	25	24	26	29	–
Zinfandel	–	–	–	–	–	–	–	–	–	–	–	26	26	–	
Italian:															
Tuscany	–	–	–	–	25	22	25	20	29	24	28	26	25	–	–
Piedmont	–	–	–	27	28	–	23	27	27	25	25	28	23	–	–